MICROSOFT

ACCESS & EXCEL

FOR BEGINNERS & POWER USERS

The Concise Microsoft Access & Excel 2021
A-Z Mastery Guide for All Users

Tech Demystified

Copyright © 2021 *Tech Demystified*

All rights reserved. No part of this publication may be reproduced, distributed, or transmitted in any form or by any means, including photocopying, recording, or other electronic or mechanical methods, without the prior written permission of the publisher, except in the case of brief quotations embodied in critical reviews and certain other noncommercial uses permitted by copyright law.

ISBN: 9798517005540

TABLE OF CONTENT

TABLE OF CONTENT _____ i

BOOK ONE _____ ix

MICROSOFT ACCESS _____ ix

INTRODUCTION _____ x

CHAPTER ONE _____ 1

INTRODUCING ACCESS 365 _____ 1
   What Is Access? _____ 1
   Why Should You Use Access? _____ 2

CHAPTER TWO _____ 4

MICROSOFT ACCESS OBJECTS _____ 4
   What Is A Database _____ 4
   Tables _____ 4
   Query _____ 5
   Form _____ 5
   Report _____ 6
   Macro _____ 6
   Module _____ 7
   Microsoft Access Data Types _____ 7

CHAPTER THREE _____ 10

CREATING A DATABASE FILE _____ 10
   Creating A Blank Database File _____ 11
   Creating Database From Template _____ 12

The Navigation Pane _____ 13
   Managing The Navigation Pane _____ 14
   Show Or Hide The Navigation Pane _____ 14
   To Select A Predefined Category _____ 15
   Filter By Group _____ 15
   Sort Objects _____ 16
   Finding Objects In Database _____ 17
   Changing How Objects Are Displayed _____ 17
   How To Hide And Unhide Objects And Groups _____ 18
   To unhide or display hidden objects or groups _____ 19

Customizing The Navigation Pane 20
Creating A Custom Category 20
Renaming A Custom Category 21
Deleting A Custom Category 22
Creating A Custom Group 23
Renaming A Custom Group 24
Deleting A Custom Group 25
Creating A Custom Group From A Database Object 25
Designing A Database 26
Deciding What Information You Need 26
Separating Information Into Different Database Tables 27
Choosing Fields For Database Tables 27
Deciding On A Primary Key Field For Each Database Table 28
Mapping The Relationship Between Tables 28

CHAPTER FOUR 29

BUILDING YOUR DATABASE TABLES 29

Creating A Database Table 29
Creating a database table by importing database table from another database 29
Creating A Database Table From A Template 30
Importing A Table From Another Database 32
Opening And Viewing Tables 32
Opening Table In Design View 33
Opening Table In Datasheet View 33

Switching Between Views With The View Buttons *34*

To switch between the view buttons 34
Switching Between Views On The Status bar 34
Switching Between Views By Right Clicking 35
Entering And Altering Table Fields 35
Creating A Field 35
Creating A Field On Your Own 35
Using The Ready-Made Fields 36
The Data Types 36
Designating The Primary Key Field 37
Moving, Renaming, And Deleting Fields 37
Moving A Field 37
Renaming A Field 38
Deleting A Field 38

    Understanding Field Properties _____ 38
    Creating A Lookup Data-Entry List _____ 41
    Creating A Drop-Down List On Your Own _____ 42
    Getting List Items From A Database Table _____ 44
    Indexing For Faster Sorts, Searches, And Queries _____ 47
    The Indexed Property Settings _____ 48
    Indexing One Field In A Table _____ 48
    Indexing Bases On More Than One Field. _____ 48
    Deleting An Index _____ 49
    Viewing And Editing Index _____ 50

CHAPTER FIVE _____ 51

TIPS AND TRICKS ON ACCESS _____ 51

    Every Table Should Have A Primary Key _____ 51
    Keep Your Access Database Fields As Small As Possible _____ 51
    Don't Over Index _____ 51
    Choose The Optimal Data Types _____ 51
    Validating Your Access Data _____ 52
    Use Simple And Direct Names In Access _____ 52
    Shortcut Keys And Controls _____ 52
    Frequently Used Shortcuts Keys _____ 52
    Navigating Through The Ribbons Shortcut Keys _____ 53
    The Shortcut Keys For Database Files _____ 54
    The Shortcut Keys For Access Workplace _____ 55
    The Shortcut Keys For Menus _____ 55
    The Shortcut Keys For Dialog Boxes _____ 56
    The Shortcut Keys For Wizard _____ 57
    The Shortcut Keys For Property Sheets _____ 57
    The Shortcut Keys For Text Box _____ 58
    The Shortcut Keys For Combo Or List Box _____ 58
    The Shortcut Keys For Working With Objects _____ 59
    The Shortcut Keys For Working Design, layout, or Datasheet View ____ 59
    The shortcut Keys For Datasheet View _____ 60
    The Shortcut Keys For Subdatasheets In Datasheet View _____ 61
    The shortcut Keys To Navigate In A Design View _____ 62
    The Shortcut Keys For Editing Using Controls In the Form And Report Design View _____ 64
    The Shortcut Keys To Navigate Between Fields And Records _____ 64
    The Shortcut Keys To Navigate In Forms With More Than One Page ___ 65

The Shortcut Keys To Navigate Between A Main Form And A Subform _ 65
The Shortcut Keys To Navigate In Print Preview And Layout Preview __ 66
The Shortcut Keys For The Diagram Pane _____ 66
The Shortcut Keys For Grid Pane _____ 67
The Shortcut Keys For The Field List Pane _____ 68
The Shortcut Keys To Select A Field Or Record _____ 68
The Shortcut Keys To Select Text In A Field _____ 68
The Shortcut Keys To Extend A Selection _____ 69
The Shortcut Keys To Find And Replace Text Or Data _____ 69
The Shortcut Keys To Move The Insertion Point In A Field _____ 69
The Shortcut Keys To Copy, Move, Or Delete Text _____ 70
The Shortcut Keys To Undo Changes _____ 70
The Shortcut Keys For Entering Data In A Datasheet Or Form View _____ 71
The Shortcut Keys To Refresh Field With Current Data _____ 71
The Shortcut Keys To Work Around In Tables And Cells _____ 71
The Shortcut Keys For Get Help With Access _____ 72
Miscellaneous Keyboard Shortcuts _____ 73

CONCLUSION ON ACCESS _____ 74

BOOK TWO _____ 75

MICROSOFT EXCEL 365 _____ 75

PREFACE _____ 76

INTRODUCTION _____ 78

CHAPTER ONE _____ 80

OVERVIEW OF MICROSOFT EXCEL _____ 80
Origin of Excel _____ 80
Meaning of Excel _____ 80
Relevance of Excel _____ 80
What Is Excel 365? _____ 81
Differences Between Excel 365 And Traditional Excel Such As (2013, 2019 And Others) _____ 81
Similarities Between Excel 365 And Traditional Excel (Such As 2013, 2019 And Others) _____ 85
Importance of Excel 365 _____ 86

CHAPTER TWO _____ 87

START YOUR EXPLOIT WITH EXCEL _____ 87

Creating and Opening A New Excel Workbook _____ 87
Getting Familiar with The Excel Interface _____ 89
Understanding Rows, Columns, And Cell Addresses _____ 91
Workbooks And Worksheet_____ 93
Entering Data in The Worksheet Cell_____ 94
The Basic Knowledge of Entering Data _____ 95
Typing Your Text _____ 98
Typing Numeric Value _____ 100
Typing Dates and Time Values_____ 101
Taking Advantages of Flash Fill And Autofill Commands By Entering Specific Lists and Serial Data _____ 104
Applying Formatting to Numbers, Dates, Money, And Times Values __ 109
Essential Guide to Data Validation _____ 113

CHAPTER THREE_____ 120

IMPROVING YOUR WORKSHEET_____ 120

Editing Your Worksheet Data _____ 120
Navigating Around the Worksheet _____ 121
Giving Your Worksheet A New Appearance _____ 122
Freezing and Splitting Columns and Rows_____ 123
Hide and Unhide The Columns and Rows _____ 126
Comments for Documenting Your Worksheet _____ 134
Selecting Cells (S) In A Worksheet_____ 139
Deleting, Copying, And Moving Data _____ 142
Managing the Worksheets in A Workbook _____ 145
Restricting Others from Meddling with Your Worksheets _____ 150
Hiding Your Worksheet _____ 150
Protecting Your Worksheet _____ 152

CHAPTER FOUR _____ 155

COMPUTING DATA WITH FORMULAS AND FUNCTIONS _____ 155

About Formulas _____ 155
Referencing the Cells Via Formulas _____ 155
Referencing Formula Results in Subsequent Excel Formulas _____ 157
Operators and Precedence of Excel Formulas_____ 158
Arithmetic Operators_____ 158
Concatenation Operator _____ 159
Reference Operator _____ 159
Comparison operator_____ 160

The Order of Operator Precedence in Excel Formulas _____ 160
Changing Excel Order with Parenthesis _____ 161
Foreknowledge of Entering A Formula _____ 162
The Fast-Track Method to Observe in Entering A Formula _____ 164
Reference Cells in The Worksheet by Clicking on The Cells _____ 171
Inserting A Cell Range _____ 171
Creating Cell Range Name for Formulas' Use _____ 172
Pointing to Cells in A Worksheet for Formula Purpose in A Different Worksheet _____ 177
Ways of Copying Formulas from One Cell to Other Cell _____ 179
Discovering and Adjusting Formulas Error _____ 180
Frequent Message Error for Entering Wrong Formulas _____ 181
Discover More About the Error and Adjusting It _____ 181
Tracing Cell References _____ 182
Making Use of Error Checkers Button _____ 184
Stepping into A Function _____ 185
Understand the Use of Argument in Function _____ 186
Checking Out the Necessary Argument for A Given Function _____ 186
ENTERING A FUNCTION FOR BUILDING A FORMULA _____ 188
Glancing Through Generally Used Function _____ 190
Using COUNT and COUNTIF To Count Data Item in A Cell Range _____ 191
Joining Text with Value with Concatenate _____ 192
Using Average for Averaging Point Value _____ 193
PMT For Estimating Periodic Payment of Loan _____ 194
Project Time Measuring with NETWORKDAY and TODAY _____ 195
LEN For Counting Text Character _____ 196
Compares the Range of Values with LARGE And SMALL _____ 197
Text Capitalizing with PROPER Function _____ 199
LEFT, MID, AND RIGHT for Data Extraction _____ 204
IF For Analytical Identification _____ 206

CHAPTER FIVE _____ **208**

CONSTRUCT WORKSHEET FOR EASY COMPREHENSION _____ **208**
Spreading Out Worksheet in An Orderly Manner _____ 208
Numbers and Text Alignment in Rows and Columns _____ 208
Text Merging and Centering Over Multiple Cells _____ 212
Delete and Insert Rows and Columns _____ 214
Deleting rows or columns _____ 217
Adjusting Rows and Columns Size _____ 218

- Adjusting the Height of The Rows _____ 219
- Adjusting the Column Width _____ 223
- Furnishing A Worksheet with Borders and Colors _____ 225
- Quick Way of Formatting Worksheet with Cell Style _____ 225
- Making Use of Excel Built-In Cell Style _____ 226
- Customizing Your Cell Style _____ 227
- Using Table Style to Format A Cell _____ 229
- Creating Border on The Worksheet Cells _____ 231
- Colorize Your Worksheet _____ 236
- Be Prepared to Print A Worksheet _____ 237
- Setting Up A Worksheet to Fit the Page _____ 237
- Present A Worksheet in An Attractive Manner _____ 244
- Repeat Rows and Columns Heading on Every Page _____ 249
- Removing Row and Column Headings _____ 251

CHAPTER SIX _____ 253

TOOLS AND TECHNIQUES FOR DATA ANALYSIS _____ 253

- What Are the Sparklines? _____ 253
- Conditional Format Application for Certain Data That Need Important Attention _____ 255
- Taking Care of The Information List _____ 258
- Sorting List of a Data _____ 259
- Filtering List of Data _____ 261
- Exploiting Goal Seek Command _____ 264
- Analysing Data with Data Table and What If Analysis _____ 267
- Using A One Input Data Table for Analysis _____ 268
- Using A Two Input Data Table for Analysis _____ 271
- Using Pivot Table for Data Analysis _____ 274
- Using Recommended Pivot Table _____ 275
- Creating A New Pivot Table _____ 277
- ADDING FINAL TOUCHES TO THE PIVOT TABLE _____ 279

CHAPTER SEVEN _____ 282

EXCEL 365 SHORTCUTS, TIPS AND TRICKS _____ 282

- Useful Shortcuts _____ 282
- Formula Shortcuts _____ 282
- General Excel Shortcuts _____ 283
- Indispensable Tips And Trick For Quick Command _____ 286
- Absolute and Relative Reference _____ 286

Quick Analysis Tool _____ 289
Autofit Column Width _____ 291
XLOOKUP Function _____ 293
Remove BLANK _____ 295

CONCLUSION _____ **299**

INDEX _____ **300**

BOOK ONE
MICROSOFT ACCESS

INTRODUCTION

Microsoft Access is a database management system (DBMS), provided by Microsoft to analyze large amounts of information and manage data efficiently. Access 365 is a member of the Microsoft 365 suite of applications that are included in the Professional and higher editions or sold separately. The Microsoft Access stores in its format based on the Access Jet Database Engine, import or link directly to data stored in other applications and databases.

Virtually, every organization benefit from the use of Access to organize, store, and document important information. With Microsoft Access, data such as inventory and customers' information, order details, and vendors can be effectively organized, analyzed, and processed.

Here in this book, with the use of Access 365, you will be familiar with commonly used data management software and learn some basic functions associated with it.

By the end of this book, you should be able to:

- Create a table from the scratch or use the template
- Create field from the scratch or use the template
- Get conversant with the use of the Access shortcut keys etc.

To use this book, especially as a beginner, you must have the following

- A good computer system with a strong and stable internet connection
- Installed Access 365 or 2019 version on the computer system

With all these available, becoming proficient in Access 365 is much easier than you must have thought.

See you in the next stage!

CHAPTER ONE
INTRODUCING ACCESS 365

What Is Access?

Microsoft Access is a database management system (DBMS) that is used to store and manage data. This is a member of the Microsoft 365 suite of applications which is made for business and enterprise users.

Microsoft Access is also an Information Management Tool that allows you to store information for referencing, reporting, and also analyzing.

Just like Microsoft Excel, Access allows the users to view and edit data. One of the features that make Access better than Excel is that it can take in more data at a stretch.

Microsoft Access provides the users, the features of a database, and the programming proficiencies to create an easy-to-navigate screen (Forms). Not only that, Access helps to process a large bunk of information and manages them effectively and efficiently.

Microsoft Access saves data in its format based on the Access Jet Database Engine, and can also link or import directly to the data that are stored in other applications or databases.

Just like every other Microsoft application, Access also supports the use of Visual Basic for Application (VBA)

To use Microsoft Access, you will need to follow the procedures below

- **Database Creation:** The first thing to do is create a database and indicate what type of data to be stored in the database
- **Data Input:** After creating a database, the next thing to do is enter the data into the database.
- **Query:** This is a process of retrieving information from a database

- **Report:** This is where information from the database is organized in a nice and presentable manner that can be printed out in an Access report

Why Should You Use Access?

There are many benefits attached to the use of Microsoft Access and some of them will be outlined below

- **Cost Of Development**: One of the benefits of using Microsoft Access is that it is less expensive compared to the larger database systems like Oracle, SOL server, etc., which requires a huge amount of set up and high maintenance costs
- **Software Integration**: One of the notable features of Microsoft Access being a product of the Microsoft Office suite is that it can integrate well with two other apps in the MS office suite.
- **Legacy Data**: Microsoft Access can easily import many data formats, in such a way that the existing data is retained and not lost. It does not only save 100's of hours of input time but can remove potential human input errors.
- **Distribution**: Microsoft Access has its Jet Database format that contains both the application and data in one file. With the ability of having the application and data together in one place, it is convenient to distribute the applications to many users, who can, in turn, run the apps in disconnected environments.
- Microsoft Access provides a fully functional, relational database management system in a few minutes.
- Microsoft Access can function well with many of the development languages that work on Windows OS.
- With Microsoft Access, you can create tables, queries, forms, reports, and connect using the macros.
- Microsoft Access allows the users to link data from its existing location and manipulate it for viewing, updating, querying, and reporting.
- Microsoft Access allows for customizing according to personal and company needs.

- Microsoft Access executes any challenging or difficult office or industrial database tasks.
- Access in its uniqueness can function with the most popular databases that are compatible with Open Database Connectivity (ODBC) standards, including SQL Server, Oracle, and DB2.
- With Access, software developers can use Microsoft Access to develop application software
- Microsoft Access requires less code to get work done unlike SQL server and some other client-server database).
- Microsoft Access is a very good tool for creating database applications with a large array of readily available functionality.
- Another reason you need to use Access is that it is flexible i.e., it allows you to put together a custom database and later change as needs are likely changes as needs arise.
- Access can be used alongside VBA, a programming language. Developers can create a custom solution for their database using the VBA code, an effective programming language that contains codes or commands for specific programs.
- Microsoft Access allows users to choose any of the four ways to view reports:
    - Report view
    - Print view
    - Layout view
    - Design view
- Microsoft Access is a simple desktop application that does not need any particular hardware or license to function. Thus, making it more suitable and cost-effective for individual users and smaller teams who do not need larger and complicated databases for an extra price.
- Users of Access do not need to undergo any special training to get the skills needed to use this application. In a nutshell, Access is easy to master especially to users who are conversant with the use of Excel

CHAPTER TWO
MICROSOFT ACCESS OBJECTS

Here in this section, we will be learning about the basic objects in MS Access. These objects are what Access uses to help its users list and organize information and prepare specially designed reports. When a database is created, Access provides the users with objects such as tables, queries, forms, reports, macros, and modules.

What Is A Database

A database is a tool that is used for the collection and organization of information. The database can store information about people, products, orders, etc. The database stores its information in a single file and the file contains database objects, which are the components of the database. The database consists of six components which are listed below

- *Tables*
- *Queries*
- *Forms*
- *Reports*
- *Macros*
- *Modules*

Tables

This is the heart of the database where data are defined and stored in rows and columns. Here, you can create as many tables as you need to store all kinds of information. The following are what you should keep in mind when using the table

- Each field must carry a unique name and data type

- The table must contain fields or columns that must be able to take in different kinds of data, such as name, address, and a row that collects information about the subject, and such information can be details about the employee or customer.
- You can also define the primary key in a table.

Query

This is one of the objects in the database that gives a custom view of data from one or more tables. The query selects sorts and filters data based on the search criteria. Take note of the following hints when using the query

- Running a query is compared to asking an in-depth question of your database
- Building a query in Access implies that you are defining the specific search conditions to find precisely the data you need
- You can define your queries to Select, Update, Insert, or Delete data
- You can also set queries that create new tables from the data in one or more existing tables

Form

Form is also one of the databases objects that is mainly created for data input, display, or control of application executions. Forms can be used to modify the presentation of data that the application extracts from queries or data. Not only that, forms give an easy way to view or change information in a table. Note the following about forms

- Forms is a database object used for creating a user interface for database application
- Forms are used for entering, customizing, and viewing records
- Forms are used from time to time because they are easy to guide people to entering data correctly

- When you input data into a form in Access, the data goes precisely the database designer wants it to go in one or more related tables
- Forms also display live data from the table. This aimed at easing the process of entering or editing data.

Report

Report is also an object of the database that is used to format, calculate, print, and summarize selected data. The report helps to print some or all of the data in a selected data. Report allows you to choose where the information is displayed on the printed page, and how it is grouped, sorted, and formatted. Take note of the following when working with report

- You can view or display a report on your screen before printing it out
- Report is for output purposes
- Reports are very important because they permit for the displaying of the database components in an easy-to-read manner
- You can modify the report's appearance to make it more attractive
- You can create a report from the table or query

Macro

Macros are mini computer programming constructs that the users to set up commands and processes in the forms. Some of the activities in the form include searching, moving to another record, and running of formula. With macros, you can customize your data, even without being a programmer. Take note of the following tips about macro in the Microsoft Access

- The macros can be used to open and execute queries, to open tables, or to print or view reports.

- You can run other macros or Visual Basic procedures from within a macro
- Macros can attach data directly to table events such as inserting new records, editing existing records, and deleting records
- Data macros in web apps can also be stand-alone objects which can be called from other data or macro-objects.

Module

A module is an object in the database that contains the procedures which are used in the Visual Basic for Application (VBA). With these procedures, you can do anything. The modules give a more distinct flow of actions and permit the users to trap errors. Take note of the following when using the modules to execute any operation in Access

- Whatever can be done in the macro can also be done in the modules
- Modules are most suitable when the users intend to write codes for a multi-user environment, unlike the macros which cannot do error handling
- The modules being a standalone object can be called from anywhere in the application, or they can be linked with a form or a report to react to events on the associated form or report.

Microsoft Access Data Types

The data types are the properties of each field in a table. These properties are what define the features and performance of the fields in a table. The Datatypes determine the type of values the users can store in any given field. Below is the table of the most common data types that can be used in the Microsoft Access database

TYPE OF DATA	DESCRIPTION	SIZE
Short Text	These are texts and numbers which do need calculation e.g., mobile numbers	Up to 255 characters
Long Text	This data type is used for lengthy text or combination of texts and numbers	Up to 63,999 characters
Number	These are numerical data used for storing mathematical calculations	1,2,4, 8, and 16 bytes
Date/Time	This stores data and time for the years 100 through 9999	8 bytes
Currency	This allows you to store currency values and numeric data used in mathematical calculations involving data with one to four decimal places	8 bytes
Auto Number	This assigns a unique number when a new record is created or added to a table.	Four bytes (16 bytes if it is set as a Replication ID)
Yes/No	It stores only logical values Yes and No	1 bit
Attachment	This stores file such as digital photos and multiple files can be attached per record	Up to 2 GB of data can be stored.
OLE objects	OLE objects can store audio, video, other Binary Large Objects.	Up to about 2 GB
Hyperlink	Text or combination of texts and numbers stored. The text is used as hyperlink address	The Hyperlink data type allows you to store a maximum of 2048 characters

| Calculated | This creates an expression that uses data from one or more fields. | You can create an expression that uses data from one or more fields |

CHAPTER THREE
CREATING A DATABASE FILE

Here in this chapter, we will be learning how to create a database. Here, we will be learning how to create a database by using a template or building a database from the scratch

Before we create a database file, we will need to open Microsoft Access and to open Microsoft Access, follow the steps below

- Click on the **Windows icon** where you will find the list of installed programs
- Search and click on **Access** to open it

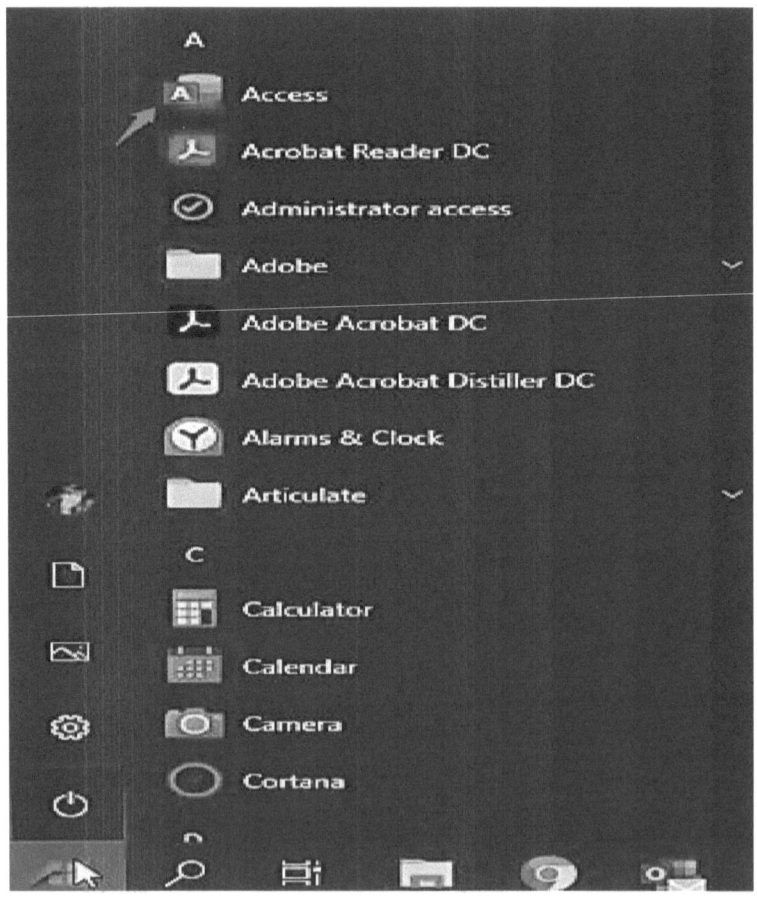

Creating A Blank Database File

To create a new blank database file

- Open the Microsoft Access
- From the right panel of the screen, click **on Blank database** and enter the name of the database.

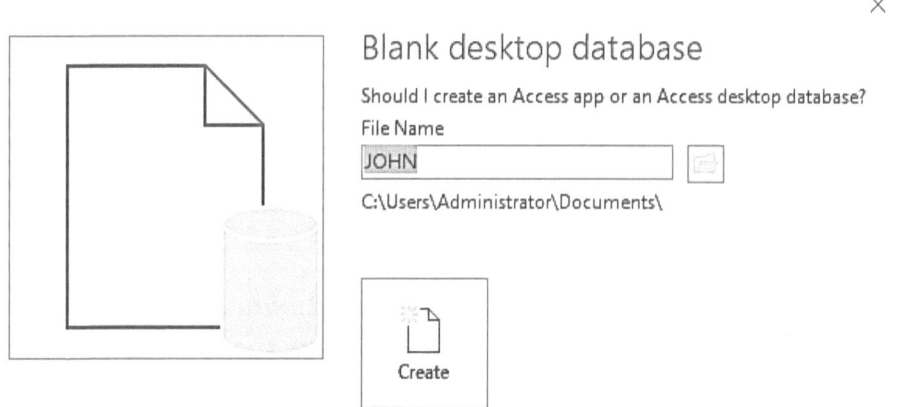

- Choose the folder where you want to store your data

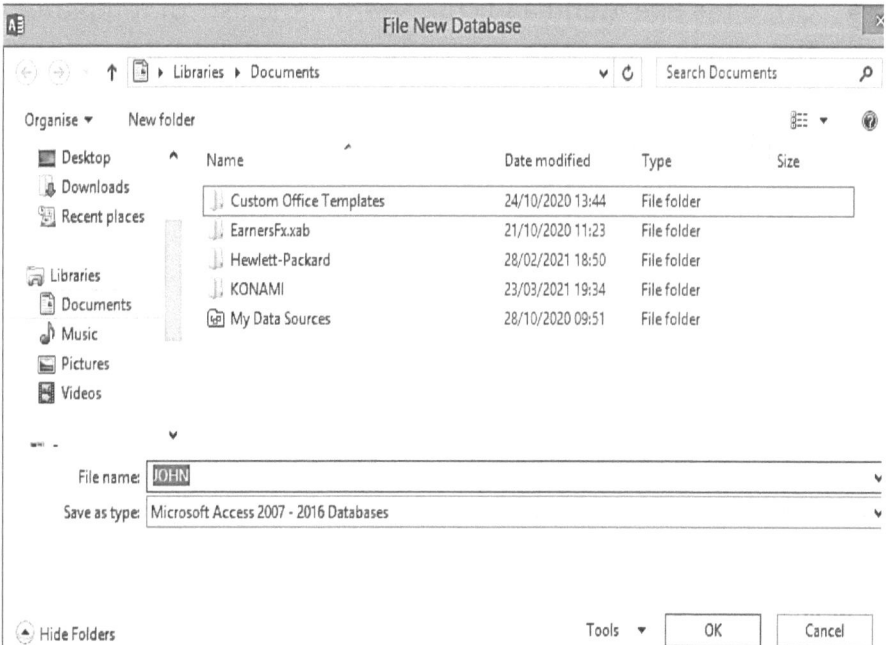

- Click on the big **Create button** under the file name box, and Access will open a blank table

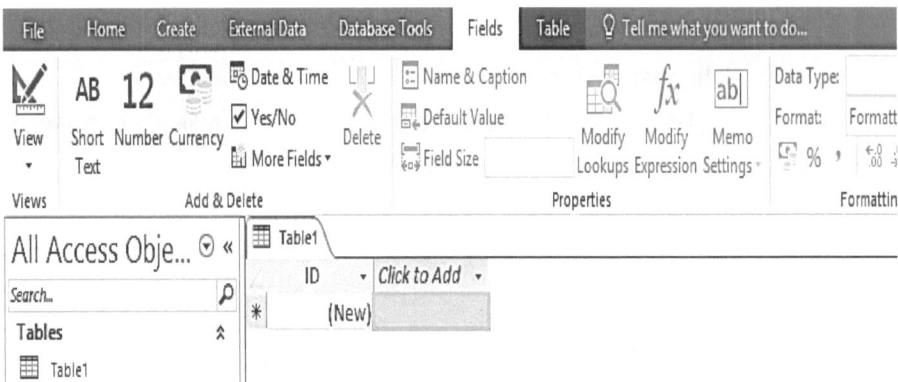

Creating Database From Template

An Access template is a ready-made file that, when opened, creates a complete database application. The template contains all the tables, forms, forms, reports, queries, and macros needed to achieve your goals.

To create a database from a database

- Go to the **File menu** and choose from the lists of templates or use the search feature to search for any template among the list of templates

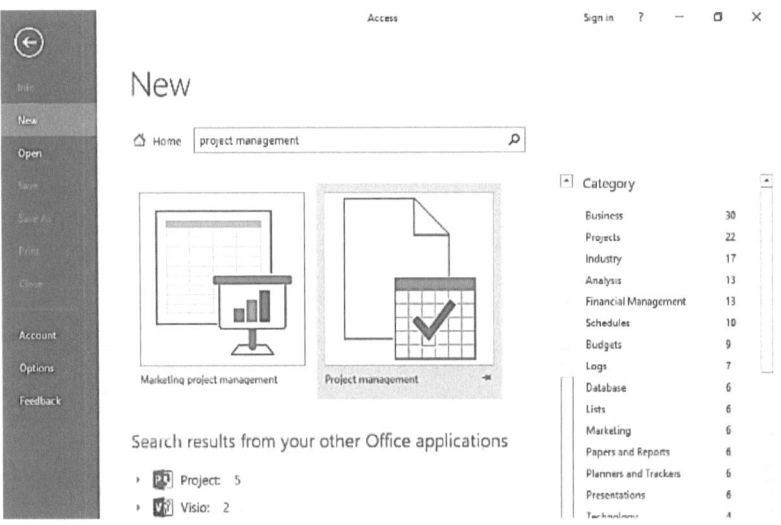

12

- When you click on the template, a preview panel will pop up, displaying the description of the database and a preview of the database fields. If the template suits your need, click on **Create button**, and the database will launch for usage.

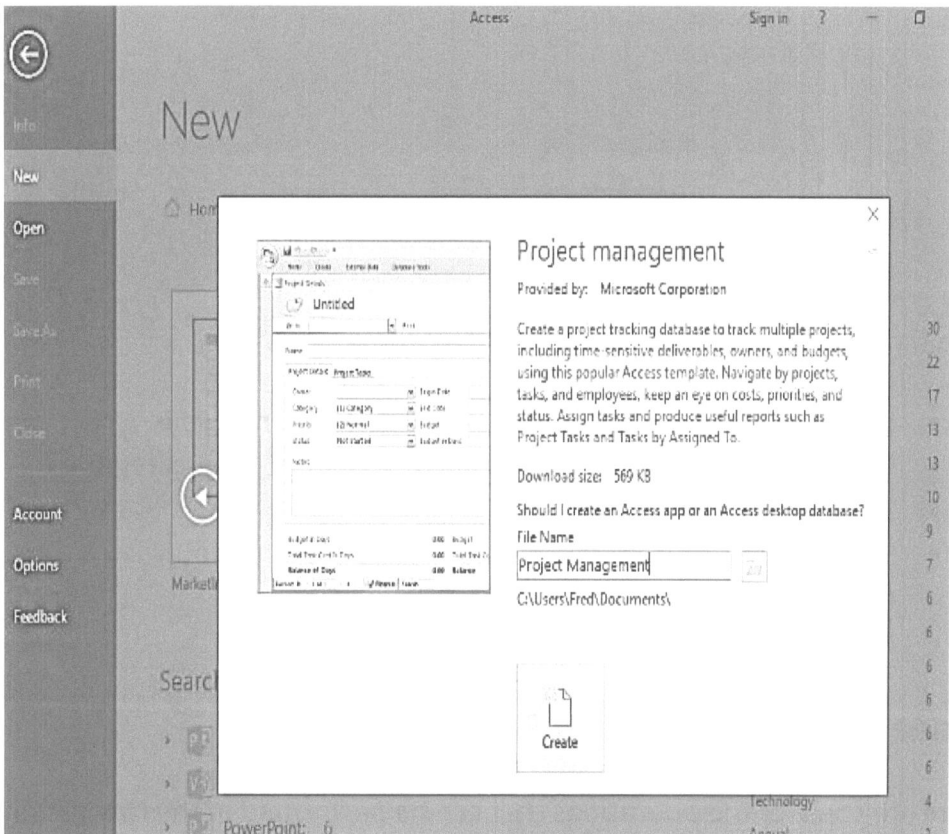

The Navigation Pane

The Navigation Pane is the center point of the database that displays or shows objects, tables, queries, forms, reports, and macros that allows you to filter, and search through these objects to locate the one you are looking for in the database. The Navigation Panel is a rectangular object located at the left session of the database.

The Navigation Panel by default appears as a rectangular box with a tile on top, a yellow down pointing button, and Shutter Bar Open/Close Button

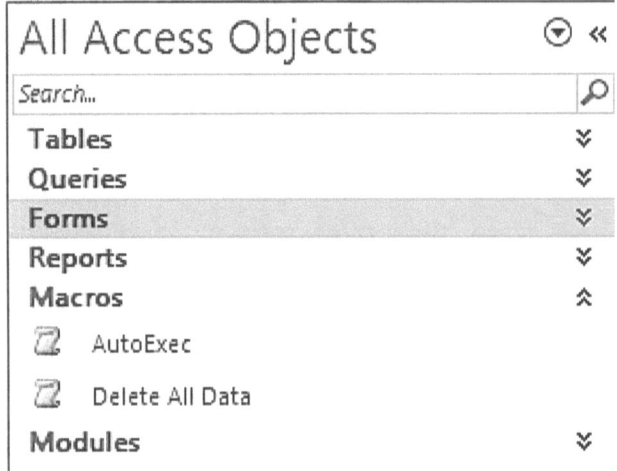

The Navigation Pane has the following features

- Easily show and hide the Access navigation panel view
- Select a type of category including the custom-built categories
- Sorting items and groups
- Searching for objects create and modify custom group
- Copy and paste Access objects
- Hide and unhide objects.

Managing The Navigation Pane

Here are some of the operations that can be performed in the Navigation Pane

Show Or Hide The Navigation Pane

To show or hide the Navigation Pane in Access, follow the steps below:

- To show the Navigation Pane, click on the shutter bar or press F11

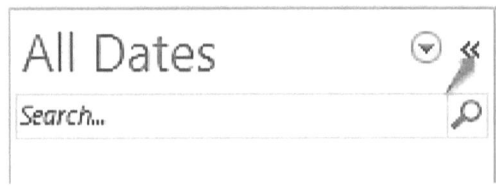

- To hide the Navigation Pane, click on the shutter bar or press F11

To Select A Predefined Category

When a new database is created, the category that is displayed by default is **Tables** and **Related Views** and the group is **All Tables**. But you change the categories to whichever one you desire.

- To display the **Navigate to category**, click on the title bar of the Navigation Pane
- Then select the predefined category

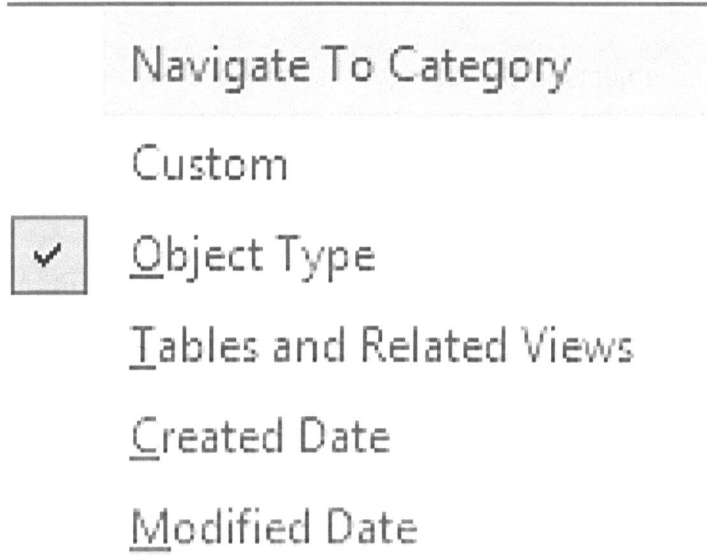

Filter By Group

While working on your database, you may want to display a particular set of database objects, to help your focus. By default, under the Filter by group are Tables, Queries, Forms, and Reports

- To display the **Filter by Group** menu, click on the title bar of the Navigation Pane
- Then select a group

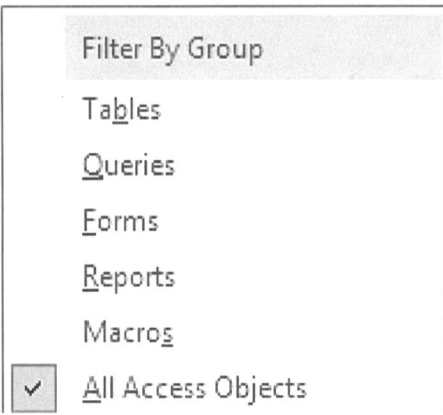

Sort Objects

By default, the objects in the Navigation Pane are sorted by object type in ascending alphabetical order. However, you can change the sorting order of the objects by following the steps below

- Right-click on the top of the Navigation Pane
- Select **Sort by** and then click on any of the sorting options

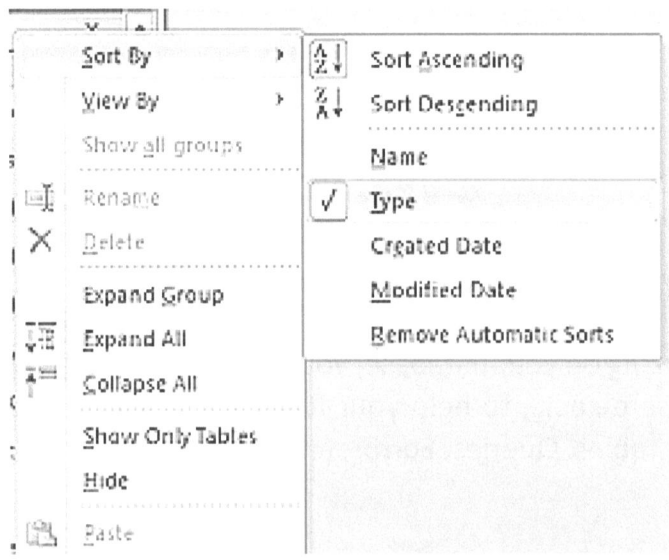

Finding Objects In Database

You can search for any object in the database using the Navigation Pane. Access allows you to search for objects in the categories and groups that are currently displayed or shown in the Navigation Pane.

To find any object in the Navigation Pane

- Click on the **Search box** in the **Navigation Pane**
- Input the name of the characters you need to find and it will be displayed for you to see.

- In case you need to carry out another search, click on the **Clear Search String**, or press **BACKSPACE** to delete the previous character, and then enter another character you wish to search for

Changing How Objects Are Displayed

Objects in the database can be displayed any way you want in the Navigation Pane. To indicate how objects should be displayed, follow the steps below

- Right-click on the top of the Navigation Pane

- Select **View By** and then click on any of the viewing options (**Details, Icon, or List**)

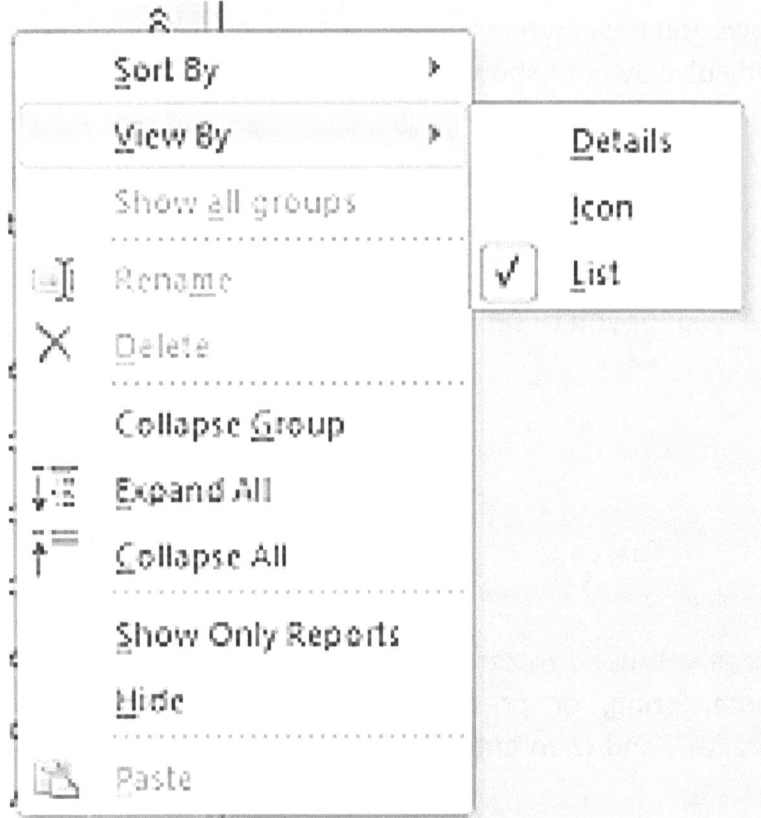

How To Hide And Unhide Objects And Groups

Rather than deleting an object or group from the database, you can hide the object or group and later unhide it.

To hide an object or group

- To hide an object, right-click on the object and then select the **Hide in this Group**
- To hide an entire group, right clock on the group, and then select **Hide**

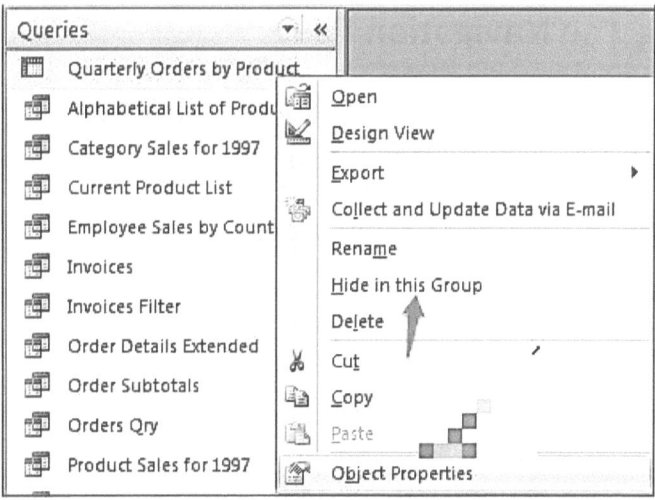

To unhide or display hidden objects or groups

To do this

- Right-click on the **Navigation Pane** and then click on the **Navigation Options**
- In the **Navigation Options** dialog box, click on the **Show Hidden Objects** check box. Then click on **OK**

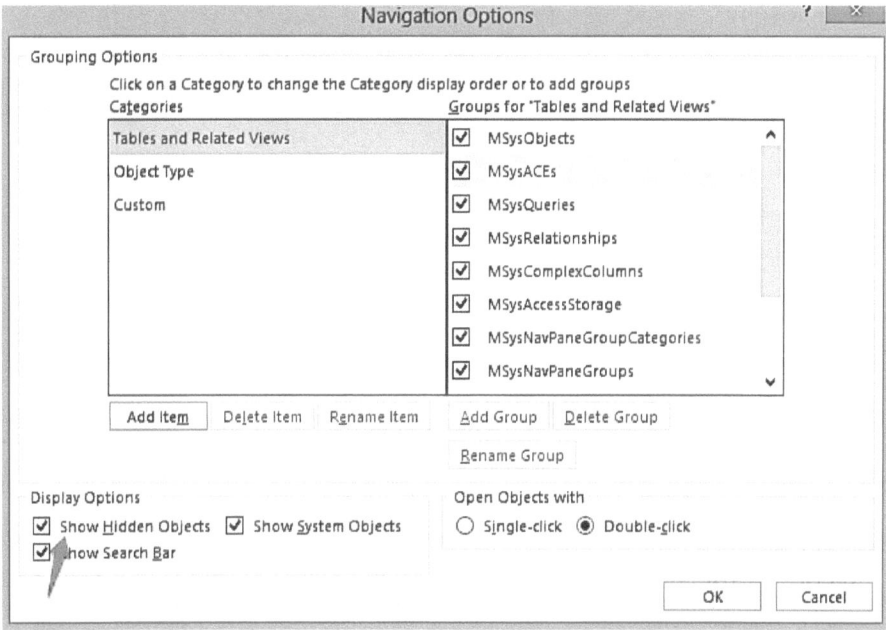

Customizing The Navigation Pane

The Navigation Pane is one of the most important features of Access. To organize the objects in the database the way you want, Then you will need to customize your Navigation Pane. Customizing your Navigation Pane involves creating custom categories and groups, renaming and deleting categories and groups, and lots more. In few minutes, we will be learning how to customize with the Navigation Pane.

Creating A Custom Category

To create a custom category in the database, follow the steps below

- Right-click on the top of the Navigation Pane and then select **Navigation Options**
- In the **Navigation Options** dialog box under the **Categories list,** click on **Add Item**
- Input the name of the new category and then press **Enter**

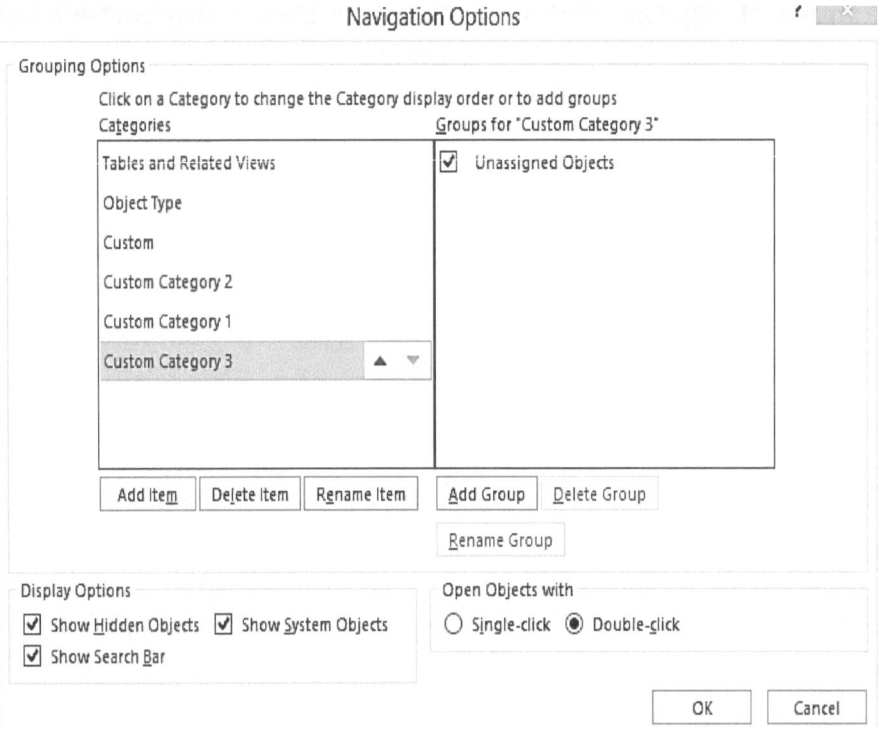

Renaming A Custom Category

To rename a custom category to whatever name you want, follow the steps below:

- Right-click on the top of the Navigation Pane and then select **Navigation Options**
- In the **Navigation Option** dialog box under the **Categories list,** select the item you want to rename, and then click on **Rename Item**
- Input the new name of the category and then press **Enter**

Deleting A Custom Category

- Right-click on the top of the Navigation Pane and then select **Navigation Options**
- In the **Navigation Option** dialog box under the **Categories list**, select the item you want to delete, and then click on **Delete Item**
- A dialog box will pop up, asking if you want to delete the item from the Categories, then click on **Ok** for the item to be permanently deleted

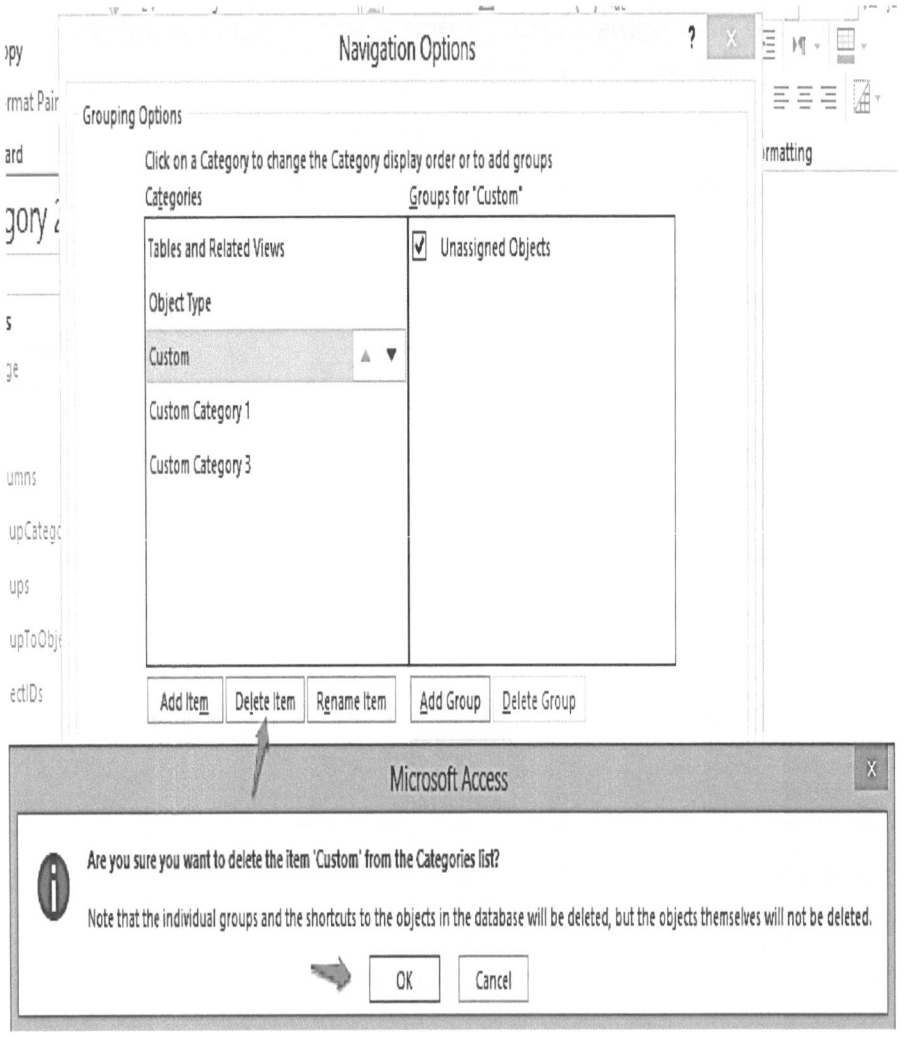

Creating A Custom Group

- Right-click on the top of the Navigation Pane and then select **Navigation Options**
- In the **Navigation Option** dialog box under the **Categories list**, select the category you wish to add the new group
- Click on **Add group** under **Groups**
- Then input the name of the new group and then press **Enter**

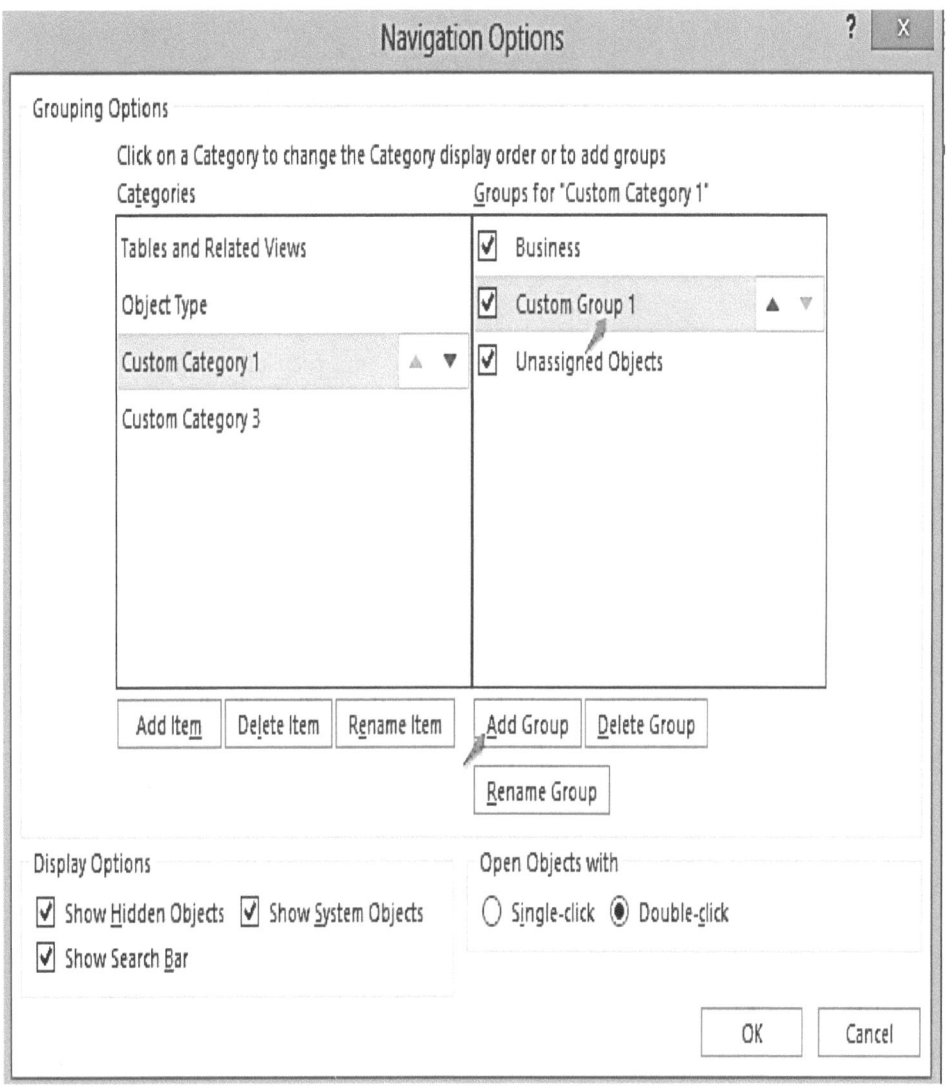

Renaming A Custom Group

- Right-click on the top of the Navigation Pane and then select **Navigation Options**
- In the **Navigation Option** dialog box under **Group for**, select the group you wish to rename
- Click on **Rename Group**, input the new name of the group, and then press **Enter**

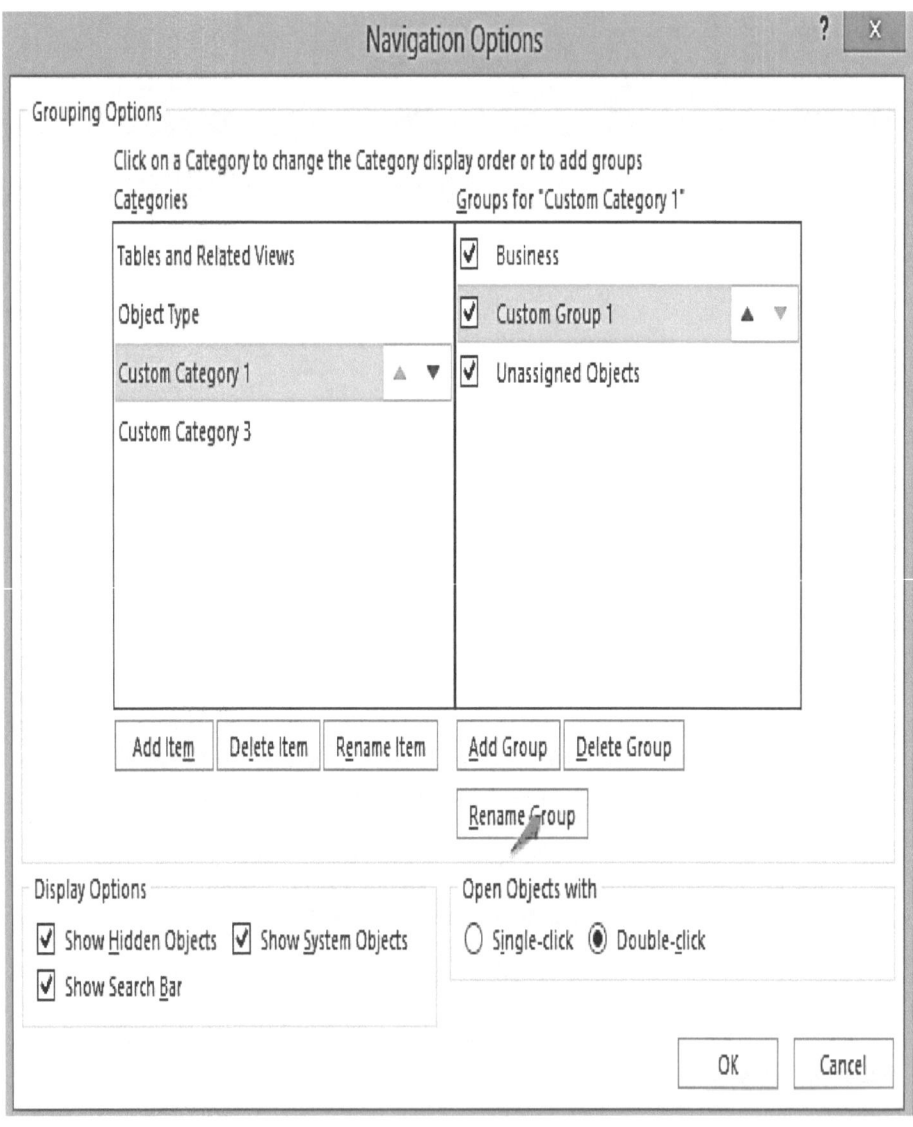

Deleting A Custom Group

- Right-click on the top of the Navigation Pane and then select **Navigation Options**
- In the **Navigation Option** dialog box under **Group for**, select the group you wish to delete
- Click on **Delete Group**, and a dialog box will be displayed asking if you want to delete the group. Click on **Ok** and the group will be deleted

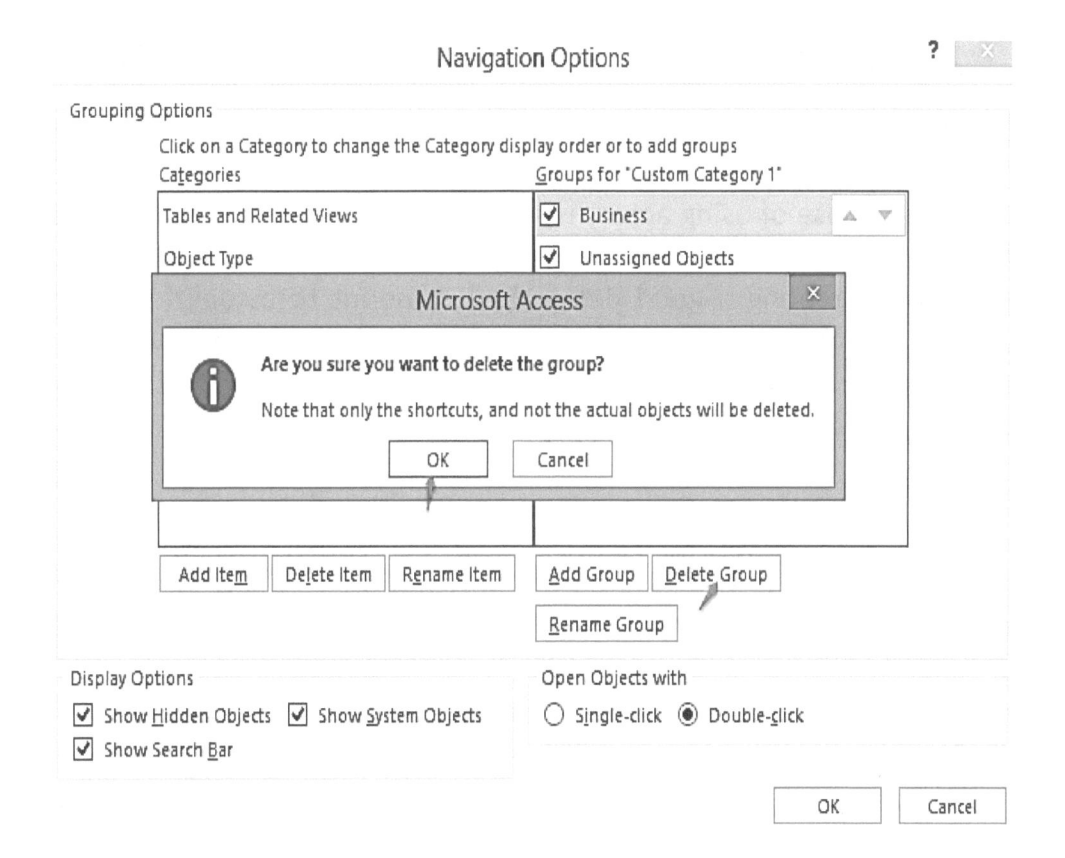

Creating A Custom Group From A Database Object

- **Right-click on the object you wish to put in a new group**
- Move to **Add to group,** and then click **New Group** (A new group will appear in the Navigation Pane)
- Then input the name of the new group and press **Enter**

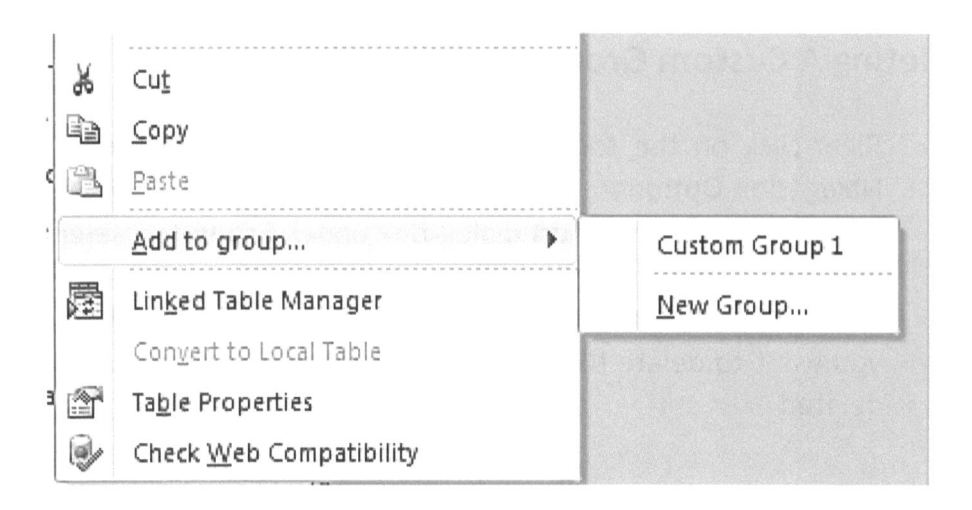

Designing A Database

The main purpose of using access is to be able to create a database and not just anyhow database, but one that provides up-to-date and accurate information. Creating a good design is paramount to actualizing your goals while working with the database. With a good database, you can enter information accurately and you can also get the right information from it when needed.

Here in this section, the guidelines to be considered when designing a database. Here, you will get to learn how to decide what information you need, how to decide the information into the appropriate tables and columns, etc.

To design the database, the following guidelines must be put into consideration

Deciding What Information You Need

The first thing to put into consideration is the kind of information you want in the database. This could be customers' information or the record of the purchase orders. With this being put into consideration, you will be able to get every piece of the information required by the organization's record.

To find the kind of information required by an organization, you can start by examining or checking the previous forms used to record the information used by the organization.

While deciding on what information you need, ensure that each piece of information is broken into smallest useful parts.

Separating Information Into Different Database Tables

After deciding on what information you need to put in the database, the next thing to do is to think of how to separate the information into database tables.

Deciding on the numbers of database tables, you need and how to separate data across the different tables is one of the most difficult parts of designing.

Below are the rules to apply when separating into different tables

- Limit a table to one subject only each table in the database should contain information about a single subject.
- Avoid duplicate information i.e., do not keep the same information more than once in a database or duplicate information across different.

Choosing Fields For Database Tables

For all the tables that the information is separated into, there must be at least one field. The table is the subject while the fields are the details or facts about the subject.

To create a field that will be added to the database table, follow the guidelines below

- Ensure to break down information into smaller logical parts. For instance, create separate fields for the first and last name. With this, you can easily sort out the tables using the fields.

- Ensure to give clear and detailed descriptive names to the fields, to know exactly what they are meant for, and also avoid errors
- While separating information into different database tables, do not include calculated data. This implies that you should not store the result of calculations in tables. Rather, let the Access execute the calculation you which to see the results.
- As you begin to input the information into the table, include the field for each piece of information. Do not wait until the information is entered into the table before adding the fields, because this can be so stressful and tiring.

Deciding On A Primary Key Field For Each Database Table

For each table in the database, there must be a primary key field.

The primary key field is the unique identification number which can be ID number, serial number, etc. The primary key field prevents you from inputting or entering duplicate data into two different records by displaying a dialog box, warning you not to insert duplicate data. In the query, the primary key field is also important, this allows access to search for information and obstructs you from obtaining the information twice.

Mapping The Relationship Between Tables

When the database contains more than one table, there is a need to map how the table relates to one another. With this in place, the information from different tables is linked or brought together in a meaningful way.

The relationships are usually formed between the primary key field in the table and the corresponding field, which is known as the foreign key in another table.

CHAPTER FOUR

BUILDING YOUR DATABASE TABLES

The database tables are the foundation or building blocks of a database. These are what contain or hold the raw data that are later manipulated

Here in this chapter, you will be learning how to create database tables from scratch or the template.

Creating A Database Table

One of the most important things to learn while using the database is to learn how to create tables, and how the data are entered. In few minutes, we will be learning how to create a table using the three methods

- Creating a database table from scratch
- Creating a database table from a template

Creating a database table by importing database table from another database

Creating A Database Table From The Scratch

To create a database table from the scratch, follow the steps

- Open **Access,** go to the **Create tab,** and click on the **Table Design button**

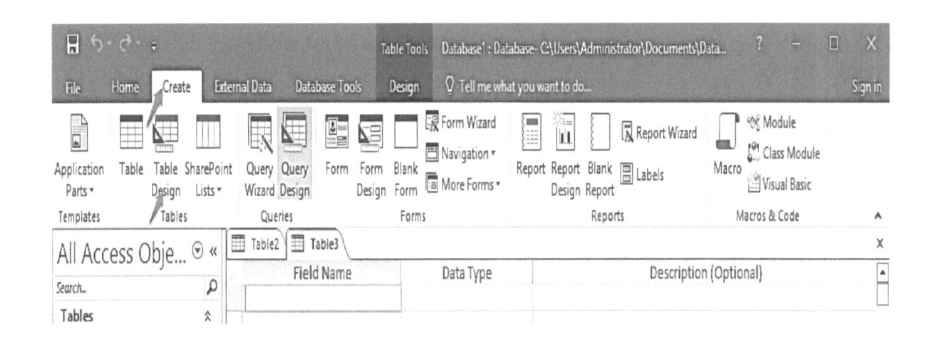

- Click on the **Save button** on the **Quick Access toolbar**
- In the **Save As** dialog box, input the descriptive name of the table and then click on **OK**

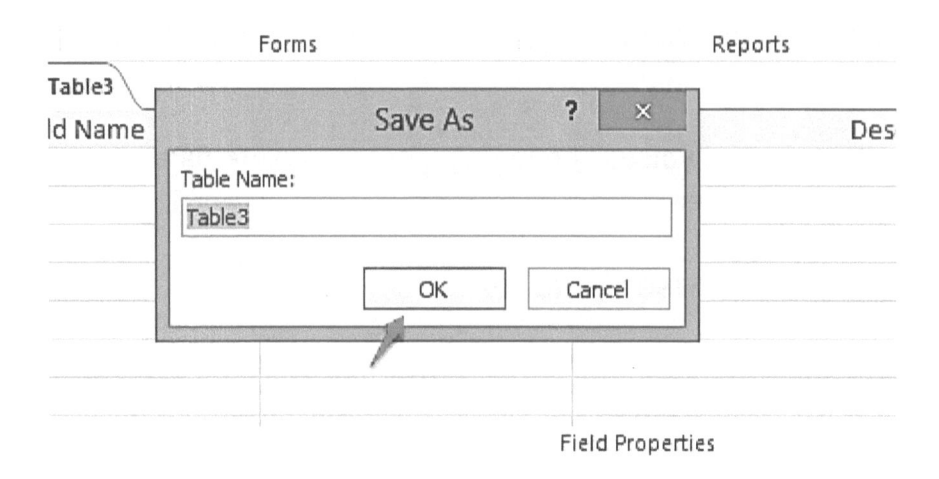

Creating A Database Table From A Template

Access provides four templates' types to create a table which are

- **Contacts:** This is used for storing contact addresses and phone numbers
- **Issues:** For prioritizing issues
- **Tasks:** This is used for tracking projects and their status
- **User:** For storing email addresses

Just like using a template for tables. Access also offers ready-made queries, forms reports.

To create a table using a template, follow the procedures below

- Open **Access,** go to the **Create tab,** and click on the Application Parts button
- In the drop-down list, under Quick Start; you can select **Contacts, Issues, Tasks, or Users**

- In the **Create Relationship** dialog box, click on **There is no relationship** and then click on **Create.**

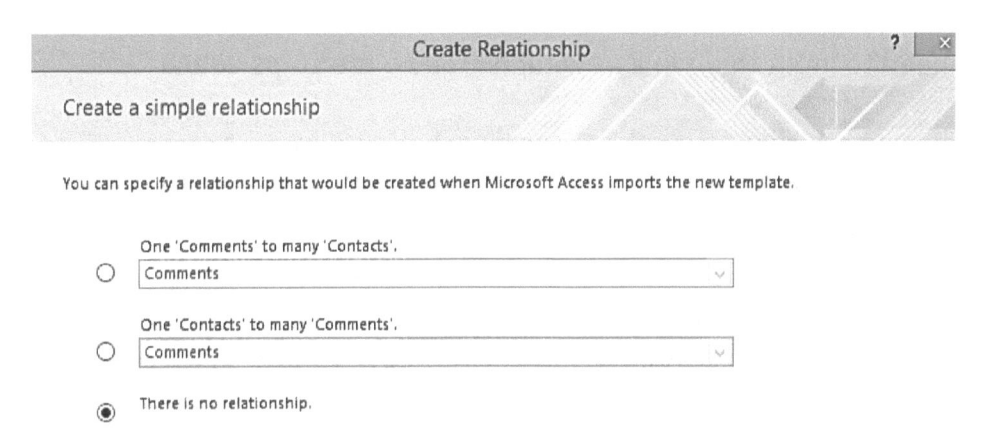

- On the Navigation pane, right-click on the name of the table you created and then select **Design View** (The Design view displays the names of the fields in the tables)

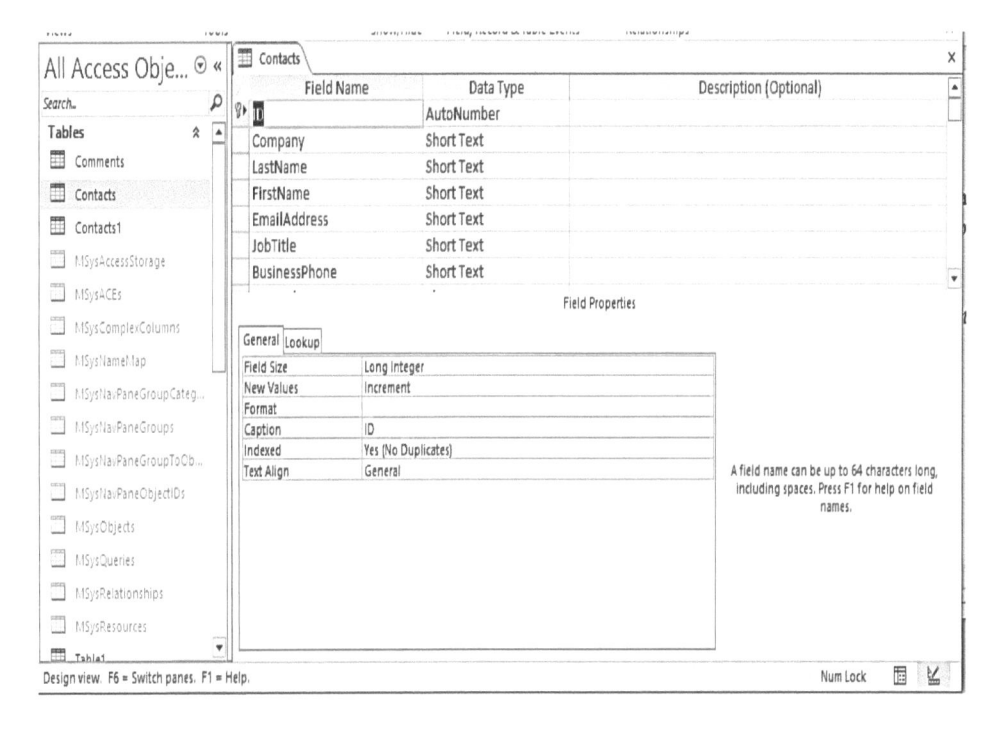

NOTE: Before you create a database table using a template, ensure that all objects that are opened are closed

Importing A Table From Another Database

Assuming the records, you need have been inputted in another table and you need to input them in a new table, follow the steps below

- Open **Access,** go to the **External tab,** and click on **Access**
- In the **Get External Data – Access Database dialog** box, click on Browse.
- In the File Open dialog box, select the Access database with the table, and then click on Open
- Select the first option button (Import, Tables, Queries, Forms Reports, Macros, and Modules) and click Ok
- Select the database table you want from **the Tables tab** and then click **on Ok**

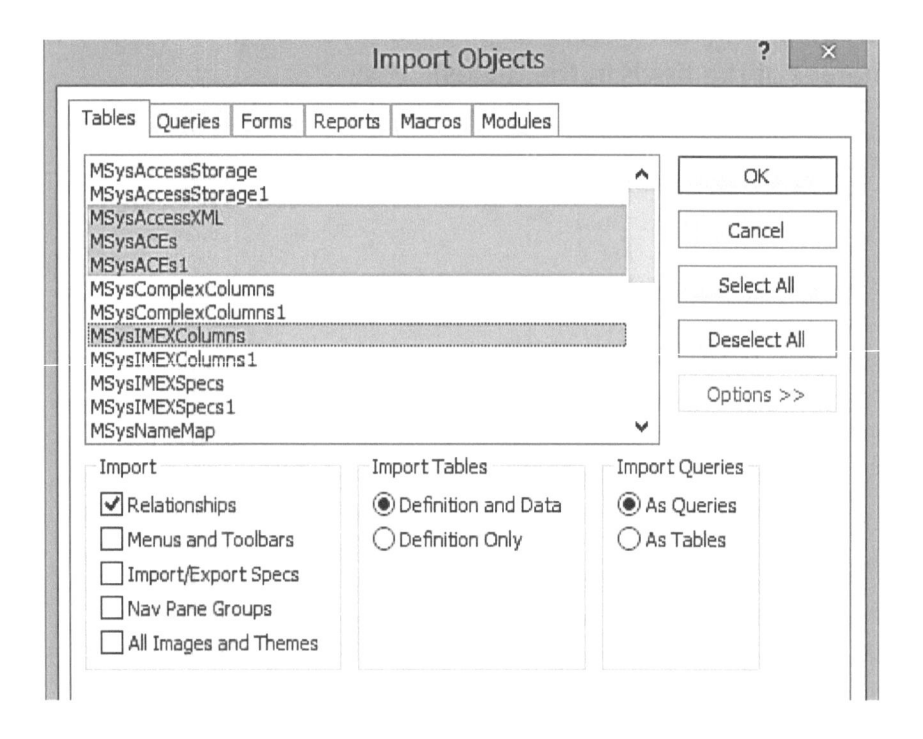

Opening And Viewing Tables

To open a table, you will need to go to the Navigation pane and to view the names of the database table you created, you will need to select the Table group.

While opening and viewing tables in the database, there are two keywords you need to know

- **Datasheet View**: This is used for entering and checking data in a table
- **Design View**: This is used for creating fields and giving details about their parameters

To open and view the tables in the database, there are several ways to go about it. Below, are the ways to open and view tables

Opening Table In Design View

To open the table in the design view

- Select the table in the **Navigation Pane** and right-click on it
- In the shortcut menu, select **Design view,** and the objects in the table open as a tab on the work surface

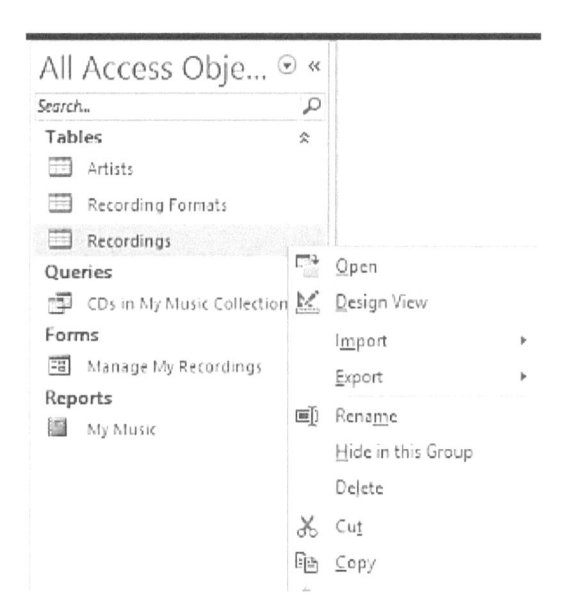

Opening Table In Datasheet View

To open the table in the Datasheet View

- Select the table in the **Navigation Pane** and right-click on it
- In the shortcut menu, select **Open** and the objects in the table opens as a tab on the work surface

Switching Between Views With The View Buttons

To switch between the view buttons

- **Select the table and move to the Home tab**
- **Select View Button** and choose **Database Sheet View** or **Design View**

Switching Between Views On The Status bar

To switch between views on the Status bar

- Select the table and move to the Status bar to either choose **Datasheet View** or **Design View**

Switching Between Views By Right Clicking

To switch between views by right-clicking, all you need to do is right-click on the table's tab and either choose **Datasheet View** or **Design View**

Entering And Altering Table Fields

After you must have a created a table, the next thing to do is to input the fields. You can also allow Access to create the tables for you and manipulate the fields to your liking.

Here in this section, we will be taking a tour on how to insert fields into the database table

Creating A Field

Let's quickly learn how to create a field from the scratch or using the ready-made fields available in Access.

Creating A Field On Your Own

To create a field on your own, follow the steps below

- Open the table you need to enter a new field
- Switch the view to **Design View**
- Insert a new row to the field; to do this, right-click on the new field and then click on **Insert Row**
- Input a name in the **Field Name** column
- Click on the **Data Type** column to choose the data type from the drop-down list
- You can enter a description in the **Description column** when necessary

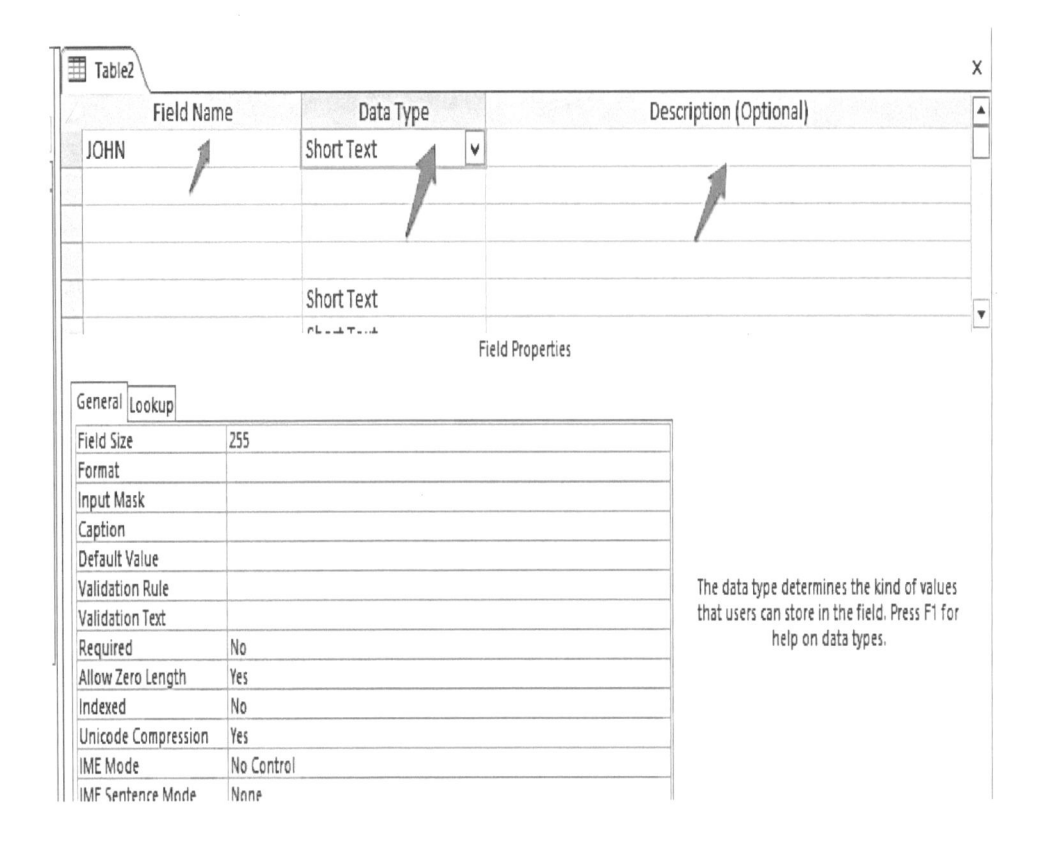

Using The Ready-Made Fields

To create a field using the ready-made field, follow the steps below

- Switch to **Datasheet View** and select the field you intend for your new field to look like
- On the **Field tab,** click on **More Field b**utton, and select the name of the field you want on the drop-down menu
- Go to the **Add & Delete in the Field button** to select the data type
- After all these have been done, switch back to **Design View** to check the field properties

The Data Types

In chapter 1 of this book, I discussed explicitly on the data types in a tabular form, in case you have forgotten what we discussed on data type, you can go back to read all over again

36

Designating The Primary Key Field

In the course of creating a table, the primary key field is one of the most essential parts of the table that cannot be overemphasized, and Access won't permit the closing of the table unless a primary key field is created. As earlier said about the primary key field, the primary key field does not allow duplicate and null data into the table.

To make a field in the database to be a primary key field, follow the steps below

- Go to the **Design View**, select the field you want to make the primary key
- Right-click on the field and then click on the **Primary key button** (Here, a small symbol appears on the row selector to indicate which of the fields is a primary key field.

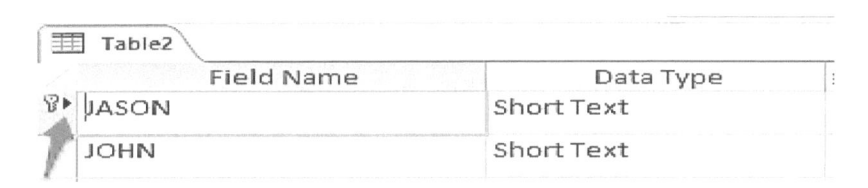

Field Name	Data Type
JASON	Short Text
JOHN	Short Text

To remove a primary key from a database table, click on the row selector and then select the Primary key all over again. With this being done, the primary key will be removed from the field.

Moving, Renaming, And Deleting Fields

In case you need to move, rename and delete fields in the database table, and you are wondering how to go about it, switch over to the Design View and follow the steps below

Moving A Field

To move a field, do the following
- Click in the Field's row and release the mouse button
- Click and drag the selector to the desired location

Renaming A Field

To rename a field in a table, follow the steps below

- Click in the Field Name box where the old name is
- Erase the old name and type the new name

Deleting A Field

To delete a field in a table, follow the steps below

- Click in the Field Name
- Navigate to the **(Table Tools) Design tab**
- Then click on the **Delete Rows button**

Understanding Field Properties

Every table in the Access database comprises fields and each field has its properties. The properties of the fields are what describes the characteristics and behavior of the data that are found in the field.

The properties of the field determine the type of data that can be entered into the fields.

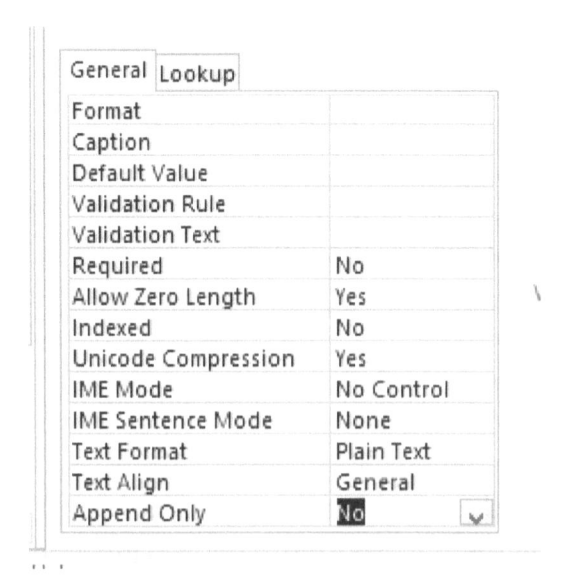

Below are the field properties:

- **Field Size**: The field size contains the text field and the number field. The text field allows for a maximum number of 255 characters that can be inputted in the field, and the default setting is 50. The Number field, just like the Text field allows for maximum numbers of 255 characters, and the numbers are stored as Byte, Integer, Long Integer, Single, Double, or Replication ID.
- **Format:** The Format property is what allows you to set the way or manner in which an Access will display or print out the data located in the table. The Format property can be displayed in form of text, numbers, dates, and times
- **Decimal Places:** This indicates the number of decimal places Access can display. The default specification is Auto, which allows Access to display two decimal places for the Currency, Fixed, Standard, and Percentage format and the number of decimal places.
  You can also set the number of the decimal places, ranging from 0 to 15.
- **Input Mask:** The Input Mask creates a pattern on how data must be entered into a particular field. For instance, when you enter a phone number into a field, the Input Mask by default, allows the number to take the phone number format. The Input Mask supports the following data types; Text, Number, Date and Time, and Currency.
- **Caption:** This property allows the user to give a fully descriptive detail about a field in which the Access displays in form of labels and report headings. When the caption is not entered, Access uses the field name as the caption. The field property supports all data types.
- **Default Value:** This property allows the user to specify or indicate a default value for a field that Access automatically uses for a new row if there is no value given. If a default value is not set, the field will be null when the user refuses to input a value. The Default Value supports Text, Memo, Numbers, Date and Time, Currency, and Yes/No data types

- **Validation Rule**: This is the field property that allows you to supply an expression that limits or controls the values that can be inputted in the field. To set a validation rule, enter an expression in the Validation Rule text box. The following are the instances of the validation rules
    - \>100 means that the value entered must greater than 100
    - <=200 means that the value entered must be less than or equal to zero
    - \>#1/2/2020# means that the date to be entered must be greater than February 1, 2020 (Each time a date is used in an expression, the date must be enclosed in a number sign (#)
- **Validation Text:** This is the message that is displayed by Access when the data entered does not follow the validation rule. You can also create your message. If the default message is not suiting for you. To do this, enter the custom message in the Validation Text dialog box.
- **Required**: This is one of the important properties of the field that helps to specify whether or not a value must be entered in the field. By default, the property is set to No. If No is selected, no entry is required to be entered, but if Yes is selected, an entry must be made otherwise, a message box will be displayed telling you to ensure that an entry is made.
- **Allow Zero Length:** This property allows the user to input zero-length strings i.e. a string containing no characters. The Zero-length text strings come in handy when you want to enter data in a field, and some data do not exist. For instance, you want to enter a person's data but he does not have an email address, and there is a space for it. All you need to do is to enter the zero-length string. To enter the zero-length text string in the cell, type ".
- **Indexed:** This is the property that indicates if the user wants to index the field to speed up searches and sorts operations performed on the field. By default, this is set to No
- **Unicode Expression:** This is a property setting of the field that compresses data stored in Unicode when set to Yes, thus saving space in the database file.

- **Smart Tags:** This property allows you to enter a smart tag name and actions in the field, by clicking the three dots next to the Smart Tags box and selecting an option in the Action Tags dialog box.
- **Text Align:** The Text Align property determines how the texts in the column, forms, or reports are to be aligned (Left, Right, Center, or Distribute). When you select General, Access determines how the texts are aligned.
- **Text Format:** This property allows Access to set the text format to either Rich text or Plain text. The Rich text allows to make words bold, italics, underline, and change font sizes and colors. The Plain text makes words plain without formatting. The Text format is only available in the Long Text field.
- **Append Only:** This property allows Access to add data to a Long Text field to collect a history of comments. This property is only available in Long Text fields.
- **Show Date Picker:** This property displays the built-in date picker control to select a date when the field receives focus in a table datasheet or query. This property is only available in the Date/Time fields.
- **IME Mode/IME Sentence Mode:** This property is what is used in Access to convert characters and sentences from the East Asian version of Access.

Creating A Lookup Data-Entry List

The Lookup Data-entry List is one of the most important features in Access that allows one to enter data correctly in the database. With this feature, you can enter the data into the database, without having to type them. This feature saves time and avoids the entering of invalid data into the database.

There are two ways of creating a drop-down list

- Creating the lists by entering the items yourself
- Get the items from another database table

Creating A Drop-Down List On Your Own

You can create a drop-down list on your own with entries you type by following the steps below

- Go to the **Design View** and select the Field that you wish to apply the drop-down lists
- Go to the **Data Type** drop-down list and choose **Lookup Wizard**
- In the **Lookup Wizard dialog**, select the second option **I Will Type in the Value That I want**, and then click on the **Next button**

- In the next dialog box, under **Col1** and then type the item you want to appear in the drop-down list. Then click on the **Next** button

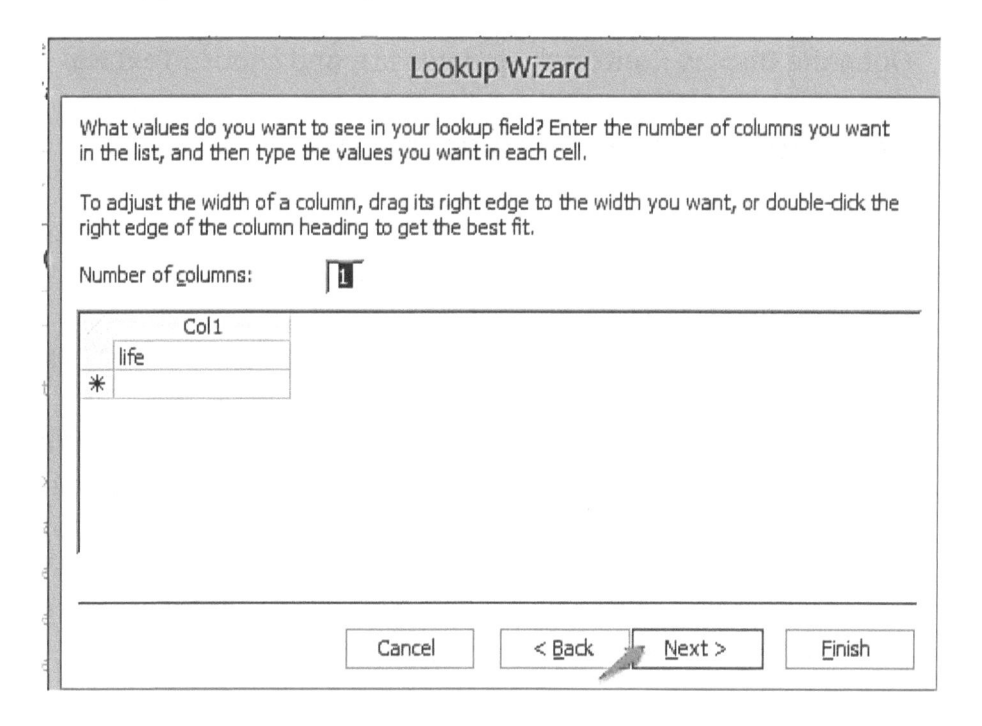

- Input the name for the field and then click on the **Finish** button

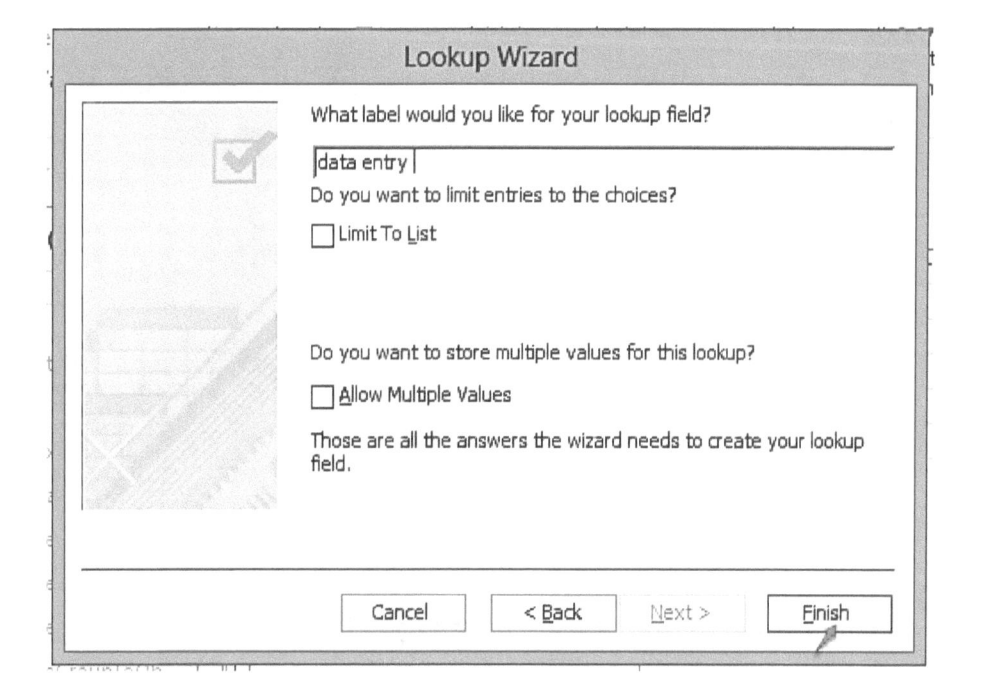

To remove the lookup list from the field

- Select the field, go to the **lookup tab** in the **Design View** window
- Open the **Display Control** drop-down list, and choose **Text Box**

Getting List Items From A Database Table

You can get items in a drop-down list from another database table, follow the steps

- Go to the **Design View** and select the Field that you wish to apply the drop-down lists
- Go to the **Data Type** drop-down list and choose **Lookup Wizard**
- In the **Lookup Wizard dialog**, select the first option **I Want the Lookup Field to Get the Values from Another Table or Query,** and click **Next**.

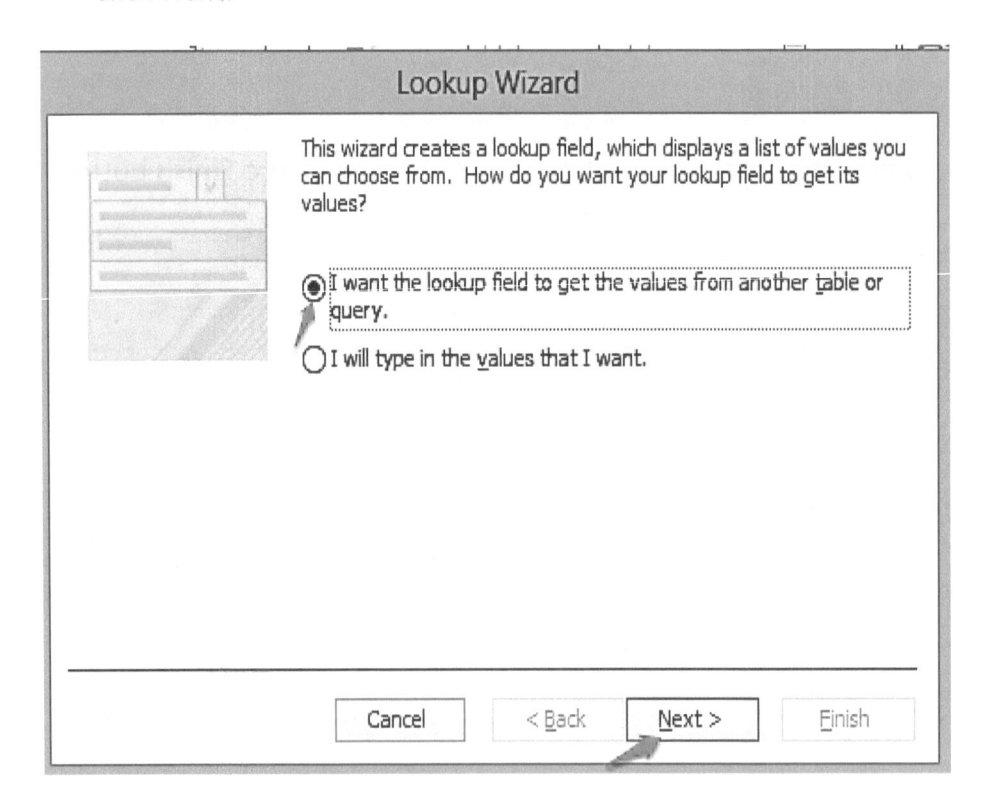

- **In the Lookup Wizard,** select the table with the data you need and click on the **Next button.**

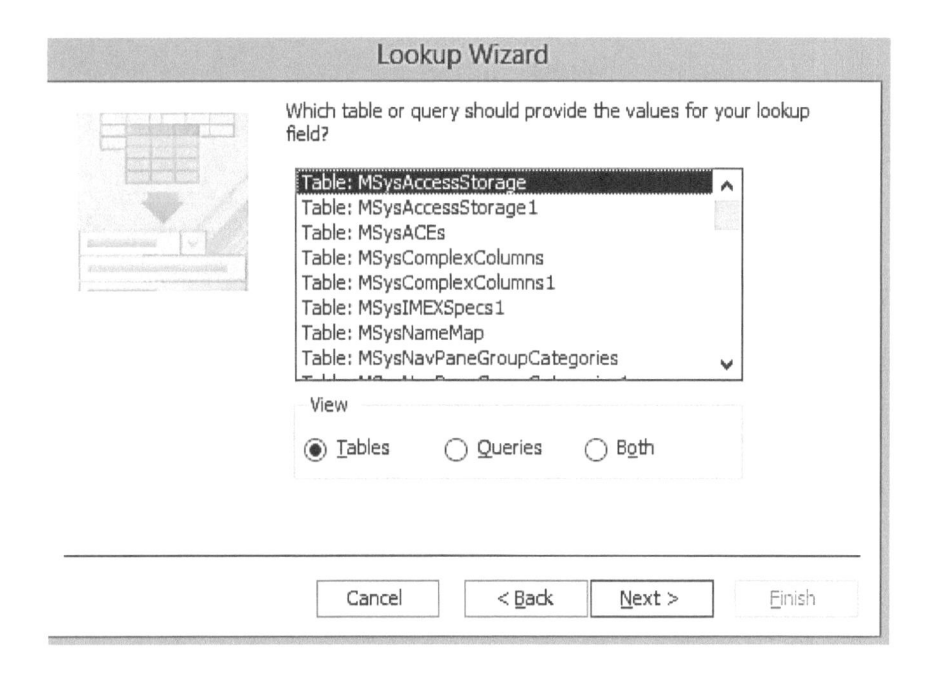

- Select the field where the data for your list is stored, select the > button, and then click on the **Next** button.

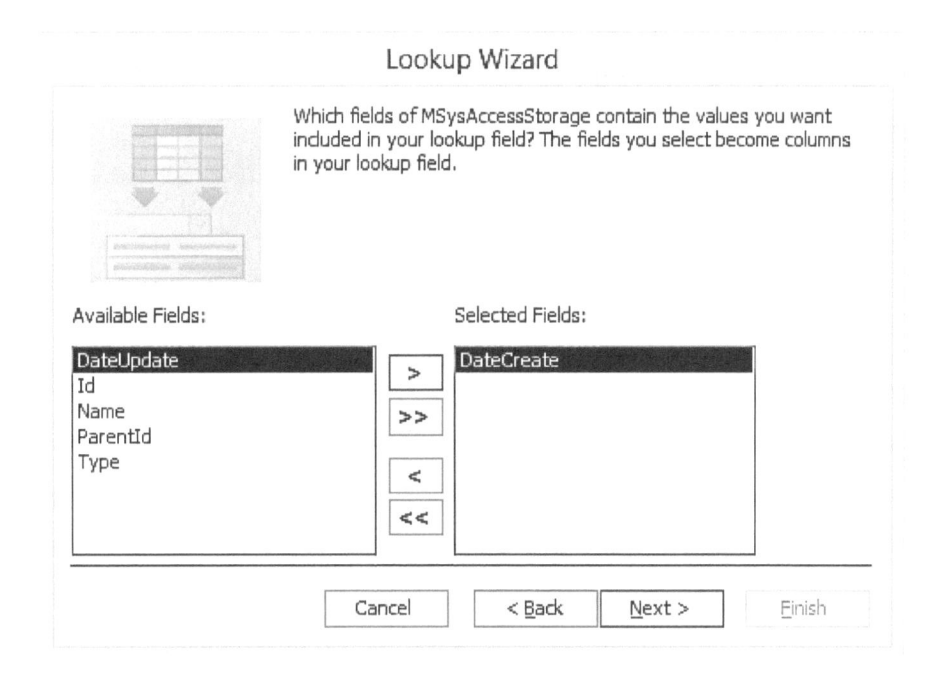

- On the next page, you will be asked, what sort of order do you want for the items in your list box (Ascending or descending order). Then click on **Next.**

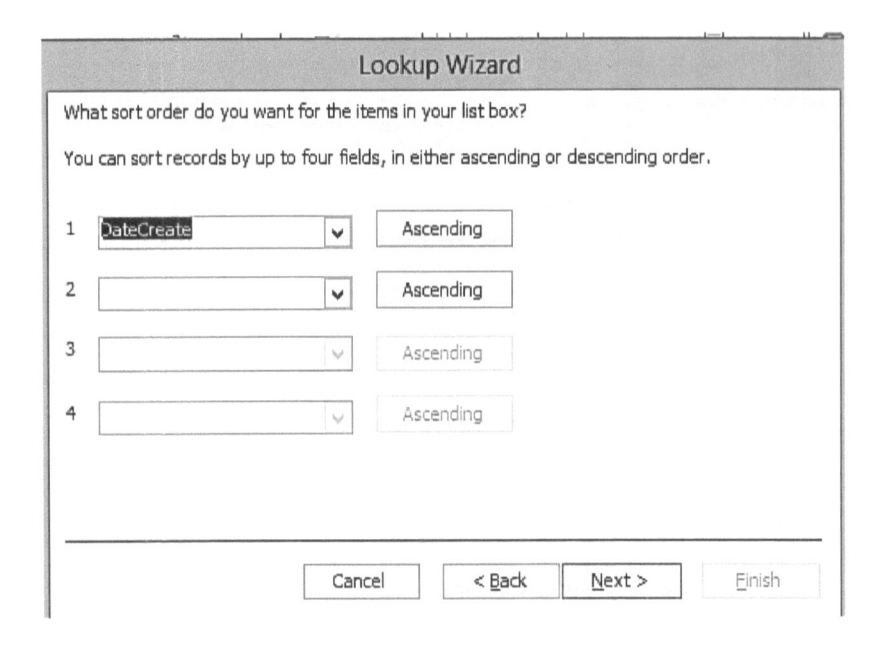

- Here on this page, you will be asked, how wide you like the columns in your lookup field; just place the cursor in between the line, until it becomes a cross sign, adjust the width of the column and then click on **Next.**

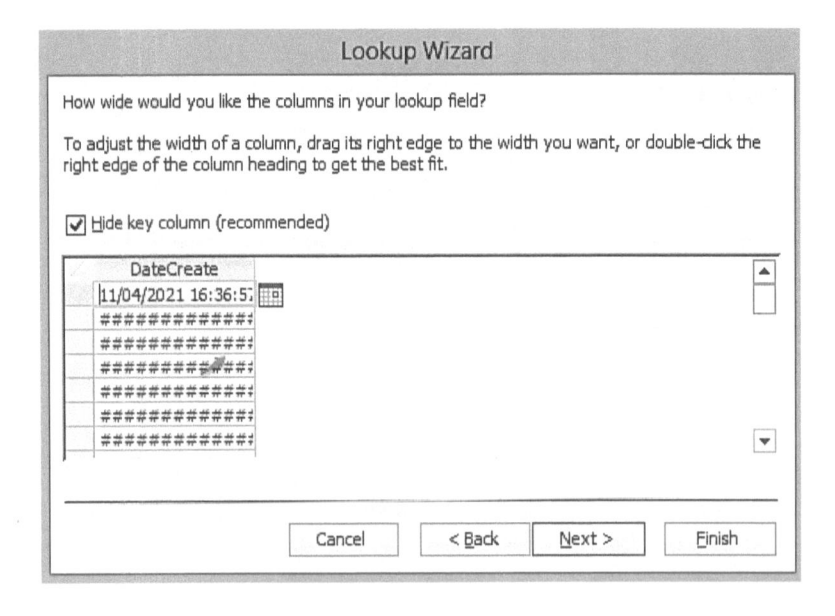

- Input the name for the field and then click on the **Finish** button.

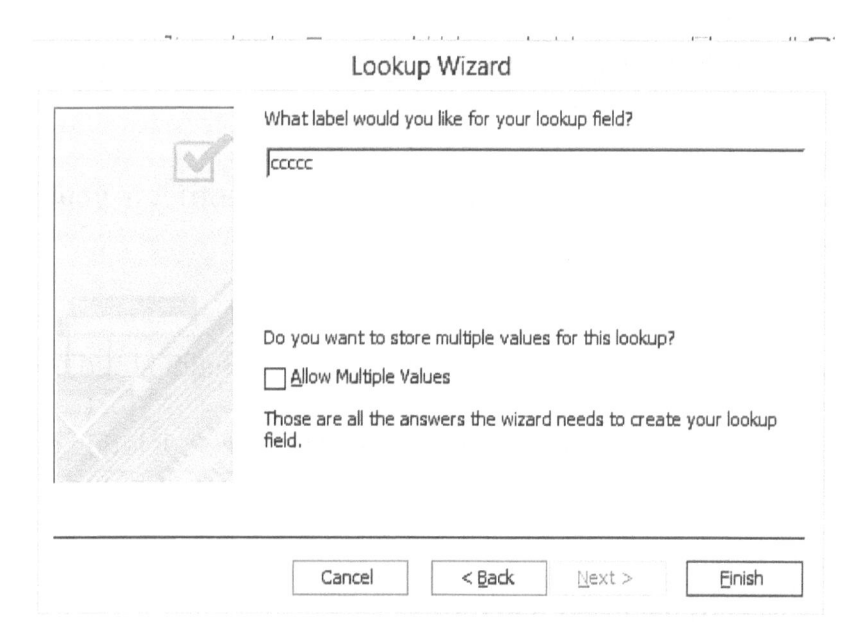

Indexing For Faster Sorts, Searches, And Queries

Indexing is a process in Access of keeping information about data in one or more fields. With indexing, Access does not have to go through the long process of searching through every record in the database table to sort data, search for data, or even run a query, rather Access checks through its data where it is stored.

Indexing data in the fields helps the Access to speed up queries and sorts especially in a large database table. In a nutshell, indexing helps Access to improve the speed of its data retrieval process.

By default, the field you select as the primary key field is indexed. If you do queries and searches very well, it is recommended to add other fields to the primary key field for indexing.

Below are some important notes about indexes:

- Since indexes speed up searching and sorting, it is recommended to index the fields that are used frequently to search and sort.

- Avoid indexing too many fields in a table. The more fields you index, the slower the searches and sort will be.
- Index supports all data types except for memo, OLE, and hyperlinks fields.
- By default, the primary key fields are indexed.
- Indexing helps prevent duplicate and invalid entries in your table.

The Indexed Property Settings

The Indexed property has three functions which are highlighted below

No: This does not allow the field to be indexed and even deleting existing indexes.

Yes (Duplicate OK): This allows the field to be indexed and allow duplicate values to be entered in the field

Yes (No Duplicate): This allows the field to be indexed but does not allow duplicate values to be entered. This works like the primary key fields.

Indexing One Field In A Table

To index a field, follow the steps below

- Switch to the **Design View**, select the field you wish to index
- Go to the **General tab** of the field property, open the **Indexed** drop-down list and choose any of the options available

Indexing Bases On More Than One Field.

To index more than one field. Follow the steps below

- Switch to the **Design View**, go to the **Table Tools (Design tab)** and click on the Indexes button where the Index windows appear
- In the Index Name column, in the first blank row, type a name for the index

- In the Field Name column, open the drop-down list and select the first field you want for the multi-field index
- In the next row, leave the **Index Name** column blank and then enter the second field for the index in the **Field Name** column until you have selected the fields to be indexed

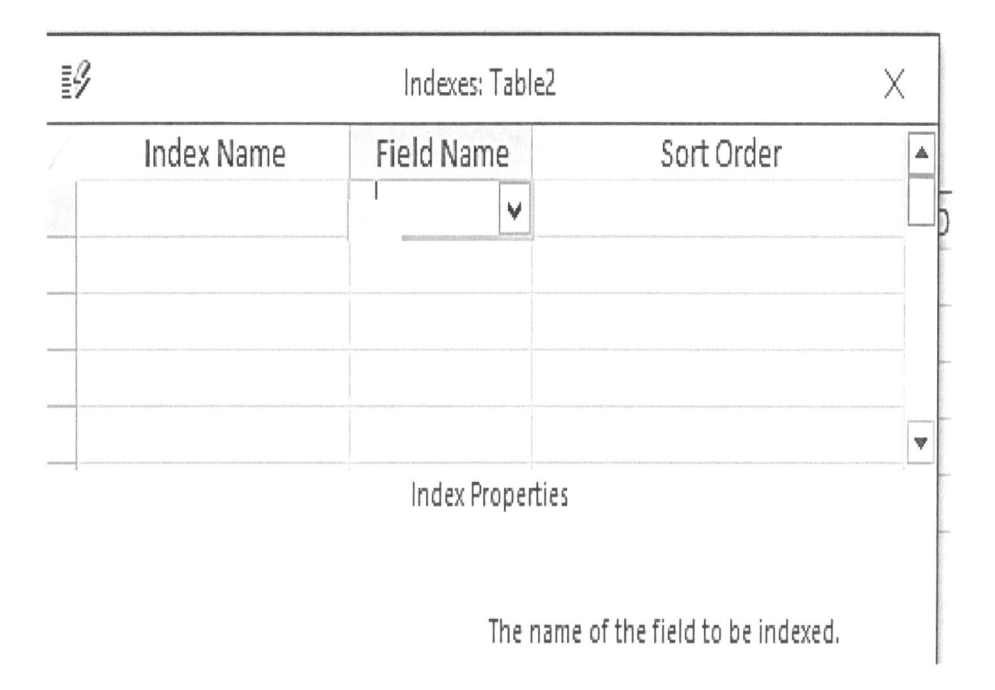

- In the **Sort Order column,** you can either choose **Descending** or **Ascending** order
- Then click on the **Close button**

Deleting An Index

To delete an index in a field

- Switch to the **Design View**, select the field you wish to delete the index
- Go to the **Table Tools (Design tab)** and click **Index**
- In the **Index** window, select the rows that contain the index you wish to delete and then press **DELETE**

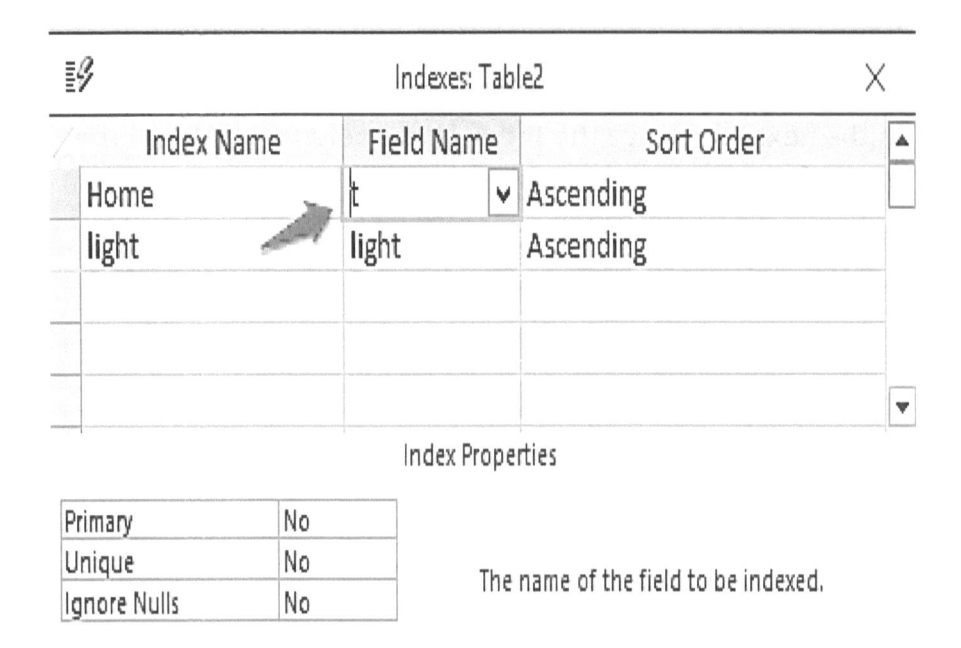

Index Name	Field Name	Sort Order
Home	t	Ascending
light	light	Ascending

Index Properties

Primary	No
Unique	No
Ignore Nulls	No

The name of the field to be indexed.

- Then close the **Index** window

Viewing And Editing Index

To view or edit indexes is the same way as following the steps involved in deleting an index. The difference here is that; you are not deleting but viewing or making changes to the indexes

To view and edit the index

- Switch to the **Design View**, select the field you wish to view, and edit the index.
- Go to the **Table Tools (Design tab)** and click **Index**
- In the **Index** window, view and edit the indexes to meet your needs
- Then close the **Indexes** window

CHAPTER FIVE
TIPS AND TRICKS ON ACCESS

In this chapter of this book, you will be learning some of the tips and tricks that will help you to get the best of Access, and at the same time utilize it for the desired goals. Below are some of the tips and tricks in Access

Every Table Should Have A Primary Key

Ensure that every table in Access has a primary key. This helps the database to locate specific records easily and faster. Also, it helps the data to be indexed by default.

Keep Your Access Database Fields As Small As Possible

While building the tables, ensure that the text fields are in the right format size. By default, the setup text for Access is Short Text which holds 255 characters. To adjust the file size, go to the **Field size s**ettings on the **General tab** in the **Design view**

Don't Over Index

In as much as indexing is very important, do not index the fields you don't need. Indexing all the fields may cause it to load slowly when it wants to update, delete or add records to the database

Choose The Optimal Data Types

While entering data into the fields, you should choose the best data types for your fields. Selecting the optimal data type helps to reduce the disk space used to store data, and the time it involves for Access to retrieve, manipulate, and write data.

Validating Your Access Data

Validating the data in your tables is one of the ways to prevent bad data from being entered into your table.

The amazing thing about this is that you can set the validation rule to what suits the purpose of your table without compromising.

Use Simple And Direct Names In Access

Before creating a table or database, ensure to have simple and direct names to tag your database file, fields, and tables. This helps to remember what your database is all about even if you have not opened it for a long period. Also, another can quickly relate with information on the database, even without you being there

Shortcut Keys And Controls

The following are shortcut keys and their functions used in Access 365

Frequently Used Shortcuts Keys

Shortcut keys	Functions
Alt or F10	To select the active tab of the ribbons and activate keyTips
Alt + H	To open the Home tab
Alt + Q	To open the Tell me box on the ribbon
Shift + F10	To show the shortcut menu for the selected item
F6	To move the focus to a different pane of the window
Ctrl + O	To open an existing database
F11	To show or hide Navigation Pane
F4	To show or hide a property sheet
F2	To switch between Edit mode and Navigation mode in the Datasheet or Design View
F5	To switch from Design view to Form view

Shortcut	Function
Shift + Tab	To move to the next or previous field in the Datasheet view
Alt + F5 (type the record number in the record number box, and then press Enter	Navigate to a specific record in the Datasheet view
Ctrl + P	To open the Print dialog box from Print
S	To open the Page Setup dialog box
Z	To zoom in or out on s part of the page
Ctrl + F	Open the Find tab in the Find and Replace dialog box in the Datasheet view or Form view
Ctrl + Plus Sign	To add a new record in Datasheet view or Form view
F1	To open the Help window
Alt + F4	Exit Access

Navigating Through The Ribbons Shortcut Keys

Shortcut	Functions
Alt + F	To open the File page
Alt + C	To open the Create tab
Alt + X	To open the External Data tab
Alt + Y	To open the Database Tools tab
Alt + J,B	To open the Fields tab
Alt + J, T	To open the Table tab
Alt + X, 2	To open the Add-ins tab
Alt + Q, and then enter the search term	To open the Tell me box
The Tab key or Shift + Tab	To move focus to commands on the ribbon
Ctrl + F1	To expand or collapse the ribbon

Shift + F10	To display the shortcut menu for the selected item
F6	To move the next or previous command on the ribbon
The Tab key or Shift + Tab	To move to the next previous command on the ribbon
Spacebar or Enter	To activate the selected command or control on the ribbon
Spacebar or Enter	To open the selected menu or gallery on the ribbon
The Down Arrow Key	To open the selected list on the ribbon e.g. Font list
The Tab Key	To move between items in an open menu or gallery
Enter	To modify a value in a control on the ribbon, and move the focus back to the document

The Shortcut Keys For Database Files

Shortcuts	Functions
Ctrl + N	To open a new database
Ctrl + O or Ctrl + F12	To open an existing database
Enter	To open the selected folder or file
Backspace	To open a folder one step above the selected folder
Delete	To delete the selected folder or file
Tab	To move forward through options
Shift + F10	To display a shortcut menu for a selected item such as a folder or file
Shift + Tab	To move backward through options
F4 or Alt + I	To open the Look in list
Ctrl + S	To save a database object
Ctrl + P	To print current or selected object
P or Ctrl +P	To open the Print dialog box from the Print Preview

S	To open the Page Setup dialog box from the Print Preview
C or Esc	To cancel Print Preview or Layout Preview
Esc	To return to the database from the Backstage

The Shortcut Keys For Access Workplace

Shortcut Keys	Functions
Ctrl + F	To go to the Search box in the Navigation Pane
F6 or Shift + F6	To switch to the next or previous pane in the workplace
Enter	To restore the selected minimized window when all windows are minimized.
Ctrl + F8	To Turn on Resize mode for the active window, when it is not minimized.
Ctrl + W or Ctrl + F4	To close the active database window
Alt + F11	To switch between the Visual Basic Editor and the previous active window
Ctrl + F10	Maximize or restore a selected window

The Shortcut Keys For Menus

Shortcut keys	Functions
Alt + Spacebar	To display in the program icon menu.
The Down or Up arrow key	To select the next or previous command with the menu or submenu visible
The Left or Right arrow key	To select the menu to the left or right. Also, when a submenu is visible, it is used to switch between the main menu and the submenu
Home or End	To select the first and the last command on the menu or submenu

Spacebar or Enter	To open the selected menu or execute the action assigned to the selected button
Shift +F10	To open a shortcut menu or open a drop-down menu for the selected gallery item
Page Up or Page Down	To scroll up or down in the selected gallery list
Ctrl + Home or Ctrl + End	To move to the top or bottom of the selected gallery list.
Alt	To close the visible menu and submenu at the same time
Esc	To close the visible menu

The Shortcut Keys For Dialog Boxes

Shortcut keys	Functions
Ctrl + Tab	Switch to the next or previous tab in the dialog box
Ctrl + Shift + Tab	To switch to the previous tab in a dialog box
The Tab Key or Shift + Tab	To move to the next or previous option or option group.
Ctrl + Shift + Tab	To switch to the previous tab in a dialog box
The Tab Key or Shift + Tab	To move to the next or previous option or group.
Arrow key	To move between options in the selected drop-down list box, or move between options in a group of options
Spacebar	To execute the action assigned to the selected button, or clear the check box
Alt + Down Arrow	**To open selected drop-down list box**
Esc	**To close the selected drop-down list box**
Enter	**To perform the action assigned to the default button in the dialog box**

The Shortcut Keys For Wizard

Shortcut Keys	Functions
The Tab Key	To toggle the focus forward between controls in the wizard
F6	To toggle the focus between sessions of the wizard
Alt + N	To move to the next page of the wizard
Alt + B	To move to the previous page of the wizard
Alt + F	To complete the wizard

The Shortcut Keys For Property Sheets

Shortcut Keys	Functions
F4	To show or hide property sheet
Alt + Enter	To display a property sheet in Design view
The Down or Up Arrow Key	To move among choices in the control drop-down list one item at a time
Page Down or Page Up	To move among choices in the control drop-down list one page at a time
The Tab Key	To move to the property sheet tabs from the control selection drop-down list
The Left or Right Arrow key	To move among the property sheet tabs with a tab selected, but no property selected.
The Tab Key	With a property selected, move down one property on a tab
Shift + Tab	With a property selected, move up one property on a tab, or if at the top, move to the tab.
Ctrl + Tab	To toggle forward between tabs when a property is selected.
Ctrl + Shift + Tab	To toggle backward between tabs when a property is selected.

The Shortcut Keys For Text Box

Shortcut Keys	Functions
Home	To move to the beginning of the entry
End	To move to the end of the entry
The Left or Right Arrow Key	To move one character to the left or right
Ctrl + Left Arrow or Ctrl + Right Arrow	To move one word to the left or right
Shift + Home	To select from the insertion point to the beginning of the text entry
Shift + End	To select from the insertion point to the end of the text entry
Shift + Left Arrow	To change the selection by one character to the left
Shift + Right Arrow	To change the selection by one character to the right
Ctrl + Shift + Left Arrow	To change the selection by one word to the left
Ctrl + Shift + Right Arrow	To change the selection by one word to the right

The Shortcut Keys For Combo Or List Box

Shortcut Keys	Functions
F4 or Alt + Down Arrow	To open a combo box
F9	To refresh the content of the Lookup field list box or a combo box
The Down Arrow Key	To Move down one line
Page Down	To move down one page
The Up Arrow key	To move up one line
Page Up	To move up one page
The Tab Key	To exit the combo box or list box
Ctrl + E	To open the Edit List Items dialog box

The Shortcut Keys For Working With Objects

Shortcut Keys	Functions
F2	To rename a selected object
The Down Arrow Key	To move down one line
Page Down	To move down one window
End	To move to the last object
The Up Arrow Key	To move up one line
Page Up	To move up one window
Enter	To open selected table or query in Datasheet view
Enter	To open the selected form or report
Enter	To run the selected macro
Ctrl + Enter	To open the selected table, query, form, report, macro, and module in the Design view
Ctrl + G	To display the Immediate window in the Visual Basic Editor

The Shortcut Keys For Working Design, layout, or Datasheet View

Shortcut Keys	Functions
F2	To switch between Edit mode and Navigation mode in a datasheet
Esc	To exit Navigation mode and return to Edit mode in a form or report
F4 or Alt +Enter	To switch to the property sheet in the Design view and Layout view in forms and report.
F5	To switch to the Form view from the Design view
F6	To switch between the upper and lower portions of a window in the Design view of queries, macros, and the Advanced Filter or Sort window

F6	To cycle through the field grid, property, field property, the Navigation Pane, Quick Access Toolbar, and KeyTips on the ribbon in the Design view of tables
F7	To open the Choose Builder dialog from a selected control on a form or report
F7	To open the Visual Basic Editor from a selected property in the property sheet for a for or report
Alt + F11	To switch from the Visual Basic Editor back to the form or report Design view
Ctrl + Right Arrow or Ctrl + Comma	To toggle forward between views when in a table, query form, or report
Ctrl + Left Arrow or Ctrl + Period	To toggle forward between views when in a table, query form, or report

The shortcut Keys For Datasheet View

Shortcut Keys	Functions
The Tab Key or Right Arrow Key	To move to the next field
End	To move to the last field in the current record
Shift + Tab or The Left Arrow Key	To move to the previous field
Home	To move to the first field in the current record
The Down Arrow Key	To move to the current field in the next record
Ctrl + Down Arrow Key	To move to the current field in the last record
Ctrl + End	To move to the last field in the last record
The Up Arrow Key	To move to the current field in the previous record
Ctrl + Up Arrow	To move to the current field in the first record

Ctrl +Home	To move to the first field in the first record
Alt + F5 (In the record number box, type the record number and press Enter	To go to a specific record
Page Down	To move up one screen
Page Up	To move down one screen
Ctrl + Page Down	To move right one screen
Ctrl + Page Up	To move left one screen
Ctrl + Spacebar	To select the current column or cancel the column section, in Navigation mode only
Shift + Right Arrow key	To extend the selection one column to the right, if the current column is selected.
Shift + Left Arrow key	To extend the selection one column to the left, if the current column is selected.
Ctrl + Shift + F8 (Then press the Right or Left arrow key to move the selected columns to the right or left	To turn on Move mode

The Shortcut Keys For Subdatasheets In Datasheet View

Shortcut Keys	Functions
Tab Key	To enter the Subdatasheet from the last field of the previous record in the datasheet
Shift + Tab	To enter the Subdatasheet from the first field of the following record in the datasheet
Ctrl + Tab	To exit the Subdatasheet and move to the first field of the next record in the datasheet

Ctrl + Shift + Tab	To exit the Subdatasheet and navigate to the last field of the previous record in the datasheet
The Tab Key	To enter the next field from the last field in the Subdatasheet
The Down Arrow key	To bypass the Subdatasheet and move to the next record in the datasheet.
The Up Arrow Key	To bypass the Subdatasheet and move to the next record in the datasheet.
Alt + F5(In the record number box, type the record number and press Enter)	To go to a specific record in a Subdatasheet
Ctrl + Shift + Down Arrow Key	To move from the datasheet to the record's Subdatasheet
Ctrl + Shift + Up Arrow Key	To collapse the Subdatasheet

The shortcut Keys To Navigate In A Design View

Shortcut keys	Functions
F2	To switch between Edit mode and Navigation
F4 or Alt + Enter	To open or close the property sheet
F5	To switch to Form view from form
F6	To switch between the upper and lower portions of a window (in the Design view of queries, macros, and the Advanced Filter or Sort window
F6	To toggle forward between the design pane, properties, Navigation Pane, ribbon, and Zoon controls (in the Design view of tables, forms, and reports)
F7	To open the Visual Basic Editor from a selected property in the property sheet for a form or report
Alt + F8	To show or hide the Field List pane

Shift + F7	This switches from the Visual Basic Editor to the form or report Design view, when the code module is open
Shift + F7	To switch from a control's property sheet in form or report Design view to the design surface without changing the control focus
Ctrl + C	To copy the selected control to the Clipboard
Ctrl + X	To cut the selected control and copy it to the Clipboard
Ctrl + V	To paste the content of the Clipboard in the upper –left corner of the selected section
The Right Arrow key	To move the selected control to the right pixel along the page's grid
The Left Arrow Key	To move the selected control to the left by a pixel along the page's grid
The Up Arrow Key	To move the control selected up by a pixel along the page's grid
The Down Arrow Key	To move the control selected down by a pixel along the page's grid
Ctrl + Right Arrow key	To move the control selected to the right by a pixel, regardless of the page's grid
Ctrl + Left Arrow Key	To move the control selected to the left by a pixel, regardless of the page's grid
Ctrl + Up Arrow key	To move the control selected up by a pixel, regardless of the page's grid
Ctrl + Down Arrow key	To move the control selected down by a pixel, regardless of the page's grid
Shift + Right Arrow Key	To increase the width of the control selected to the right by a pixel
Shift + Left Arrow Key	To decrease the width of the control selected to the left by a pixel
Shift + Up Arrow Key	To decrease the height of control from the button by a pixel
Shift + Down Arrow Key	To increase the height of the control selected from the bottom by a pixel

The Shortcut Keys For Editing Using Controls In the Form And Report Design View

Shortcut Keys	Functions
Ctrl + C	To copy the selected control to the Clipboard
Ctrl + X	To cut the selected control and copy it to the Clipboard
Ctrl + V	To paste the content of the Clipboard in the section selected
Ctrl + Right Arrow Key	To move the selected control to the right
Ctrl + Left Arrow	To move the selected control to the left
Ctrl + Up Arrow Key	To move the selected control up
Ctrl + Down Arrow Key	To move the selected control down
Shift + Down Arrow Key	To increase the height of the selected control
Shift + Right Arrow Key	To increase the width of the selected control
Shift + Up Arrow Key	To reduce the height of the selected control
Shift + Left Arrow Key	To reduce the width of the selected control

The Shortcut Keys To Navigate Between Fields And Records

Shortcut Keys	Functions
The Tab Key	To move to the next field
Shift + Tab	To move to the previous field
End	To move to the last control on the form and remain in the current recor7d
Ctrl + End	To move to the last control on the form and set focus in the last record
Home	To move to the first control on the form and remain in the current record

Ctrl + Home	To move to the first control on the form and set focus in the first record
Ctrl + Page Down	To move to the current field in the next record
Ctrl + Page Up	To move to the current field in the previous record
Alt + F5	To go to a specific record

The Shortcut Keys To Navigate In Forms With More Than One Page

Shortcut Keys	Functions
Page Down	To move down one page
Page Up	To move up one page

The Shortcut Keys To Navigate Between A Main Form And A Subform

Shortcuts	Functions
The Tab Key	To enter the subform from the preceding field in the main form
Shift + Tab	To enter the subform from the following field in the main form
Ctrl + Tab	To exit the subform and move to the next field in the master form or next record
Ctrl + Shift + Tab	To exit the subform and move to the previous field in the main form or previous record

The Shortcut Keys To Navigate In Print Preview And Layout Preview

Shortcuts	Functions
Ctrl + P	To open the Print dialog box from print
S	To open the Page Setup dialog box
Z	To zoom in or out on a part of the page
C or Esc	To cancel Print Preview or Layout Preview
The Down Arrow Key	To scroll down in small increments
Page Down	To scroll down one full screen
Ctrl + Down Arrow Key	To move to the bottom of the page
The Up Arrow Key	To scroll up in small increments
Page Up	To scroll up one full screen
Ctrl + Up Arrow Key	To move to the top of the page
The Right Arrow Key	To scroll to the right edge of the page
End	To move to the right edge of the page
Ctrl + End	Move to the lower right corner of the page
The Left Arrow Key	To scroll to the left in small increments
Home	To move to the left edge of the page
Ctrl + Home	To move to the upper-left corner of the page
Alt + F5 (type the page number and press Enter)	To move to the page number box

The Shortcut Keys For The Diagram Pane

Shortcuts	Functions
The Tab Key	To move among tables, views, and functions
The Arrow Keys	To move between columns in a table, view, or function
Spacebar or Plus Sign (+)	To choose the selected data column for output h

Spacebar or Minus Sign (-)	To remove the selected data column from the query output
Delete	To remove the selected table, view, or functions, or join the line from the query

The Shortcut Keys For Grid Pane

Shortcuts	Functions
The Arrow, the Tab key, or Shift +Tab	To move among cells
Ctrl + Down Arrow Key	To move to the last row in the current column
Ctrl + Up Arrow Key	To move to the first row in the current column
Ctrl + Home	To move to the upper-left cell in the visible portion of the grid
Ctrl + End	To move to the bottom-right cell
The Up or Down Arrow Key	To move in a drop-down list
Ctrl + Spacebar	To select an entire grid column
F2	To toggle between the Edit mode and cell selection mode
Ctrl + C	To copy selected text in cell to the Clipboard
Ctrl + X	To cut selected text in a cell and place it on the Clipboard
Ctrl + V	To paste text from the Clipboard
The Insert Key	To toggle between insert and overtype mode while editing in a cell
Spacebar	To toggle the check box in the Output column
Delete	To clear the selected contents of a cell
Delete	To clear all values for a selected grid column

The Shortcut Keys For The Field List Pane

Shortcut Keys	Functions
Alt + F8	To show or hide the Field List pane
Enter	To add the field selected to the form or report details
The Up Arrow Key and the Down Arrow Key	To move up or down the Field list pane
The Tab Key	To move between the upper and lower panes of the Field List

The Shortcut Keys To Select A Field Or Record

Shortcut Keys	Functions
The Tab Key	To select the next field
F2	To switch between the Edit mode (with insertion point displayed) and Navigation mode in a datasheet
Esc	To exit the Navigation mode in a form or report
Shift + Spacebar	To switch between selecting the current record and the first field of the current record in Navigation mode
Shift + Up Arrow	To extend the selection to the previous record, if the current record is selected
Ctrl + A	To select all records

The Shortcut Keys To Select Text In A Field

Shortcuts	Functions
Shift + Right Arrow Key	To change the size of the selection by one character to the right
Ctrl +Shift + Right Arrow Key	To change the size of the selection by one word to the right

Shift + Left Arrow Key	To change the size of the selection by one character to the left
Ctrl +Shift + Left Arrow Key	To change the size of the selection by one word to the left

The Shortcut Keys To Extend A Selection

Shortcut Keys	Functions
F8	To turn on Extend mode
The Left or Right Arrow Key	To extend a selection to adjacent fields in the same row in Datasheet view
The Up or Down Arrow Key	To extend a selection to adjacent rows in Datasheet view
Shift + F8	To undo the previous extension
Esc	To cancel Extend mode

The Shortcut Keys To Find And Replace Text Or Data

Shortcut Keys	Functions
Ctrl + F	To open the Find tab in the Find and Replace dialog box in the Datasheet view and Form view only.
Ctrl + H	To open the Replace tab in the Find and Replace dialog box in the Datasheet view and Form view only.
Shift +F4	To find the next occurrence of the text specified in the Find and Replace dialog box, if the dialog is closed in the Datasheet view and Form view only.

The Shortcut Keys To Move The Insertion Point In A Field

Shortcut Keys	Function
The Right Arrow Key	To move the insertion point one character to the right
Ctrl + Right Arrow	To move the insertion point one word to the right

The Left key Arrow	To move the insertion point one character to the left
Ctrl + Left Arrow	To move the insertion point one word to the left
End	To move the Insertion point to the end of the field, in single-line fields, or move it to the end of the line in multi-line fields
Ctrl + End	To move the Insertion point to the end of the field, in multi-line fields
Home	To move the Insertion point to the beginning of the field, in single-line fields, or move it to the beginning of the line in multi-line fields
Ctrl + Home	To move the Insertion point to the beginning of the field, in multi-line fields

The Shortcut Keys To Copy, Move, Or Delete Text

Shortcut Keys	Functions
Ctrl + C	To copy the selection to the Clipboard
Ctrl + X	To cut the selection and copy it to the Clipboard
Ctrl +V	To paste contents of the Clipboard at the insertion point
Backspace	To delete a character to the left of the insertion
Delete	To delete a character to the right of the insertion
Ctrl + Delete	To delete all characters to the right of the insertion

The Shortcut Keys To Undo Changes

Shortcuts Keys	Functions
Ctrl + Z or Alt + Backspace	To undo tying
Esc	To undo changes in the current field or current record

The Shortcut Keys For Entering Data In A Datasheet Or Form View

Shortcuts Keys	Functions
Ctrl + ;	To insert the current date
Ctrl + Shift + :	To insert current time
Ctrl + Alt + Spacebar	To insert the default value of a field
Ctrl + '	To insert the value from the field in the previous record
Ctrl + +	To add a new record
Ctrl + -	To delete the current record in a datasheet
Shift + Enter	To save changes to the current record
Spacebar	To switch between the values in a check box or option button
Ctrl + Enter	To insert a new line in a Short Text or Long Text field

The Shortcut Keys To Refresh Field With Current Data

Shortcut keys	Functions
F9	To recalculate the field in the window
Shift + F9 or F5	To requery the underlying tables
F9	To refresh the contents of a Lookup field list box or combo box

The Shortcut Keys To Work Around In Tables And Cells

Shortcut Keys	Functions
The Tab key	To move to the next cell
Shift + Tab	To move to the preceding cell
The Down Arrow key	To move the next row
The Up Arrow key	To move to the preceding row
Ctrl + Tab	To insert a tab in a cell

Enter	To start a new paragraph
The Tab Key at the end of the last row	To add a new row at the bottom of the table
The Left Arrow Key	To move one character to the left
The Right Arrow Key	To move one character to the right
Ctrl +Left Arrow Key	To move one word to the left
Ctrl + Right Arrow Key	To move one word to the right
End	To move to the end of the line
Home	To move to the beginning of the line
Ctrl + Up Arrow Key	To move up one paragraph
Ctrl + Down Arrow key	To move down one paragraph
Ctrl + End	To move to the end of a text box
Ctrl + Home	To move to the beginning of a text box
Shift + F4	To repeat the last Find action

The Shortcut Keys For Get Help With Access

Shortcut Keys	Functions
F1	To open the Help window
Alt + Home	To go back to Access Help Home
The Tab Key	To select the next item in the Help window
Shift + Tab	To select the previous item in the Help window
Enter	To act as the selected item
Enter	To expand or collapse the selected item in the AccessHelp topics
The Tab Key	To select the next hidden text or hyperlink, including Show All or Show All at the top of a topic
Shift + Tab	To select the previous hidden text or hyperlink
Enter	To act for
Alt +Left Arrow or Backspace	To move the back to the previous Help topic (Back button)

Alt +Right Arrow	To move the back to the next Help topic (Forward button)
The Up or Down Arrow Key	To scroll a small amount up or down within the currently displayed Help topic
Page Up or Page Down	To scroll larger amount up or down within the currently displayed Help topic
Esc	To stop the last action (Stop button)
F5	To refresh the window (Refresh button)
Ctrl + P	To print the current Help topic
F6 + Enter	To change the connection state
F6	To switch among areas in the Help window e.g. the toolbar and Search list
The Up or Down Arrow key	To select the next or previous item in the table of contents
Enter	To expand or collapse the selected item in the table of content

Miscellaneous Keyboard Shortcuts

Shortcuts Keys	Functions
F2	To display the complete hyperlink address (URL) for a selected hyperlink
F7	To check spellings
Shift +F2	To open the Zoom box to conveniently enter expressions and other text in small input areas
Ctrl + F2	To invoke a Builder
Print Screen	To copy a screenshot of the entire screen to the Clipboard
Alt + Print Screen	To copy a screenshot of the current window to the Clipboard
Ctrl + Down Arrow Key	To display the full set of commands on the task pane menu
Alt + F4	Exit Access

CONCLUSION ON ACCESS

Amidst the applications available in the Microsoft Office suite, Access is no doubt, one of the most resourceful and a must-learn application for every organization, which desires to have a well-planned and detailed way of gathering and analyzing data that will be of help to the organization.

In the world at large especially in the business world, there is a need to be proficient with the use of Access. With this in place, every organization out there will have the opportunity to gather, managed, and process a large bunk of data, which in no time be of great help to the organization.

Therefore, as you take your time to explore this book, ensure to have Access 365 software installed on your computer with a strong internet connection.

With all that has been said so far, I wish you all the best as you explore this user guide.

See you at the top!

BOOK TWO
MICROSOFT EXCEL 365

PREFACE

It is the new era of Excel and we are all aware that Excel is nothing else but a spreadsheet application that you can make use of in recording and analyzing data, probably number, statistic, and text data. Above all this, Microsoft has done it again with the advent of Excel 365, an Excel with a subscription-based version that comes with a lot of features that you can use to leverage modern Excel everywhere and on any device.

Without much repetition, permit me to introduce to you what Excel 365 has in stock. Excel 365 has come to help us in carrying out general formatting on the list of numbers, texts, dates, times, and symbols such as percentage and currency. It improves the splitting and freezing feature which allows you to freeze and split the area of your worksheet, hiding and unhide, comments, as well as protecting and hiding the worksheet from unauthorized access, I also include the diverse ways of navigating a worksheet within the workbook.

Part of its features include essential function and formula for the computation of data such as formulation of a formula, proper uses of an argument, and indispensable functions such as LARGE, SMALL, AVERAGE, SUM, and many more, it also includes error detection, correction within a formula, and effective error checker on the worksheet.

I must also discuss appealing tools with Excel 365 for aligning the text and data horizontally or vertically, as well as inserting and deleting of both rows and columns, including the decoration of the worksheet with suitable colors and borders and also procedures for printing a worksheet by setting the worksheet to fit the page and shifting of the page break to print the specified area of the worksheet.

Furthermore, Excel 365 improved the use of the Pivot table by analyzing data in a new way and rearranging a broad and long worksheet. With this Excel pivot, you can convert Excel into a driving force that can combine considerable volumes of data from numerous sources and construct a connection between them, and What-if analysis also can help you change one or more variables through its analysis and also check out the effect of such on the estimated data.

Last but not least of Excel 365 features that will be discussed are the advanced techniques for various analysis of diverse data to meet various needs, such techniques are the importance and use of Sparkline, sorting for arranging data, Filtering for isolating useful data in the list, Goal-seek for getting variable of a particular result, conditional formatting for carrying out special order with the data set, using one and two input data for carrying out a special experiment on the data to derive other essential variables or elements. This guide stretches its teaching to necessary formatting techniques by altering the appearance of each data in the worksheet. These are just to mention a few of what comes with Excel 365.

Sit comfortably and begin the journey of a new era with the Excel online-based version. Happy exploring.

INTRODUCTION

Excel Office 365 is a new update patching into an excel program and it uses a more powerful tool that can allow you to create a document in a better way and to work with others conveniently. Excel 365 permits you to put together a lot of information from various people and sectors into a single worksheet, above all, you will be permitted to work with two or more persons on a similar worksheet at the same time which in turn improves efficiency and leads to a new vision for an organization as information is shared with all relevant personalities within the organization. In the same vein, it introduces an Excel pivot that can let you convert Excel into a driving force that can combine considerable volumes of data from numerous sources and construct a connection between them.

It is the free version of Excel that allows you to use a web browser by signing up for a Microsoft account with a new email or an existing email address with monthly or yearly payment to have access to Excel 365 features as well as the privilege to update to the latest version and effective security updates and bug fixes.

Above all, it securely stores all your document into the cloud with 1 TB of one cloud storage, nevertheless, you can access this cloud anywhere.

Do not get it twisted, Online Excel remains Microsoft Excel with a few differences from the traditional Excel. For instance, you run Excel on your computer by navigating to the start menu, search for Excel and click on it to open it, while Excel Online runs on the cloud and it can only be accessed with your web browser over the Internet by using Outlook.com or Gmail.com.

Once you acquaint yourself with the traditional Excel, you will find Online Excel interface very easy to work with because they are very similar in major aspects, though with little but significant differences, and thus there won't be a problem using Excel 365.

This is a well-designed user guide for all levels of users that is produced to grant you the prerequisite skills and knowledge you need to produce an accurate worksheet be it from a blank document or template with the necessary formulas for all data and text values input.

CHAPTER ONE

OVERVIEW OF MICROSOFT EXCEL

Origin of Excel

Microsoft has been in existence since early 1980 but it began to come into the limelight in 1987/1988 when Excel version 2.0 was released. It started to gain significance during the release of Excel version 5.0 with the inclusion of VBA (Visual Basic for Application) which opened many opportunities for crunching data and present the result to offices and organizations for use.

The present version of Excel is the newest release of Excel version 2019 and Excel 365 which because of their capability and the change they bring to every business demand has helped them to gain popularity and be used in the universe. Using Excel with other Microsoft applications will do greater leveraging because there can only be little that will be unachievable when they come together.

Meaning of Excel

Excel is a spreadsheet application with the major purpose of organizing and carrying out calculations on data. It is a tool for recording, analyzing data, and representing such data on a graph or chart. It is the most potent electronic application for data analysis and documentation. It comprises several rows and columns, which in turn comprises data or pieces of fact through which you can build a formula or edit it.

Relevance of Excel

The relevance of Excel cannot be overemphasized, this makes it a preferable spreadsheet application over other spreadsheet programs, and this is the key reason why it always finds expression in both small and big offices. To say the fact, we can't talk about all Excel relevance, but we will touch the essential ones.

Among what makes Excel relevant are the following:

1. It is used in keeping track of expenditures you made and for monthly budget preparation.
2. Effective modeling and practically analyzing every data
3. It is used to create a formula and edit the formula.
4. Good for finance and accounting analysis.
5. It is used to create a check and balance of a report and checkbook.
6. Performing work easier and faster.
7. Performing better in making a concise and accurate prediction.
8. Virtually developing the new feature on every new release for proper calculation such as CONCATENATE and TEXTJOIN in Excel 2019.
9. It is used in storing and manipulating data.

What Is Excel 365?

Excel 365 is an online-based version of Excel with a monthly or yearly subscription which you can operate on the Web or Cloud and thereby grant you the privilege of getting new features anytime there is a new release of any kind. It permits you to save your document both on the Cloud and hard disc or storage device.

Differences Between Excel 365 And Traditional Excel Such As (2013, 2019 And Others)

Talking about Excel 365 and traditional Excel, there may be many similarities, nevertheless, there are few differences, they may be few, but significant. Let us delve into those differences in a jiffy:

PRICING METHODS (EXCEL 365)

It involves continuous monthly or yearly payments. It is just like leasing a house, immediately you stop paying, you stop enjoying the features, though it may be a continuous payment, yet, it is very little compared to an exorbitant one-time purchase.

	Monthly cost	Annualized cost	Number of users
Office 365 Personal	$7	$84	1
Office 365 Home	$10	$120	6
Office 365 Business	$8.25	$99	5 PCs/Macs for 1 user

TRADITIONAL EXCEL (2016, 2019, etc.)

It involves a one-time purchase and when you pay for it once, you enjoy it forever, nevertheless, you will not enjoy the new features unless you will have to pay for such. For instance, when new versions come, perhaps version 2022, 2025, etc. to enjoy any feature that comes with the newer version, you are going to pay an exorbitant price that comes with it.

UPDATED VERSIONS AND FEATURES (EXCEL 365)

It always stays updated whenever there is a release of newer versions or features including security updates and bug fixes. For instance, if there is a release of Excel 2022 or 2023 in the future, you will be informed when it is out and you will get the features of such version to your application with a single click on the **update** option and it will be downloaded to your system. In short, no need for any future payments aside from the monthly and yearly payments you have been paying.

TRADITIONAL EXCEL (2016, 2019, etc.)

It does not stay updated, when there is a release of a newer version, you will not even get to know, unless other users tell you. Besides that, you will have to pay another exorbitant amount before you can enjoy any newer features or versions including security update and bug fixes. In short, before you can enjoy a new feature, you will have to make a substantial payment again unless if your version will not be updated and you continue with the older version and features.

DOCUMENT SAVING TYPES (AUTOSAVING OR AUTO RECOVER)

EXCEL 365

It has an Autosaving format of saving a document, by saving automatically to OneDrive. When you are working with Excel 365, you do not have an issue with system crash or power breakdown and thus, you have nothing to lose, even if the system you are using gets destroyed or gets lost. In short, it has an ever-reliable saving format because you can access such documents anywhere in the world.

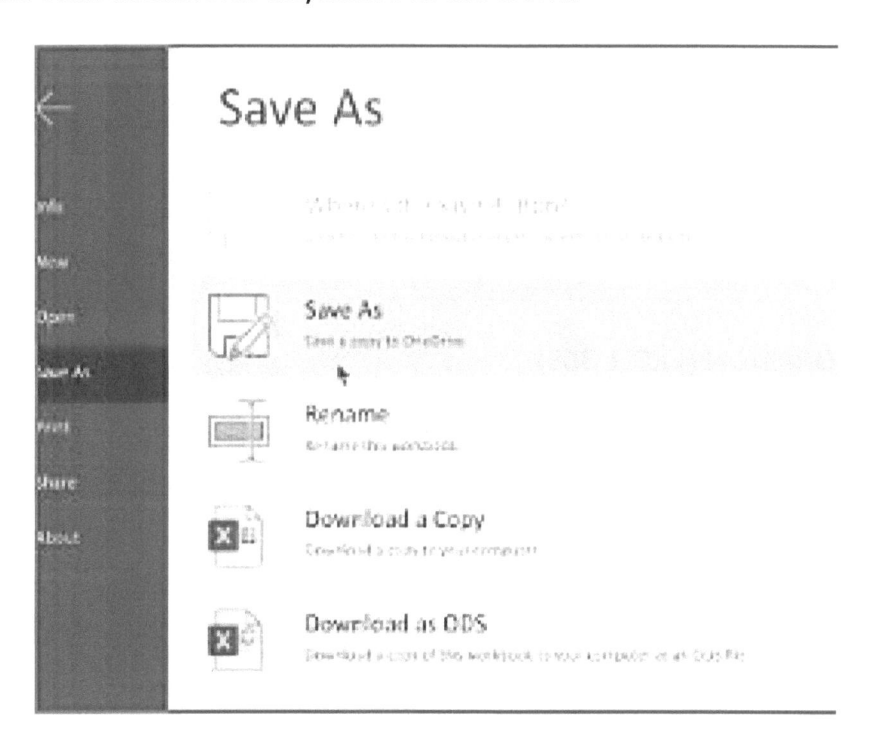

TRADITIONAL EXCEL (2016, 2019, etc.)

It has an Auto recover format of saving a document, by helping you recover the document you forgot to save maybe as a result of power breakdown or other things which may necessitate auto recovering of a document. Note that you have to meet the conditions of auto recovering before it can recover such a document. Nevertheless, it has a limitation, if the system crashes or gets lost; any document recovered or saved to that system has gone with it.

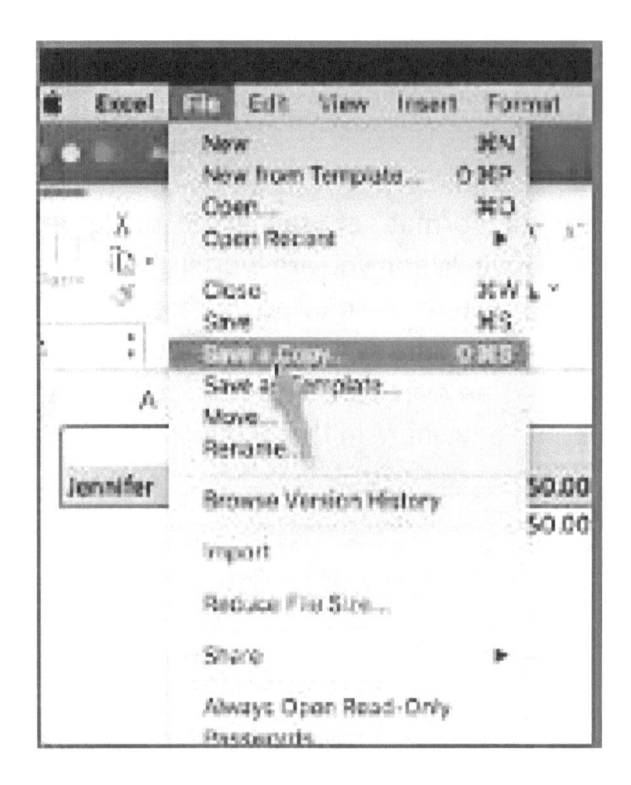

COLLABORATION (EXCEL 365)

You can collaborate and work with others through co-authoring feature which permits people to work together on a single document at the same time from anywhere in the world. This is done with an invitation via a link. To do this, single-click on "share" and enter their e-mail contact.

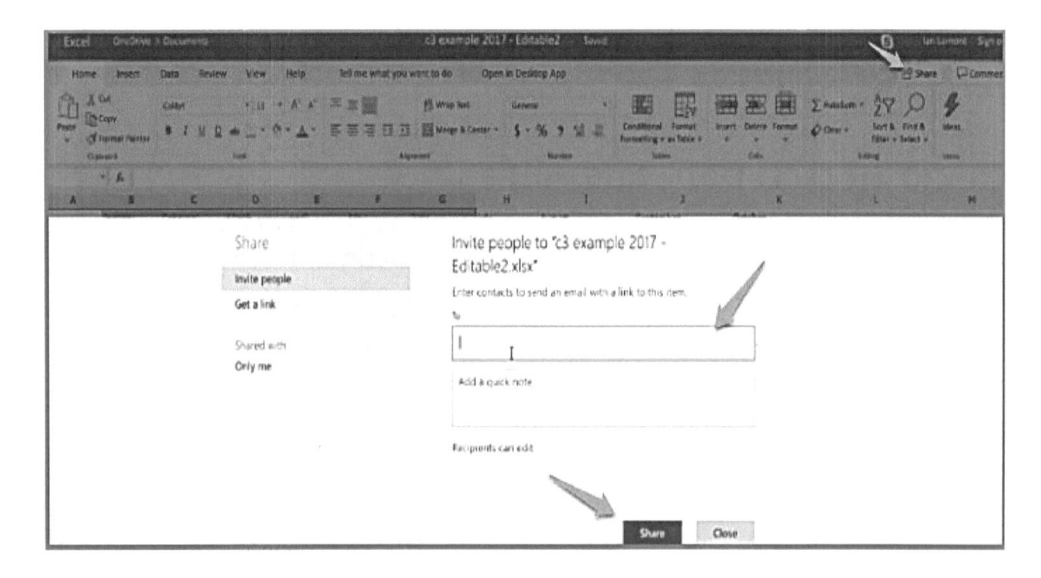

TRADITIONAL EXCEL (2016, 2019, etc.)

You can't collaborate with others, you are the only person that can work on the document unless you send the document to another email, and still, you can't work together on it at the same time with the person you sent it to.

SUB RIBBON MENU (EXCEL 365)

The sub ribbons of Excel 365 are not many; they involve basic tools for data analysis. They have a similar menu tab and you will notice they are the same but, immediately you click on each tab or ribbon, you will notice that they are little, each contains the basic tools.

TRADITIONAL EXCEL (2016, 2019, etc.)

It has full sub ribbons, it includes all the tools for data analysis and when you click on each tab or ribbon, you will observe it contains every tool you need for data analysis.

Similarities Between Excel 365 And Traditional Excel (Such As 2013, 2019 And Others)

Let us check the similarities between them, though we can't mention all, yet, we will mention the major ones.

   (1) Both are downloaded into the computer
   (2) Both are spreadsheets for recording and analyzing data.
   (3) The Window screen and menu tab are almost the same.

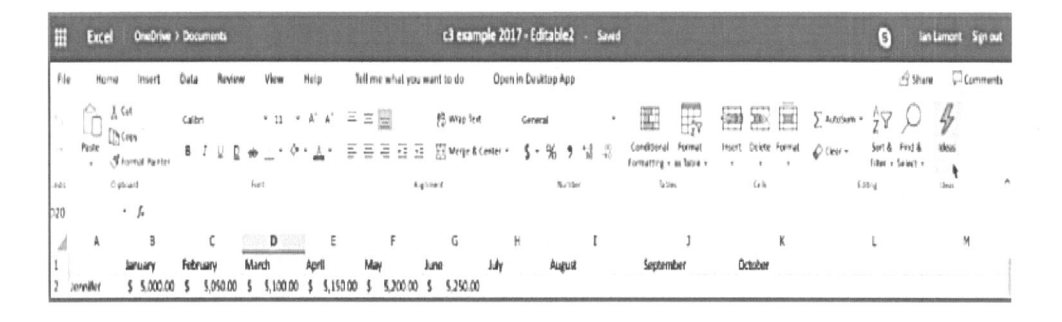

Importance of Excel 365

Excel 365 comes with a lot of benefits, but we will just make mention of the few essential ones which are:

(1) Instant communication in and out of the organization: Excel 365 helps to forward instant messages to co-workers and invite them for online meetings to rub minds together on a particular document and work on it at the same time to reach a meaningful conclusion.
(2) Security mindset priority: your Excel 365 document is scanned every minute, 24 hours a day to fight against malware of any type, and thus safeguard your document and information.
(3) Cost-conscious and flexible: aside from pay as you go, that is, paying stipends for the service you are receiving from Excel 365, you can as well stop the payment when you do not need the service anymore, and also make payments again anytime you need the service again. This allows for immediate flexibility according to the trend.
(4) 24 hours accessibility: having a consistent internet provider grants you access to the document, program, and other information on your Excel 365 program.

CHAPTER TWO

START YOUR EXPLOIT WITH EXCEL

Creating and Opening A New Excel Workbook

Before we go into creating a new excel workbook, what is a workbook? The workbook is an excel document that contains one or more worksheets that you can use to arrange your data. A workbook can be created from a blank document or an available template.

To create Excel workbook from a blank document, you have to:

- Navigate to the **start menu** and **scroll down or** you type **its name and** click on **Excel** to launch it**.**

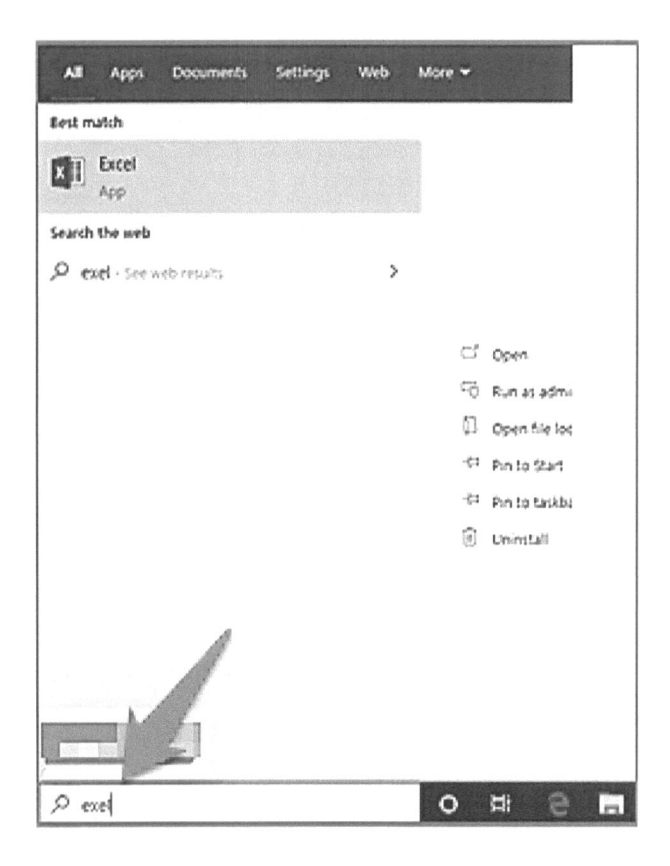

- Click on **New**, then click on **Blank Workbook**

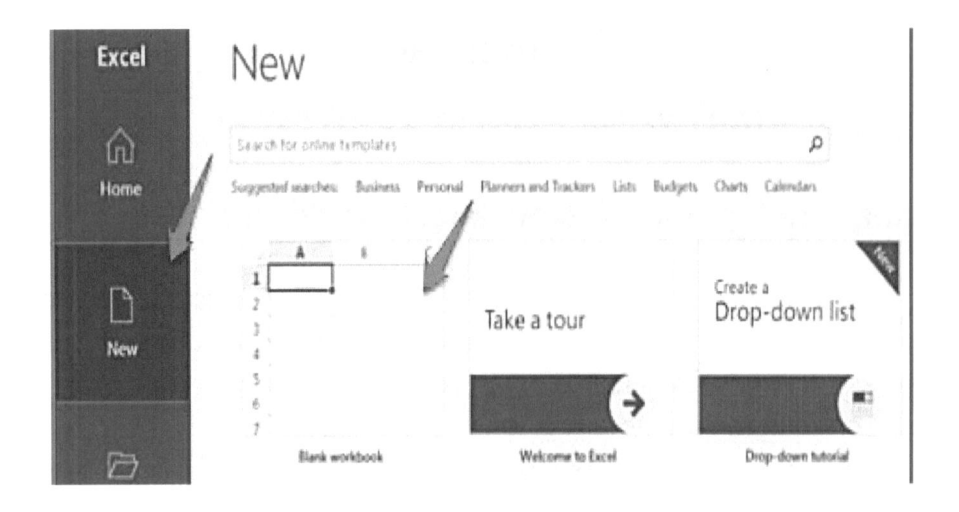

- Click on **each cell** and begin to **input data.**

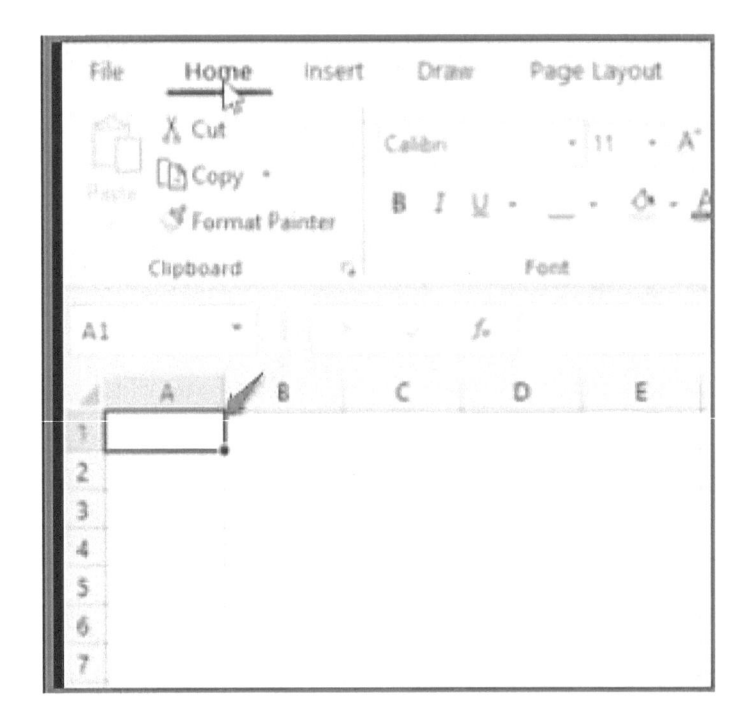

To create Excel workbook from a template, after you must have opened the Excel program, kindly:

- Search for the **desired template** by scrolling through the templates or type its name in the search box for the online template and then double-click on the desired one.

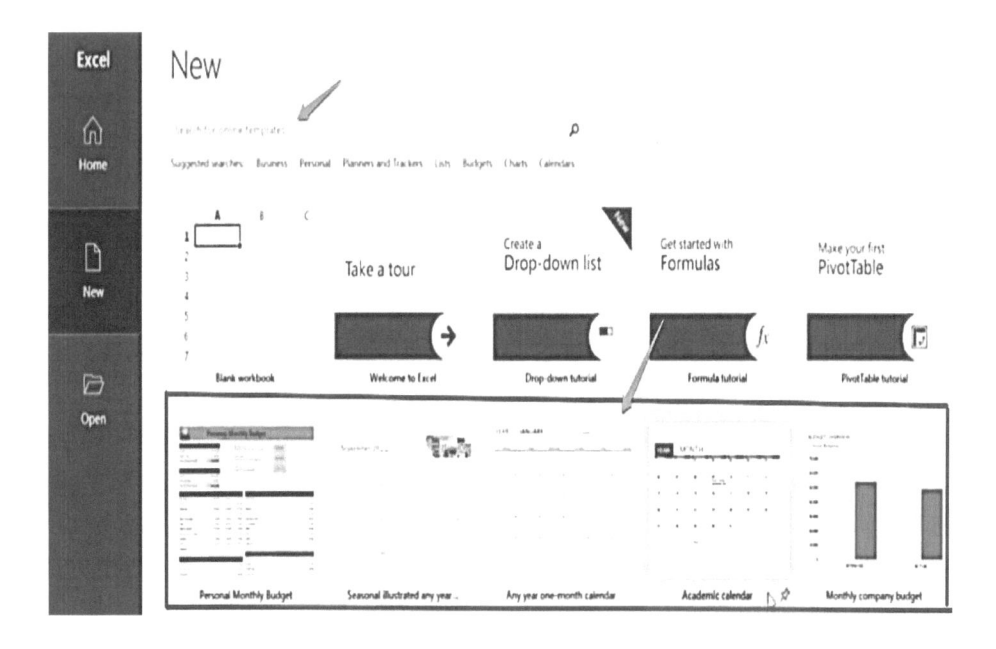

- Click on **each cell** and begin to input your data.

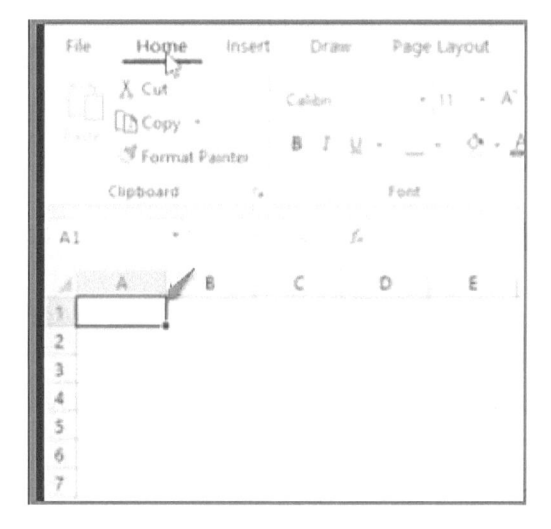

Note: Excel connects you to the online database with more than thousands of databases you can make use of.

Getting Familiar with The Excel Interface

Excel interface comprises of several keys which you can use together to produce a meaningful assignment, such as:

(1) **Excel document:** Excel document is called **a workbook**; the default name is **book 1**.
(2) **Excel ribbon:** it is broken into tabs, such as File, Home, Insert, and so on, they are used to perform specific commands. When you click on each tab, you will be able to see the various sub-grouping.
(3) **Name and formula bar:**
    a. **The name box** is located at the upper left side above the Excel column and it usually displays the address of the current cell.
    b. **The formula bar** is located after the **name box** to the right side and it is used to display the content of the current cell.
(4) **Column, row, and cell:**
    a. **Columns** are the cells arranged vertically in the spreadsheet.
    b. **Rows** are the cells arranged horizontally in the spreadsheet.
    c. **A cell** is the intersection of row and column; it is represented by a rectangular box.
(5) **Worksheet navigation key:** this is a button that permits worksheet forward and backward movement within a workbook with a single click on each button.
(6) **Status bar:** it tells you the current mode of each worksheet such as:
    a. **Ready mode:** it means you have not entered anything into the worksheet.
    b. **Enter mode**: this means you are currently typing something into the worksheet.
    c. **Edit mode**: it means you are correcting the current cell that has data inside. This is done by double-clicking on the cell to be corrected.
(7) **Plus icon**: this is a link to add more worksheets to your workbook. The more you click on it, the more worksheet you will be having within your workbook.
(8) **Worksheet:** this is the whole workspace where you can insert the numbers, letters, and formulas to carry out intended calculations.

(9) **Scroll bar**: it is the bar that navigates you to any other position within the worksheet and also an indicator of your current position.

(10) **Zoom Slider**: it is used to adjust the worksheet view by increasing or reducing the zoom ratio of the worksheet.

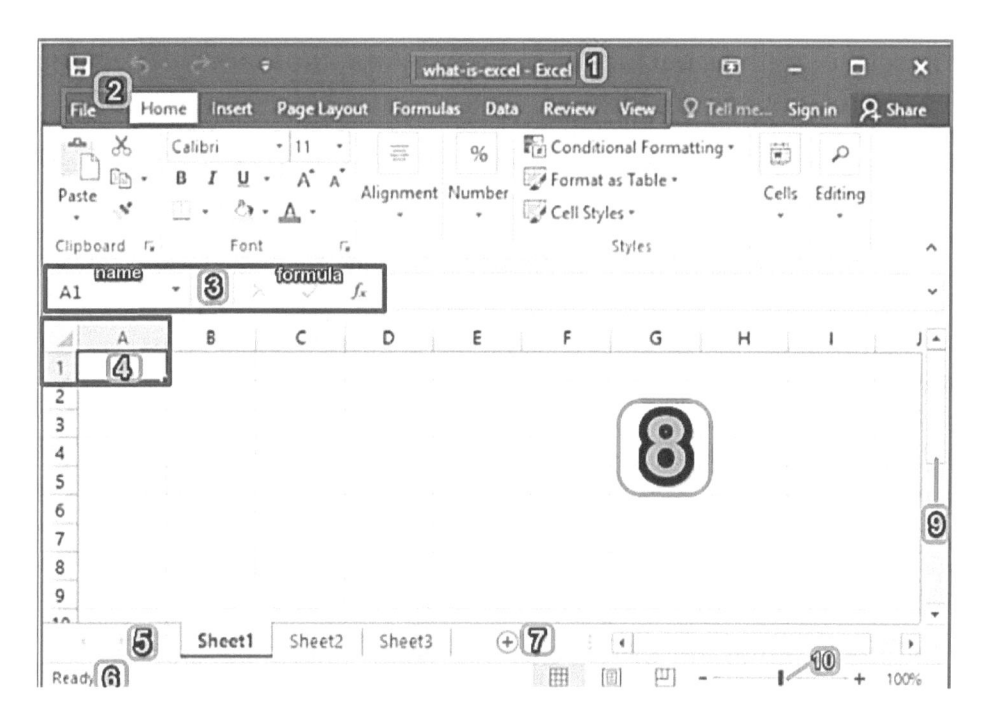

Understanding Rows, Columns, And Cell Addresses

Row carry headings with numbers, they are in the vertical level of the worksheet, and are identified with **numbers 1, 2, 3,** and so on. It ranges from 1 to 1048576.

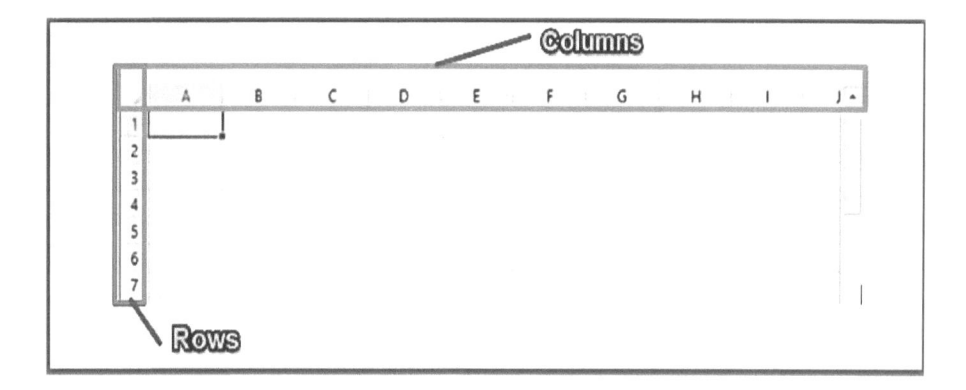

Column carry headings with letters, they are in the horizontal level of the worksheet, and are identified with **letters A, B, C,** and so on. It ranges from A to XFD.

A cell is a rectangular box that represents a point of intersection between columns and rows. This point of intersection is called cell reference, and it is used to address each cell. There are over thousands of rectangles (cell) inside a single spreadsheet.

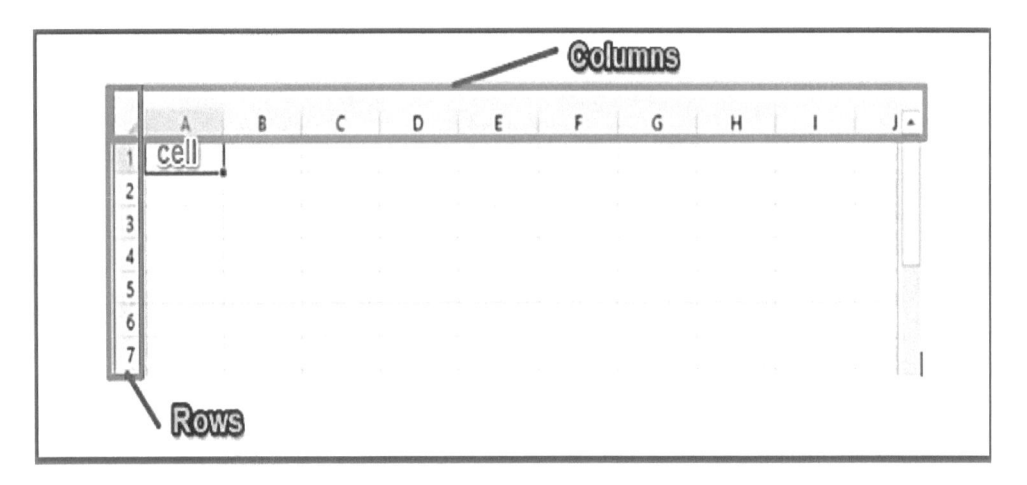

Cell range is the group of two or more cells. Cell range is addressed by **the first** and **last cell** in the cell range. For instance, the selected cell here is (A1:A8)

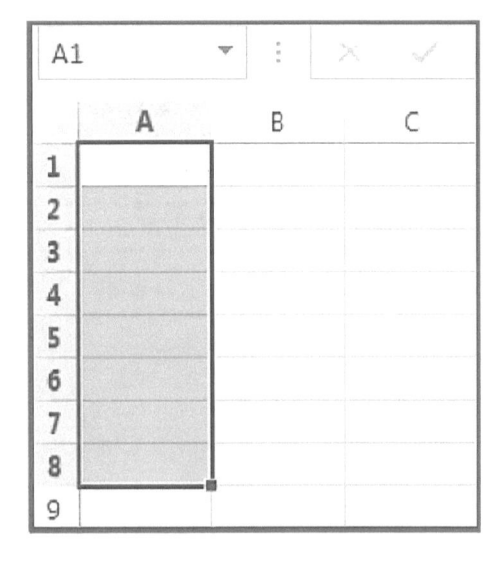

Workbooks And Worksheet

Excel Workbook is simply a file, or a document, or a book that consists of one or more worksheets with countless kinds of connected information. The workbook contains many worksheets with the drive to organize and arrange relevant data in a single place but in a different grouping which is known as a worksheet. Workbooks can hold unending amounts of worksheet depending on the size and magnitude of the data.

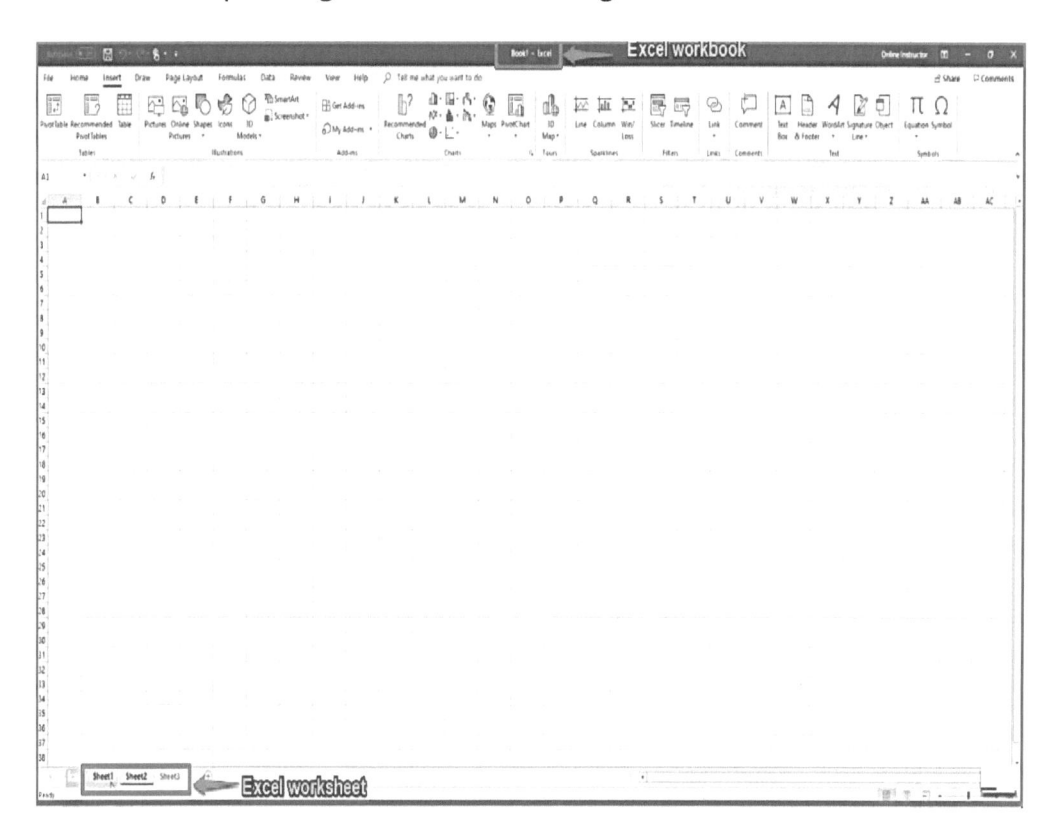

Excel worksheets can be likened to a single work page or spreadsheet in which Excel users can write, edit, and control data while the collection of such is what is referred to as a **workbook**. Though the worksheet is a single work page, it is a complete work page that contains a box of rectangular cells which is the intersection of rows and columns that you can use to reference each cell (Address). You can have as many as possible worksheets inside the workbook because there is no limit to the number of the worksheet that can be inside the workbook.

Entering Data in The Worksheet Cell

Data can be inserted in various ways in Excel. You can insert your data in a single cell, in many cells, or even more than a single worksheet at once. The data carries different forms such as texts, numbers, dates, or time.

Note: perhaps you cannot enter or edit data in a worksheet, such a worksheet might have been protected to avoid data being changed unintentionally either by you or another user. A locked/protected worksheet will allow you to view what is inside the cell but will not permit you to type or edit the cell. To **unprotect the worksheet**:

- Go to the **Review tab.**
- Move to the **Changes** group and then to the **unprotect sheet** option and below, click **OK**. If it has a password, you will have to input the **password** before you can unprotect it.

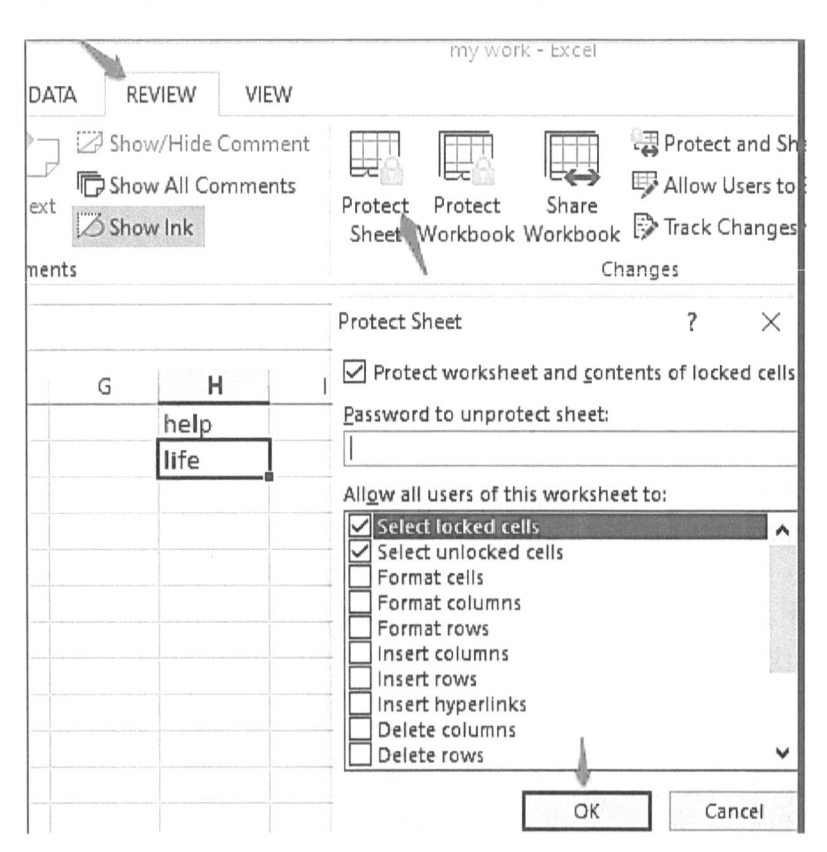

The Basic Knowledge of Entering Data

To enter data into an Excel worksheet, you have to understand what you have to avoid and what you have to practice to avoid frustration and difficulty later on and such basic knowledge will make using Excel tools, functions, and features very easy to use. The following are what you should put at the top of your mind as you begin entering data into the worksheet:

(1) **Do not leave an empty row or column as you are entering associated data:** any empty row or column inside a range of data or data table obstructs appropriate use of several Excel features such as charts, specific functions, pivot tables, and so on.

	A	B	C	D	E	F
1				Restaurant sales book		
2				April	may	june
3	Revenue from sales:					
4	pawpaw			$150	$180	$150
5	orange			$300	$250	$400
6	pearl			$100	$500	$180
7						

The nonexistence of empty spaces aid Excel to select related data when using a range of features such as sorting, filtering, or Auto sum.

(2) **Do not use figures as column headings and do not put units with the data:** simply use heading at the top of the column, not figures such as 200, 300, and 400, etc. when you use word heading such as equipment, advertising, etc. and not figures, it will make sorting easier

	A	B	C	D	E	F
1				Restaurant sales book		
2	Revenue from sales:					
3				2018	2019	2020
4	pawpaw			$150	$180	$150
5	orange			$300	$250	$400
6	pearl			$100	$500	$180
7	Total income			=SUM (D3:D6)		

If you use numbers as row and column headings, such may be mistakably included in the calculations, and also, using formula and function may not give adequate result when it includes all numbers in the calculation.

(3) **Keep unconnected data separately:** it is expedient to keep similar data together and at the same time it is very paramount to separate every unconnected data. Ensure to put a blank row or column between unalike data range on the worksheet so that excel will choose the correct connected ranges or tables of data.

(4) **Excel aligns texts to the left and numbers to the right:** this is the default alignment of the data which gives you the clue if you have input your data correctly and if it is formatted correctly in the worksheet.

(5) **Using cell references and named ranges in using formulas:** endeavor to use cell references and named ranges when you are using formulas so that the formulas and whole spreadsheet will be error-free and accurate.

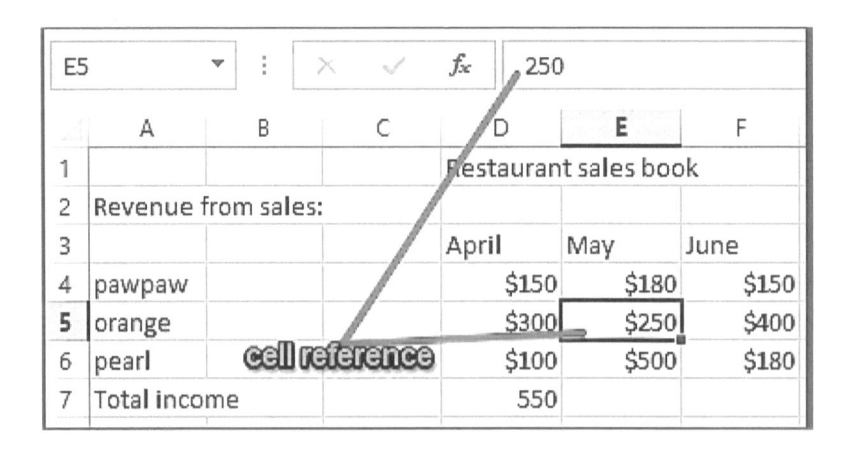

E5   fx   250

	A	B	C	D	E	F
1				Restaurant sales book		
2	Revenue from sales:					
3				April	May	June
4	pawpaw			$150	$180	$150
5	orange			$300	$250	$400
6	pearl		cell reference	$100	$500	$180
7	Total income			550		

Tips: cell references recognize the position of the data by combining the row of numbers and column of letters (a single cell) while named ranges are used to recognize a range of cells in a worksheet (multiple cells combine).

(6) **Use of percent and Unit (currency, temperature, distance, and other units) symbols:** do not type percent and units' symbol along with numbers because Excel will recognize them as text, therefore, ensure you enter all your numbers to the worksheet then after the insertion of the numbers you can format the cell to display the accurate figures either as a percentage, currency or other units. Nevertheless, some Excel recognizes the British pound (£) and dollar ($) currency sign if you type them along with numbers in the cell, but every other currency symbol are not recognized and thus they will be interpreted as text, though, this is not the same for all Excel versions. To prevent such occurrence, enter the amount first then later format the cells to input currency instead of typing currency symbols along with the amount.

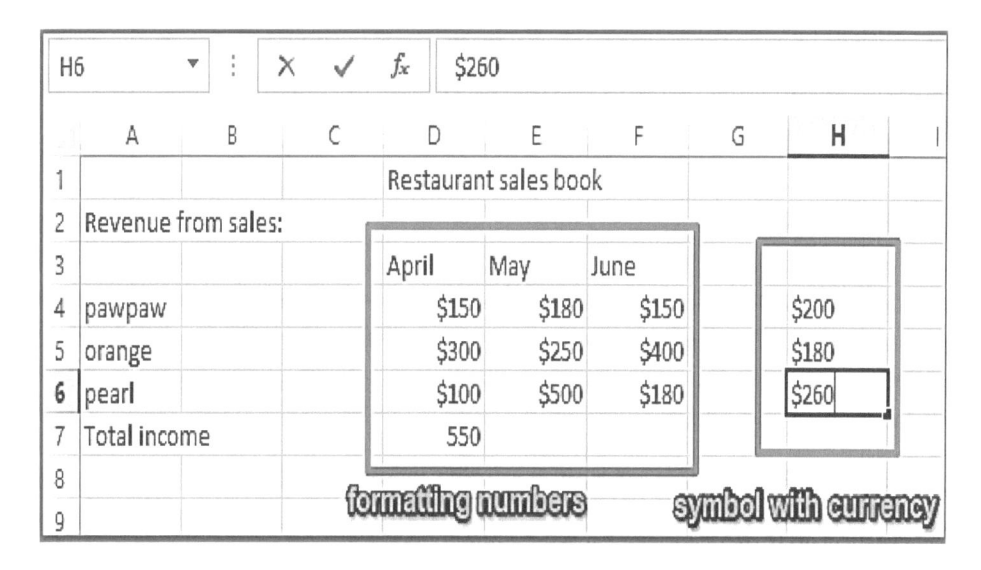

	A	B	C	D	E	F	G	H	I
1				Restaurant sales book					
2	Revenue from sales:								
3				April	May	June			
4	pawpaw			$150	$180	$150		$200	
5	orange			$300	$250	$400		$180	
6	pearl			$100	$500	$180		$260	
7	Total income			550					

formatting numbers — symbol with currency

(7) **Pointing at the data:** pointing to the Excel data in a cell to enter the reference into the formulas minimizes the risk of error that may be caused by typing the wrong cell reference or address and range name misspelling.

(8) **Select the data to be sorted:** Excel has an interest in the exact range of cell data you need to sort and therefore identifies those related areas of data, even if there are:
- a. Empty rows and columns between areas of related data.
- b. No empty rows and columns between areas of related data.

	A	B	C	D	E	F
1				Restaurant sales book		
2	Revenue from sales:					
3				April	May	June
4	pawpaw			$150	$180	$150
5	orange			$300	$250	$400
6	pearl			$100	$500	$180
7	Total income			550		
8				D3:D7		

Notes: Excel automatically excludes rows with field names from sorting. However, letting Excel choose the sorting area can be risky particularly when large data is involved.

Typing Your Text

The first assignment inside the worksheet is entering some headings into the rows and columns. Before you can make any data input into the worksheet, you have to make your preferred cell in which you want to input data an active cell by clicking on the cell first before typing. For instance, let us open a new blank workbook and enter some text:

1. Click **cell A2** to make it an active cell and type **Skateboarding**, press **"Enter"** to go down to another cell to make it an active cell. If you observe the text you just inserted, it seems like it stands in both A2 and B2 cells, but really, it is only in cell A2, B2 simply permits the rollover because there is no data in it. Believing the text is in cell B2 is a delusion.

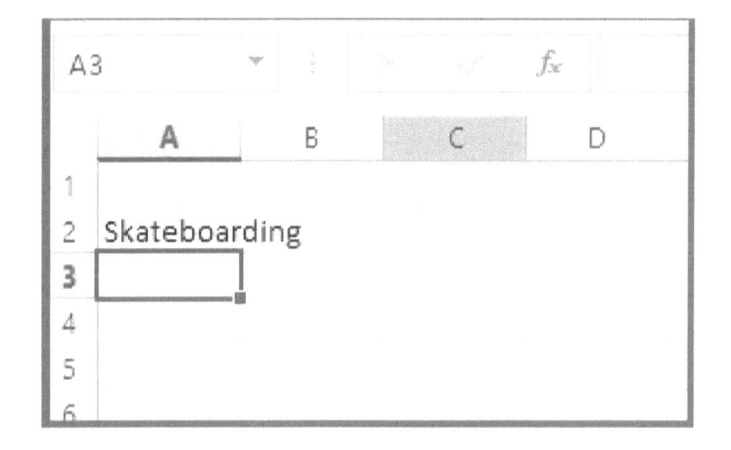

2. Let us continue and type Basketball, then press **"Enter"**.

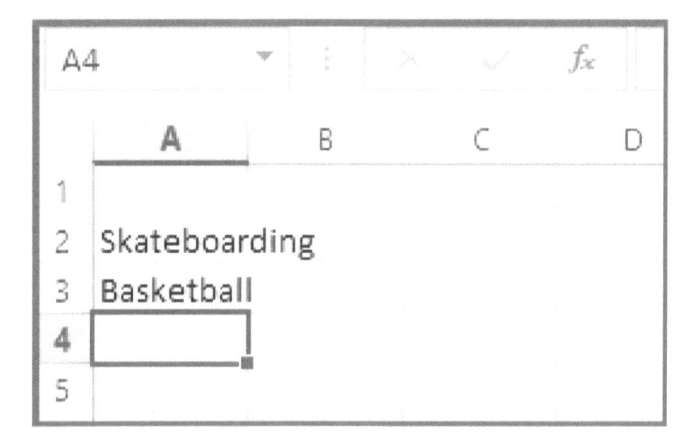

3. Repeat the above process to enter the remaining sport types in column A as shown below.

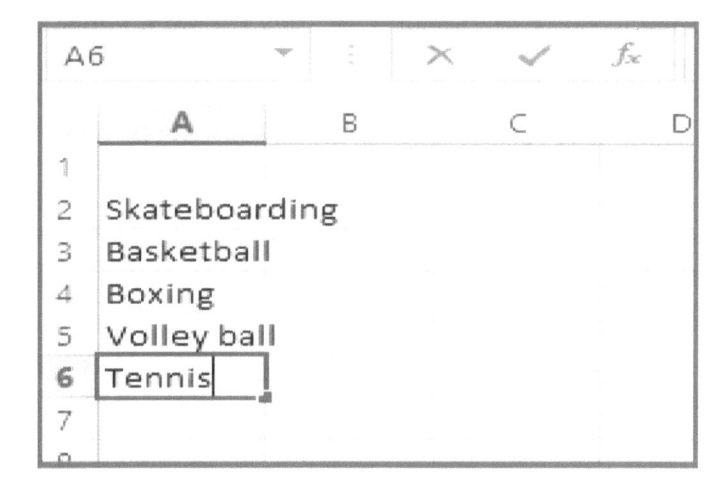

4. Click on **cell B1** and type **China**, then press **Tab** to navigate the cell to the right to make it an active cell.

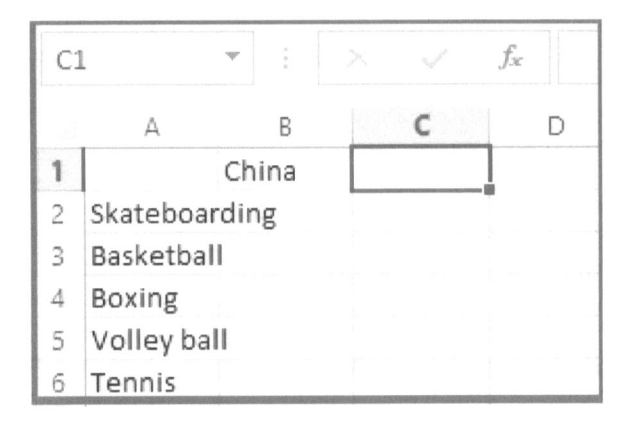

5. Enter the remaining country names in **row 1** as shown below.

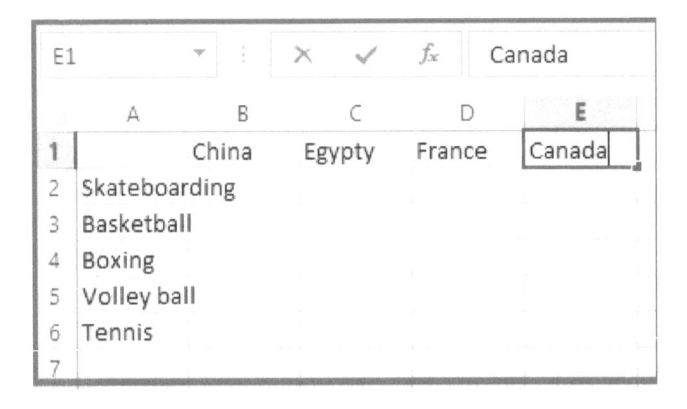

Tips: you are not restricted to use the enter or tab keys to make the cell active, you may use the arrow keys to click on each cell you want or in moving up, down, right, or left.

Typing Numeric Value

Typing number is the same way you type letters or text, by just clicking on the cell and make it active, then type the number inside. The only exception is that of the alignment, that is, the numbers will align themselves to the right side of the cell while letters align themselves to the left side of the cell, both alignments are by default. To examine how to type numbers, let us continue with the above text exercise by:

1. Clicking on **cell B2** to make it active, then type **15300,** and press **Enter** or the **down arrow**. If you observe very well, some of the texts in the left cell are not visible anymore, it is because cell B now has information inside and it has to show superiority of ownership over the texts that should not be in cell B, though some of the texts in cell A are still there.
2. Enter the remaining figures in the other cells to complete the illustration as shown below.

	A	B	C	D	E
1		China	Egypt	France	Canada
2	Skateboar	15300	10000	5800	12000
3	Basketbal	18500	15400	8000	6000
4	Boxing	15900	20000	24500	17000
5	Volley bal	53400	18000	16800	5000
6	Tennis	12000	6000	40000	24100

Note: to be sure of what is inside a cell (contents), click on such cell, and go to the **formula bar** at the uppermost of the worksheet to check the data contained in such active cell.

Typing Dates and Time Values

In Excel, dates are referred to a special data because immediately you insert those numbers into the cell inside the worksheet, Excel recognizes the format to which they come and instantly converts them to date. For example, 20-2, numbers like this will be converted to 20-February, from that henceforth, you can use such a date to carry out calculations.

Let us check the scenario by continuing with the previous worksheet by:

1. Clicking on **cell A8** to make it an active cell, then type **Sport at,** then tap **"Tab"** to move to the next cell.

	A	B	C	D	E
1		China	Egypt	France	Canada
2	Skateboar	15300	10000	5800	12000
3	Basketbal	18500	15400	8000	6000
4	Boxing	15900	20000	24500	17000
5	Volley bal	53400	18000	16800	5000
6	Tennis	12000	6000	40000	24100
7					
8	Sport at:				

2. Type **20/03** to the active cell you have made above in (1), this number will be identified as a date and will be formatted as a date accordingly. Though you can change the format type at the latter period if you desire.

	A	B	C	D	E
1		China	Egypt	France	Canada
2	Skateboar	15300	10000	5800	12000
3	Basketbal	18500	15400	8000	6000
4	Boxing	15900	20000	24500	17000
5	Volley bal	53400	18000	16800	5000
6	Tennis	12000	6000	40000	24100
7					
8	Sport at:	20-Mar			
9					
10					

3. Click on **cell A9,** and type **appraised,** then tap **"Tab"** to move to the next cell (B9).

	A	B	C	D	E
1		China	Egypty	France	Canada
2	Skateboar	15300	10000	5800	12000
3	Basketbal	18500	15400	8000	6000
4	Boxing	15900	20000	24500	17000
5	Volley bal	53400	18000	16800	5000
6	Tennis	12000	6000	40000	24100
7					
8	Sport at:	20-Mar			
9	Appraised:				

4. Go to the **formula box** and Type = **B8 + 5** and press **Enter**. B8 + 5 is a **formula** that is referencing the date you typed above in cell B8. Formulas are used in the spreadsheet to carry out calculations just like the formula we used here by adding 5 to cell B8 (which signifies 5 days to the date).

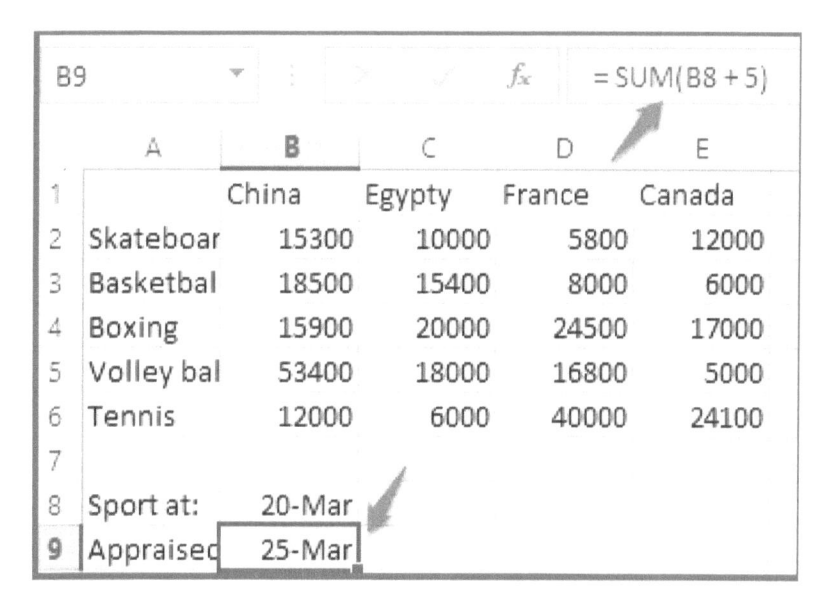

B9　　　　　　　　　　　ƒx　= SUM(B8 + 5)

	A	B	C	D	E
1		China	Egypty	France	Canada
2	Skateboar	15300	10000	5800	12000
3	Basketbal	18500	15400	8000	6000
4	Boxing	15900	20000	24500	17000
5	Volley bal	53400	18000	16800	5000
6	Tennis	12000	6000	40000	24100
7					
8	Sport at:	20-Mar			
9	Appraised	25-Mar			

Note: examine the alignment of your date, it should be to the right of the cell just like numbers. If the alignment is at the left, it means the date is invalid to Excel and it is not recognizing it as a date and thus, you have to take cognizance of how you enter your dates.

Taking Advantages of Flash Fill And Autofill Commands By Entering Specific Lists and Serial Data

Worksheet at times includes specific sequences of numbers drawn out of longer sequences. Entering and formatting these longer sequences will take a long time and therefore Excel has offered features like Flash Fill and Autofill to make such long tasks easier and faster. Let us quickly check how to use those features by starting with the Flash Fill.

A. **Combining data with Flash Fill:** let us begin the illustration by:
   1. Opening the worksheet and input employer names; start with the First name, followed by the last name, and Establishment name in row 1 and other rows after you must have made those cells active.
   2. We will assume all employers have the same format of email address which we will take as first name.last name@establishment.com.
   3. We will now try to produce an automatic email address with Flash Fill by putting the first email manually. Simply click on **cell D2** and type Albert.dent@goldminers.com.

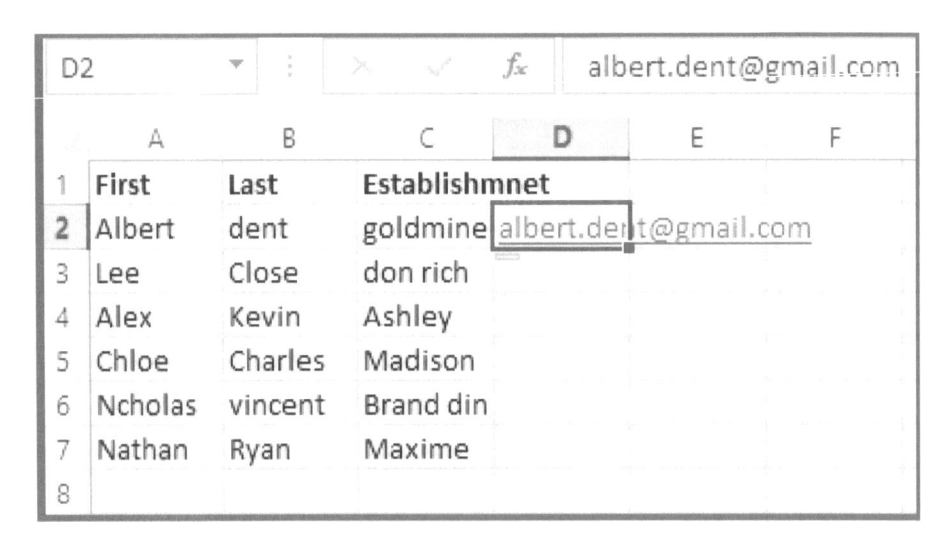

	A	B	C	D	E	F
1	First	Last	Establishmnet			
2	Albert	dent	goldmine	albert.dent@gmail.com		
3	Lee	Close	don rich			
4	Alex	Kevin	Ashley			
5	Chloe	Charles	Madison			
6	Ncholas	vincent	Brand din			
7	Nathan	Ryan	Maxime			
8						

D2 — fx — albert.dent@gmail.com

   4. Now let us check the function of Flash Fill by navigating to the **Data tab** and click on the **Flash Fill** ribbon, Excel will operate it automatically, but ensure cell D2 remains cell active before you

click on Flash Fill. Once you have done that, Excel will input the remaining employees' email by creating their email addresses based on the first email address's format.

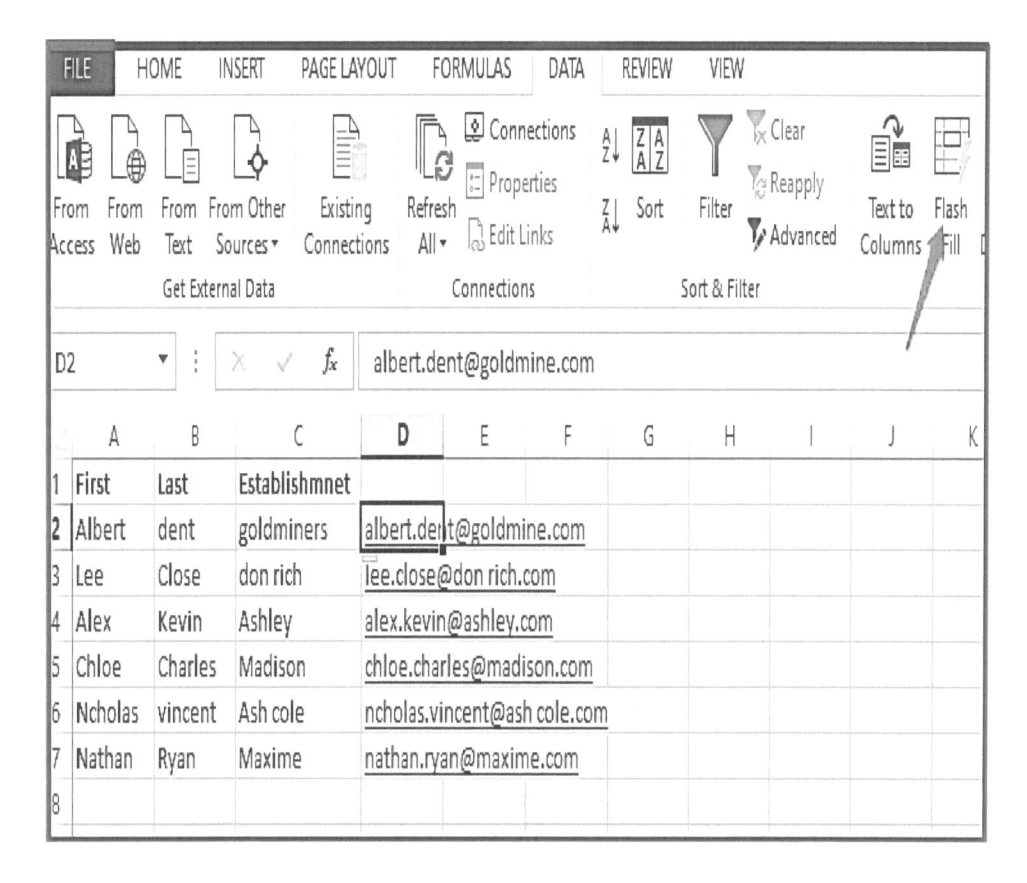

	A	B	C	D
1	First	Last	Establishmnet	
2	Albert	dent	goldminers	albert.dent@goldmine.com
3	Lee	Close	don rich	lee.close@don rich.com
4	Alex	Kevin	Ashley	alex.kevin@ashley.com
5	Chloe	Charles	Madison	chloe.charles@madison.com
6	Ncholas	vincent	Ash cole	ncholas.vincent@ash cole.com
7	Nathan	Ryan	Maxime	nathan.ryan@maxime.com

5. If you observe row 3 and row 6 email addresses. You will notice that their establishment names have two words and spaces between them and thus those spaces were included in their respective email, let us get to correct the error.

6. Navigate to **column D** and click on **cell D3**, erase the email address inside it and type lee.close@donrich.com, the space between don and rich has been removed, now go to Flash Fill, and ensure you are still having D3 as the active cell, then click on Flash Fill to apply the same formulas to the remaining email address and you will perceive that no company name will have space in the email address again irrespective of whether there is space in their establishment name or not.

	A	B	C	D	E	F
1	First	Last	Establishmnet			
2	Albert	dent	goldminers	albert.dent@goldmine.com		
3	Lee	Close	don rich	lee.close@donrich.com		
4	Alex	Kevin	Ashley	alex.kevin@ashley.com		
5	Chloe	Charles	Madison	chloe.charles@madison.com		
6	Ncholas	vincent	Ash cole	ncholas.vincent@ashcole.com		
7	Nathan	Ryan	Maxime	nathan.ryan@maxime.com		

(Cell D3 = lee.close@donrich.com)

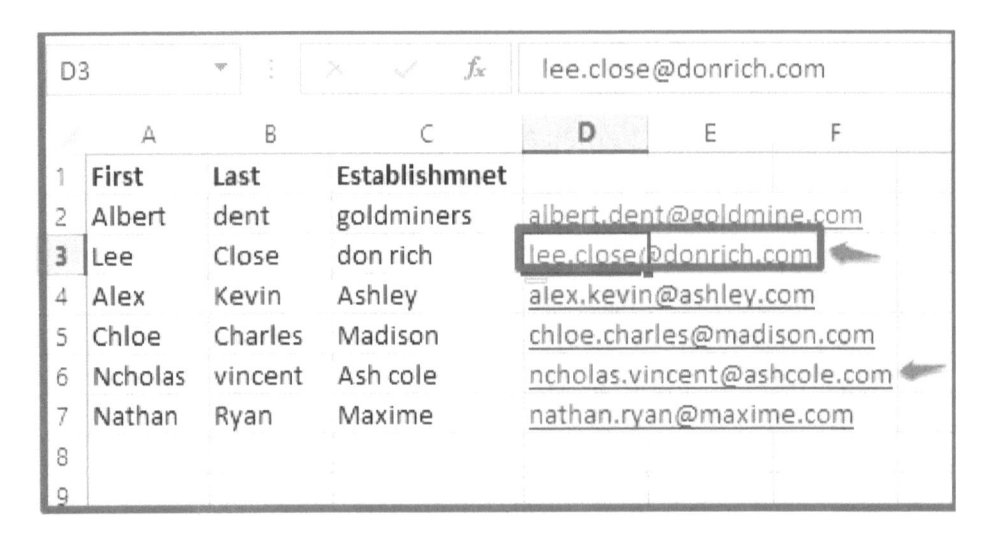

Note: remember you have to enter one cell manually and use it as a formula, to let Excel know what you are trying to do.

B. **Extracting data with Flash Fill**: as you have combined data with Flash Fill, you can as well extract data with Flash Fill. How? Let us check the below illustration:

1. We are having a first name, last name, and security serial number (SSN), but the security number is not real and the actual SSN ought to be the first two (2) numbers and the last three (3) numbers of the initial SSN. Now we will be using Flash fill to extract the real SSN by clicking on **cell D2** and type **28/293** which represents the first two and last three digits of the first SSN to tell Excel what you are trying to do and what you want to do to the remaining ones.

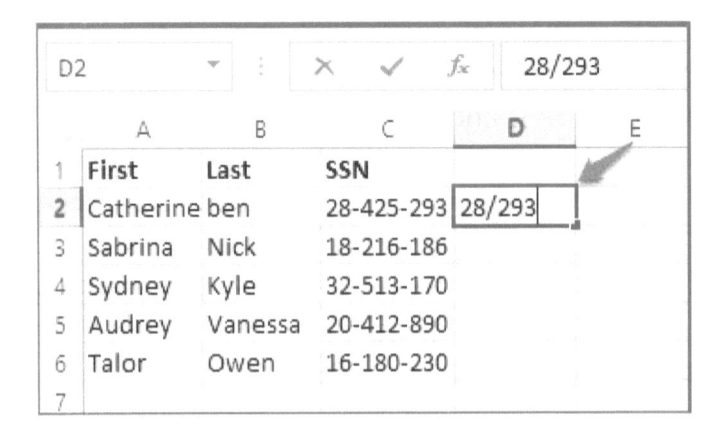

	A	B	C	D	E
1	First	Last	SSN		
2	Catherine	ben	28-425-293	28/293	
3	Sabrina	Nick	18-216-186		
4	Sydney	Kyle	32-513-170		
5	Audrey	Vanessa	20-412-890		
6	Talor	Owen	16-180-230		

(Cell D2 = 28/293)

2. Ensure **cell D2** remains the active cell, now move to click the **Flash Fill** button, and you will notice Excel has grabbed the actual digits we want to extract and even add the Separator line to the digits, this is the power of Excel using Flash Fill.

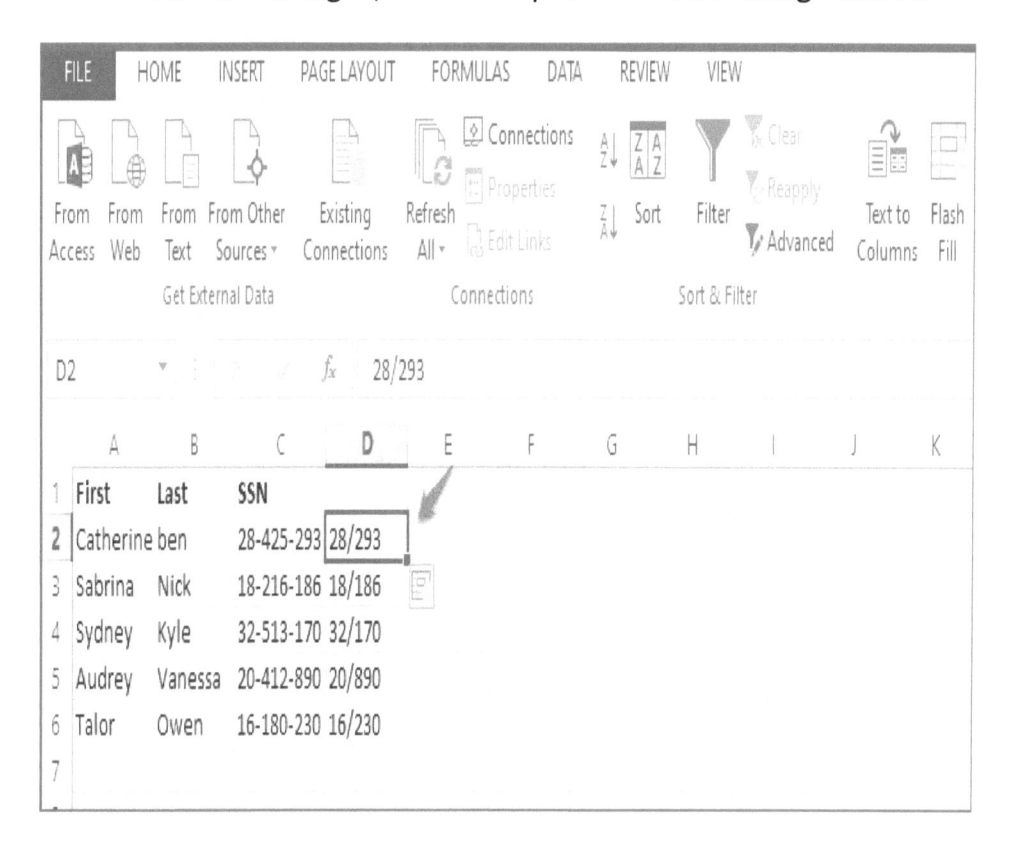

C. **Auto Fill command:** identifies a specific category of data such as consecutive numbers, dates, days of the weeks, and months of the year and therefore, instead of entering all these data manually, simply enter one or two pieces of such data and Excel will quickly fill the remaining data with the AutoFill command. To enjoy the AutoFill command, kindly observe the following processes:
1. Click **the cell** that will be the first in the sequences. For instance, list the month, and the day you want. For illustration, start with February, Wednesday, or a consecutive number such as 3.
2. Then enter the first item in sequence into the cell as stated above in (1).

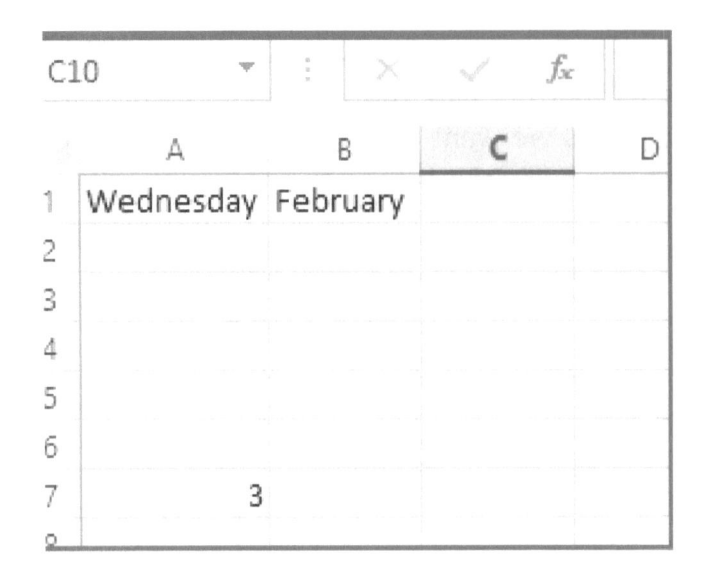

3. Move to the **next cell** perhaps in row order or column order and enter the second item in the sequences such as March, Thursday, and 6, so that Excel can perfectly understand the flow of the sequences.

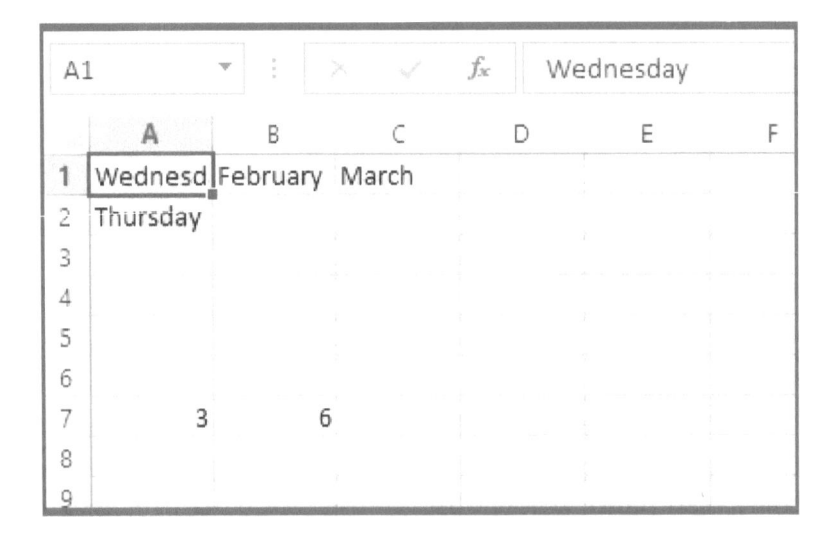

4. You can now select the **cell or cells** you have inserted your data into, either you will select one of the two cells or both cells by a click on one cell or dragging over the two cells.
5. Then click on the **AutoFill** handle and double-click to begin dragging it to the direction you want those sequences to appear on the spreadsheet.

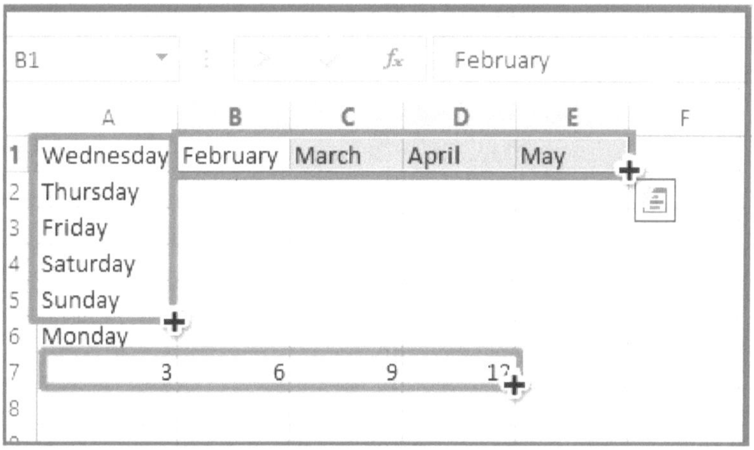
B1
February
A
B
C
D
E
F
Wednesday
February
March
April
May
Thursday
Friday
Saturday
Sunday
Monday
3
6
9

Note: **AutoFill** handle is the small green square located at the lower-right corner of the cells you selected. It is inactive until it changes to a black plus (+) sign, then you can drag it by double-clicking it. The more you drag the AutoFill handle, the more the serial data will be appearing in a pop-up box. AutoFill options appear immediately you start entering serial data, and it gives you the option to either copy or fill the cell without transferring the data along with the format.

Probably you want to enter the same item into many empty cells, drag over the cells to select those cells, then type the text or numbers you want to duplicate to other cells into the first cell in the sequence and press **Ctrl + Enter**. You can as well select those cells by holding down the Ctrl key and continue clicking on where you want the item to enter.

Applying Formatting to Numbers, Dates, Money, And Times Values

Formatting in Excel simply means changing the appearance of the numbers, dates, and times to your taste. For instance, if you type 23/3 in

a cell, Excel will change it to a date format and it will be displayed as 23-March in the cell, in the same vein you may type 11.15a, Excel will interpret it as time and show it as 11:15 AM. This format may not tally with your preference and thus you have to change it by formatting such data. To format numbers, times and dates kindly:

- Click **cell C2**, hold down the Shift key, and then click on **C7** to select a range of dates.

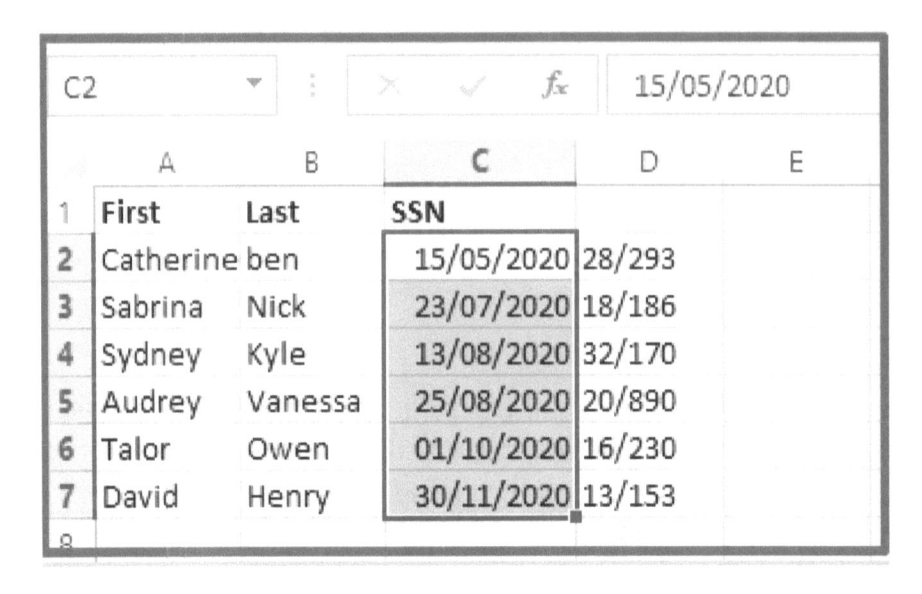

- Move to the **Menu bar** and click on the **Home tab,** then move to the **Number** group to see a number format.
- In the number group, click on the **Long date** option to change those selected short dates to a long and more explicit format.

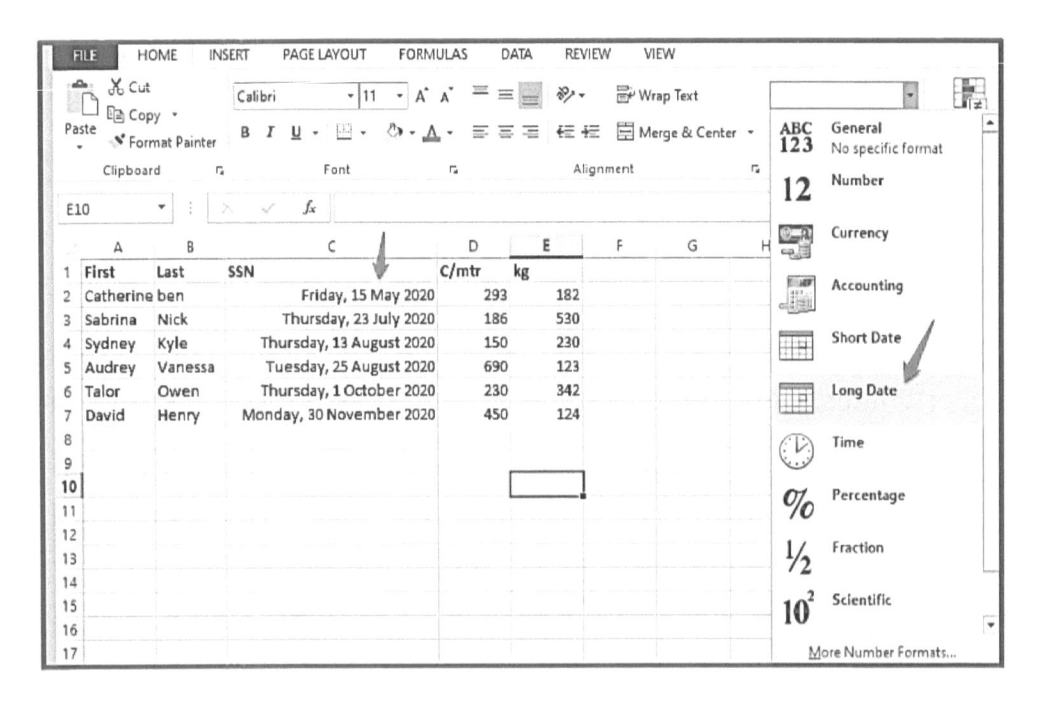

110

- For currency, select the range of cell D2 to cell D7, move to the **Number** group, then select **Currency**. The currency here is naira (#), you can check other currencies by moving to the "more number format" option to select your preferred currency.

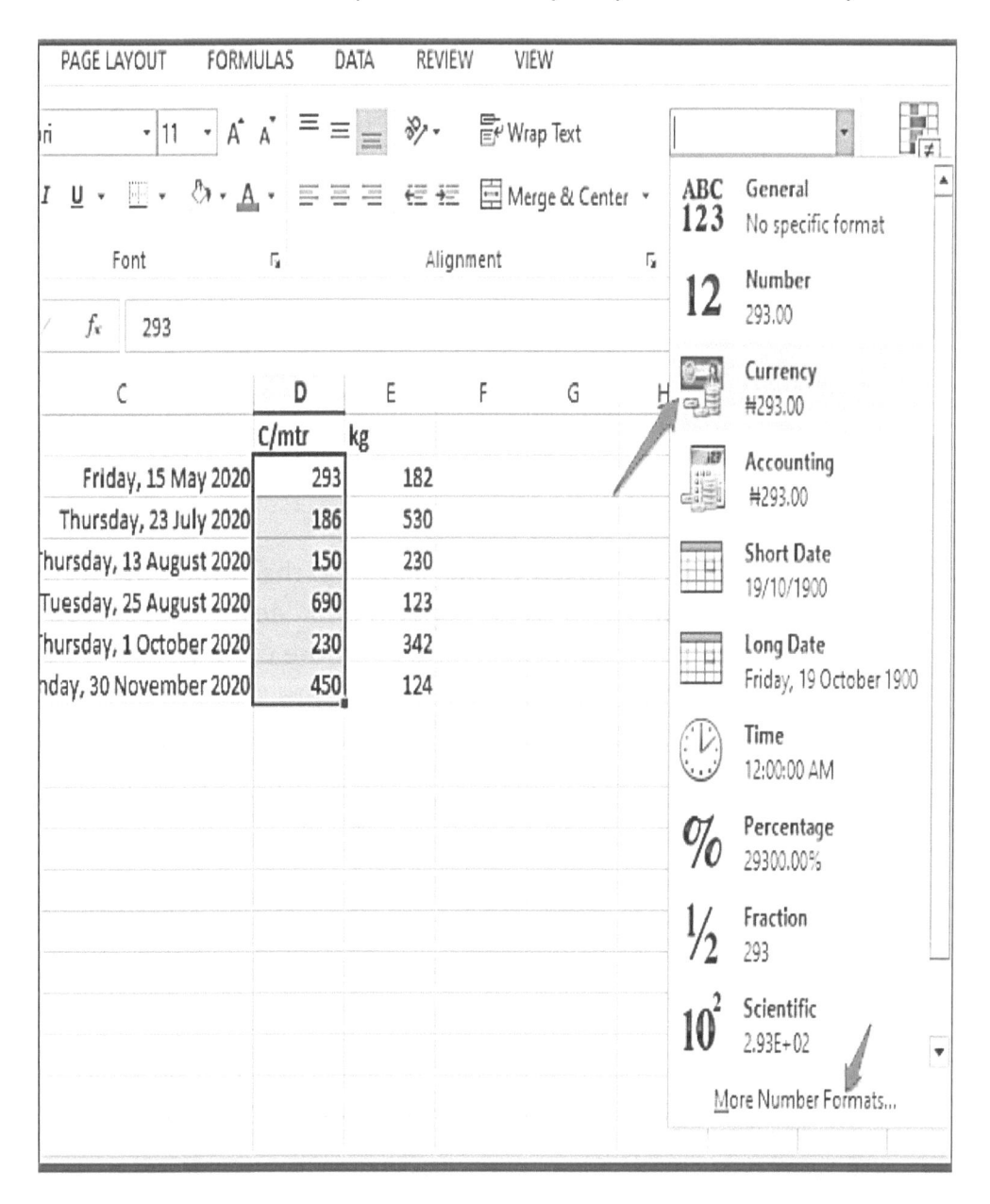

- On the Number bar, click on **Currency,** pick your preferred currency, and tap **Ok**.

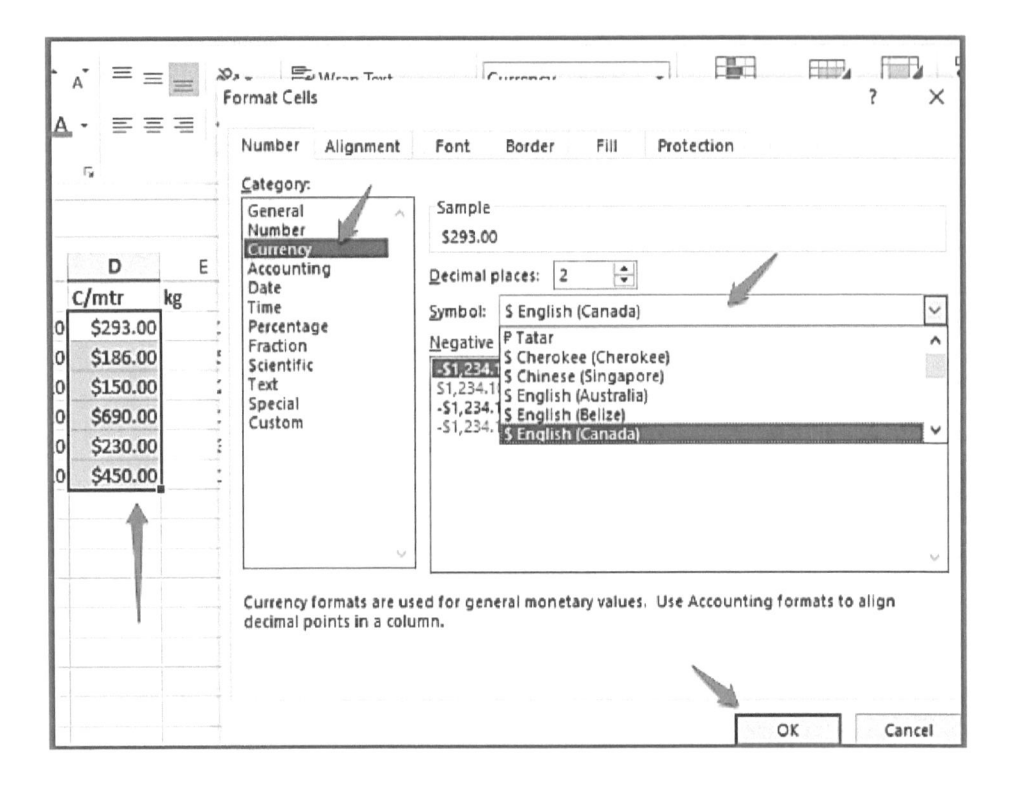

- Select a range of **Cell E2 to E7** and move to the **Number** group, then select **Number** to show numbers in two decimal places. You can still go to "More Number Format" for more options.

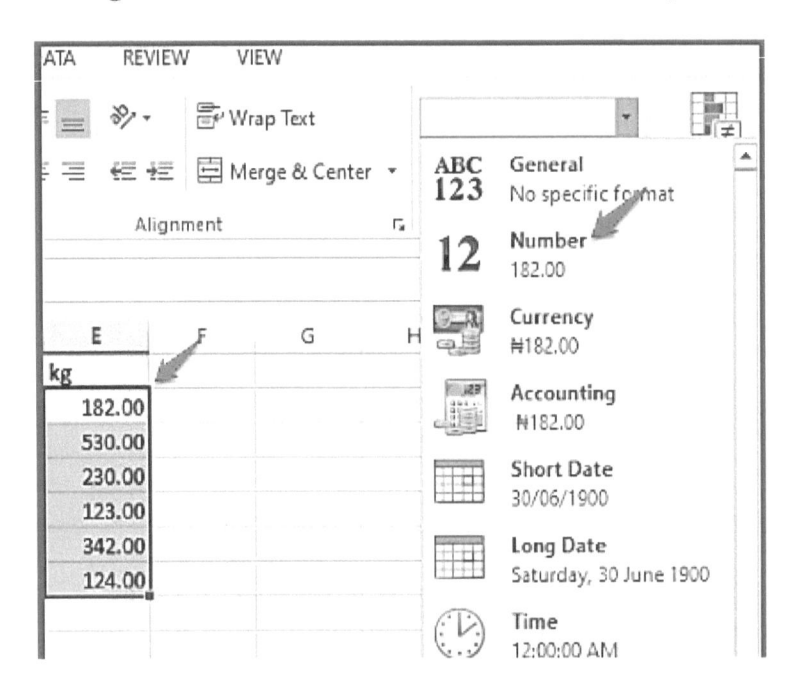

112

Note: you can press **Ctrl + 1** as a shortcut to access the "More Number Format" dialog box.

Essential Guide to Data Validation

Data validation is a special feature made by Excel that permits users to control what they enter into the cell. Data validation can help you to enter data in a preferred specified format, restrict the kind of data to be entered into the cell, and can be used to create a drop-down as well.

Let us now check types of data validation rule:

1. **Allowing whole numbers and decimal only:** to restrict the type of data that will enter into the cell such as whole numbers and decimal, you have to:
    a. Pick **the cell** you want to restrict its data.
    b. Move to the **Data tab** and select **data validation** to bring forth the data validation dialogue box.

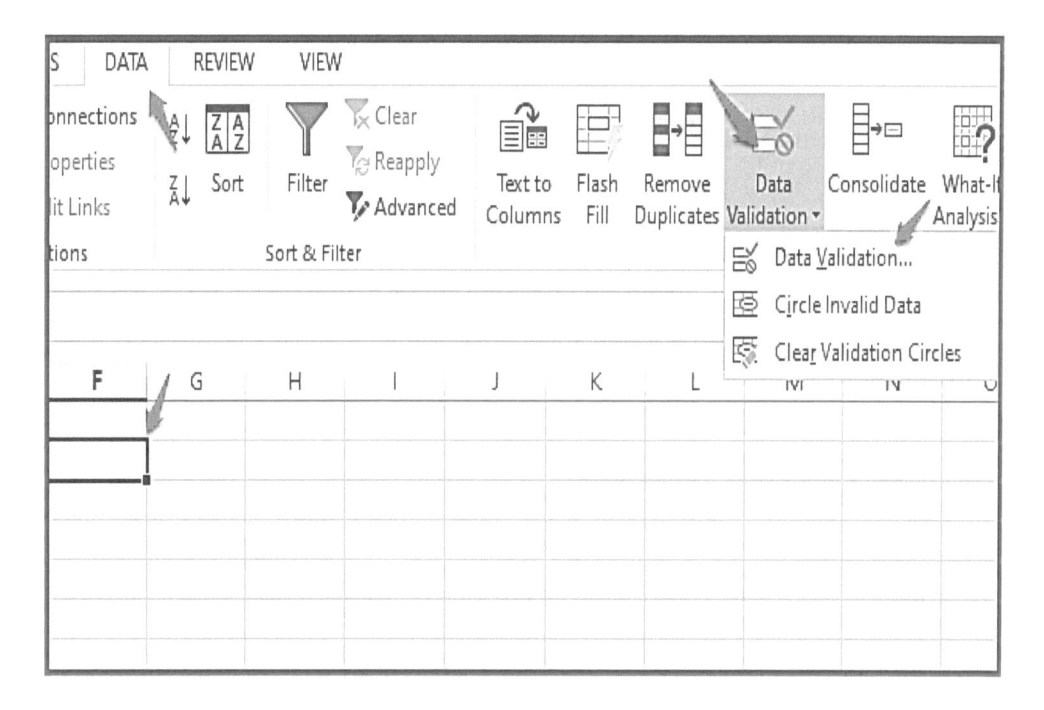

    c. Pick the **Data type** under "Allow" such as whole numbers and decimal.

113

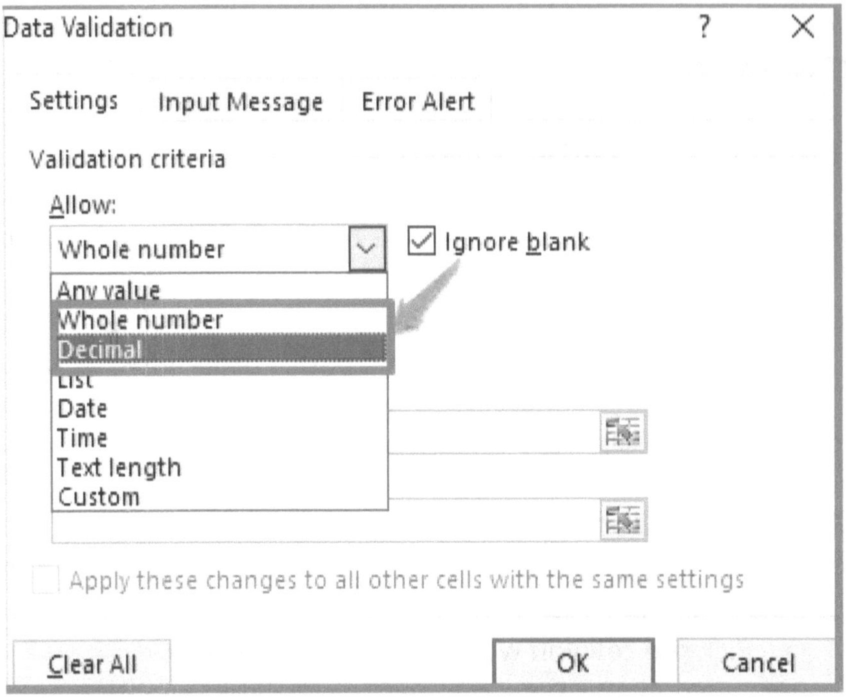
Data Validation
Settings
Input Message
Error Alert
Validation criteria
Allow:
Whole number
Ignore blank
Any value
Whole number
Decimal
List
Date
Time
Text length
Custom
Apply these changes to all other cells with the same settings
Clear All
OK
Cancel

d. Then establish the measures by choosing under **"Data"** perhaps it is between, equal to, and so on.

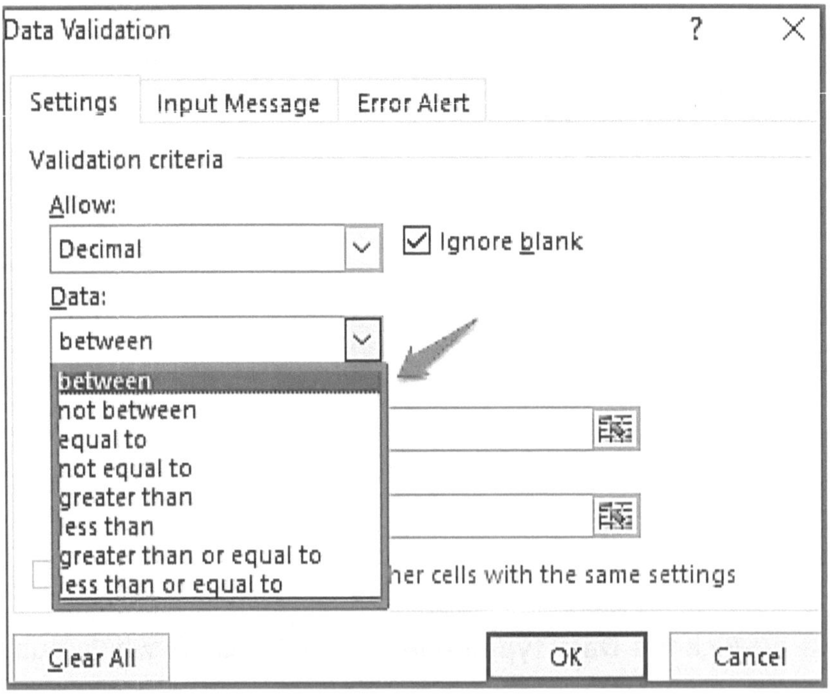
Data Validation
Settings
Input Message
Error Alert
Validation criteria
Allow:
Decimal
Ignore blank
Data:
between
between
not between
equal to
not equal to
greater than
less than
greater than or equal to
less than or equal to
her cells with the same settings
Clear All
OK
Cancel

e. Supply further information that is required for restriction guidelines such as "Minimum" and "Maximum". For instance, a filling station attendant with a customer number between 5500 to 10000 will set the minimum as 5500 and maximum as 10000. After that, tap on **Ok.**

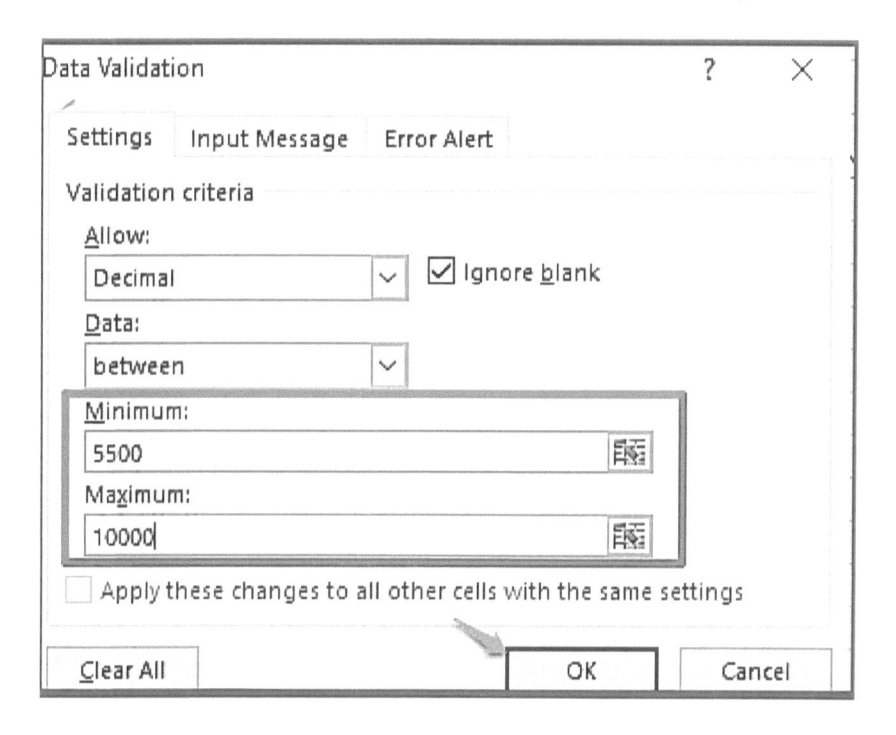

Note: immediately your data entry goes against the validation rule, there will be a prompt warning that the data doesn't match validation restrictions defined for the cell.

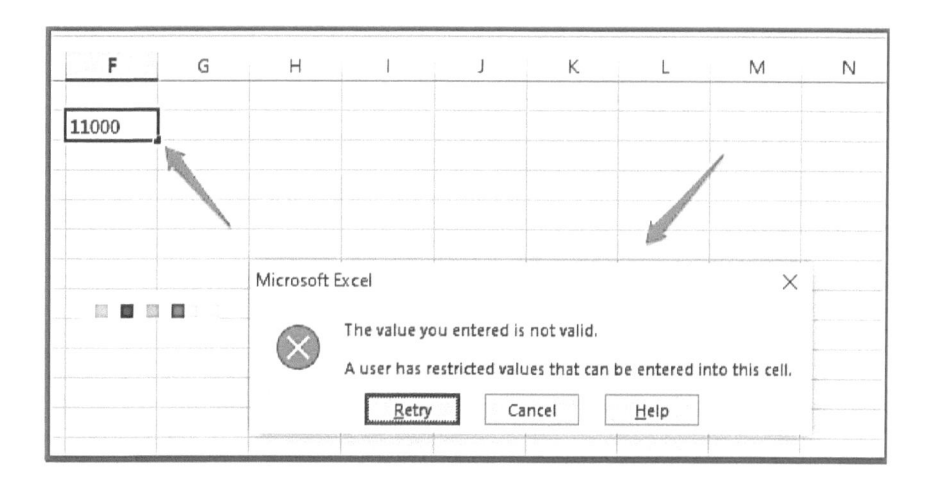

2. **Setting rules for text character length**: rules can be set for a particular text character length to limit the length of the text that can occupy the cell. To do that:
    a. Select the cell or cells that will receive the restriction guideline.
    b. Move to the **Data tab** and click on **Data Validation** to open the data validation dialogue box.

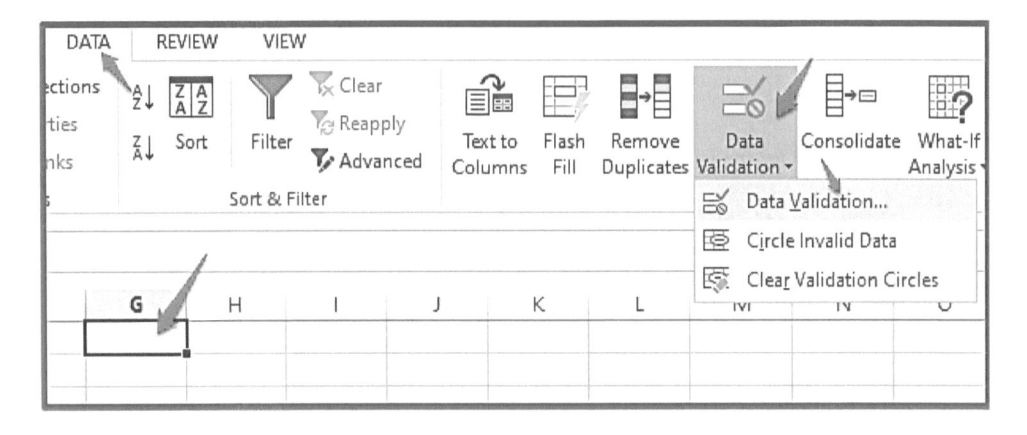

    c. Pick **"Text length"** under "Allow".
    d. Establish befitting measure under the **"Data"** option.

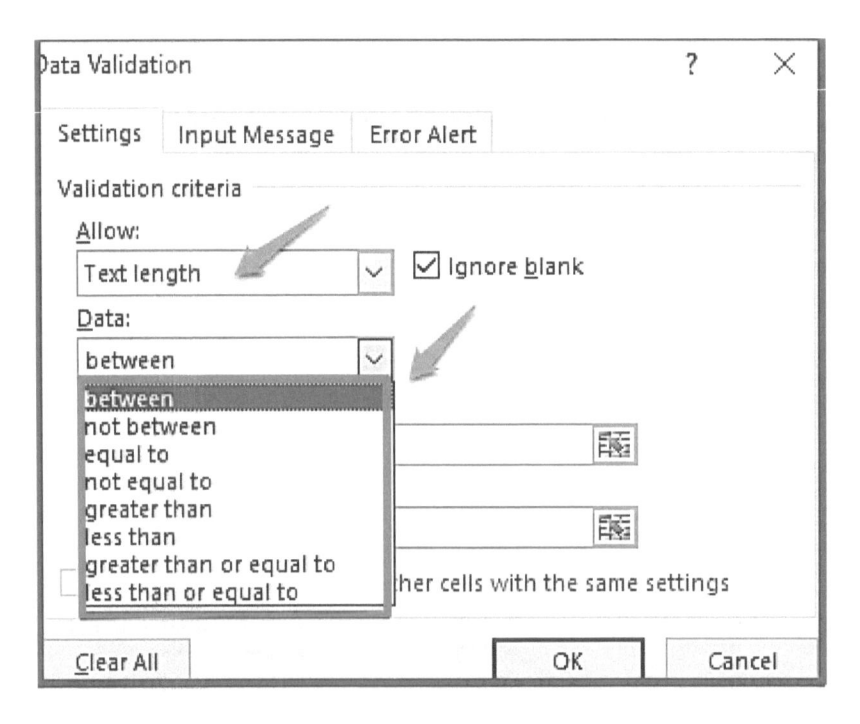

116

e. Supply further information which will stand as a restriction guide. For example, you might want the applicant's username to be within a range of 7 to 15 length in character. Input 7 in the minimum box space and 15 in the maximum box space.

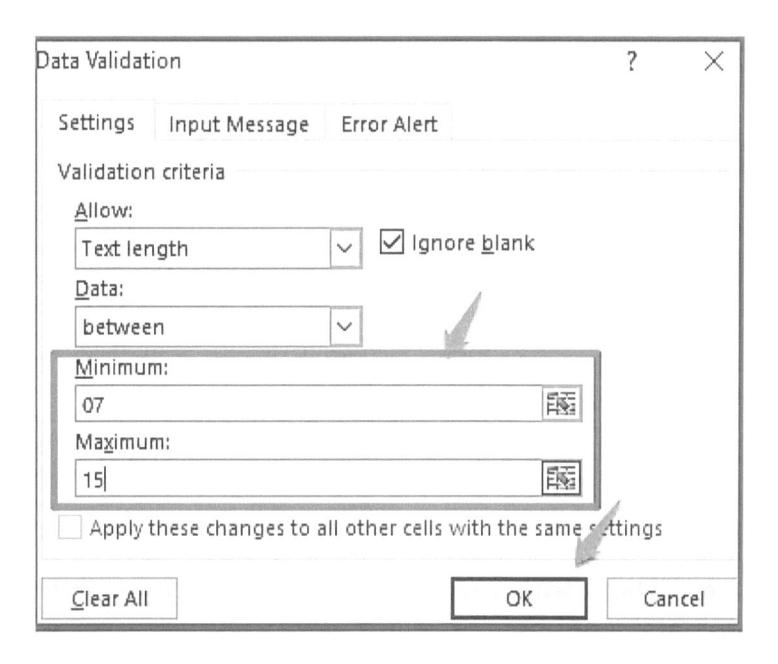

3. **Validating dates and times:** you may set a data validation rule to both the date and time to restrict specific entry into the cell. To achieve that, kindly:
   a. Choose the cell or cells that will receive the validation rule.
   b. Move to the **Data tab** and click on the **Data Validation** to open the Validation dialogue box.

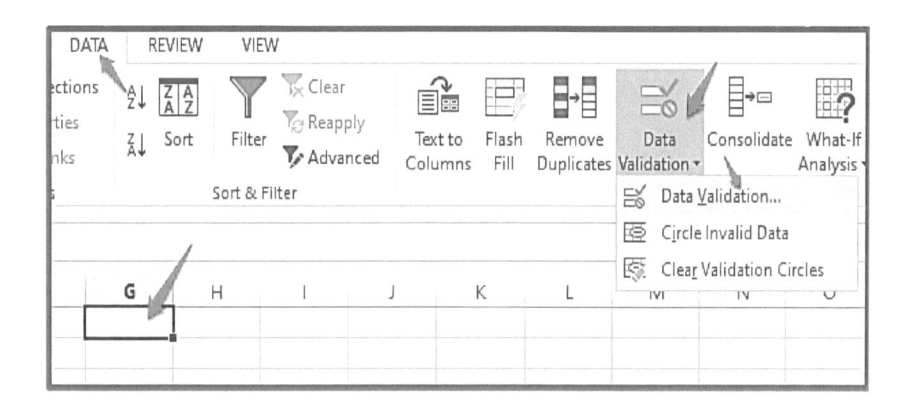

c. Pick the **"Date"** or **"Time"** option under **"Allow"** depending on the restriction item you want to incorporate first.

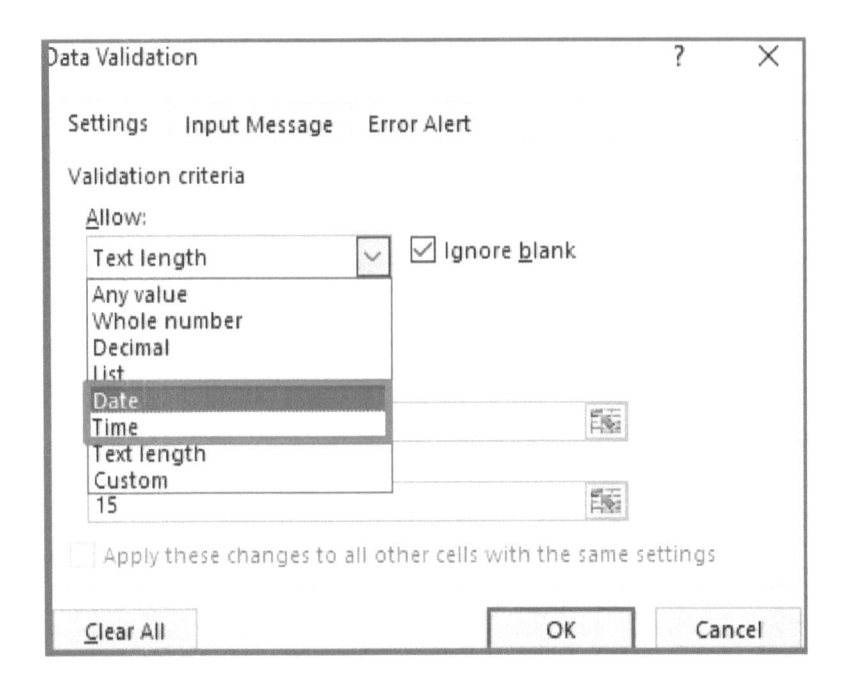

d. Pick the accurate measure that suits your preference under "Data" options.

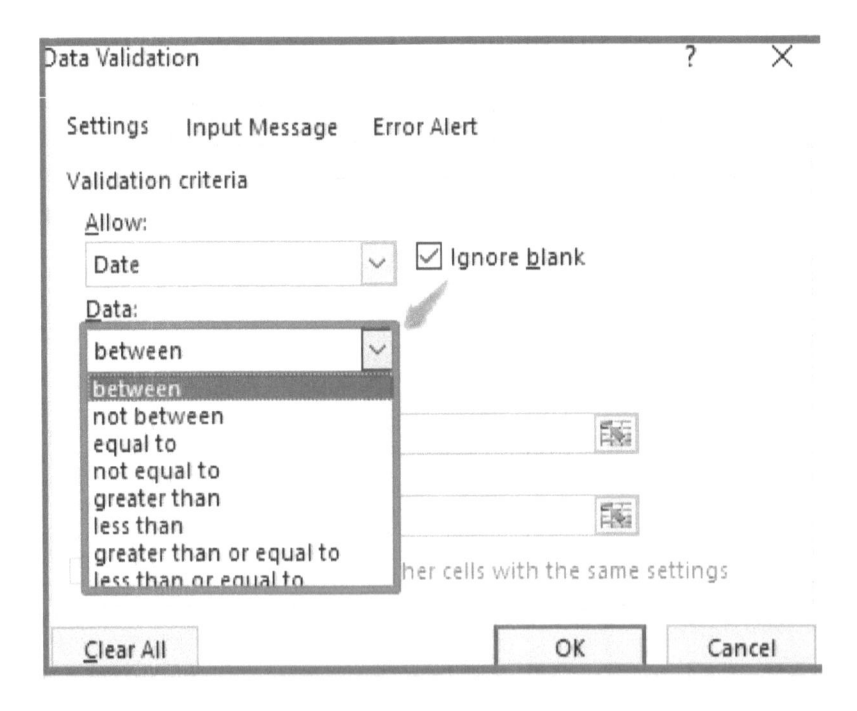

e. Supply further details needed for guideline restriction. For instance, you can choose to set employees' leave periods within the limit of a specific week in a month (10th of June to 17 June). Set the **start date** as June 10 and the **end date** as June 17.

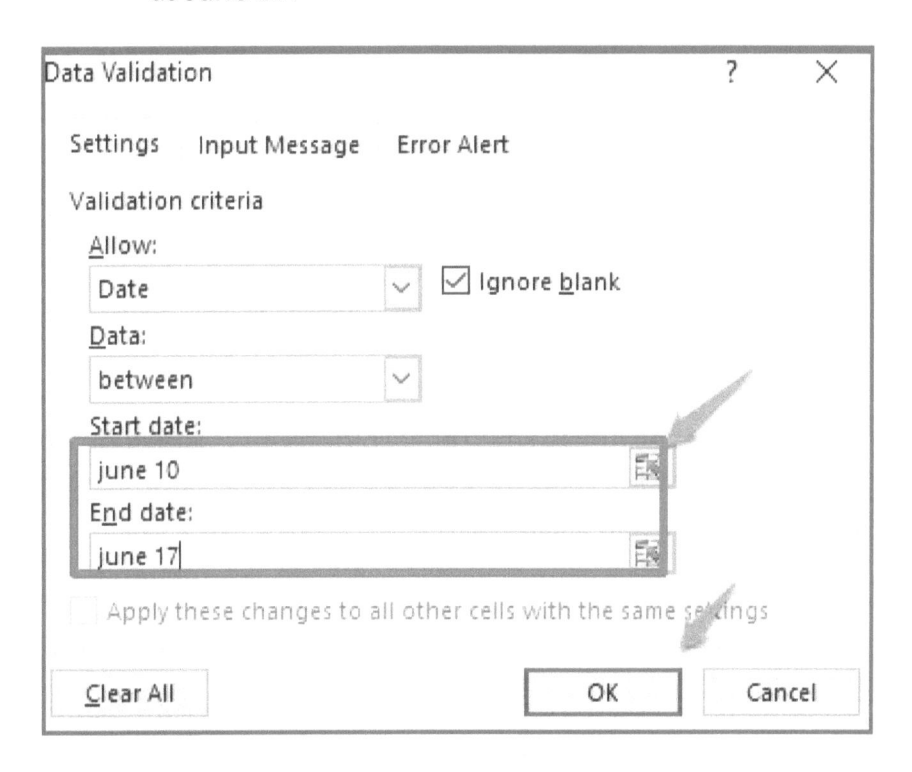

```
Data Validation                                    ?   ×

Settings    Input Message    Error Alert

Validation criteria
  Allow:
  ┌─────────────────────┐  ☑ Ignore blank
  │ Date              ∨ │
  └─────────────────────┘
  Data:
  ┌─────────────────────┐
  │ between           ∨ │
  └─────────────────────┘
  Start date:
  ┌──────────────────────────────────┐
  │ june 10                        🔲│
  │End date:                         │
  │ june 17                        🔲│
  └──────────────────────────────────┘
  ☐ Apply these changes to all other cells with the same settings

  ┌─────────┐                ┌────────┐  ┌────────┐
  │ Clear All│                │   OK   │  │ Cancel │
  └─────────┘                └────────┘  └────────┘
```

Note: Data validation guide helps Excel users to frame what they will enter within the restriction limit in such a way that it will not go beyond standard settings to avoid an error that may occur through data entry.

CHAPTER THREE
IMPROVING YOUR WORKSHEET

Editing Your Worksheet Data

Editing worksheet data simply means editing the contents of what is inside a cell either by clicking on each cell and editing it straightway or by typing data into the formula bar to edit what is inside the active cell. Any time you are editing your cell, Excel will be in editing mode.

How does Excel react in Edit mode? Some Excel users can't differentiate between Edit mode and Ready mode, Excel reacts in these two ways in Edit mode.

- In Edit mode, the "Arrow key" reacts differently, instead of moving the cursor from one cell to another cell, it will be moving from word to word within a cell.

- You can't apply special formatting or adjust the alignment of cell content in Edit mode.

How do I enter Edit mode?

To navigate into edit mode, use one of the following methods:

- Click the cell that contains the contents you want to edit, then proceed to click **the formula bar**.

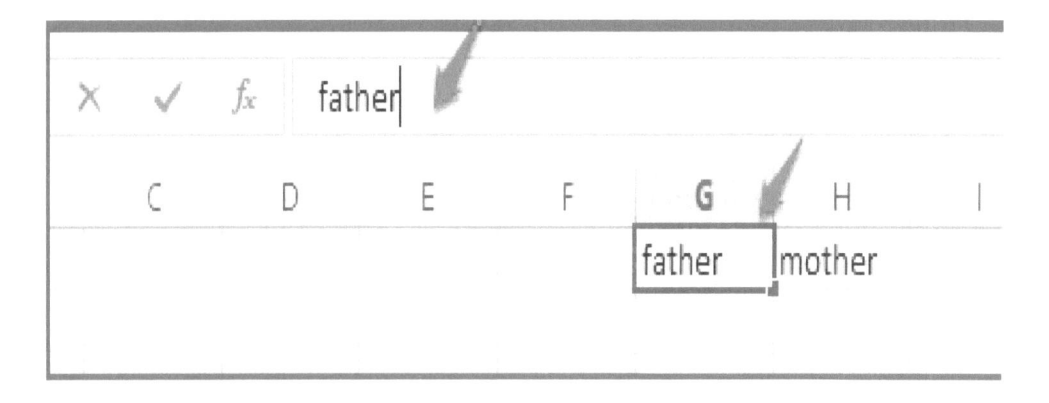

- Double-click on **the cell** that has the data you want to edit and press **"F2"** on the keyboard.

Navigating Around the Worksheet

To move around inside a worksheet, you have to make use of the cell cursor otherwise known as active cell indicator, which is the dark shape that surrounds the active cell. However, you can move round in the worksheet and alter the position of the active cell by:

1. Clicking on the cell you want to make active via the mouse.
2. Clicking on any of the four arrow keys on the keyboard to move the cell cursor in the direction of where the arrow is pointing till you get to your cell destination.

To navigate around the worksheet easily and speedily, you have to master the following shortcuts to fast-track your movement within the worksheet:

CODE	DIRECTION
Enter key	Moving to the next line near the left side.
Tab key	Moving from one cell to another in the right direction.
Shift + tab	Moving from one cell to another in the left direction.
Arrow keys	Moving cells in the direction of the arrow keys.
Home	Moving one cell to the beginning of the row that has the active cell.
Ctrl + Home	Moving one cell to the beginning of the worksheet
Ctrl + End	Moving one cell to the last cell in the worksheet.
Page down	Moving one screen down.
Ctrl + Page down	Moving to the next sheet in the workbook.
Page up	Moving one screen up
Ctrl + page up	Moving to the previous sheet in the workbook
Alt + Page up	Moving one screen to the left
Alt + Page down	Moving one screen to the right

Note: to scroll back to the active cell, perhaps you can't see it anymore on the screen, simply press **Ctrl + Backspace**.

Giving Your Worksheet A New Appearance

Programing your worksheet for a new and better look will even give you a vibe to work more on the worksheet. You have to structure your worksheet in such a way that you will be able to know which column and row you are inputting your data.

The subsequent sub-topics under this chapter describe more on how to change the appearance of your worksheet for a better display such as rows and columns hiding, freezing and splitting of rows and columns, and so on.

Freezing and Splitting Columns and Rows

Freezing: Freezing is used to lock particular rows and columns while splitting helps to generate separate Windows for the same worksheet. Freezing and splitting are needed when you have navigated deeper into the worksheet to the extent that you can't see data tags on the first row

and column which therefore makes it difficult for you to figure out where to input the data on the worksheet. For instance, if you have navigated deeper to W30 or C50, for you to make an area of the worksheet obvious as you have gone too far in the worksheet, you have to make use of Freezing and splitting.

Splitting: Splitting works better than freezing because you can drag the split line to another place whenever you split. Also, you can quickly get rid of both horizontal and vertical split by double-clicking on it, but all these do not apply to freezing (though it is only freezing that will make the top row and first column stand firm without moving, thereby, permitting you in return to view the row and column tag anywhere you are in the worksheet).

How do I freeze or split rows or columns on the screen? No qualms, follow the processes below:

1. Click **the row** that is exactly below the row you desire to freeze or split, or the column exactly at the right side of the column you desire to freeze or split.
2. Move to the **View tab**, click on **The Split Button** to split the row or column. You can take hold of the split bar, which has a small division marker that is exactly above the vertical scroll bar and exactly at the left side of the horizontal scroll bar. In splitting, you

will be able to know the position of the split bar because the pointer arrow turns to two when the pointer is on the split bar.

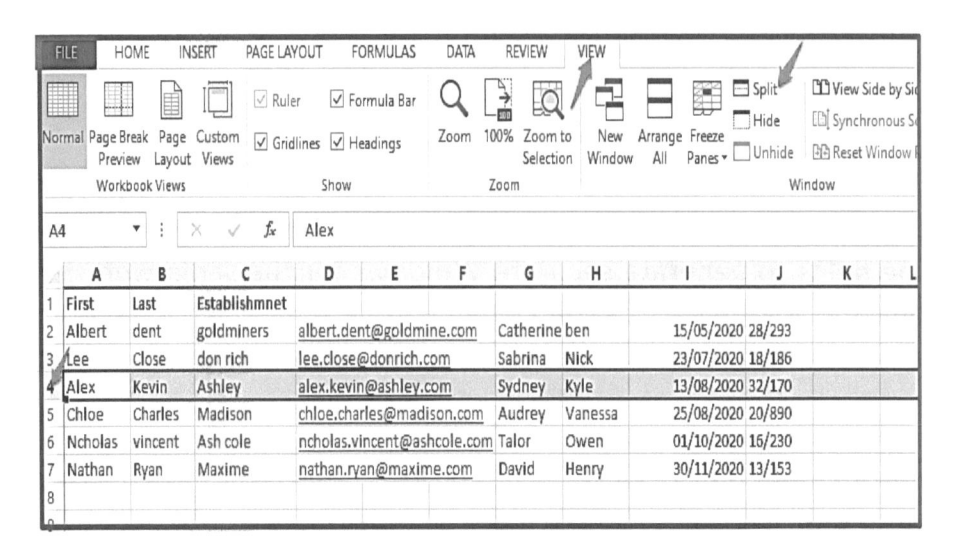

3. Click and drag **the split bar** when it turns to two arrow division to split the screen horizontally or vertically.

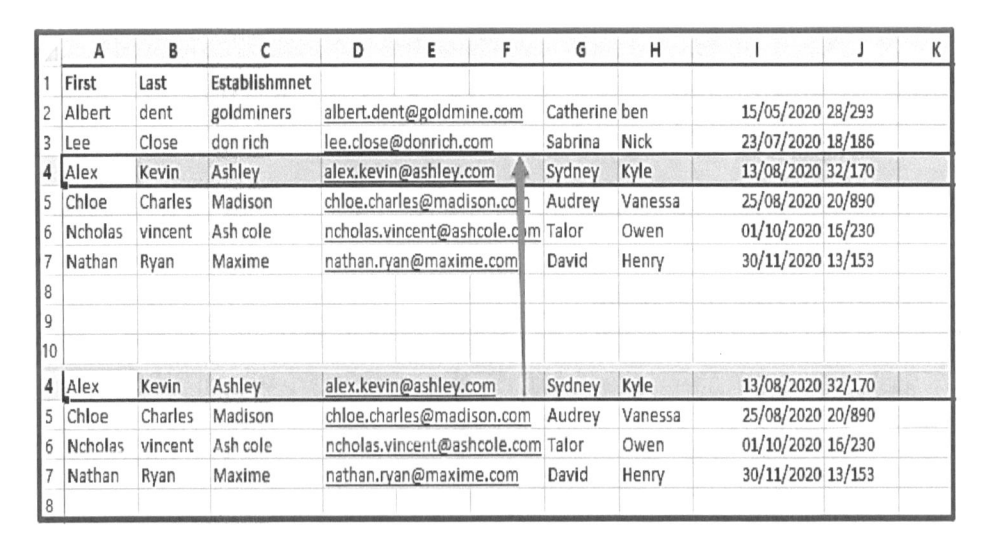

4. For freezing, kindly click on **The Freeze Panes** button, then choose either **the top row or first column** which are the 2nd and 3rd options respectively. Immediately you are done freezing and splitting, there will be a line that will be displayed on the screen which signifies those rows and column have been frozen and split.

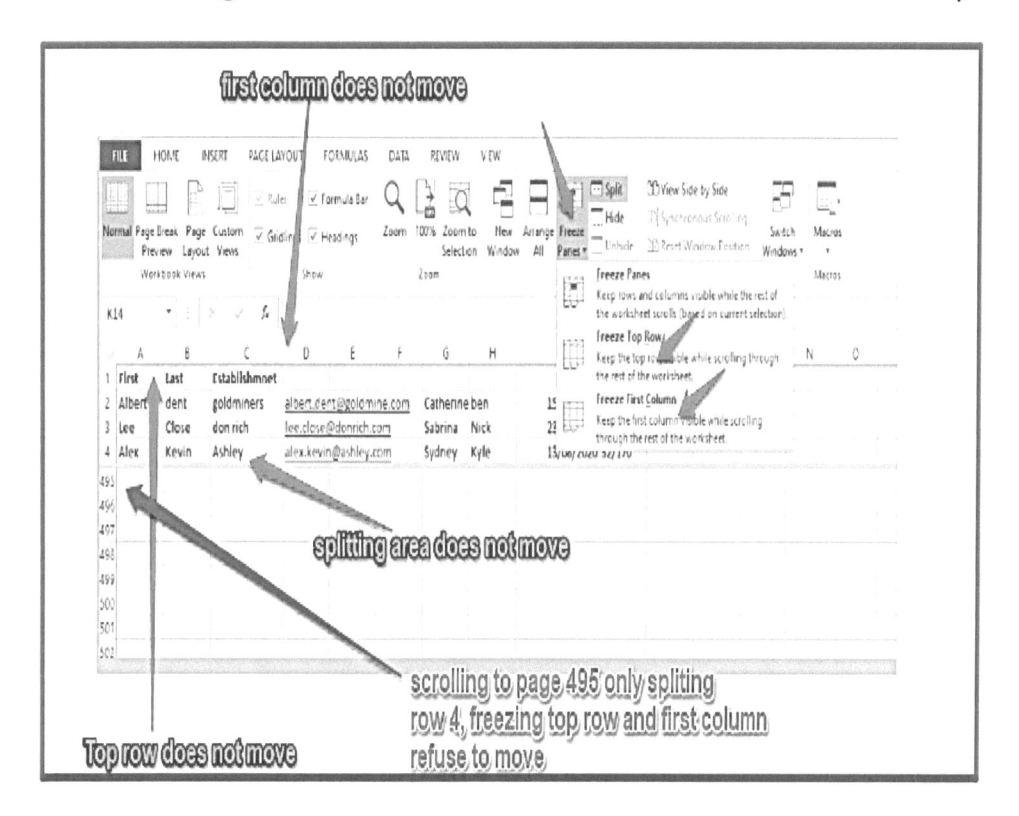

Note: Every other thing will move inside the worksheet except the frozen and split area.

Can I unfreeze and unsplit what had been frozen and split before? Yes, you can, by:

- Clicking on **the split button** once and then double-clicking either of the two bars to remove it. Drag the split bar to the top of the right or left side of the worksheet Window to unsplit rows and columns.
- Kindly click on **Freeze Panes** under the **View tab** and then proceed to pick **Unfreeze Panes** to unfreeze rows and columns.

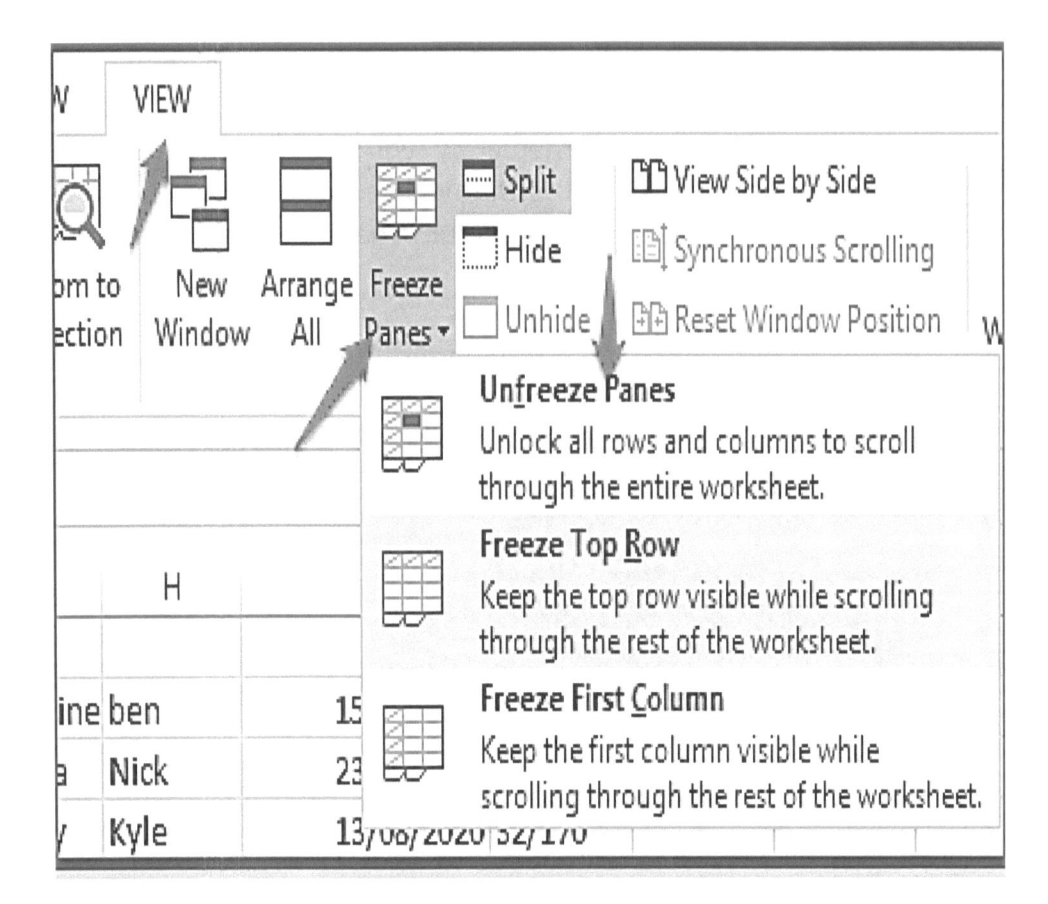

Hide and Unhide The Columns and Rows

Hiding rows and columns at times might be the best approach when you observe that you are having about thousands of rows and columns. It may be very disturbing to work in such a crowded environment, then, hiding such rows and columns will come forth as the only best option.

(1) **How can I hide a row?** This is the way:
   a. Click on **the exact row (s)** you want to hide to select them.
   b. Right-click on **the row(s)** after they have been selected and pick **hide** from the drop-down menu or you can press **Ctrl + 9** as the shortcut.

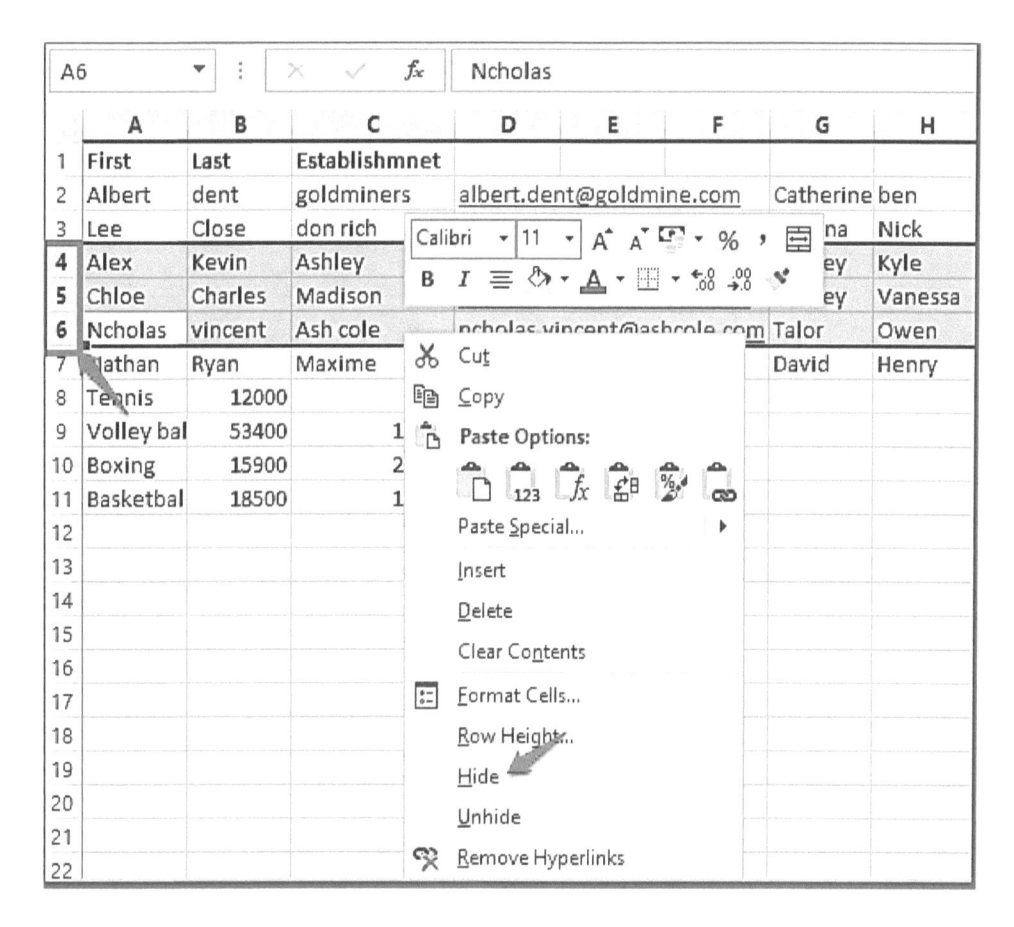

You will notice rows 4, 5, and 6 are not there anymore.

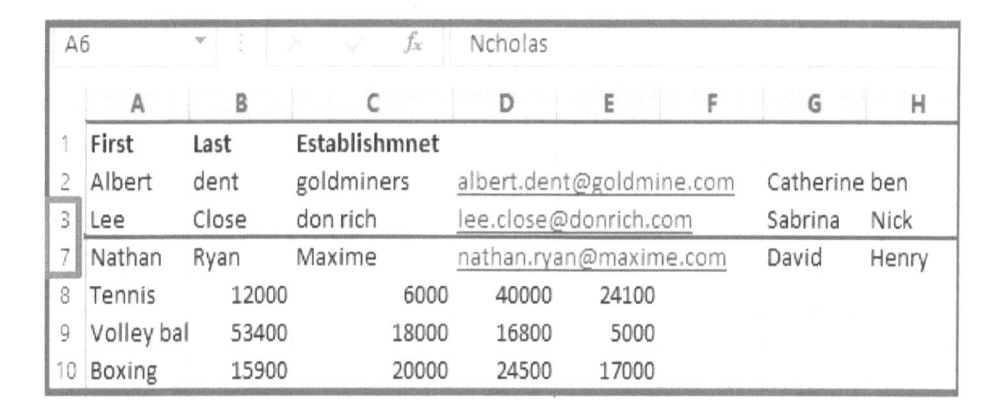

(2) Now, you have hidden rows, what if you want to unhide what you had hidden above? Let us dive into that:
    a. Select **the rows** on both sides of the hidden rows (the row at the top and the row below the hidden rows).

b. Right-click on the selected rows and pick **unhide** from the drop-down menu or you can press **Ctrl + Shift + 9** on the keyboard as the shortcut.

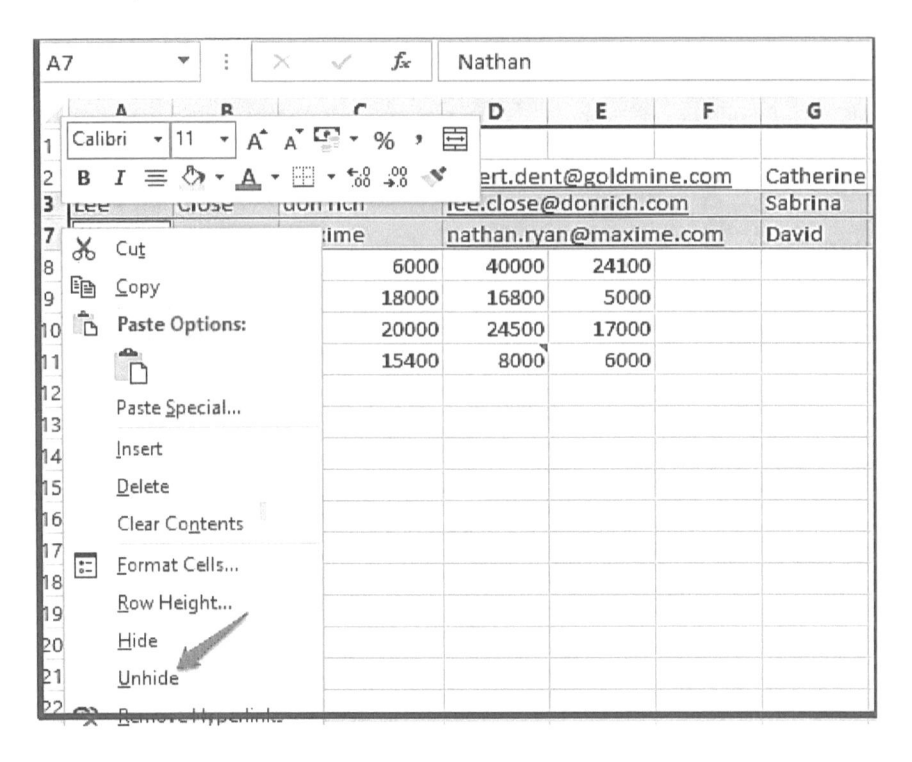

(3) However, this pattern to unhide rows can't work for the first row on the worksheet because it only has a row beneath and does not have any row above, as a result, to **unhide hidden row 1,** you have to use a different pattern:

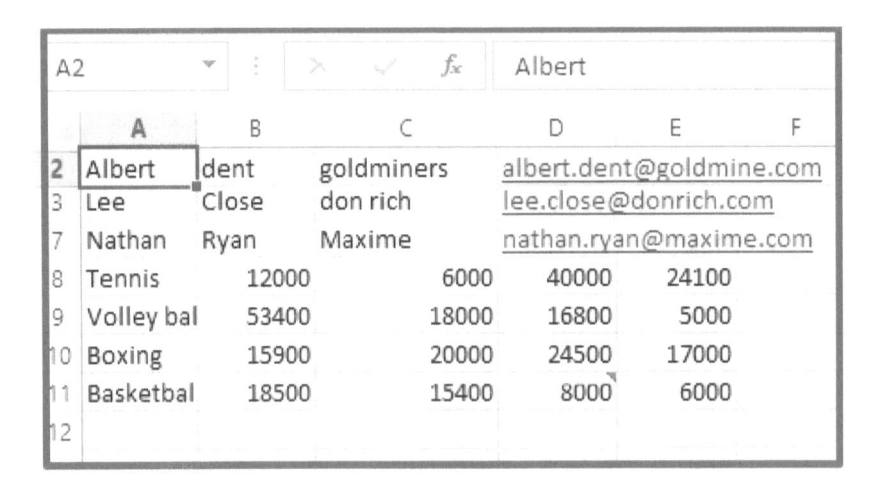

a. You will perceive row 1 of this spreadsheet has been hidden, now to unhide row 1, you will have to move to the cell selection box beside the formula bar at its left side, type A1, and press the **Enter key** so that Excel will understand you want to perform certain functions with A1.

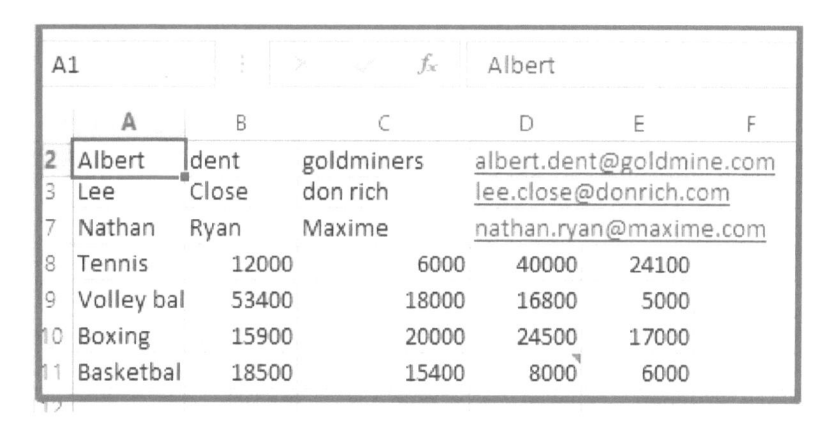

	A	B	C	D	E	F
A1			fx	Albert		
2	Albert	dent	goldminers	albert.dent@goldmine.com		
3	Lee	Close	don rich	lee.close@donrich.com		
7	Nathan	Ryan	Maxime	nathan.ryan@maxime.com		
8	Tennis	12000	6000	40000	24100	
9	Volley bal	53400	18000	16800	5000	
10	Boxing	15900	20000	24500	17000	
11	Basketbal	18500	15400	8000	6000	

b. Go to **the Home tab,** click on **Format cell** ribbon, then pick **Hide & Unhide** from the Format cell drop-down, and lastly click **unhide rows** option from the drop-down list.

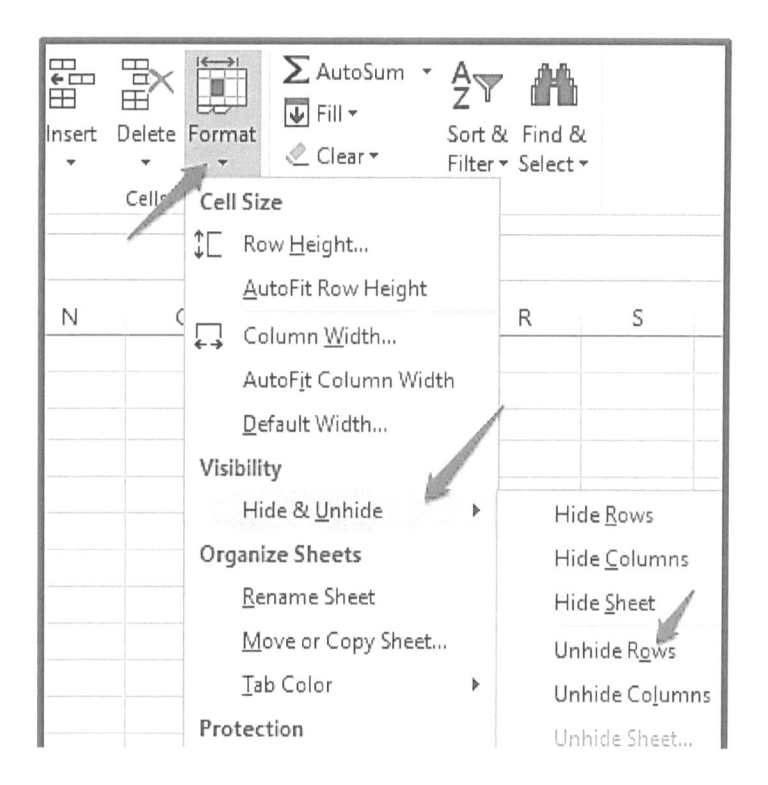

129

NOTE: You can simply press **Ctrl + Shift + 9** as the shortcut

(4) The Hide and Unhide Column is the next one. Though the patterns look similar, they are different. Let us quickly move to how to hide a column:
   a. Let's attempt to hide **column D** as an example. Click on the **D identifier** which is above cell D1 to select the whole column as illustrated below.

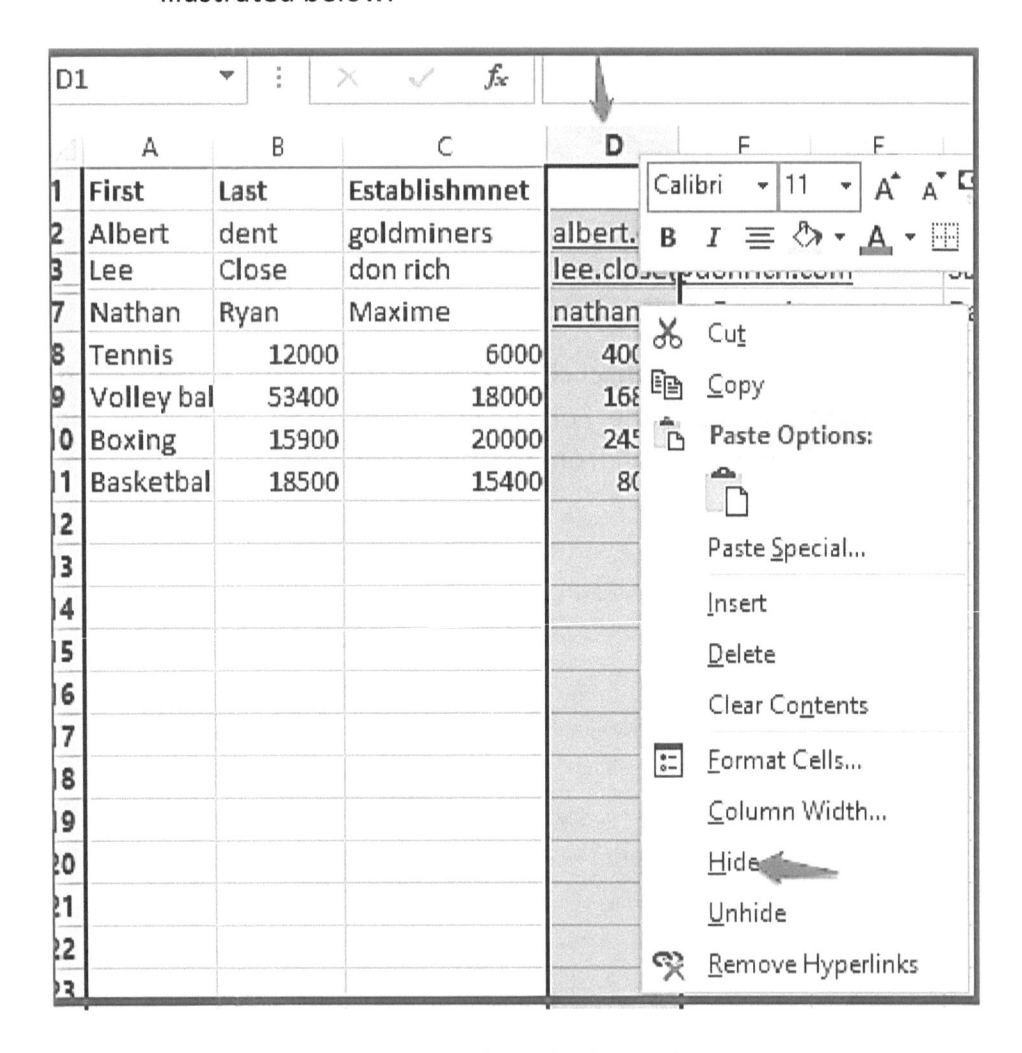

   b. Right-click on it and pick **Hide** from the context menu or you can use shortcut **Ctrl + 0 (zero)**. You will notice that column D has disappeared.

130

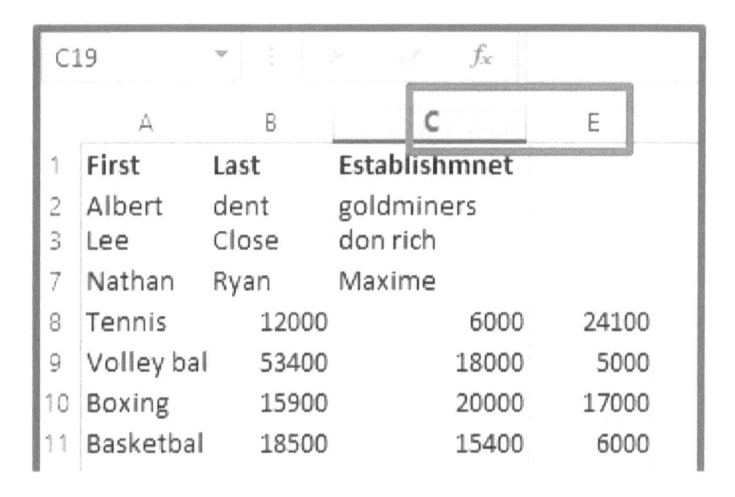

(5) To unhide the above-hidden column, you have to:
   a. Select **the column** on both sides of the hidden column and then right-click on them.
   b. Pick **unhide** from the drop-down menu or you can make use of the shortcut by pressing **Ctrl + Shift + 0 (zero)**.

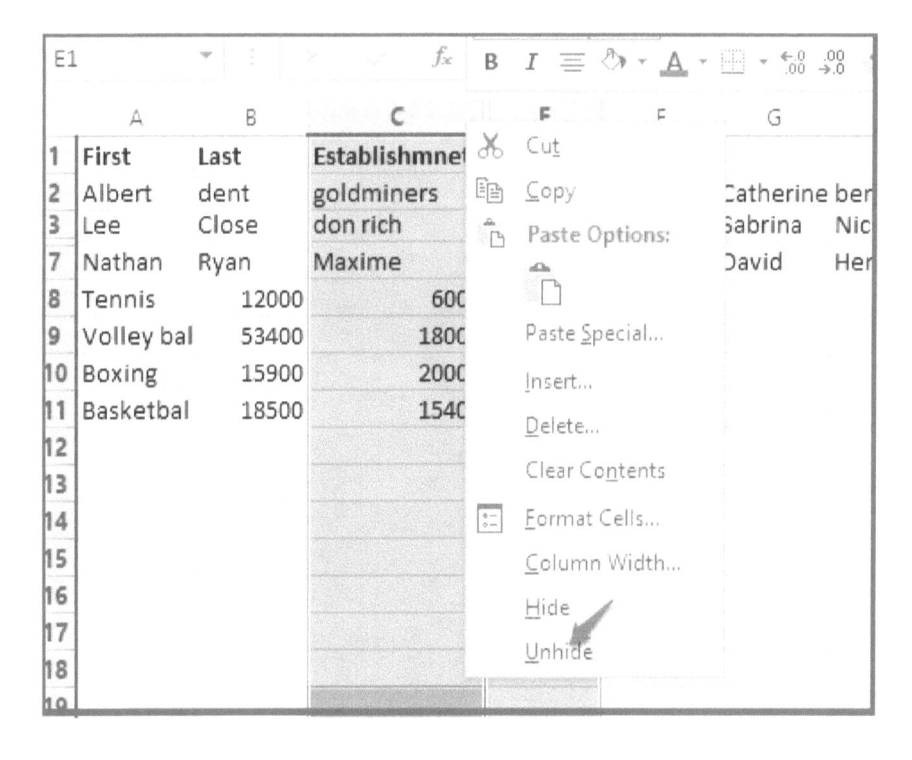

Note: probably you hide the first column, follow the same process we used in (3) above to unhide row 1 to unhide column A also;

a. Click into the **cell selection box** and input **A1.**

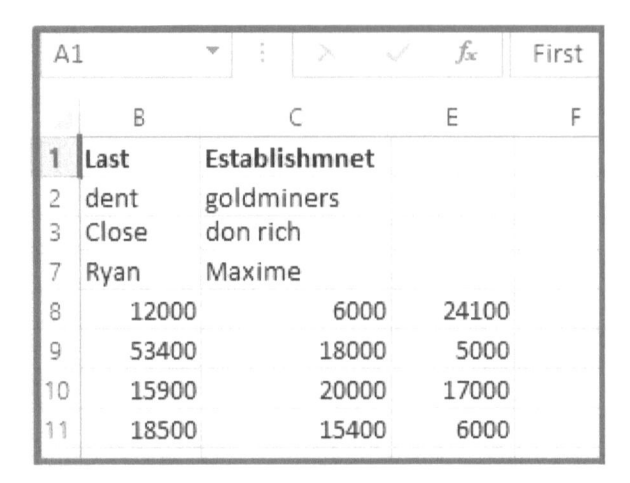

b. Navigate to the **Home tab,** and pick the **format** ribbon, and then choose **"unhide column"** from the drop-down menu.

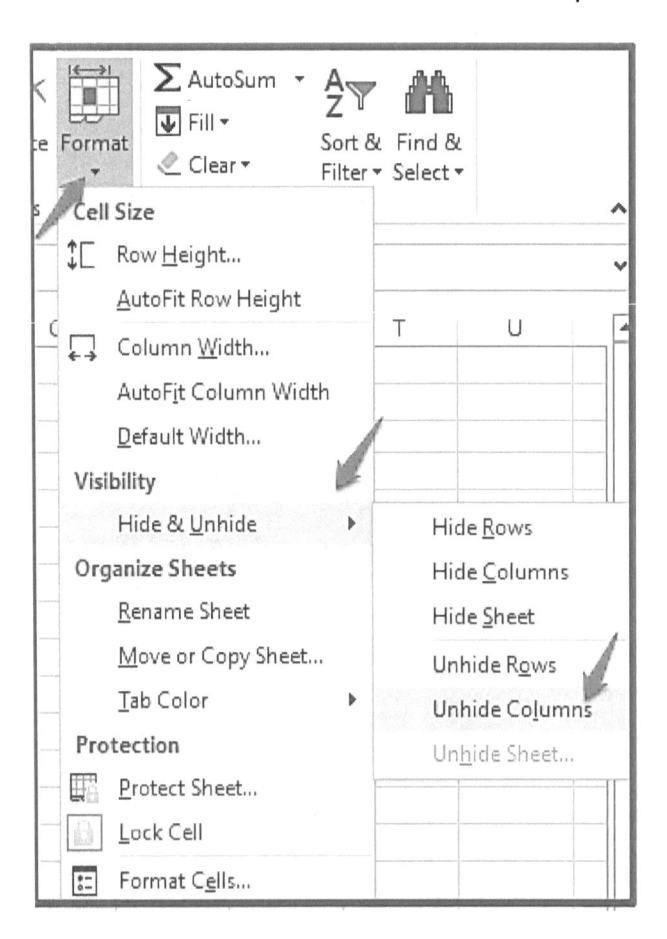

(6) **Unhide all rows and columns:** Let's assume you hid many numbers of rows and/or columns, it is not prudent to unhide them one after the other as such will take a lot of time and effort, unless you are not unhiding them all.

To unhide many rows and columns at once;

    a. Highlight all the cells in the worksheet by pressing row and column identifiers or you press **Ctrl + A,** whichever you prefer.

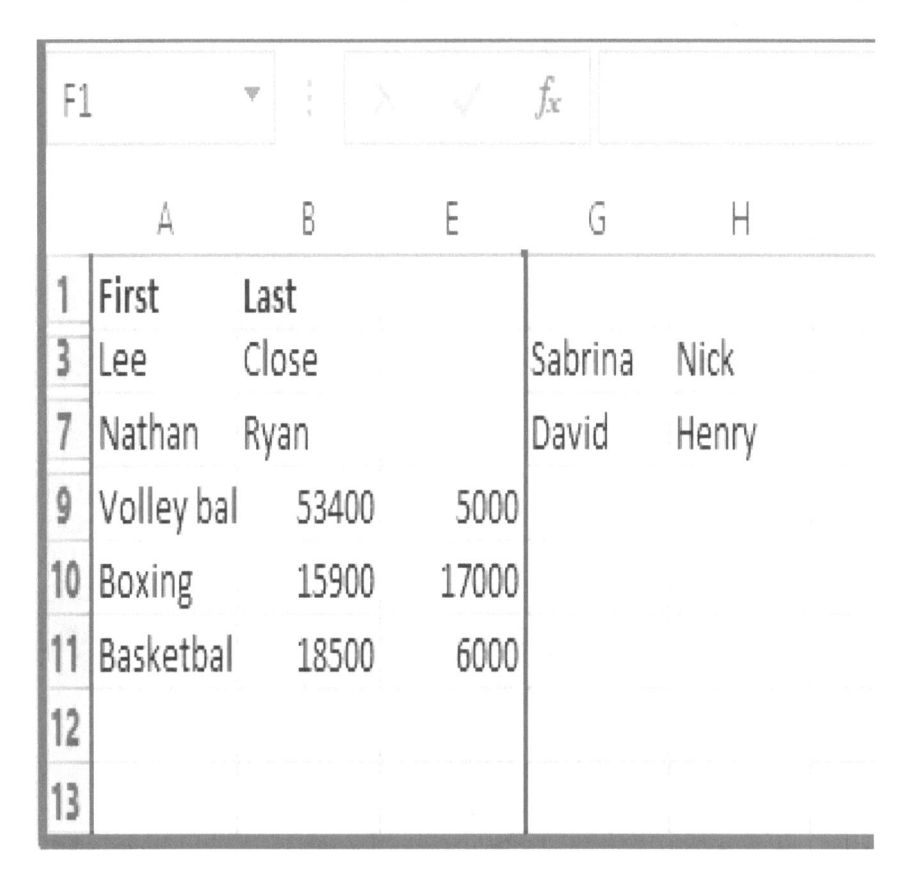

	A	B	E	G	H
1	First	Last			
3	Lee	Close		Sabrina	Nick
7	Nathan	Ryan		David	Henry
9	Volley bal	53400	5000		
10	Boxing	15900	17000		
11	Basketbal	18500	6000		
12					
13					

    b. Right-click on **row and column identifiers** and pick **unhide** from the pop-up menu or you press **Ctrl + Shift + 9** to unhide all hidden rows and columns.

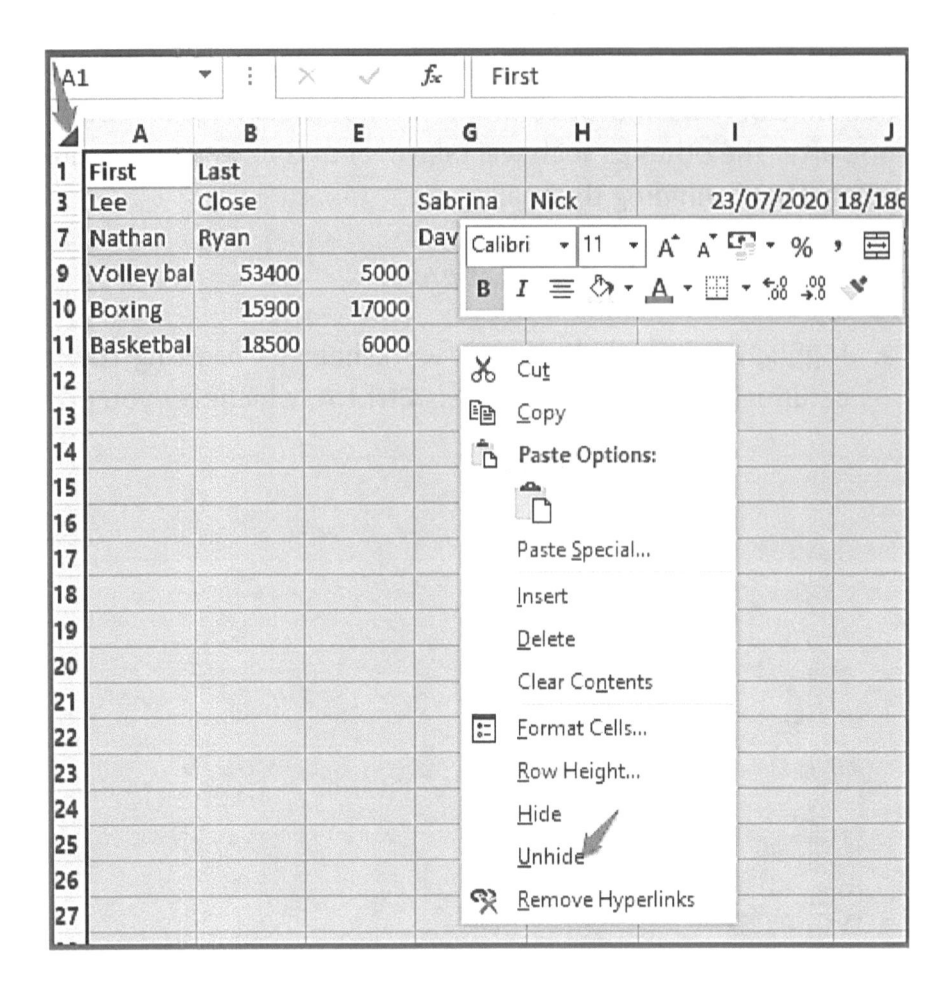

Note: perhaps you observe your worksheet is too crowded with contents, attempt to hide some rows columns to enjoy working with your worksheet.

Comments for Documenting Your Worksheet

Comments are the notes that are associated with a cell in the worksheet. They are used to give prescriptions to your worksheet. Those prescriptions give more details to the contents inside the cell, especially if it happens to be the cell with special numbers and formulas.

Comments are very easy to identify, they do have a little red triangular shape which will be displayed at the corners of each cell that has comment(s).

What do I have to know about comments? The following are the essential things you suppose to know about worksheet comments:

1. **Inserting a comment:** the first thing you can do when it comes to comment is inserting a comment. How can you do that?
    a. Tap the cell you want to attach a comment to.
    b. Move to the **Review** tab and click on the **"New comment"** option.

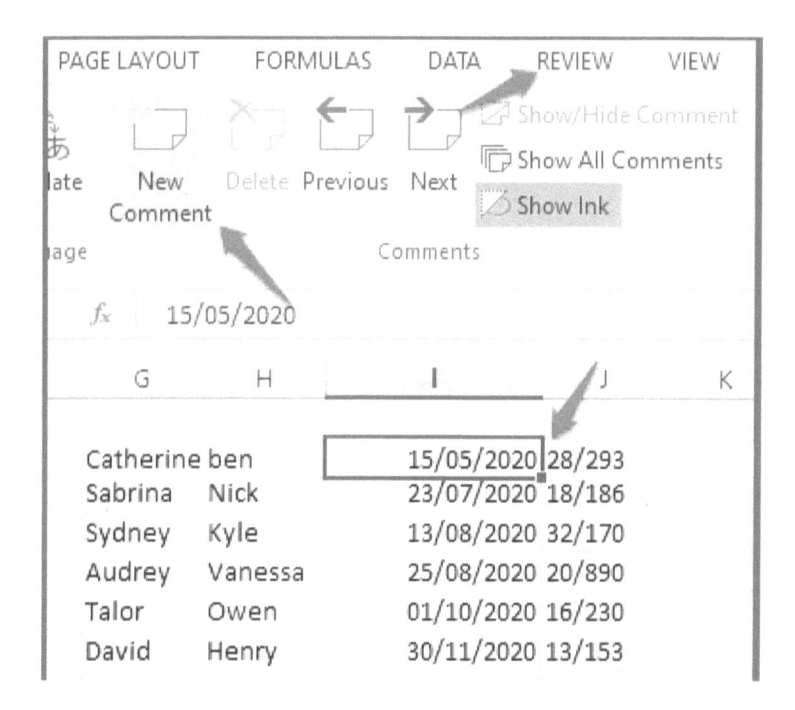

    c. Insert your comment into the rectangle pop-up box that shows up after you click on the new comment option.

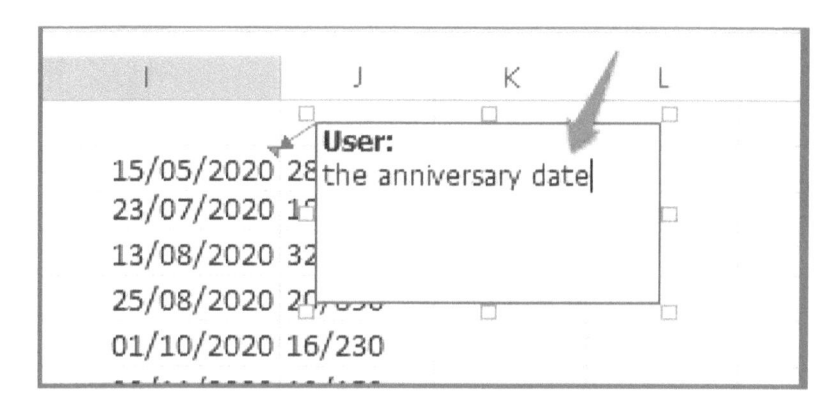

135

    d. Click on **any cell** when you are done inserting your comment.
 2. **Viewing a comment:** simply direct your mouse pointer to the little red triangle to view the comment in the pop-up box.

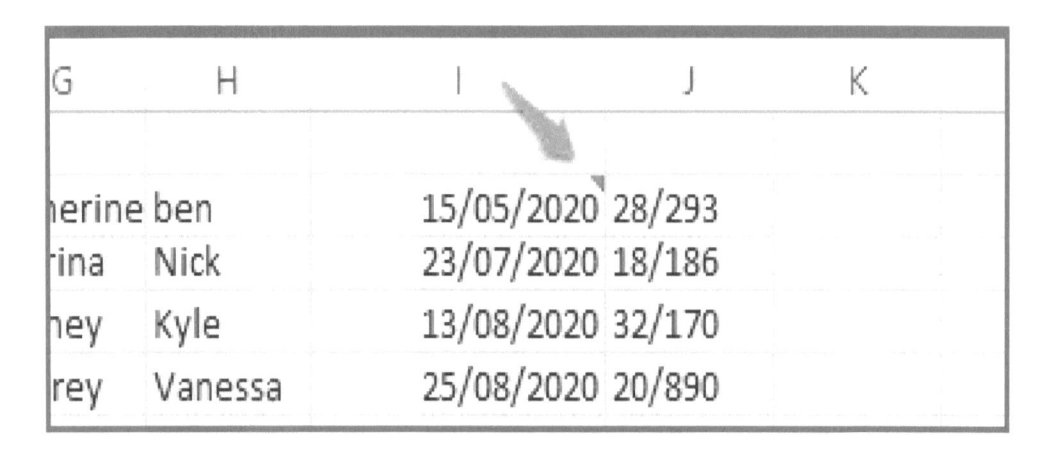

G	H	I	J	K
erine	ben	15/05/2020	28/293	
ina	Nick	23/07/2020	18/186	
ey	Kyle	13/08/2020	32/170	
rey	Vanessa	25/08/2020	20/890	

 3. **Finding comment:** go to the **Review** tab, tap on the **previous or next** button to move from one comment to another comment to find the one you are looking for.

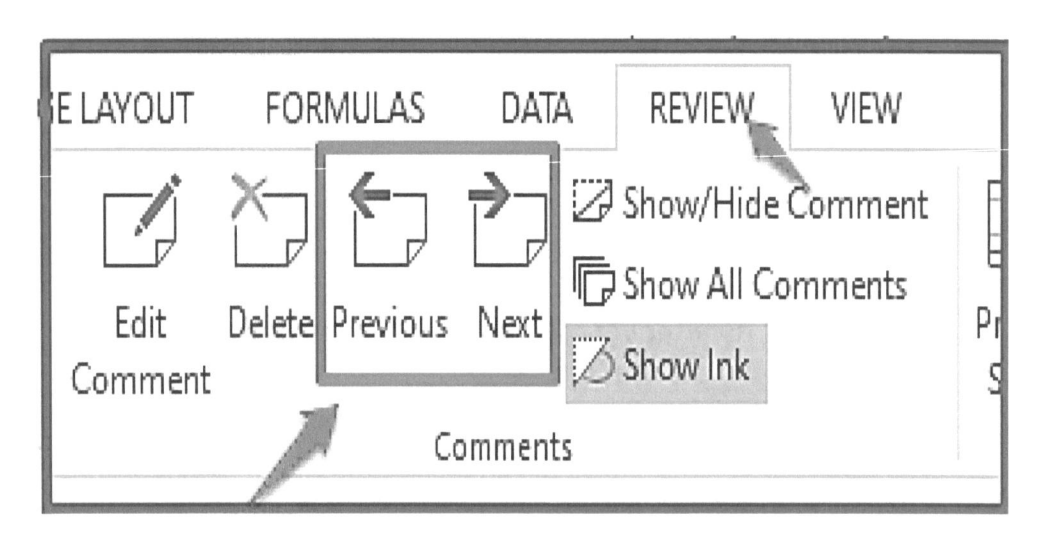

 4. **Editing a comment:**
    a. Select **the cell** with the comment.
    b. Move to the **Review** tab and tap on the **Edit comment** button to edit the comment inside the pop-up box.

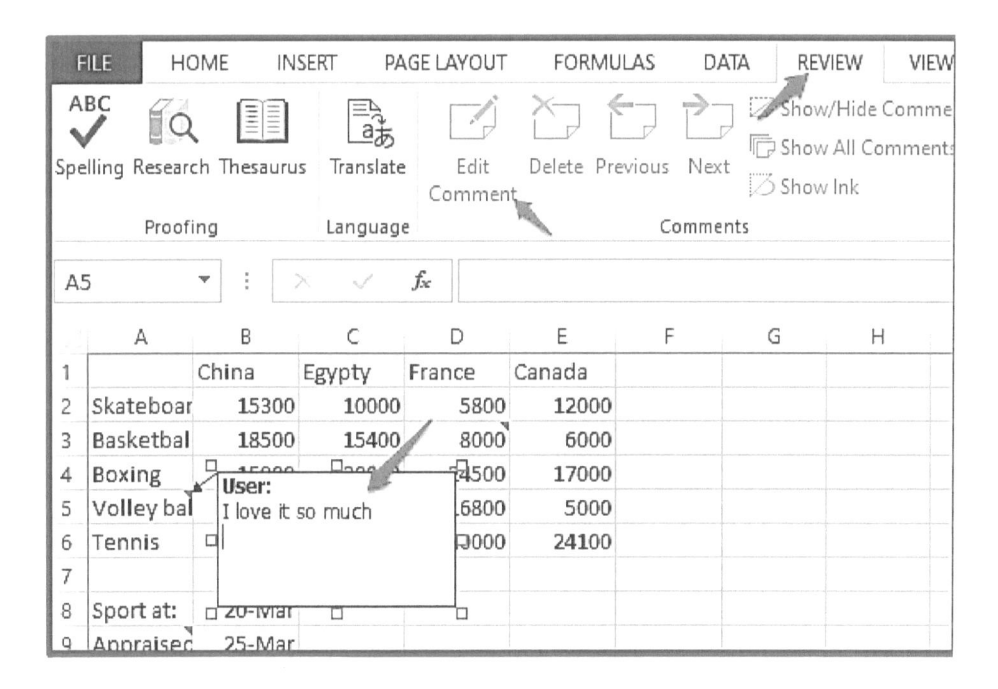

5. **Deleting all comments:** To delete comments, follow one of these methods:
    a. Highlight all the cells with comments, go to the **Review** tab and tap on the **Delete** button.

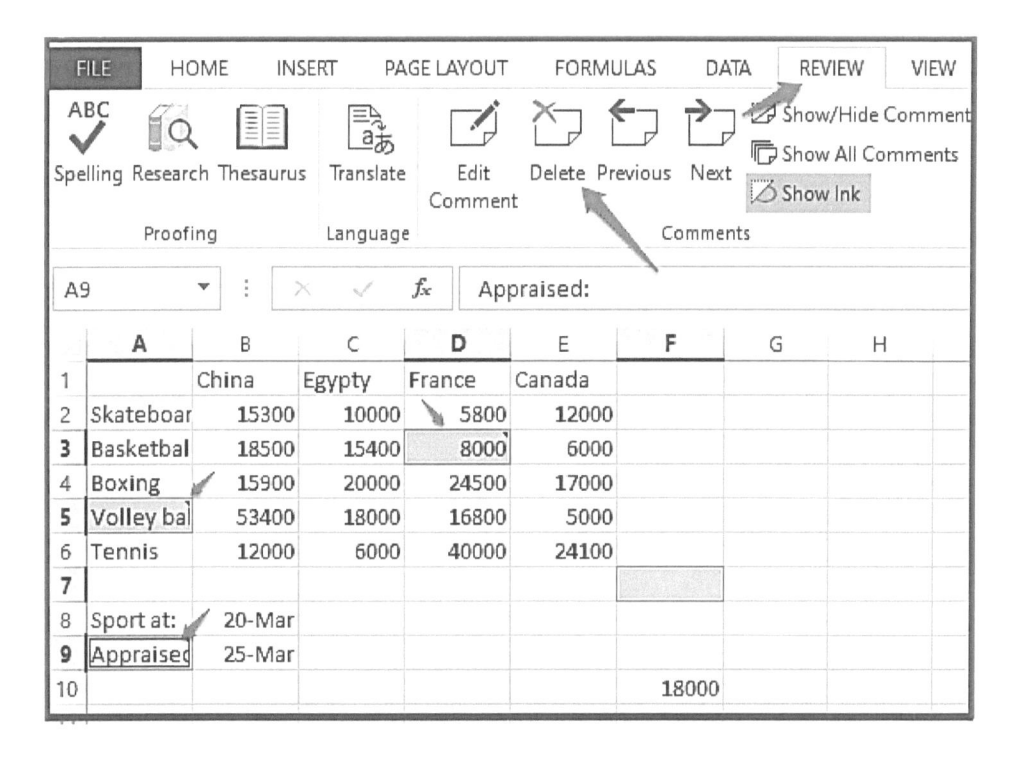

b. Alternatively, you can select all the cells with comments, go to the **"Home"** tab and then click on the **Find and Select** button.

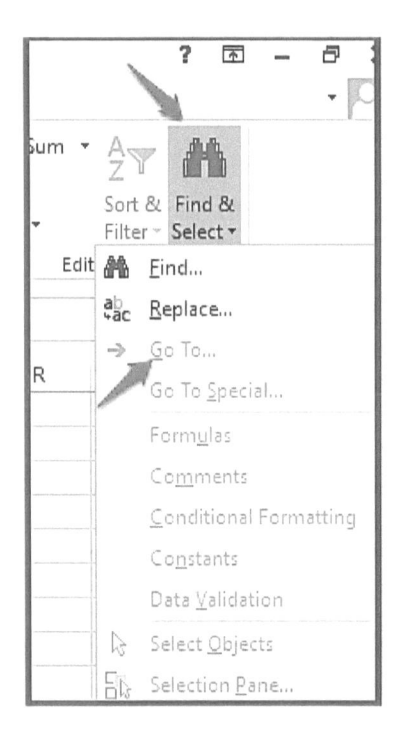

Under the **Find and Select** option, select **Go to** and tap the **Special** button.

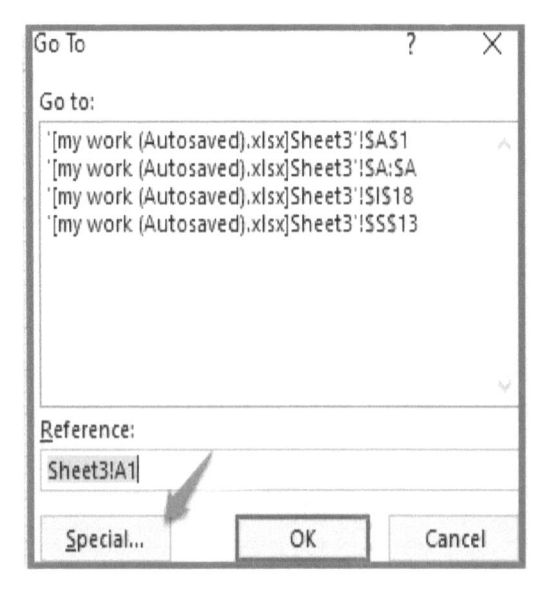

In the "Special dialog box", select **Comments** and tap **Ok**.

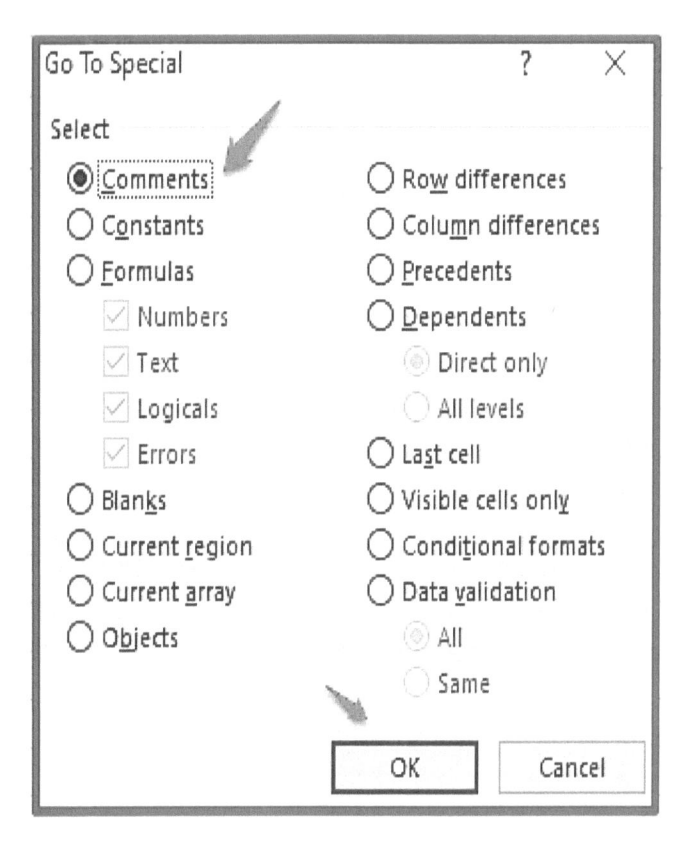

Tips: you can insert your name to the comment(s) you enter by clicking the **Office** button, select **Excel** options, and then proceed to pick a popular category from the Excel Options' dialog box where you will enter your name in the username text box.

Selecting Cells (S) In A Worksheet

You select cells most times in Excel to apply formatting effect to them or to perform a specific operation such as copy and the likes on the selected cell.

1. **How to select an individual cell:** you can select an individual cell by simply left-clicking on it. Immediately you do that, it will become an active cell, and the signal is that such cell will be surrounded by a thick box.

	A	B	C	D	E
		China	Egypty	France	Canada
	Skateboar	15300	10000	5800	12000
	Basketbal	18500	15400	8000	6000
	Boxing	15900	20000	24500	17000
	Volley bal	53400	18000	16800	5000

Alternatively, you can move arrow keys from one cell to another to select an individual cell. You can enter data in them immediately they become an active cell and you can as well edit the data you put in them by pressing F2 on the keyboard.

2. **How to select multiple individual cells:** multiple individual cells can be selected just by holding down the Ctrl key and then continue to click on the individual cells that you want to select.

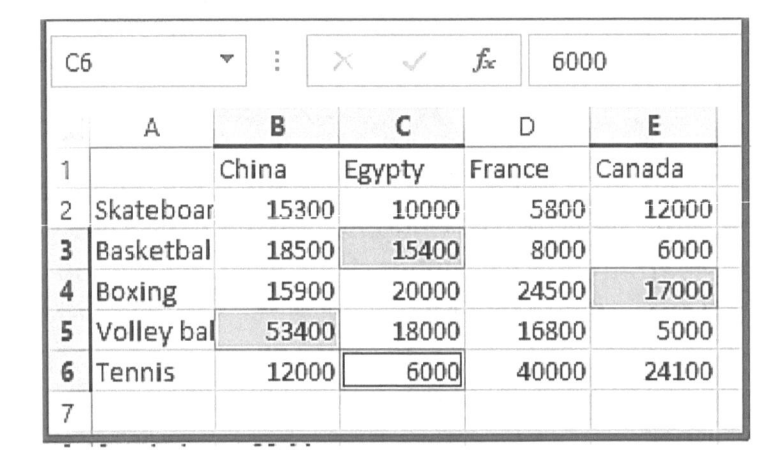

	A	B	C	D	E
1		China	Egypty	France	Canada
2	Skateboar	15300	10000	5800	12000
3	Basketbal	18500	15400	8000	6000
4	Boxing	15900	20000	24500	17000
5	Volley bal	53400	18000	16800	5000
6	Tennis	12000	6000	40000	24100
7					

Note: as you continue to select them; those selected cells will be turning to a shaded cell to specify their selection. The last active cell is also part of the selected cell but it will not indicate immediately.

3. **How to select range of cells:** to select a range of cell, you have to:
   a. Left-click via the mouse on the cell that will be the first in the range you want to select.
   b. Press and hold down the Shift key.

C2				f_x	10000			
	A	B	C	D	E	F	G	H
1		China	Egypty	France	Canada			
2	Skateboar	15300	10000	5800	12000	Garden egg	hosue fan	
3	Basketbal	18500	15400	8000	6000	table	chair	
4	Boxing	15900	20000	24500	17000	cup		
5	Volley bal	53400	18000	16800	5000			

  c. As you hold down the Shift key, move to the last cell in the range and left-click on it. For instance, you want to select cell C2 to cell G2, just left-click cell C2, then hold down the Shift key and move to cell G2 to left-click as well.

	A	B	C	D	E	F	G
1		China	Egypty	France	Canada		
2	Skateboar	15300	10000	5800	12000	Garden egg	hosue fan
3	Basketbal	18500	15400	8000	6000	table	chair
4	Boxing	15900	20000	24500	17000	cup	

Alternatively, left-click via the mouse on the first cell in the range of the cell you want to select, hold the left side of the mouse, do not release it, and then drag the mouse cursor to the last cell in the range. For instance, you want to select cell B2 through B6, left-click cell B2 and immediately without releasing the mouse, drag the mouse to cell B6.

		f_x	France	
		C	D	E
		Egypty	France	Canada
		10000	5800	12000
		15400	8000	6000
		20000	24500	17000
		18000	16800	5000
		6000	40000	24100

4. **How to select all cells:** you can select all the cells in the worksheet by:
   a. Navigating to the uppermost of the row and leftmost of the column in the worksheet.
   b. Tap on the square area that has a shaded triangle at the top of the first column and the left side of the row, instantly, all cells inside the worksheet will be highlighted.

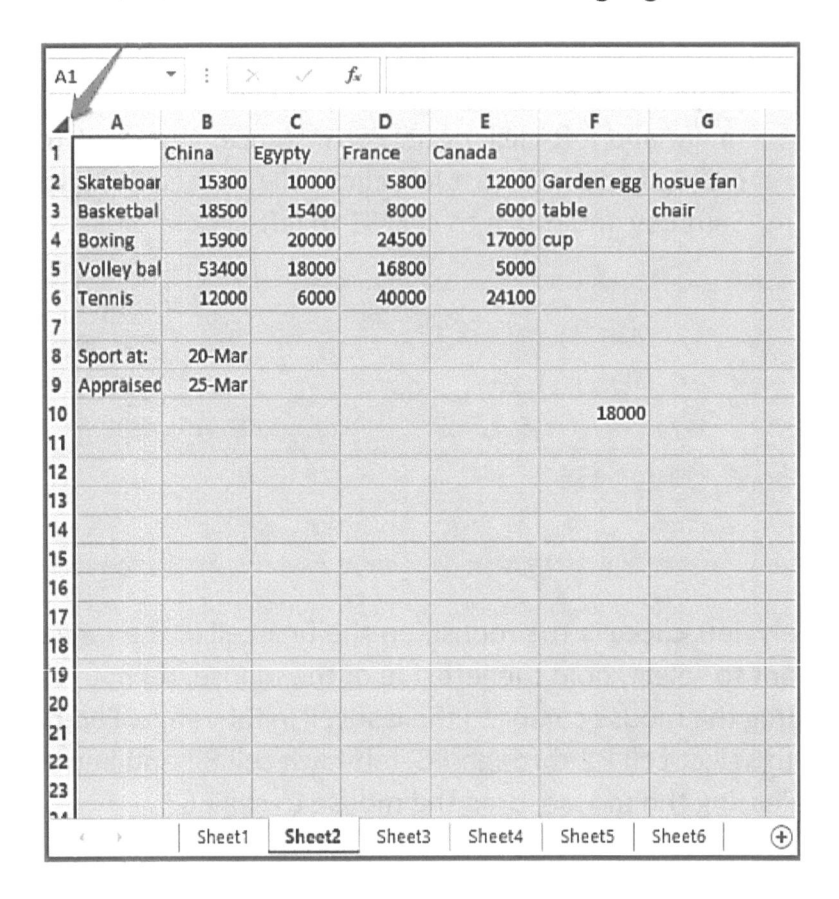

	A	B	C	D	E	F	G
1		China	Egypty	France	Canada		
2	Skateboar	15300	10000	5800	12000	Garden egg	hosue fan
3	Basketbal	18500	15400	8000	6000	table	chair
4	Boxing	15900	20000	24500	17000	cup	
5	Volley bal	53400	18000	16800	5000		
6	Tennis	12000	6000	40000	24100		
7							
8	Sport at:	20-Mar					
9	Appraised	25-Mar					
10						18000	

Alternatively, press **Ctrl + A** as a shortcut on the keyboard to select all the cells in the worksheet.

Deleting, Copying, And Moving Data

It is expedient at times to delete wrong input of data or incorrect data and in the same vein moving and copying data within and outside the worksheet can't be overemphasized.

1. **Delete your cell contents by:**
    a. Highlighting the cells to be deleted, and then press the **Delete** Key on the keyboard.
    OR
    b. Right-click the selected cells and pick the **clear contents** option or move to **the Home tab,** choose the **clear button** option, and lastly pick **clear contents.**

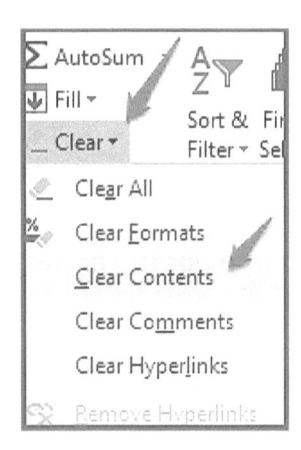

Note: Do not use the delete button on the home tab to delete cell contents because using it will delete cell contents and also the cell itself along with it.

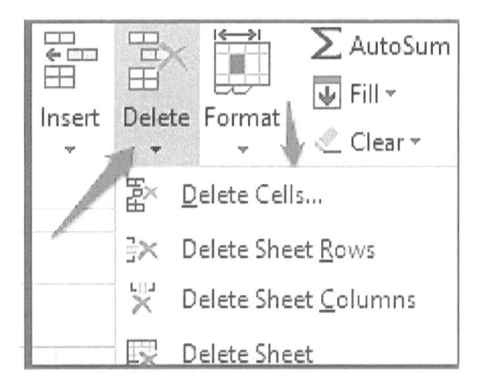

2. Moving and copying the cell contents are very similar, but has a little difference. To move and copy, kindly:
    a. Select the cell you want to move or copy its content.
    b. Right-click on the cell and pick **cut** or **copy** depending on which of it you want to do.

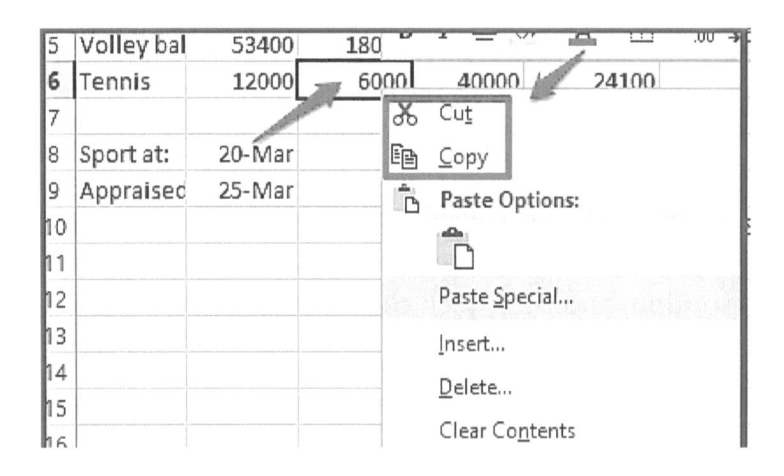

c. Go to the cell that will be the receiver of what you are moving or copying and right-click.
d. Pick **paste** from the pop-up menu, if you pick the **cut** option to cut the contents, the paste option will move the contents, and if you pick copy the content, the paste option will copy the contents.

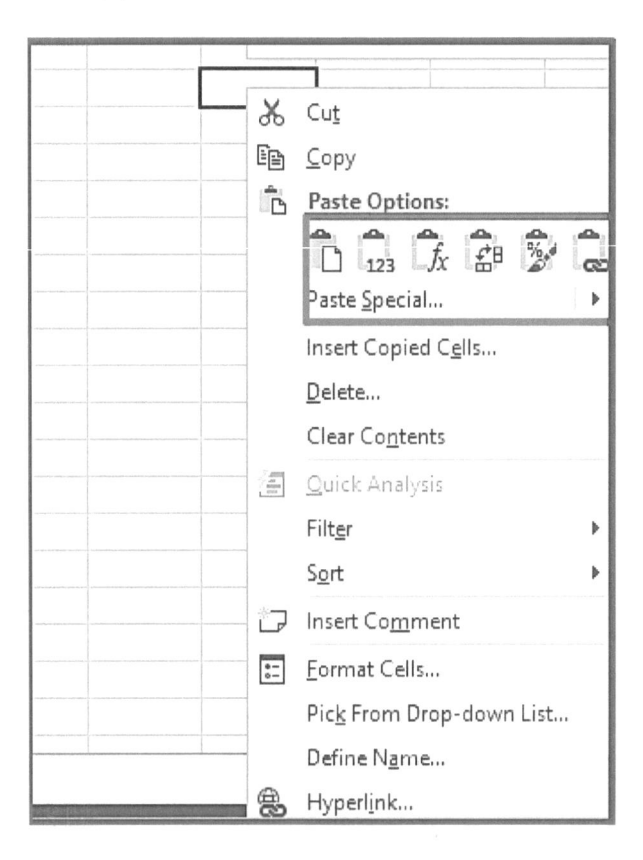

144

After you have selected the cell, and you are about to move or copy its content, then;

a. Move the pointer to the edge of the selected cell block (that is the cell that has the data inside), and wait till the pointer turns to a four-headed arrow.
b. Then double-click and start dragging to the receiver cell. You should hold the Ctrl key as you drag the four-headed arrow to the receiver cell to copy the contents, but if you want to move the contents, you should not hold the Ctrl key.

Managing the Worksheets in A Workbook

You can manage your worksheet inside the workbook by the way you handle the worksheet. Such management has to do with how to add, rename, delete and move amidst the worksheet inside the workbook.

Let us look at some ways of managing the worksheet:

1. **How to move a worksheet inside a workbook:** you can move from one sheet to another sheet in a workbook by clicking on each worksheet tab at the bottom of the screen.
   OR click on the navigation scroll button at the left side of the worksheet tabs.

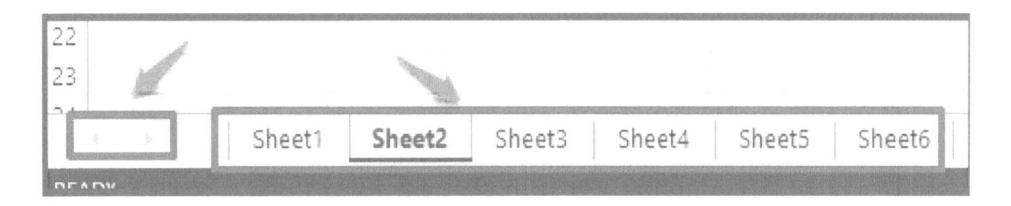

2. **How to rearrange worksheet:** worksheet can be rearranged with its tab by simply double-clicking to drag the worksheet tab to a new position. While you are dragging, you will see a little black arrow and a page icon that will appear to indicate the position of where your worksheet can be dropped to.

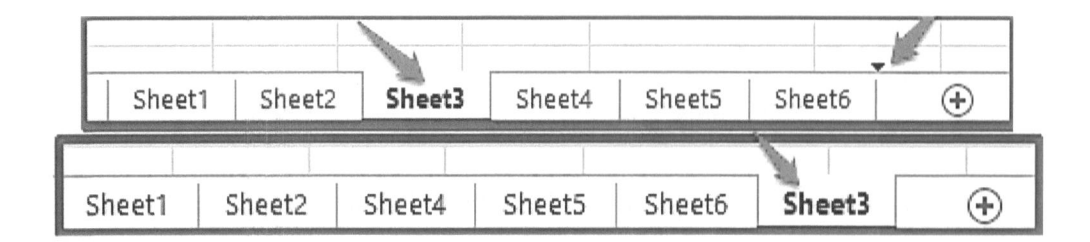

OR by:
- a. Navigating to the **Home Tab**, go to the "Cells" ribbon and select **Format**.
- b. Then choose **move** or **copy** from the drop-down menu, the dialog box will be displayed.
- c. Tap the position of the sheet where you want to drop your worksheet and tap **Ok**.

3. **How to select worksheet(s):** click on the worksheet tab to select a worksheet.
- You can as well select many worksheets at the same time by holding down the control key and continue clicking on the worksheet tabs to be selected.

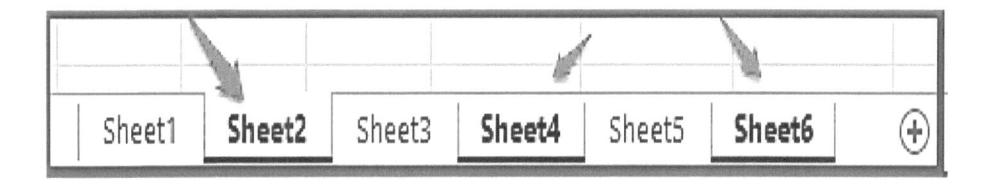

- You may also select all the worksheets by right-clicking on the worksheet tab and pick "**Select All Sheets**" from the popup menu.

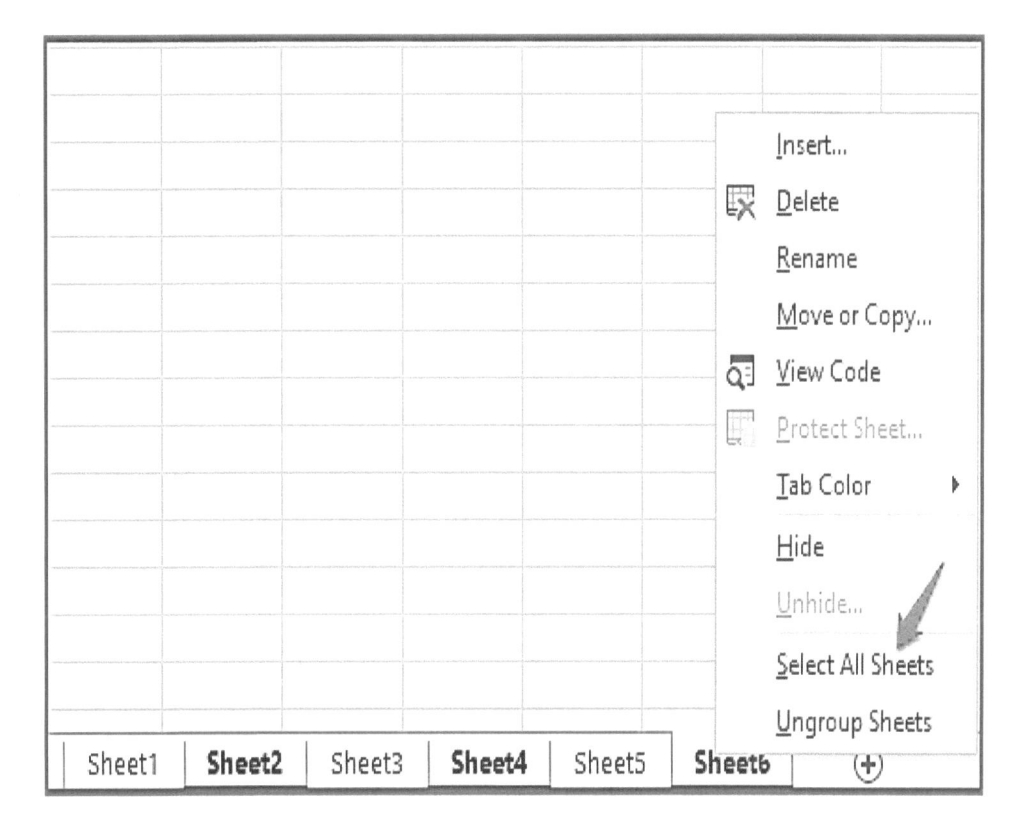

4. **How to rename a worksheet:** to rename a worksheet, you have to:
    a. Go to the **Home** tab, move to the "Cells" ribbon and select **Format**.
    b. Then select **rename** from the drop-down menu and insert a new name as desired.

Alternatively, simply right-click the **worksheet tab** and pick **rename** from the pop-up list.

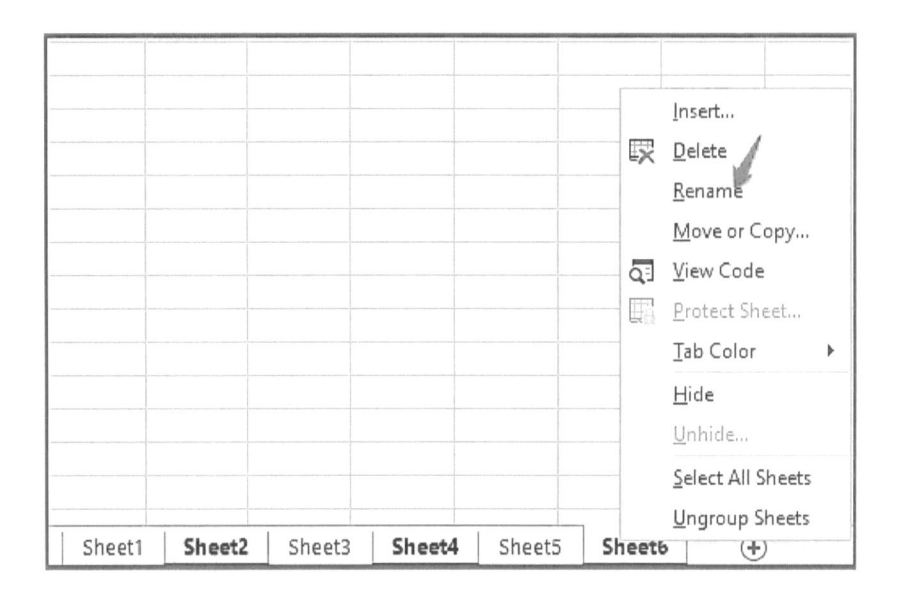

Then insert a new name and tap **Enter** to see its effect

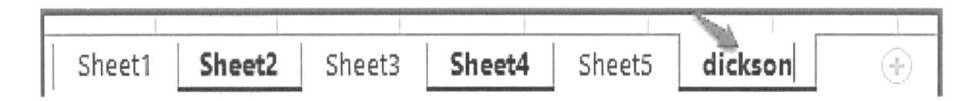

5. **How to copy a worksheet:** copying a worksheet is very easy, just hold down the Ctrl key and double-click on the worksheet you want to copy and drag it to another position.

6. **How to add a new worksheet:** click on the **new worksheet icon (+)** that is located at the right side of the worksheet tabs, and a new worksheet will come forth.

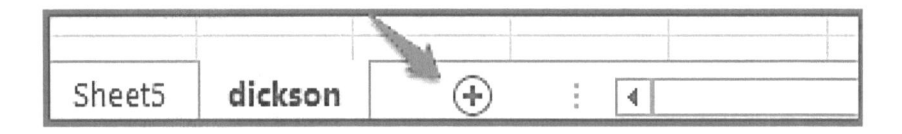

7. **How to colorize your worksheet:** add color to your worksheet by following these steps
    a. Highlight the worksheet and move to the **Home** tab, go to the "Cells" ribbon and select **Format**.

b. Select **tab color** from the drop-down menu and pick the color you want on the submenu.

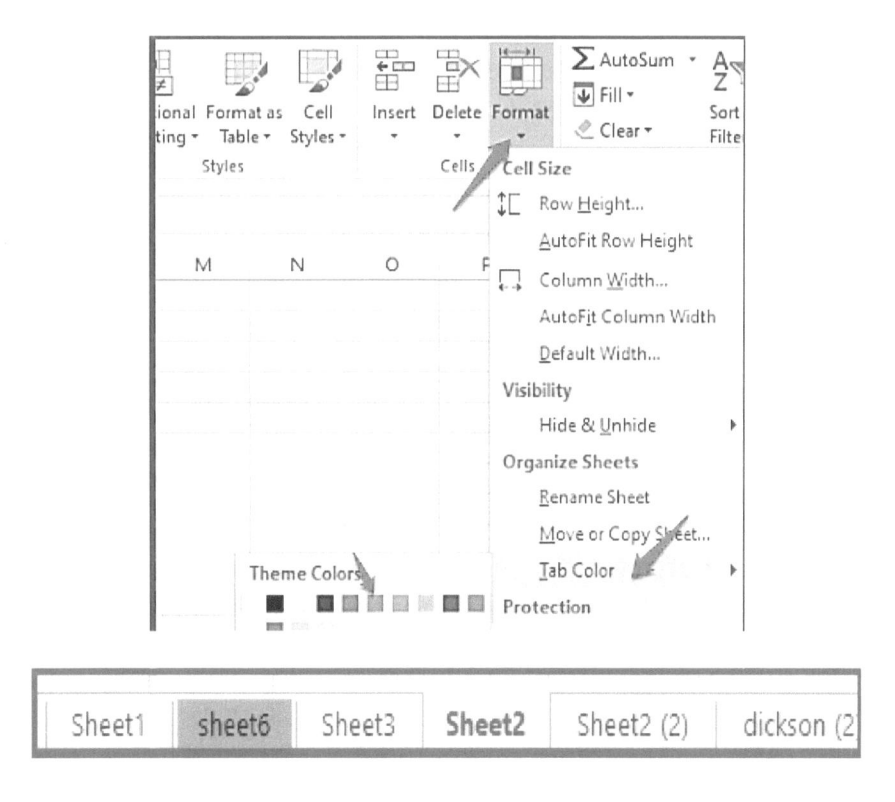

8. **How to delete a worksheet:** to get a worksheet deleted, kindly:
   a. Select the worksheet you want to delete, go to the **Home** tab, locate the **delete** option under the "**Cells**" ribbon, and then select **Delete sheet** from the drop-down list.
   You can also delete a sheet by right-clicking on the **worksheet tab** and pick **Delete** from the options.

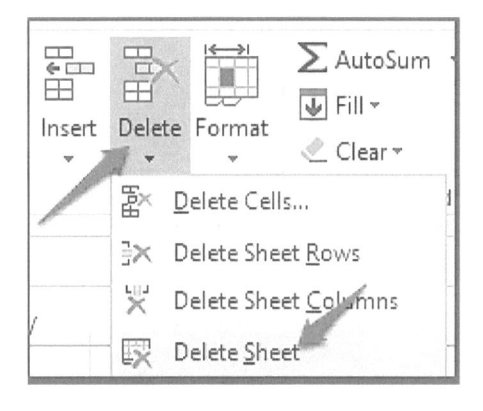

149

Restricting Others from Meddling with Your Worksheets

There are ways provided by Excel for a user to prevent others from meddling with their worksheet even if they access your PC. The two ways are worksheet hiding and protection.

Let us buttress more on these two ways. We'd start with hiding the worksheet, and then protecting the worksheet.

Hiding Your Worksheet

Observe the following steps to hide your worksheet so that others will not know it even exists except you

   a. Select the **worksheet,** move to the **Home** tab, and locate the **Format** button under the "Cells" ribbon.
   b. Select **Hide & Unhide** from the drop-down menu, and lastly, pick **Hide Sheet** from the drop-down list.

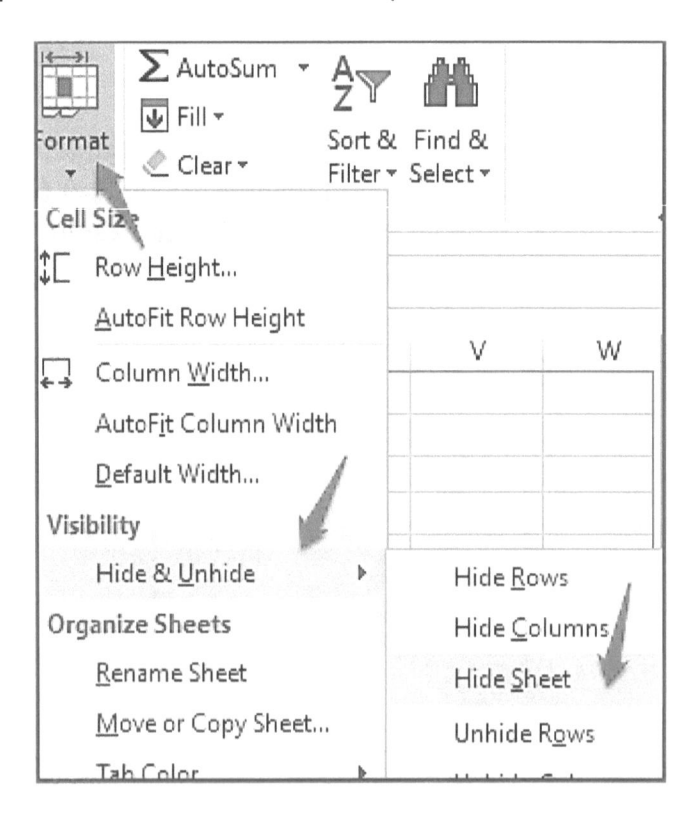

Shortcut: right-click the **worksheet tab** and pick **"Hide"** from the pop-up list.

You can as well unhide the sheet you have hidden previously by this method:

a. Move to the **Home** tab and tap on the **Format button.**
b. Then pick the **Hide & Unhide** option from the Format drop-down list and select **Unhide Sheet** from the list that pops up.

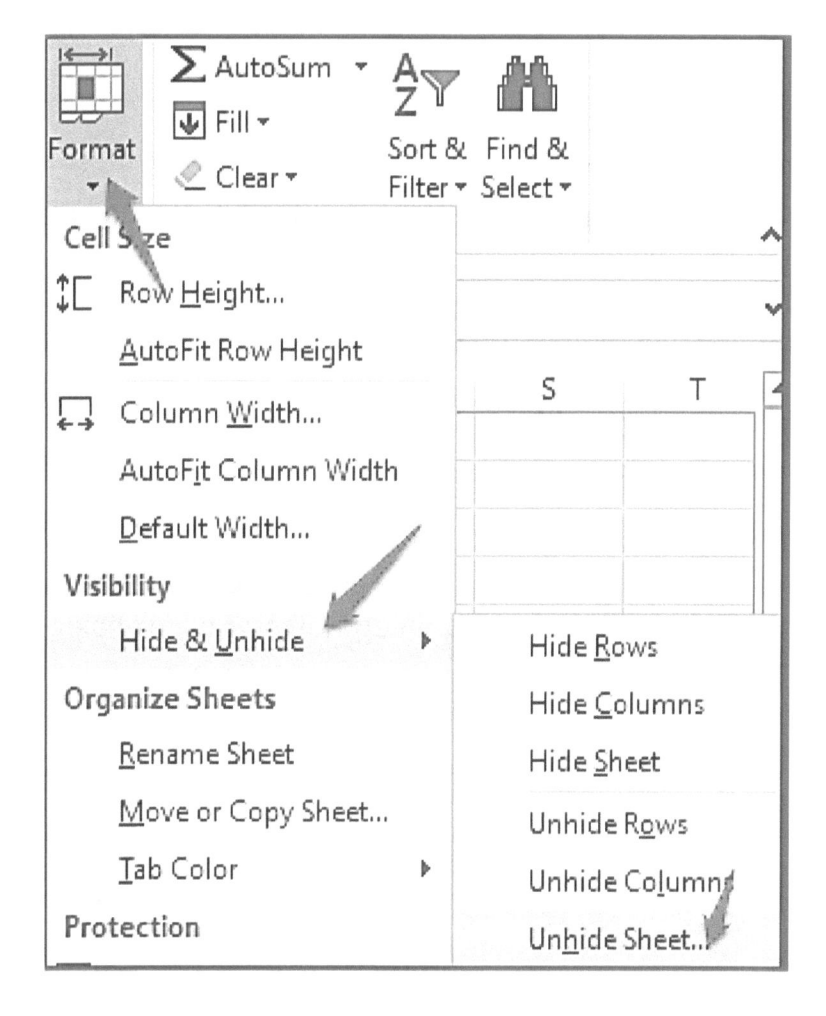

c. Immediately you click on **Unhide Sheet**, a dialog box will come up, kindly click on the **worksheet name** you want to unhide and tap **Ok.**

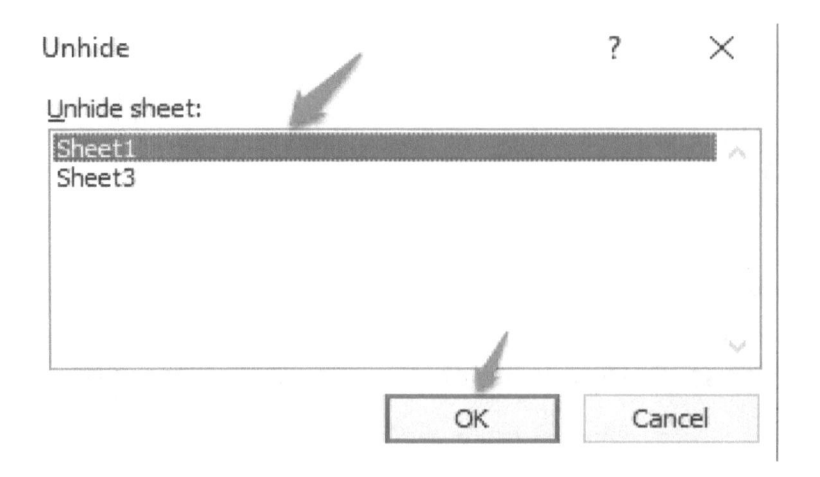

Protecting Your Worksheet

As I have said earlier, protecting one's worksheet means preventing it from any form of editing and formatting from unauthorized users. What are you preventing? They are your cell contents, rows, and columns of your worksheet, addition or removing of any row and column and so on.

Let us examine how to protect one's worksheet from an unauthorized editor:

a. Select the **worksheet** to be protected.
b. Move to the **Review** tab and tap on the **Protect sheet** button, and you will be provided with a sheet protector dialog box.

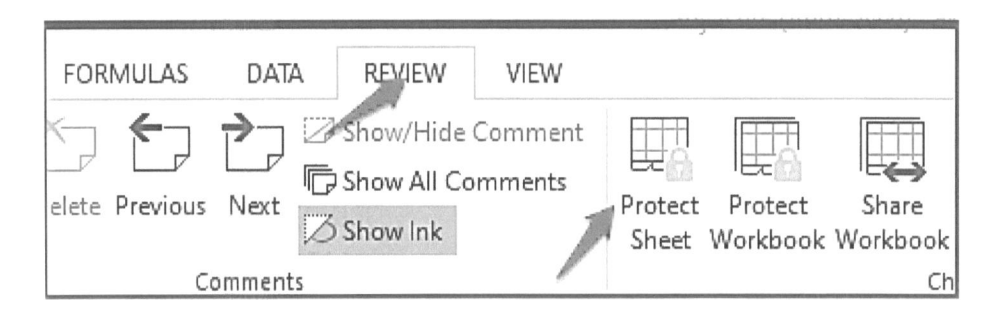

c. Input a **password** in the password space provided in the Protect Sheet box so that only those you authorize by giving them the password to unprotect it will have access to it.

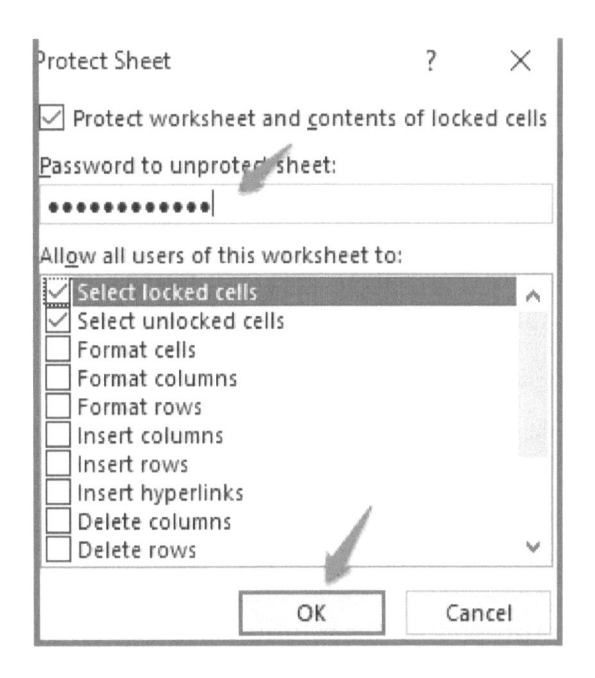

d. In the Protect Sheet box, go to **"Allow All Users of This Worksheet To:"** list, click what you want other users to do like **format cell** if you want them to format it. You only have to deselect **the "Selected locked cell"** to prevent anyone from adjusting anything on the worksheet because initially, by default, all the worksheet cells have been locked, and by deselecting the **"Selected locked Cell"**, you excellently prevent any cell from been edited.

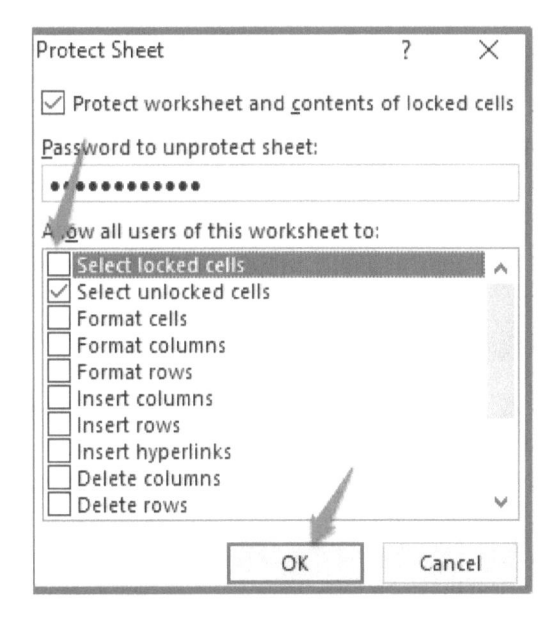

e. Tap **Ok** to effect the changes. Perhaps you entered the password in (c) above, you will have to enter it once requested for again, then you can tap **OK**.

Note: you can unprotect the sheet you have previously protected by following these simple steps:

   a. Move to the **Review** tab and click on **Unprotect Sheet**.

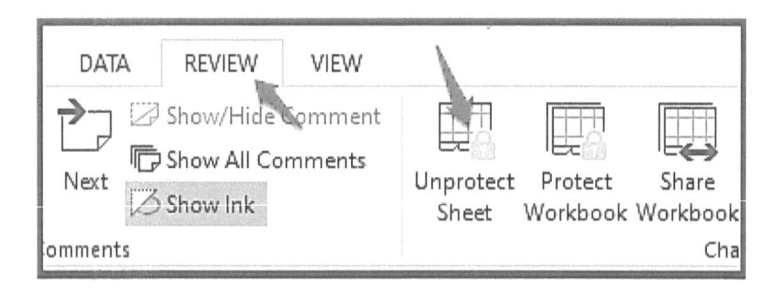

   b. Input the **password** you have previously attached to it when you were protecting it.
   c. Then tap **Ok**

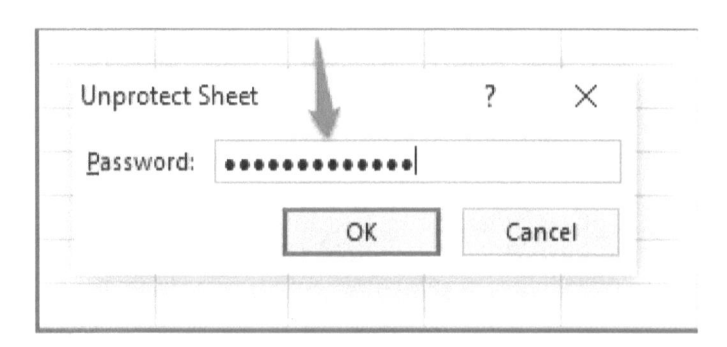

CHAPTER FOUR

COMPUTING DATA WITH FORMULAS AND FUNCTIONS

About Formulas

Excel formulas have been very helpful when it comes to numbers computation. There are certain things you will not be able to do with Excel unless you know how to structure formulas for such decisions. Excel formulas start with equal to (=), for instance, 8 + 4 = 12, that is, Excel formulas and the result. Yours is just to structure the formulas, Excel will do the computation and provide the result.

Referencing the Cells Via Formulas

Each formula you are using in Excel will be referring to some specific set of cells. Though Excel is referring to the cells, it is indirectly referring to the data or contents inside those cells to make use of them in the calculation. Let us quickly check the below illustration to get a glimpse of it:

Assuming cell C2 has 48 and cell C3 has 52, and a formula is structured in cell C4 in reference to cell C2 and C3, for example, C2 + C3, the result it will bring after you press **Enter** is 100 which is the addition of the contents that are inside cells C2 and C3. Though, Excel will not refer to the number in itself, but the cell number, therefore, if the number in cell C2 is changed to 30 and cell C3 is changed to 20, automatically, the result will be changed to 50 as well.

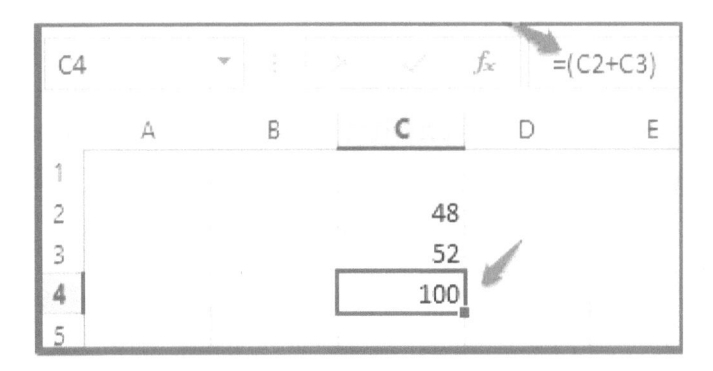

We need to study the illustration below to have the full understanding of how Excel goes in referring to cells and how it eventually makes use of the contents when it comes to formulas:

The example is about a small enterprise that forwarded its records to the worksheet with the agenda of checking the flow of income:

i. **Column B** is about the sales made and it shows all incomes from various sources.

ii. **Column C** is about the purchases made and it shows all expenses made to various sources.

iii. **Column D** is the actual profit, and it is derived by removing all the expenses from all the sales made.

	A	B	C	D	E
1					
2	Items	Sales	Purchases	Profit	
3	Toshiba	$4,500.00	$2,500.00	$2,000.00	
4	Lenovo	$3,800.00	$3,000.00	$800.00	
5	Hp	$6,000.00	$4,000.00	$2,000.00	
6	Dell	$3,000.00	$1,450.00	$1,550.00	
7	Total	$17,300.00	$10,950.00	$6,350.00	

D7 =SUM(D3:D6)

The image below gives details of how the data in the worksheet is computed:

i. Column D shows the amount of profit from various sources calculated by subtracting the Column C (purchases amount) from Column A (sales amount).

Ii The **Total** derived in Row 7 is the SUM function of the amount in column 3 to column 6.

	A	B	C	D	E
1					
2	Items	Sales	Purchases	Profit	
3	Toshiba	$4,500.00	$2,500.00	$2,000.00	
4	Lenovo	$3,800.00	$3,000.00	$800.00	
5	Hp	$6,000.00	$4,000.00	$2,000.00	
6	Dell	$3,000.00	$1,450.00	$1,550.00	
7	Total	=SUM(B3:B6)	=SUM(C3:C6)	=SUM(D3:D6)	

Cell B7: =SUM(B3:B6)=SUM(C3:

Referencing Formula Results in Subsequent Excel Formulas

Excel carries out its computation by referring to the previous formula results in the cells. Let us quickly examine the worksheet below which shows records of individual account types:

a. **Column E** displays the total aggregate savings of individuals.
b. **Column F** shows how much individual saved on average by using formula result of Total in Column E divided by 3 which stands for the total number of accounts opened by each individual.

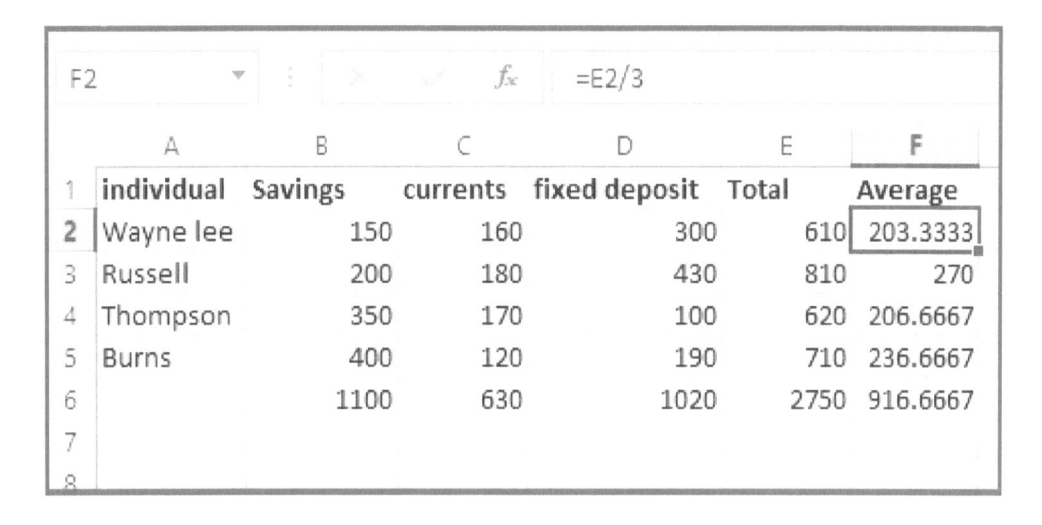

Cell F2: =E2/3

	A	B	C	D	E	F
1	individual	Savings	currents	fixed deposit	Total	Average
2	Wayne lee	150	160	300	610	203.3333
3	Russell	200	180	430	810	270
4	Thompson	350	170	100	620	206.6667
5	Burns	400	120	190	710	236.6667
6		1100	630	1020	2750	916.6667

The average point in column F is derived from the formula of total calculation results divided by the average account type which is 3.

	A	B	C	D	E	F
1	individual	Savings	currents	fixed deposit	Total	Average
2	Wayne lee	150	160	300	B2+C2+D2	=E2/3
3	Russell	200	180	430	B3+C3+D3	=E3/3
4	Thompson	350	170	100	B4+C4+D4	=E4/3
5	Burns	400	120	190	B5+C5+D5	=E5/3
6		=SUM(B2:B5)	=SUM(C2:C5)	=SUM(D2:D5)	=SUM(E2:E5)	=E6/3

Operators and Precedence of Excel Formulas

Excel users have to understand the use of operators in Excel as it indicates the kind of calculation you are about to carry out on the data as you begin to exploit the formula. There are four (4) types of Excel Operators. Let us buttress on each of them to get you acquainted with them.

1. **Arithmetic type:** This is the kind of operator that carries out basic math functions such as multiplication, subtraction, division, and many more.

Arithmetic Operators

Symbols	Meanings	Illustrations
*(asterisk sign)	Multiplication	=6*2 or = A1 * 3
+ (plus sign)	Addition	=4+6 or = B2 + 4
- (minus sign)	Negative Subtraction	=-5 = 10-4 or = E3-2
/ (right slash)	Division	=10/2 or = D7/5

158

% (percentage)	Percent of	=20%
^ (caret)	Exponentiation	=10^2

2. **Text concatenation type:** this is an operator that joins one or more values together to produce a single piece of text.

Concatenation Operator

Symbol	Meaning	Illustration
& (connector)	Connecting two value together	= Total no & B3

3. **Reference type:** this is the operator that gathers a range of cells and refers them for calculation.

Reference Operator

Symbols	Meaning	Illustration
: (colon)	It is called range operator. It is used to show the range of two or more cells by referencing those cells for computation	=SUM(D5:D8)
' (comma)	It merges multiple cell range and computes their value together to give one value	=SUM(C5:C6, G3:G7)
#	It is used to signify inadequate space, and once the cell is stretched, it will show the actual data inside	###### =SUM(D2##)
@	It indicates the indirect intersection of data items or cells in a formula	=@G1:G8 =SUM (Wednesday selling: Saturday selling)

| () space | It is used in combining the intersection of two blocks of cells, those two blocks of the cell will overlap, if not there will be an error message. | (A1:D4 B2:C3) |

4. **Comparison type:** this is the type of operator that compares one value with another and establishes reasonable outcomes, either True or False.

Comparison operator

Symbols	Meanings	Illustrations
= (Equal sign)	Equal to	= C1 = F1
< (less than sign)	Less than	= D4 < B2
>(greater than sign)	Greater than	= B2 > D4
<= (less than or equal sign)	Less than or equal to	= E8 <= A7
>= (greater than or equal sign)	Greater than or equal to	= A7 >= E8
<>	Not equal to, it only gives returns of either True or False	= D3 <> 8

The Order of Operator Precedence in Excel Formulas

There are specific orders to which Excel performs its operation, which is why you have to order your data correctly to get an accurate result for your computation. Note that Excel starts its operation from left to right.

Symbols	Details
:	Colon is used in separating all the cells you are referencing into two and gives them one reference for formulas.
'	The comma is used to collect numerous cell references into one reference.
-	Negation like -4.
%	Percentage.
^	Exponentiation or raise to the power of.
*& /	Multiplication and division.
+ & -	Addition and subtraction.
&	Two values connectors or text joint
= < > <= >= <>	Comparison.

Changing Excel Order with Parenthesis

Excel grants you the right to adjust the order by which it calculates by enclosing part of the values or formula you want to calculate into the parentheses. Let us take this scenario for example:

= 8+2*3, you should know Excel will multiply 2 by 3 before adding it with 8 in accordance to its operator order. However, if you want the addition to be done first, you can dictate to Excel your order by structuring the formula like this =(8+2)*3, this structure will cause Excel to attend to the values inside the parentheses before multiplying the result by 3.

Let us consider the example of the table in the next page, Excel will have to add D3+1000 first, after then it will divide the result with the sum of B2 through to B4, but without the parentheses, Excel will take 1000 and divide it by the sum of B2 to B4. That is the power of parentheses.

=(D3+1000)/(B2:B4).

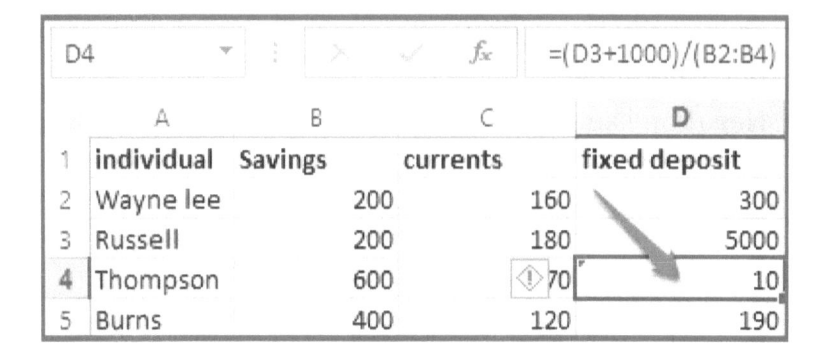

D4				f_x	=(D3+1000)/(B2:B4)
	A	B		C	D
1	individual	Savings		currents	fixed deposit
2	Wayne lee	200		160	300
3	Russell	200		180	5000
4	Thompson	600		70	10
5	Burns	400		120	190

Foreknowledge of Entering A Formula

Getting yourself familiar with the basic understanding that involves entering a formula will help you to discover other Excel formulas and make the best exploits through it. The following are the steps you should acquaint yourself with before jumping to the pool of formula entering:

1. Select an empty cell where you will put the formula so that the value inside the cell before will not be erased.
2. Double-click the cell to write inside it.

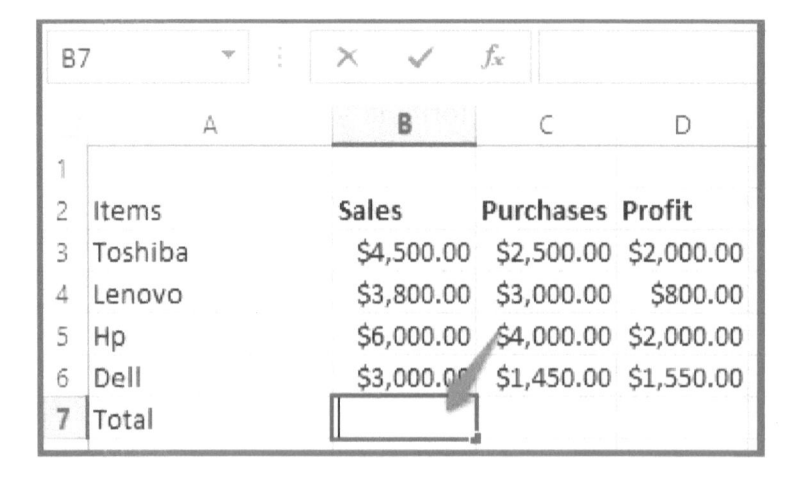

B7			× ✓ f_x		
	A		B	C	D
1					
2	Items		Sales	Purchases	Profit
3	Toshiba		$4,500.00	$2,500.00	$2,000.00
4	Lenovo		$3,800.00	$3,000.00	$800.00
5	Hp		$6,000.00	$4,000.00	$2,000.00
6	Dell		$3,000.00	$1,450.00	$1,550.00
7	Total				

3. You may decide either to write directly into the cell or you move to the formula box above and write the formula there, whichever option you take you will later arrive at the same result.
4. Before you start typing, you have to start with the **equal sign (=)** always, to tell Excel you want to perform a specific function, otherwise, everything you type into the cell will be recognized as values and not a formula.

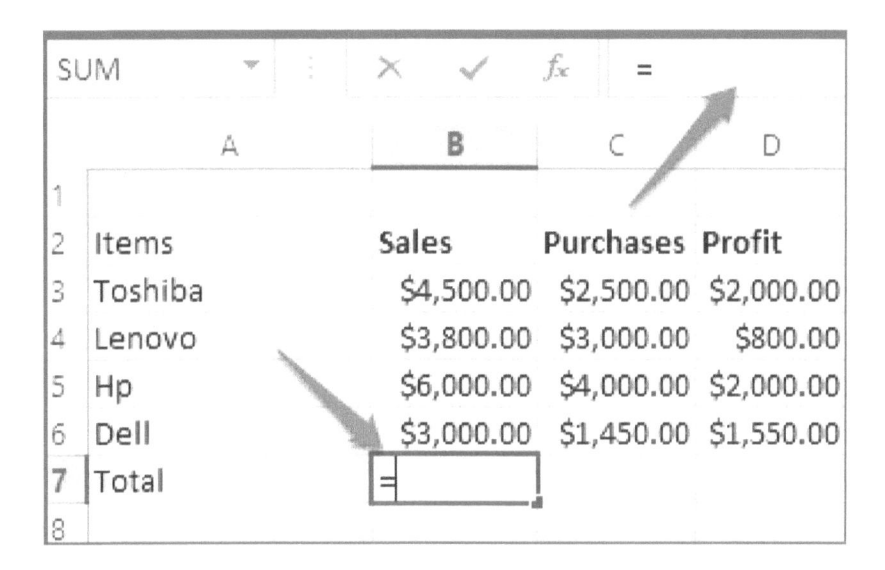

	A	B	C	D
1				
2	Items	Sales	Purchases	Profit
3	Toshiba	$4,500.00	$2,500.00	$2,000.00
4	Lenovo	$3,800.00	$3,000.00	$800.00
5	Hp	$6,000.00	$4,000.00	$2,000.00
6	Dell	$3,000.00	$1,450.00	$1,550.00
7	Total			

5. The accepted format of entering a formula is as **=(B3*5)**. It simply means Excel should find the product of the value inside cell B3 and 5.

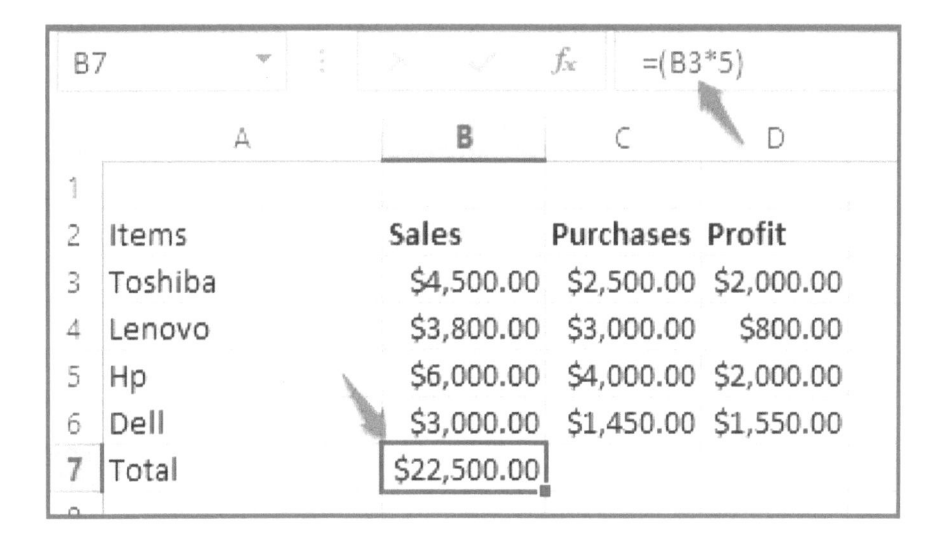

	A	B	C	D
1				
2	Items	Sales	Purchases	Profit
3	Toshiba	$4,500.00	$2,500.00	$2,000.00
4	Lenovo	$3,800.00	$3,000.00	$800.00
5	Hp	$6,000.00	$4,000.00	$2,000.00
6	Dell	$3,000.00	$1,450.00	$1,550.00
7	Total	$22,500.00		

Note: perhaps you want to use the same formula for every other cell in the same row, simply drag down the plus icon (auto command) and the formula will be assigned to other items in the cells based on the formula concerning their column.

	A	B	C	D
1				
2	Items	Sales	Purchases	Profit
3	Toshiba	$4,500.00	$2,500.00	$2,000.00
4	Lenovo	$3,800.00	$3,000.00	$800.00
5	Hp	$6,000.00	$4,000.00	$2,000.00
6	Dell	$3,000.00	$1,450.00	$1,550.00
7	Total	$22,500.00	$12,500.00	$10,000.00
8				

D7 =(D3*5)

The Fast-Track Method to Observe in Entering A Formula

Excel is capable of calculating mass formulas at once if you get it right with its pattern and method. If you can observe the following patterns of entering a formula, you will never have any problem in getting a speedy result from the Excel formulas you enter:

1. **Make all your system processors available for Excel computation**: Setting all your processors for the task will increase the speed with which Excel works because it will have sufficient processor to handle all the data. You can set up your processor by:
    a. Moving to the **File menu** to click on it and then tap on "**options**" from the drop-down list.

b. Click on **Advanced** from the Options drop-down menu and scroll down to where you can locate "**formulas**".
c. Then pick the "**Use all processors on this computer**" option, such will make your Excel calculation work faster than using the partial processor.

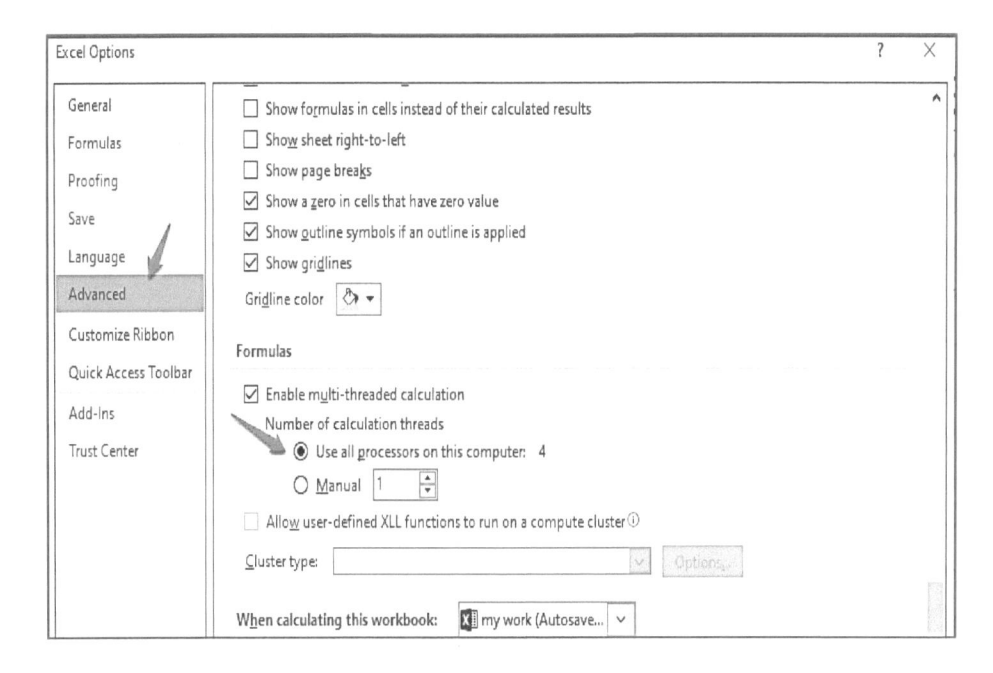

2. **Do not put the final parentheses to a function:** you should not waste time in putting a close parenthesis to your formula; Excel will do that for you automatically. For instance, = SUM (D3+D4) or =SUM (D3+D4)*5, just press **Enter,** Excel will add the parentheses and give out the result.

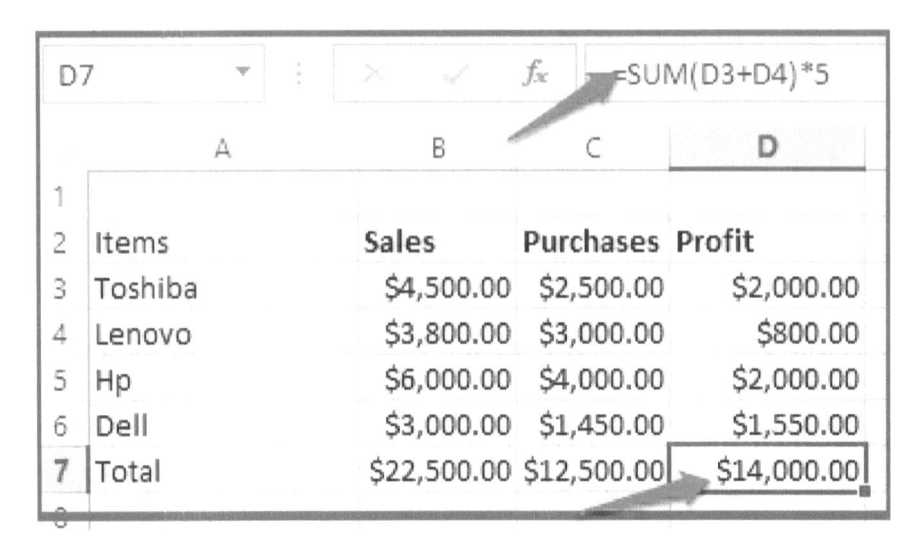

Though this tip will not work if you have more than one set of parentheses (it may be more than one parenthesis, but must not be than one set of parentheses) inside a formula, nevertheless, it will still guess the structure of what you want to type, you only need to press **Yes** if that's what you wanted to type.

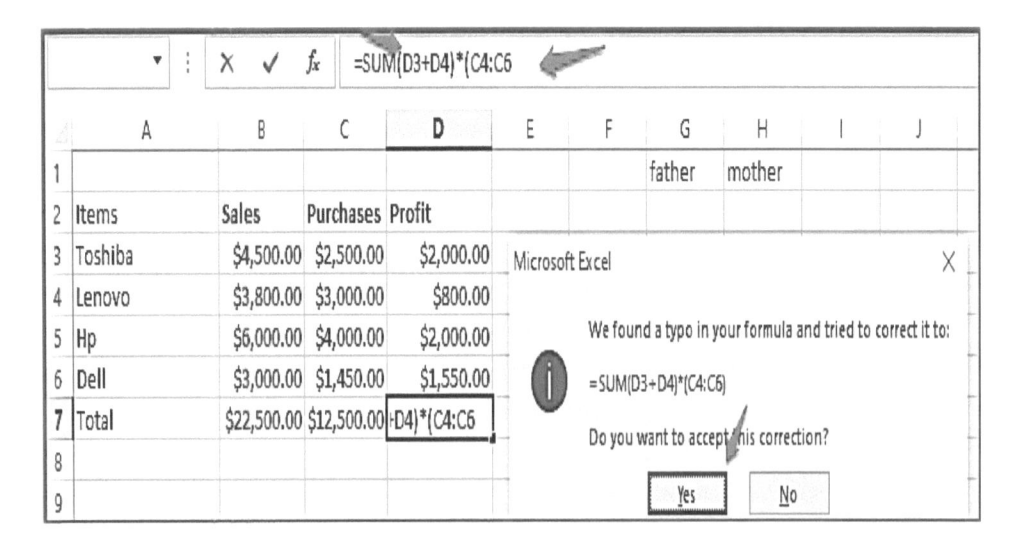

3. **Double click on the Fill handle to copy down the formulas:** when you add formulas together perhaps on the same column or inside the table, you may copy the formula used in the first row to the last row of the same column or table. Simply tap on the **Fill handle** located at the lower right corner of all your selections in Excel, immediately it turns to a plus sign **(+)**. Provided the formula in the row sits next to the other row in the same column with a complete set of data in other cells, just double-click the **Fill handle** and drag it over to copy the formula down to the bottom of the last column or table.

D3				fx	=SUM(B3+C3)
	A		B	C	D
1					
2	Items		Sales	Purchases	Profit
3	Toshiba		$4,500.00	$2,500.00	$7,000.00
4	Lenovo		$3,800.00	$3,000.00	$6,800.00
5	Hp		$6,000.00	$4,000.00	$10,000.00
6	Dell		$3,000.00	$1,450.00	$4,450.00
7	Total		$22,500.00	$12,500.00	$35,000.00

4. **Move the "formula prediction box" out of your way:** at times during insertion of formula, the formula hint may be blocking your view or blocking other data that you may want to include into the formula. When you perceive such, just recall you can move the hint box to any other place inside the worksheet by moving the cursor to the edge of the box till there is a four-headed arrow.

=AVERAGEIF(

D	E	F	G	H	I
fixed deposit	Total	Average			
160	300	660	=AVERAGEIF(		
180	5000	5380	AVERAGEIF(range, criteria,[average_range])		
170	10	780			
120	190	710			

Then click and drag to any other position in the worksheet and continue to input your formula. Note that the hint box will still be predicting formulas for you wherever it is in the worksheet.

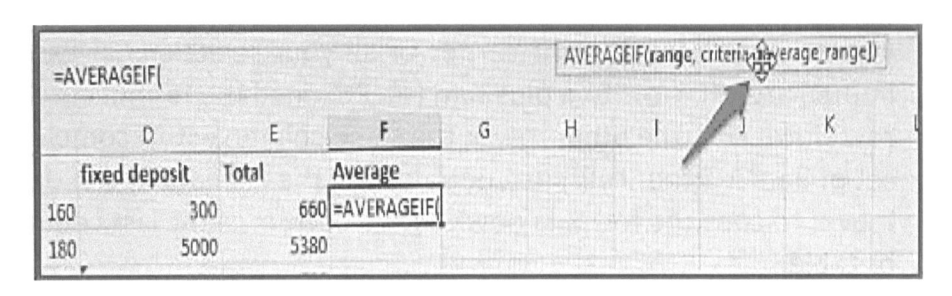

D	E	F	G	H	I	J	K
fixed deposit	Total	Average					
160	300	660 =AVERAGEIF(					
180	5000	5380					

=AVERAGEIF(
AVERAGEIF(range, criteria, average_range])

5. **Enter a formula automatically by creating a table:** when you create an Excel table, you can enter a formula faster than if you are using normal worksheet cells. Immediately you convert your data to a table, any formula you insert into the first row will be copied down to the extreme bottom of the table automatically. Excel table makes work faster and averts errors as well. To create an Excel table, simply follow this procedure:
   a. Select all the cells that involved.
   b. Then press **Ctrl + T** to draw the table over the selected cells.

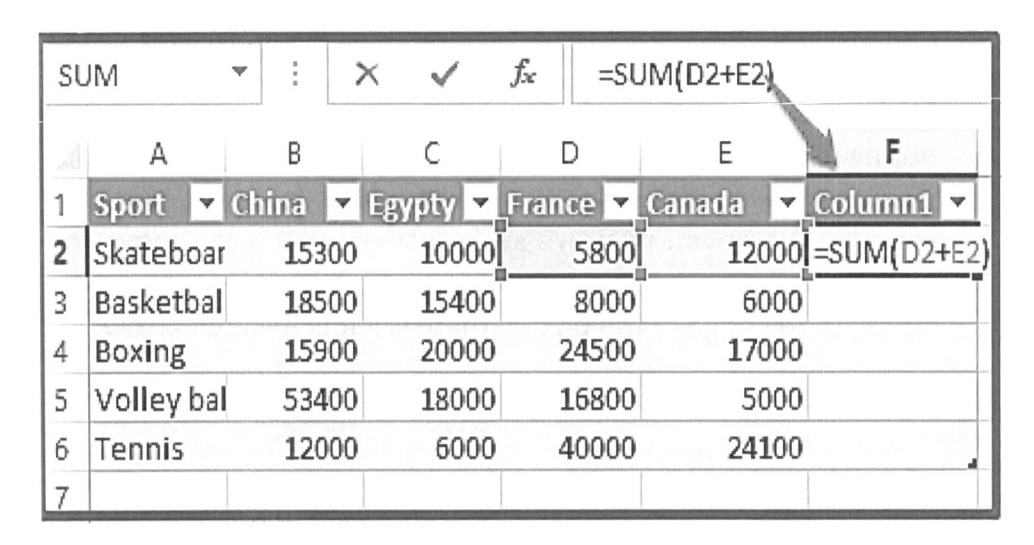

	A	B	C	D	E	F
1	Sport	China	Egypt	France	Canada	Column1
2	Skateboar	15300	10000	5800	12000	=SUM(D2+E2)
3	Basketbal	18500	15400	8000	6000	
4	Boxing	15900	20000	24500	17000	
5	Volley bal	53400	18000	16800	5000	
6	Tennis	12000	6000	40000	24100	
7						

SUM   =SUM(D2+E2)

- Excel will update every cell formula of that same column like that of the first column automatically without applying any command.

	F3				f_x	=SUM(D3+E3)	
	A	B	C	D	E	F	
1	Sport	China	Egypt	France	Canada	Column1	
2	Skateboar	15300	10000	5800	12000	17800	
3	Basketbal	18500	15400	8000	6000	14000	
4	Boxing	15900	20000	24500	17000	41500	
5	Volley bal	53400	18000	16800	5000	21800	
6	Tennis	12000	6000	40000	24100	64100	

6. **Take advantage of Auto commands, arrow key, and the tab key to enter a function:** As you are about to enter a formula,
    a. Insert **an equal (=) sign** and start typing, Excel will begin to pair the text you are entering against the huge list of the functions which is accessible in Excel. The list will correspond with the first letter you type.
    b. Scroll down with the arrow key and check the function you want. Immediately you sight the function you want, just make the arrow key remain on it and then press the **tab key,** immediately, such function will be selected.

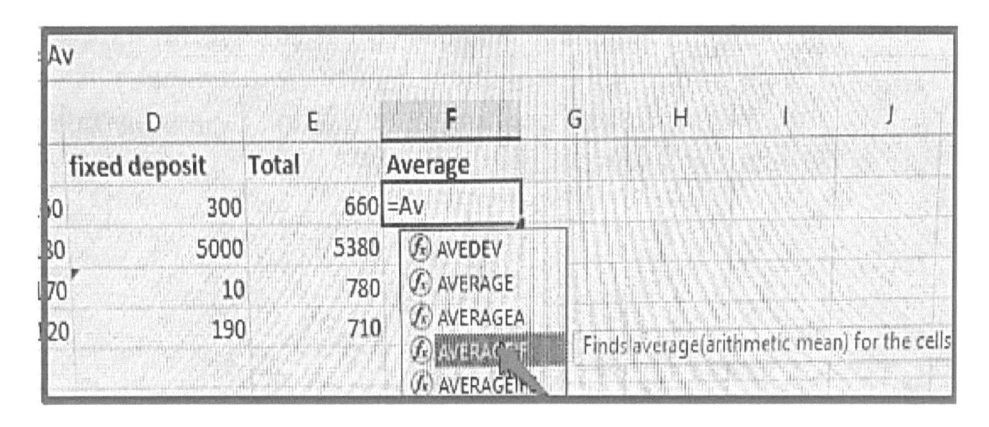

	D	E	F	G	H	I	J
Av							
	fixed deposit	Total	Average				
0	300		660	=Av			
30	5000		5380	AVEDEV			
70	10		780	AVERAGE			
20	190		710	AVERAGEA			
				AVERAGEIF	Finds average(arithmetic mean) for the cells
				AVERAGEIF	

7. **Move a formula and retain its references:** know that you can copy a formula to another position and such formula address will be adjusted to the new position, but at times, the situation may demand that you will have to retain the formula's address for an essential reason. To do that, kindly drag and drop the value to

another position, its address will remain untouched and unchanged.

	C	D	E	F	G	H	I
	ort3	Sport4	Sport5	Sport6			14000
	10000	5800	12000	17800			
	15400	8000	6000				
	20000	24500	17000	41500			
	18000	16800	5000	21800			
	6000	40000	24100	64100			

Formula bar: =SUM(D3+E3)

8. **Making use of named range makes formulas convenient and clear:** With named range, formula is easy to use, for instance using pounds or dollars always make cells' addresses more complicated. Making use of name range saves a lot of time and thereby makes formulas work faster. Creating a named range is as simple as ABC. Kindly:
    a. Select the cells you wish to name
    b. Move to the **Name box** beside the formula bar and type the name you want to use, and then press **Enter**, automatically, the cell range will name them. Hence, you can make use of it in the formula by pointing on the name range as you are structuring a formula.

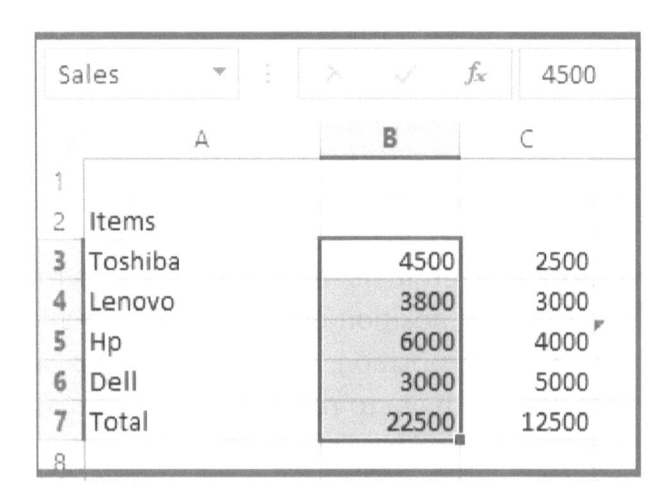

	A	B	C
1			
2	Items		
3	Toshiba	4500	2500
4	Lenovo	3800	3000
5	Hp	6000	4000
6	Dell	3000	5000
7	Total	22500	12500
8			

Name box: Sales | Formula bar: 4500

170

Note: you may also move to the **Name box** and click on the drop-down arrow to pick the name from the name box and apply it to the cell you selected.

Reference Cells in The Worksheet by Clicking on The Cells

You can click on the cells inside the worksheet to enter their references instead of typing them into the box. Let us examine the steps that are involved:

1. Click **the cell** that will be the receiver of the cells you want to reference.
2. Input an **equal (=) sign** to the cell above in (1).
3. Click **the cell** or drag it over to the groups of cells you want to make reference to, then, the names or references of those cells will enter into the receiver cell instantly after the equal sign.

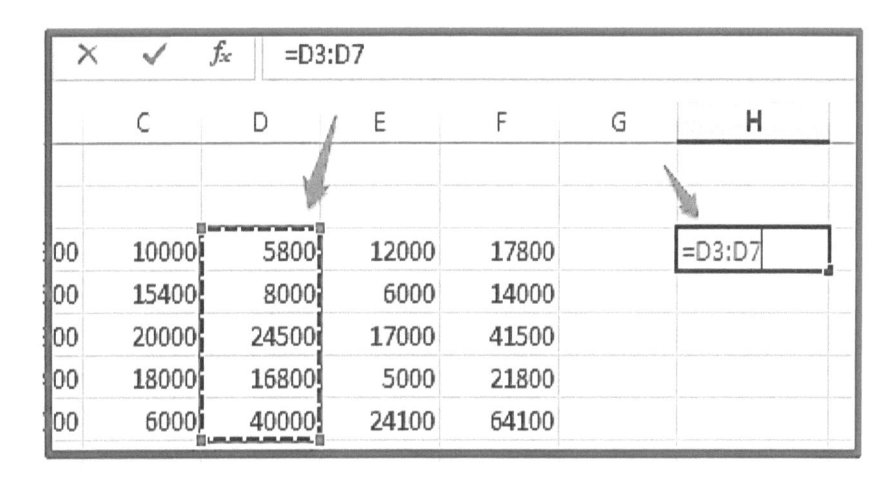

C	D	E	F	G	H
00	10000	5800	12000	17800	=D3:D7
00	15400	8000	6000	14000	
00	20000	24500	17000	41500	
00	18000	16800	5000	21800	
00	6000	40000	24100	64100	

4. Press **ENTER** to create cell references.

Inserting A Cell Range

A cell is referred to by the intersection of the column letter and its corresponding row number e.g., B2. Cell range or range of cell is called a group of adjacent cells because they are arranged next to each other, and they are separated with the use of column.

There two ways of inserting a cell range, these are:

1. Typing a cell range into the formula box.

	A	B	C
1			
2	Items		
3	Toshiba	4500	2500
4	Lenovo	3800	3000
5	Hp	6000	4000
6	Dell	3000	5000
7	Total	22500	12500

2. Dragging the cursor across the cells to be included within the range of cells.

Note: There are also two cell ranges, they are:

a. An adjacent range of cell (e.g. A3:A6), and
b. Non-adjacent cell range (e.g. C2:D6).

Creating Cell Range Name for Formulas' Use

Cell range name is the easiest way of entering data for formulas. Entering cell addresses one after the other is a very strenuous task (such as C3 + C4 + C5 + C6 + C7) and also, it may not be accurate as D4:D6. It is the cell range name that is very dependable and convenient for formulas' use. To create a cell range name, check the below guides for guidance:

1. Select the range of cells you want to name.
2. Click the **formula bar** and pick the **Define Name** button to command for the New Name dialog box.

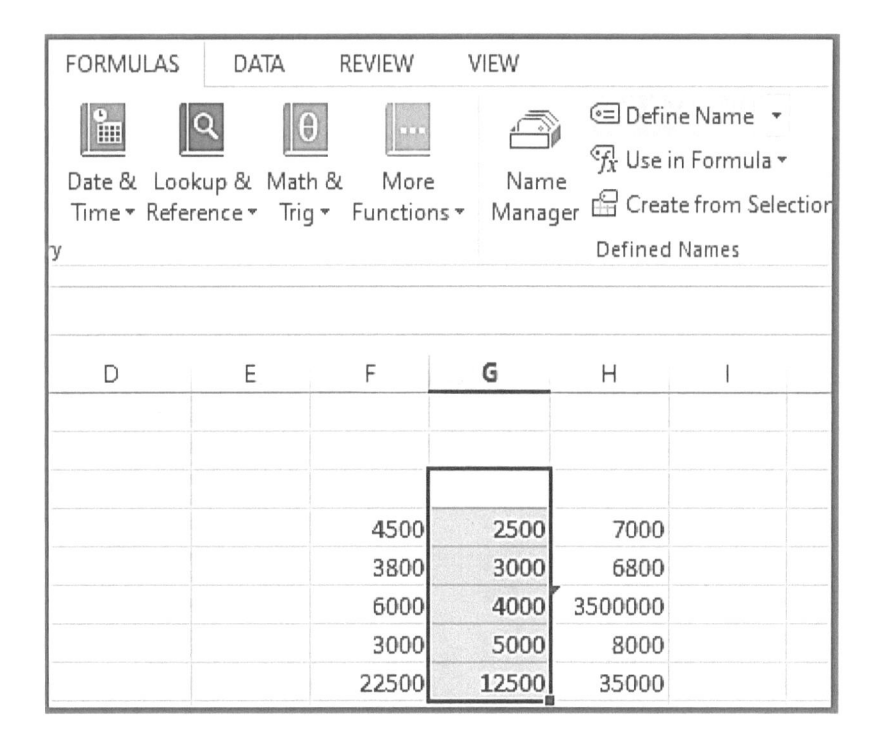

	D	E	F	G	H	I
			4500	2500	7000	
			3800	3000	6800	
			6000	4000	3500000	
			3000	5000	8000	
			22500	12500	35000	

3. Insert a brief and concise name in the provided box.
4. Move to the **Scope** drop-down list, select the **worksheet name** if the use of the range name will not go beyond the worksheet to which it is created from, but, select W**orkboo**k if you have the intention of using the name range you have just created in another worksheet.
5. Then click **OK** for confirmation.

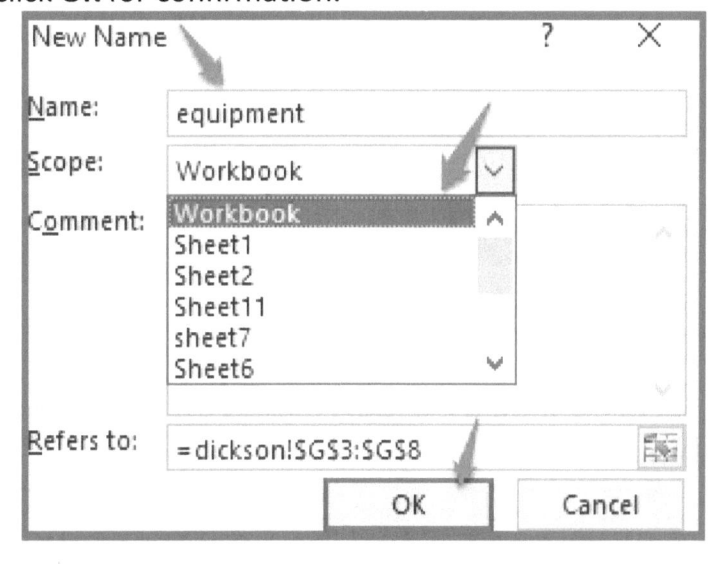

173

Note: range name reference does not change when you copy a formula with range name address from one cell to the other. A range name consistently refers to the same set of cells, and that is one of its merits.

To make use of the name range created above in a formula, simply:

a. Tap on the **Formula** bar at the place where you want to make use of the cell range name and pick the "**Use in Formula**" button.
b. Then choose **a cell range name** from the drop-down menu.

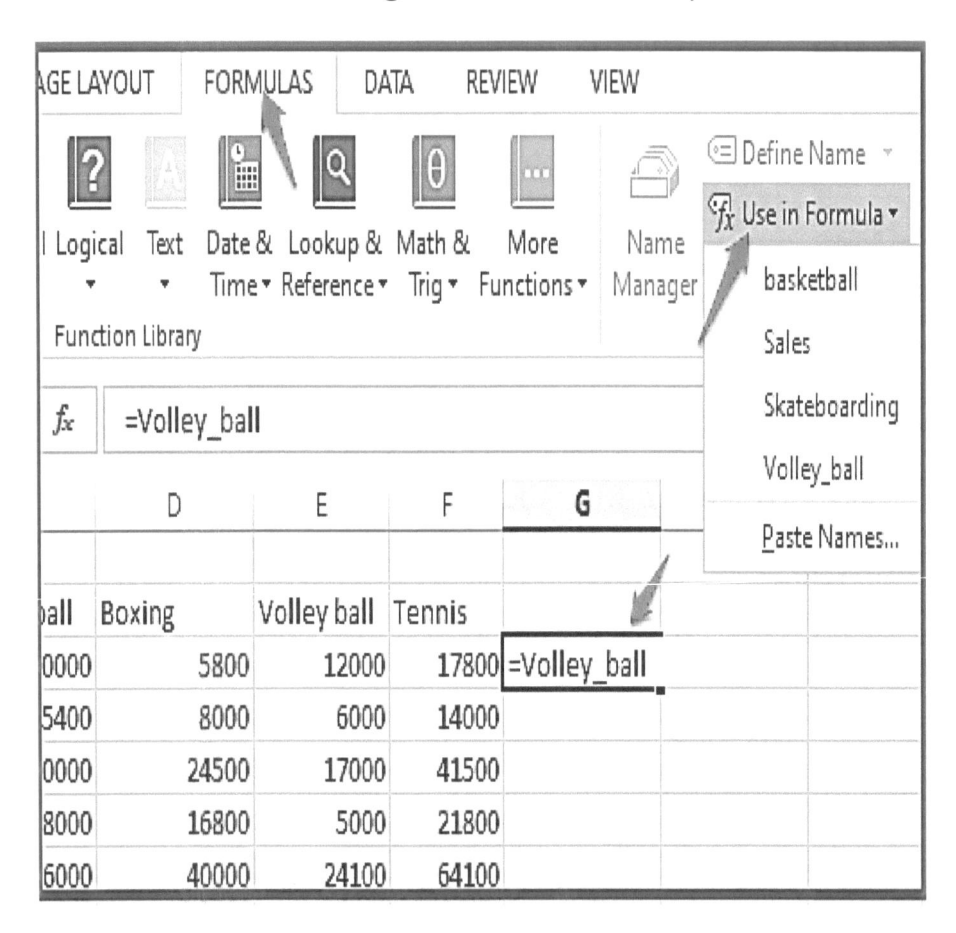

Alternatively, you can also do this:

a. Move to the **formula** button and click on it, then tap on the **"Use in Formula"** option.

```
   Define Name
fx Use in Formula ▼
      basketball
      Sales
      Skateboarding
      Volley_ball
      Paste Names...
```

b. From the "**Use in Formula**" option drop-down, pick **Paste Names,** and a paste Names dialog box will come forth.

c. Choose a cell range name and tap **Ok**.

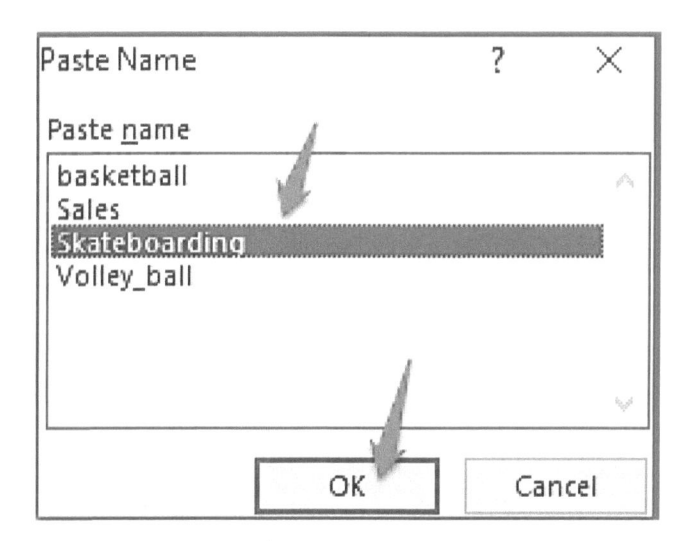

```
Paste Name                    ?   ×
Paste name
 basketball
 Sales
 Skateboarding
 Volley_ball

        OK         Cancel
```

Handling the cell range name: the cell range name belongs to you; you have all the chance to adjust it to your taste whether you want to rename or delete it. To rename or delete a cell range name, follow these processes:

a. Tap on the **Formulas** bar and click on the **"Name Manager"** button, then, the Name Manager Dialog box with a list of cell range names shows up.

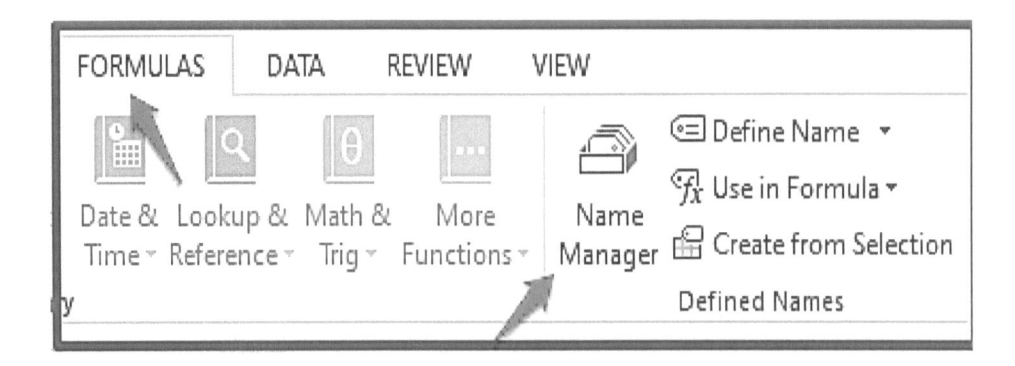

b. Simply click on the cell range name you want to adjust.
c. **To delete**, move to the top where the **Delete** button is and tap on it to delete the range name you want to delete, and then tap on **Ok** to effect the changes.

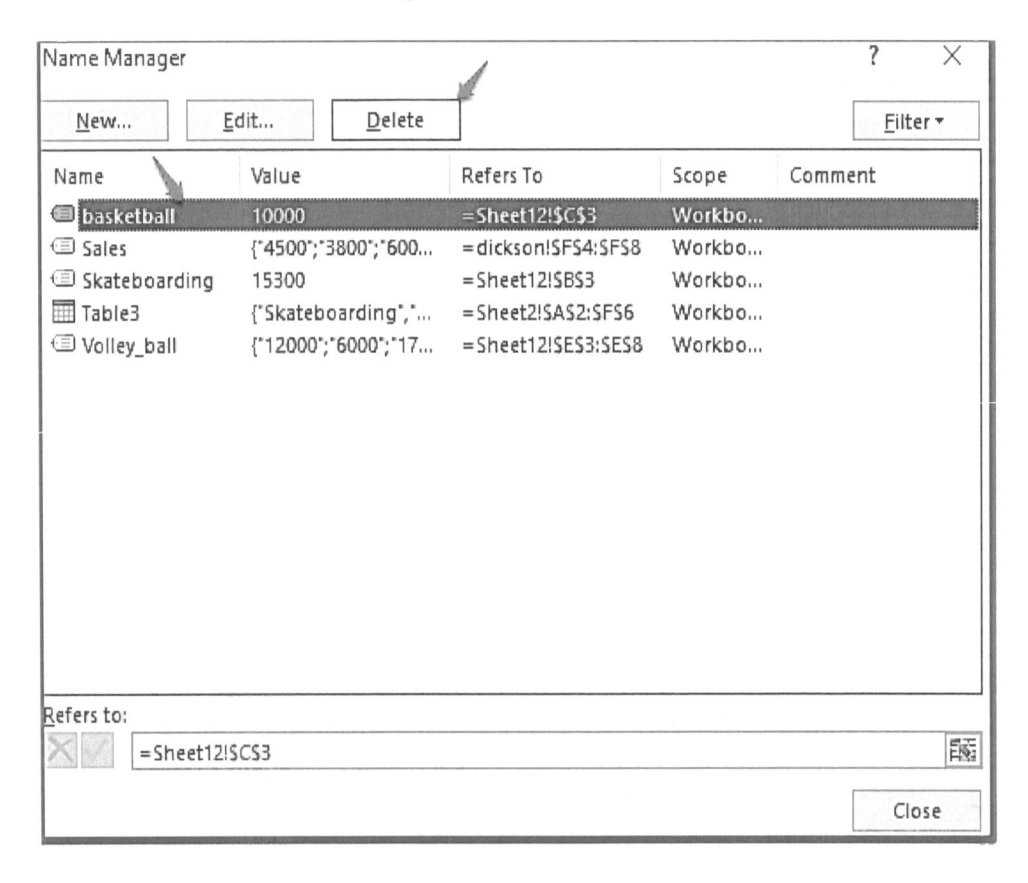

d. **To rename**, click on the **Edit** button at the top and insert the name of your choice in the Edit Name dialog box, then tap **Ok**.

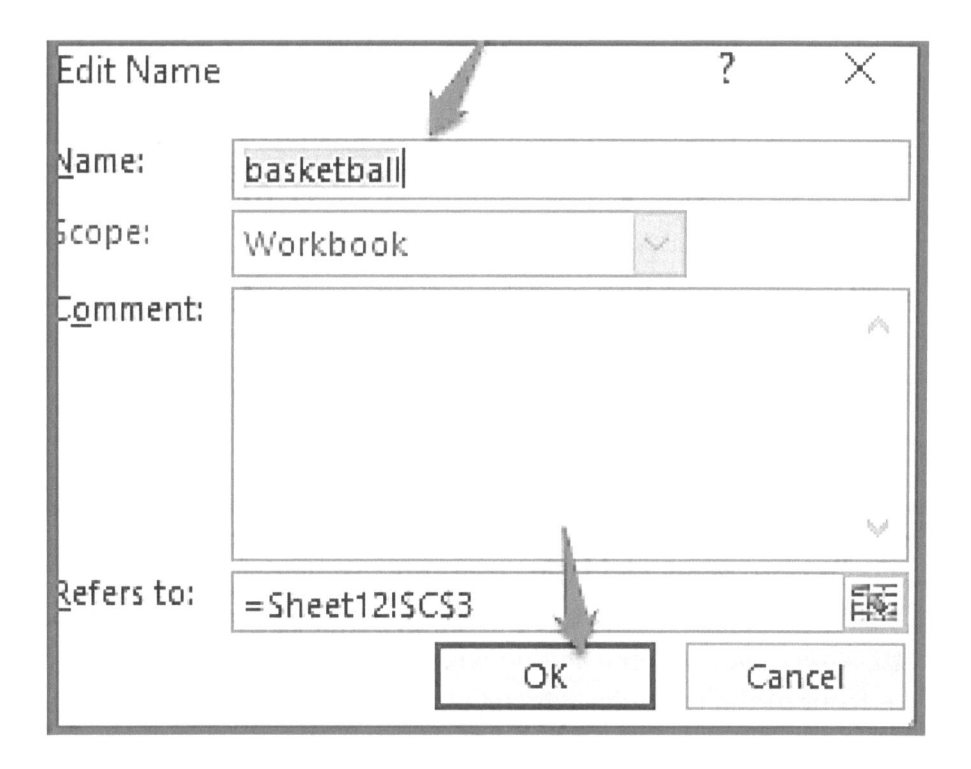

```
Edit Name                              ?    X

Name:      basketball

Scope:     Workbook

Comment:

Refers to:  =Sheet12!$C$3

                OK           Cancel
```

Pointing to Cells in A Worksheet for Formula Purpose in A Different Worksheet

You are permitted to use the cell content of another worksheet of the same workbook for your formulas since the worksheet contains the data and the contents you need for formulas computation. For example, Worksheet 1 has expenditure items for the whole month with the total aggregate amount; likewise, worksheet 2 has all income items with the total aggregate amount. If it happens that the profit establishment will take place in worksheet 2 with a formula, definitely you will need some figures in worksheet 1 before you can arrive at an exact profit figure and thus, you have to point to those cells in worksheet 1 for calculation. Let us check the below example for more comprehension of how to point to cells for the use of formulas in other worksheets.

   a. Inside **Worksheet 2** where you want to use a formula, structure it as if you want to enter a formula by starting with **=SUM(D3+D6)-AVERAGE(**

SUM	▼ : × ✓ fx	=SUM(D3+D6)-AVERAGE(					
	A	B	C	D	E	F	G	H
1								
2		Skateboard	Basketball	Boxing	Volley ball	Tennis		
3		15300	10000	5800	12000		=SUM(D3+D6)-AVERAGE(
4		18500	15400	8000	6000	14000	
5		15900	20000	24500	17000	41500	
6		53400	18000	16800	5000	21800	Sheet2
7		12000	6000	40000	24100	64100	

b. When you need to enter contents of worksheet 1, click on **worksheet 1** tab to move into worksheet 1, immediately you move to sheet 1, you will see sheet1 with an Exclamation mark (sheet1!) in front of the formulas which you are typing in sheet 2

c. Click on the **cell or group of cells** that has the contents you want to make use of by dragging over them or by typing the range in front of (sheet1!) without going back to worksheet 2 where you started the formula. For this illustration, type (E4:E6).

d. Immediately you select the cell(s), it will reflect on the formula box as a continuation of worksheet 2 formula inside sheet 1.

A3	▼ : × ✓ fx	=SUM(D3+D6)-AVERAGE(Sheet1!E4:E6)					
	A	B	C	D	E	F	G	H
3	Revenue from sales:			April	May	June		
4	pawpaw			150	180	150		$200
5	orange			300	250	400		$180
6	pearl			100	500	180		$260
7	Total income			550				
				D3:D7			sheet1	

e. After the selection, close the parentheses and press **Enter**. Immediately you tap the enter key, you will be moved from sheet 1 to sheet 2 where you will see the result of the formulas you completed in sheet 1. Nothing will show again in sheet 1.

	A	B	C	D	E	F	G
1							
2		Skateboard	Basketball	Boxing	Volley ball	Tennis	
3		15300	10000	5800	12000		22290
4		18500	15400	8000	6000	14000	
5		15900	20000	24500	17000	41500	
6		53400	18000	16800	5000	21800	sheet2
7		12000	6000	40000	24100	64100	

G3 fx =SUM(D3+D6)-AVERAGE(Sheet1!E4:E6)

Ways of Copying Formulas from One Cell to Other Cell

Excel provides a means of copying formulas from one cell to other cells instead of typing formulas again. Since the formula is of the same pattern, Excel will only amend the cell reference but will still be the same pattern of the formulas. Copying formulas from one cell to another is the easiest and fastest means.

To copy Excel formulas from cell to cell, kindly:

a. Choose **the cell** that has the formula you want to pass across to others.

	A	B	C	D	E	F	G
1							
2		Skateboard	Basketball	Boxing	Volley ball	Tennis	Total
3		15300	10000	5800	12000	5000	48100
4		18500	15400	8000	6000	14000	
5		15900	20000	24500	17000	41500	
6		53400	18000	16800	5000	21800	
7		12000	6000	40000	24100	64100	
8							

G3 =SUM(B3:F3)

b. Place the cursor to the lower part at the right side and wait till it turns to a black plus sign (+) so as to make use of it in **Autofill handle by dragging it** over the cell you want to copy the formulas to.
c. Release the mouse button to finish the process, and then go back to the cell that you copied it to, click on it and check if the formula pattern is correlated with what you want, because at times, you might have missed something in the formula and it will reflect on the subsequent result.

Discovering and Adjusting Formulas Error

Making an error in Excel formulas can't be overemphasized. One mistake inside Excel formulas can pollute all the calculations inside the worksheet. When a formula error occurs in Excel, you will discover by the presence of a small green triangle at the upper left side of the cell. Once you discover an error, the next action is an amendment. There are various errors that users can make in Excel formulas; let us quickly check those frequent errors that can occur during Excel formulas:

Frequent Message Error for Entering Wrong Formulas

Error symbols	The actual mistake
#NAME	Using a range name that is not well defined such as adding certain symbols to the range name. check the name and restructure it.
#NULL	Referring to a cell range that is not entered correctly.
#DIV/0!	Wrongly divide the number by something that does not exist, like zero.
#REF	Referring to a range name that does not exist
#VALUE	This occurs a lot, it occurs when formulas are being miswritten or you used incorrect functions.
#NUM	Using unacceptable and incorrect argument.

To amend any formula blunder you committed in Excel, there are ways of adjusting errors; we will look at them one after the other:

Discover More About the Error and Adjusting It

a. Select the **cell with signal error** (small green triangle at the upper left corner of the cell).
b. Then click the **Error Checking button** to know more about the error and a means of correcting it.

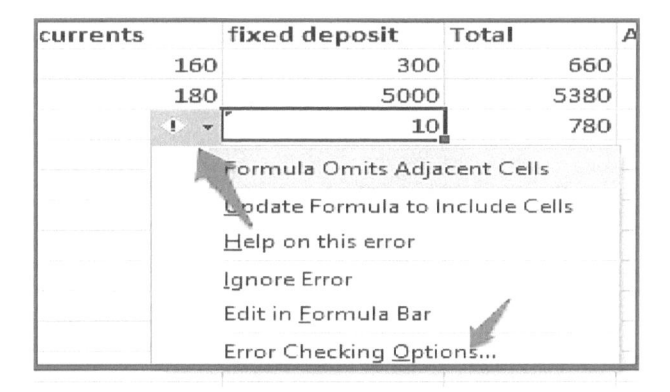

currents	fixed deposit	Total
160	300	660
180	5000	5380
	10	780

Formula Omits Adjacent Cells
Update Formula to Include Cells
Help on this error
Ignore Error
Edit in Formula Bar
Error Checking Options...

Tracing Cell References

This is meant for a crowded worksheet that is loaded with a lot of formulas even formulas from the neighbor worksheet. Tracing the cell reference will give you a hint of how the formulas are structured, and the error contains also a means of restricting the formulas. To trace cell reference, Excel has two types of cell tracer. Both show a connection about the cell you used in carrying out the formulas. A cell tracer shows a blue arrow in tracing the connection that exists between the formulas. Let us quickly run a quick check on the two cell tracers that are available in Excel:

1. **Tracing Precedent:** tracing a precedent helps Excel Users to discover those cells you used in arriving at the result of the formula. It points an arrow to all the cells that contain the data used in arriving at the result of the formula. To make use of Trace precedents, simply:
    a. Select the **cell(s)** that has the formula inside and move to the **Formulas** tab.
    b. Inside the formulas tab, click on the "**Trace Precedent**" button to check the cells that contribute to the formula and check if there should be a necessary adjustment to the data inside those cells.

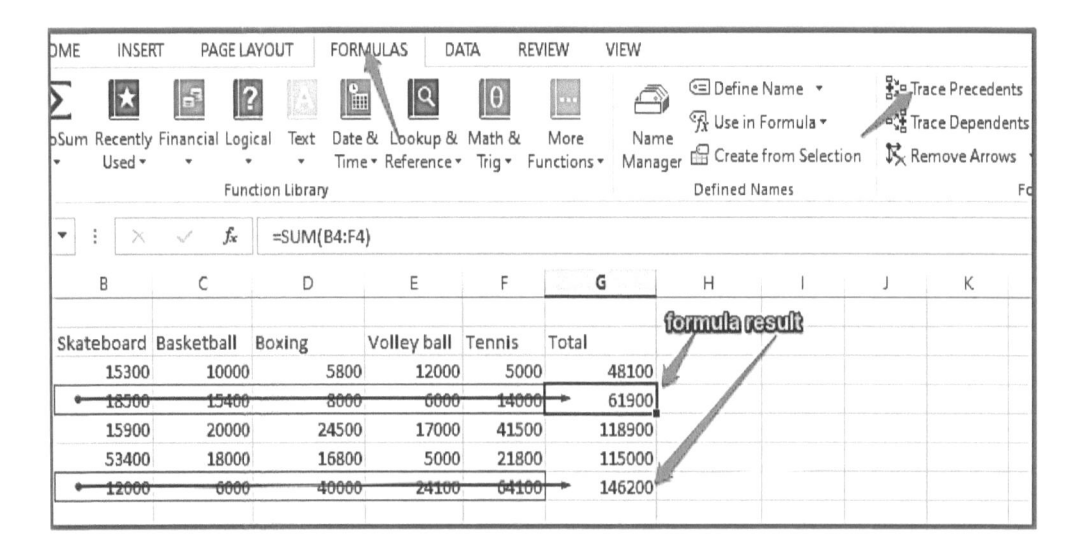

2. **Tracing dependents:** this is just the exact opposite of tracing precedent. Here the cell may have a formula or value inside, but its value or formula is used in producing formula result in another cell. And thus, cell tracer will trace from the cell selected (that is the cell that contributes to another cell formula result) to the cell where its formula or value is used (the cell with the total formula result). To make use of the Trace dependents, you have to:
   a. Select **the cell** you want to trace its dependence.
   b. Maneuver to the **formulas** bar and pick the **"Trace dependent"** button, check the relationship and amend any necessary item that needs amendment.

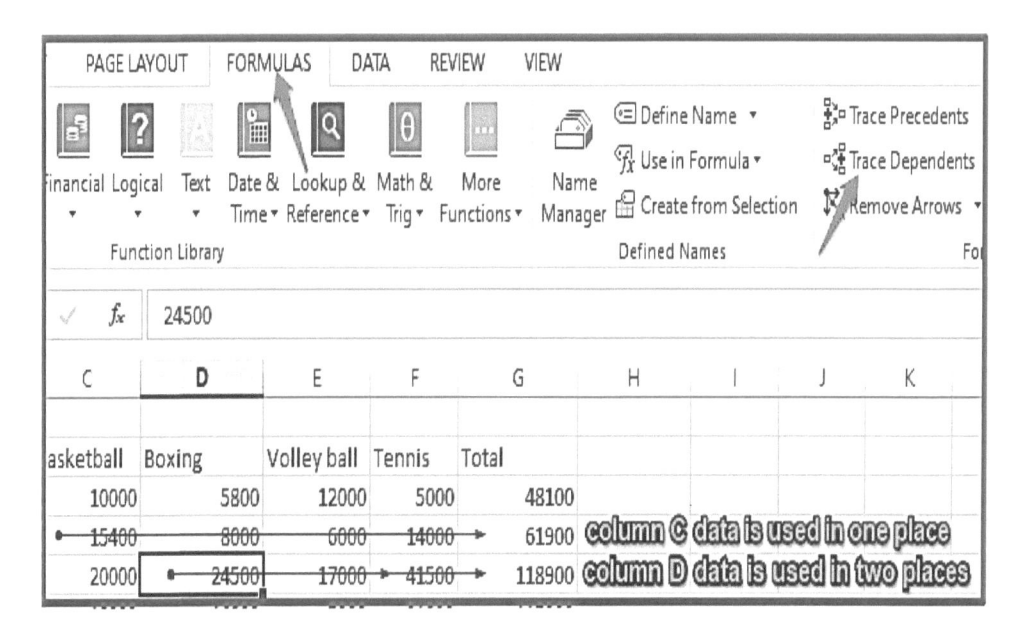

Immediately you are done tracing the cells in either option (precedent or dependent), and you are also done establishing the connection you want to establish, you can proceed to remove the cell tracer so you can have a real worksheet back by: following these steps:

a. Move to the **formulas** bar and tap on the **"Remove Arrows"** button below the precedent and dependent arrow.
b. Select either **Remove Precedent or Dependent** depending on the one you want to remove.

Making Use of Error Checkers Button

Error checker will move to the worksheet and check for any available error, once it detects the error, it will pass the details to you inside the dialog box, and then you can make the necessary adjustment.

How do I run the Error Checker? By:

a. Maneuver to the **formulas** tab and tap on **Error Checker** Button.
b. You will see the state of the error and the causative factor. Tap on **"Edit in Formula Bar"** inside the dialog box and adjust it there.

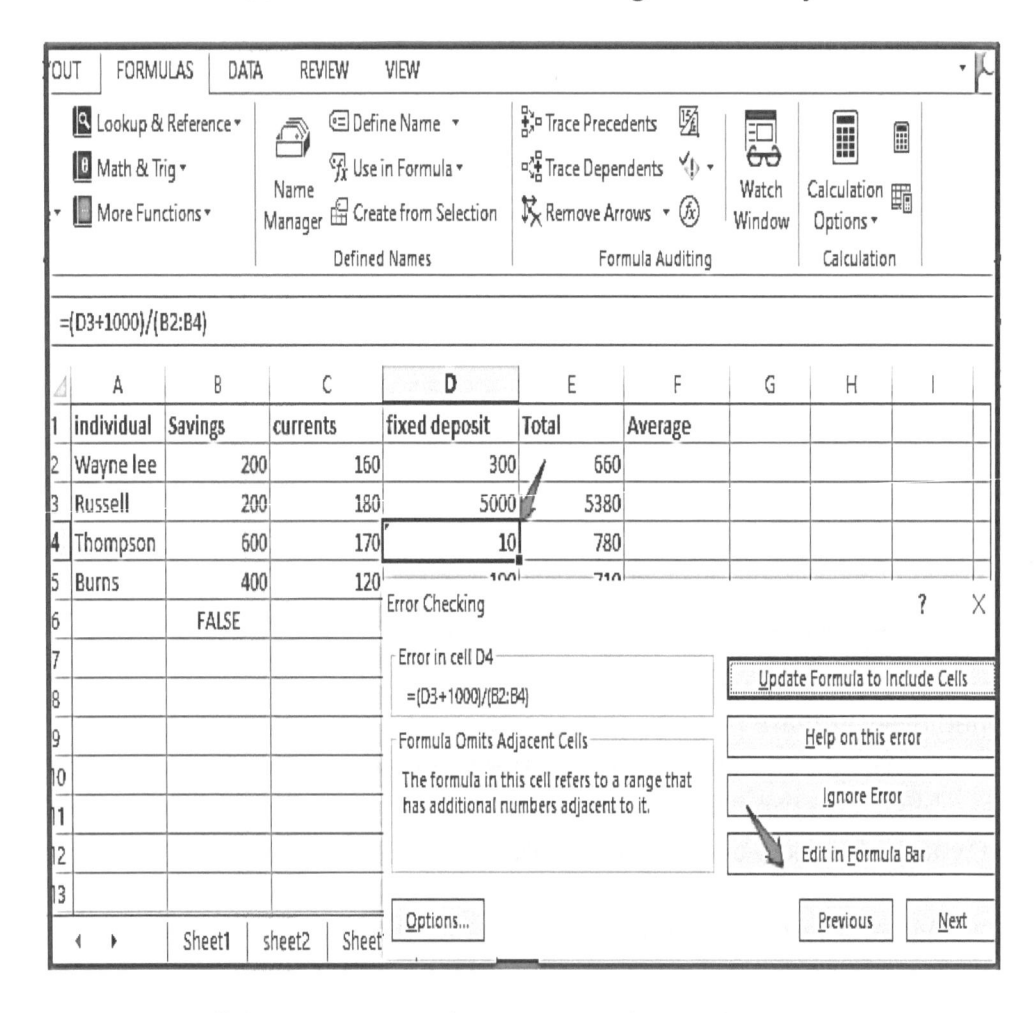

c. Then click on **Resume** when you are done adjusting.

Note: immediately you done adjusting one error, you have to click on the **Resume** option so that every other key will be active again, then click on the **"Next"** button to check the worksheet's next error, but if the error needs no adjustment, tap on the **Ignore** button and you will be moved to the next error.

Stepping into A Function

A function is an embodiment of a formula that you can use in Excel. Excel has a lot of Functions, though areas of their use depend on the Excel user's discipline, nevertheless, there are general functions that cross all disciplines such as **AVERAGE, SUM, PRODUCT,** and other most used functions. They are all located in the formulas tab. This guide will explain more on the general workable functions and how to make them find expressions in formulas to Excel users.

Understand the Use of Argument in Function

Argument is any information you supply after the insertion of a function for instance, let us use SUM function and give it a correct argument, =SUM(B3:B7); (B3:B7) is an argument, though some function does not require an argument, for example, **=TODAY() and =NOW(),** these two functions require no argument, both of them are used to get actual date and time, that is why the parenthesis is empty.

B	C	D	E	F	G
gs	currents	fixed deposit	Total	Average	
200	160	300	660		24/03/2021
200	180	5000	5380		24/03/2021 13:03
600	170	10	780		
400	120	190	710		

Note: using more than one argument for a function needs a comma, for example, =LARGE(B2:B4, 3).

Checking Out the Necessary Argument for A Given Function

At a time, you may not know the specific argument for the function you are about to use, no qualms, for any function you want to insert, simply:

a. Click on a cell and input the equal (=) sign.
b. Insert the **function** and get the parentheses opened like =AVERAGE (double click on the Function replica in the guessing box.

	B	C	D	E	F	G
X ✓ fx	=AVERAGE(					
gs	currents	fixed deposit	Total	Average	
	200	160	300	660	=AVERAGE(	24/03/2021
	200	180	5000	5380	AVERAGE(number1, [number2], ...)	
	600	170	10	780		
	400	120	190	710		

c. Immediately, Excel will activate a hint of all the arguments that are available for the function you have entered, follow it to explore any Function that you do not know its argument.

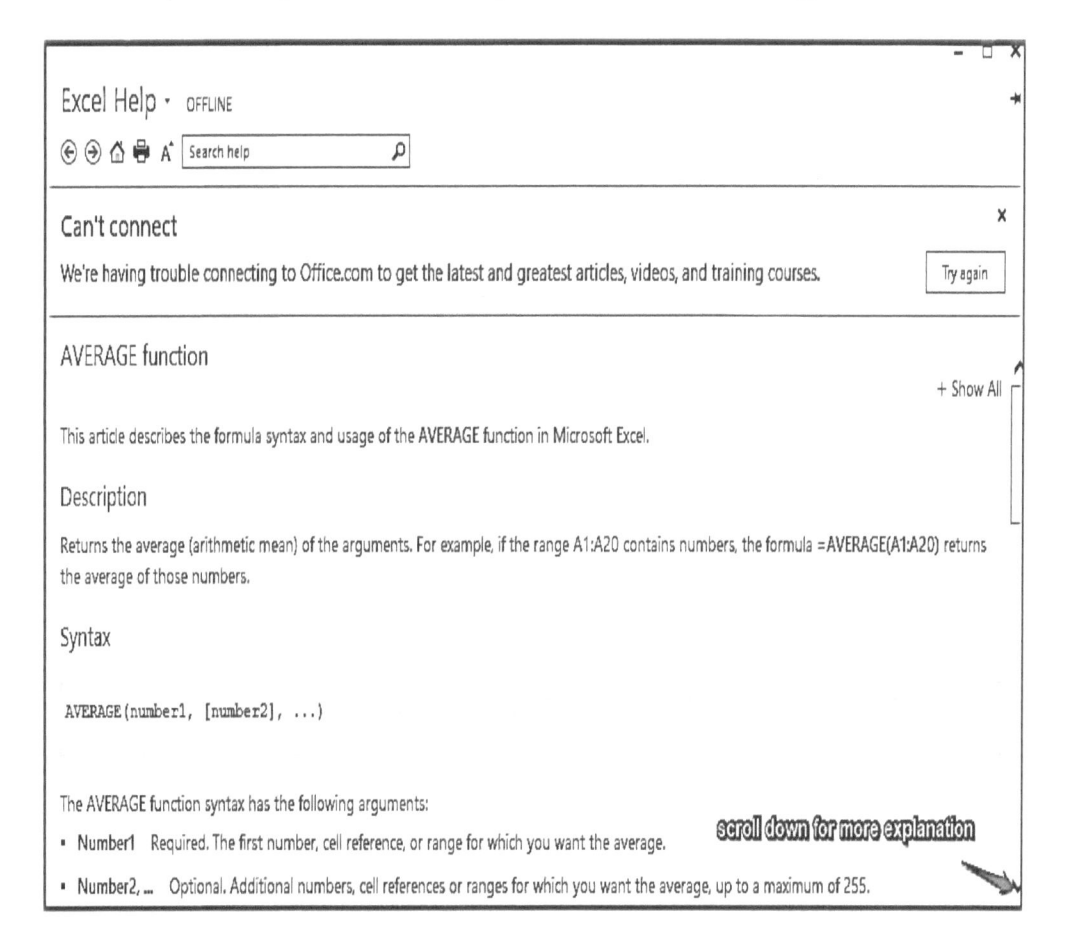

Excel Help · OFFLINE

Can't connect
We're having trouble connecting to Office.com to get the latest and greatest articles, videos, and training courses. [Try again]

AVERAGE function

+ Show All

This article describes the formula syntax and usage of the AVERAGE function in Microsoft Excel.

Description

Returns the average (arithmetic mean) of the arguments. For example, if the range A1:A20 contains numbers, the formula =AVERAGE(A1:A20) returns the average of those numbers.

Syntax

`AVERAGE(number1, [number2], ...)`

The AVERAGE function syntax has the following arguments:

- **Number1** Required. The first number, cell reference, or range for which you want the average.
- **Number2, ...** Optional. Additional numbers, cell references or ranges for which you want the average, up to a maximum of 255.

scroll down for more explanation

Note: those arguments in the bracket are optional, while those that are not in the bracket are required arguments for example = **NETWORKDAY(2/4/2021-4/6/2021, [today])**.

ENTERING A FUNCTION FOR BUILDING A FORMULA

You can either insert a function either by typing it in the formula bar or inviting Excel to guide you through, let us quickly examine the two ways:

1. **Typing into the formula bar or directly into the selected cell:**
    a. Select **the cell** where you want the formula to be created.
    b. Type the equal (=) sign directly into the cell after the selection of the cell or in the formula bar
    c. Type the **function,** open parentheses and insert your argument, then close the parentheses and press **Enter.**

D	E	F	G	H
Boxing	Volley ball	Tennis	Total	
5800	12000	5000	48100	85975
8000	6000	14000	61900	
24500	17000	41500	118900	
16800	5000	21800	115000	
40000	24100	64100	146200	

=AVERAGE(G3:G6)

Note: you may enter the function in small letters to fast-track your speed, Excel will change it to upper case automatically.

2. **Invite Excel to guide you in inserting the function:**
    a. Select **the cell** where you want the formula to reflect.
    b. Maneuver to the **formulas** tab and select the **Insert Function** to open the Insert function dialog box.

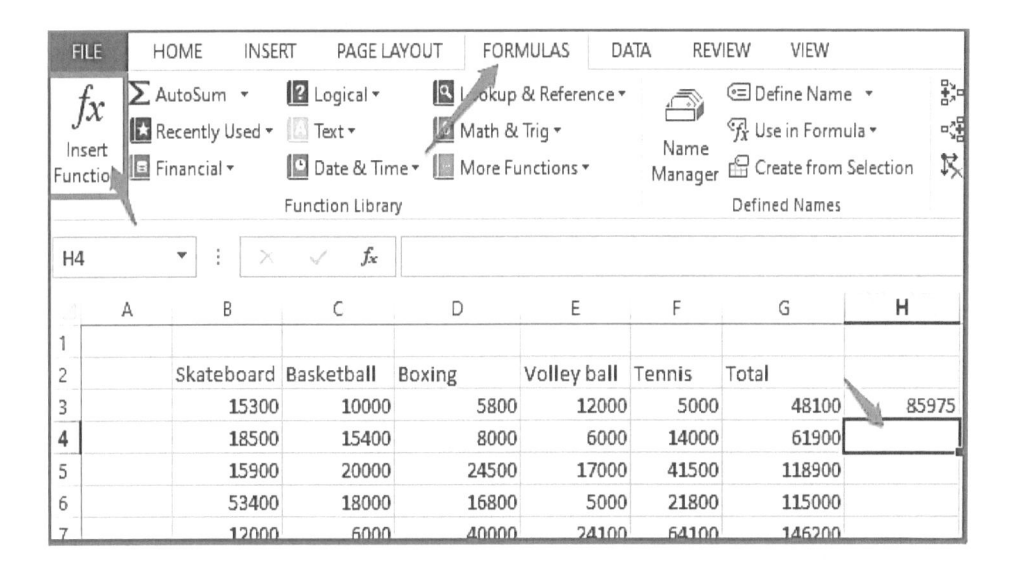

c. Choose a category from the **"select a category"** option which includes the most recently used, show all, and other categories.
d. Then choose a function from the **"Select a function"** list and tap **Ok**, another dialog box will appear where you will select the cells to be included in the formula.

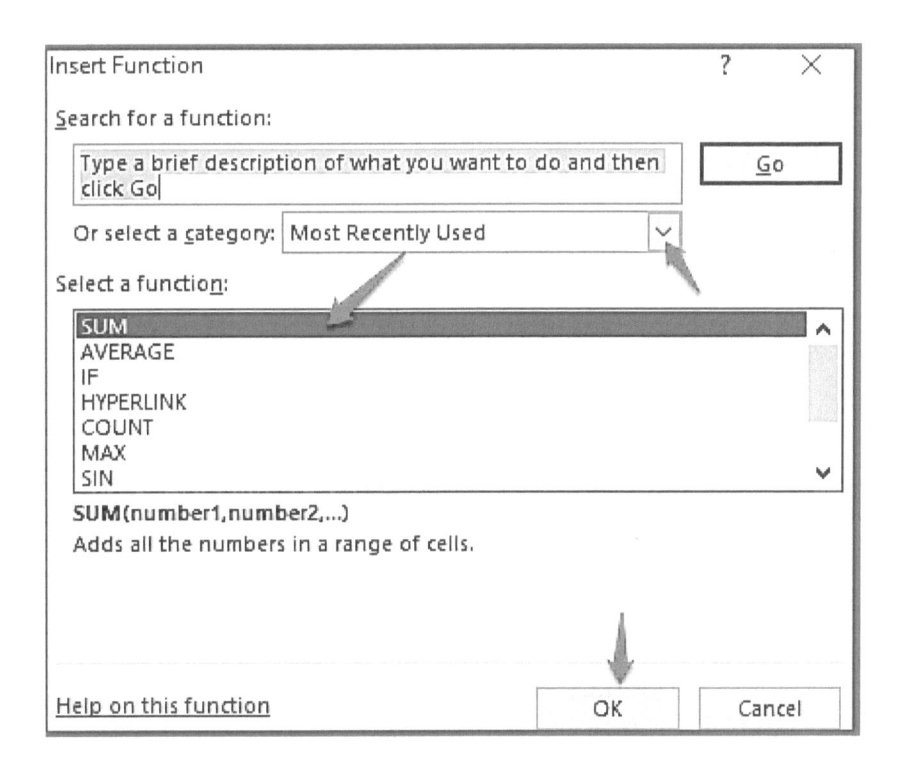

e. Select **the cells** you want to include by typing the cell address into the provided box or by clicking the first cell then drag it over the cell you want to include in the formula

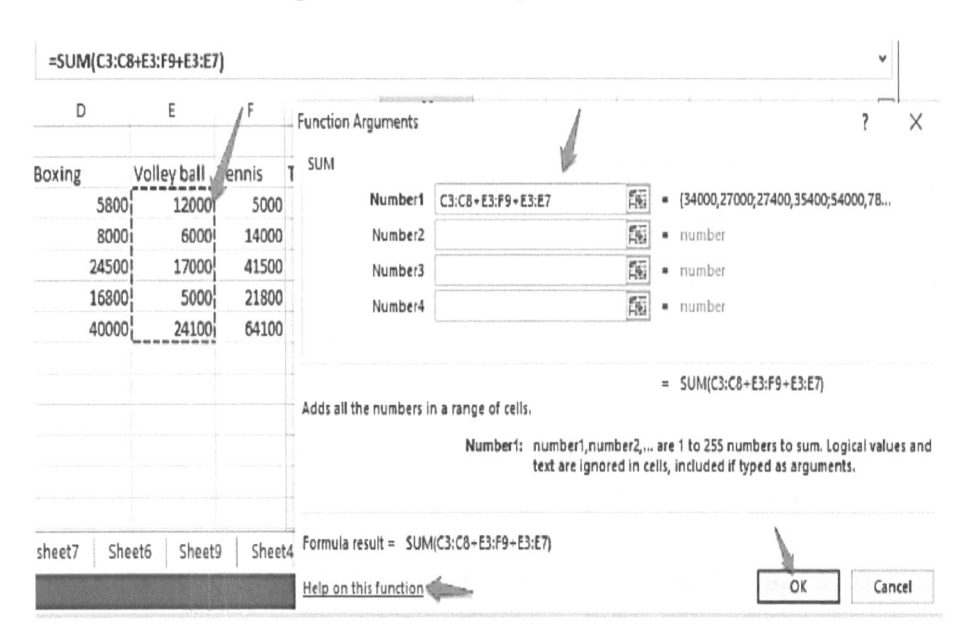

Note: each function has a separate box for the second Window dialog box. If you do not have an understanding of a specific function, call on Excel to help you out by clicking on the "Help on this function" located at the bottom left of the "Insert Function Dialog Box" and Excel will proffer a way out.

Glancing Through Generally Used Function

GENERALLY USED FUNCTION	DESCRIPTION
SUM	Addition of total cells listed in the argument.
AVERAGE	The average value of the cells recommended in the argument.
PRODUCT	The product or multiplication of the listed cell in the argument.
MAX	The largest value out of the listed cell in the argument.

MIN	The smallest value out of the listed cell in the argument.
COUNT	It represents the total number of cells listed in the argument
STDEV	Computation of a standard deviation per the sample of the cells listed in the argument.
STDEVP	Computation of a standard deviation per all the cells in the argument.

Using COUNT and COUNTIF To Count Data Item in A Cell Range

The **COUNT** function is used in counting the number of the data item you have in a selected range of cells, take for instance, =COUNT(B3:B7)

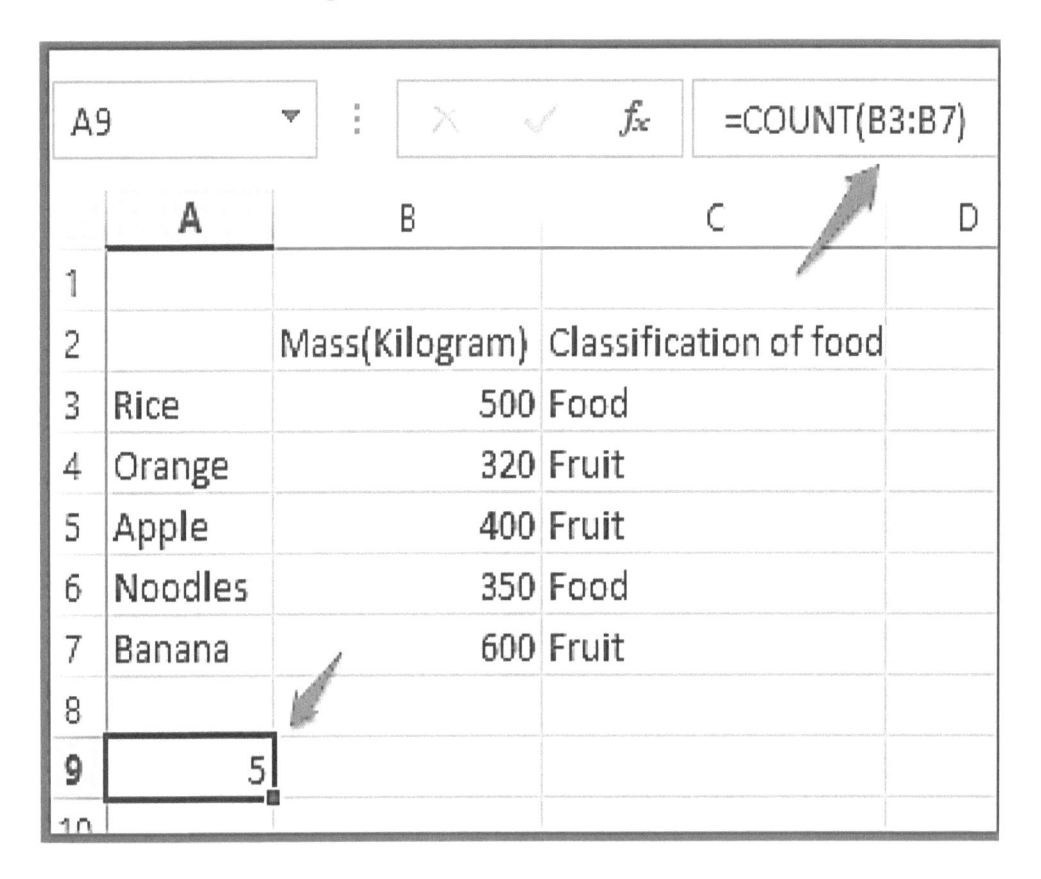

	A	B	C	D
1				
2		Mass(Kilogram)	Classification of food	
3	Rice	500	Food	
4	Orange	320	Fruit	
5	Apple	400	Fruit	
6	Noodles	350	Food	
7	Banana	600	Fruit	
8				
9	5			

Cell A9: =COUNT(B3:B7)

While COUNTIF function works very close to the COUNT function with the exception that the COUNTIF function adds A CRITERION to the argument. It counts how many cells are in the range of selected cells and how many have a particular value, and therefore to use the COUNTIF function you will be having two arguments (Cell range, and the Criterion). The criterion will be enclosed with quotation marks. Take for example, to know how many fruits are in the classification of food, the formula will be structured like this, =**COUNTIF(B3:B7, "Fruit").**

	A	B	C	D
1				
2		Mass(Kilogram)	Classification of food	
3	Rice	500	Food	
4	Orange	320	Fruit	
5	Apple	400	Fruit	
6	Noodles	350	Food	
7	Banana	600	Fruit	
8				
9	5			
10	3			

A10 =COUNTIF(C3:C7, "Fruit")

Joining Text with Value with Concatenate

Concatenate Function is about value combination from different cells and merging such into a single cell for a particular purpose, take, for instance, having a three-column name joined together to produce a single full name. The structure of the Concatenate function is like this: =**CONCATENATE(text1, text2,text3,…….).** In combining texts, you have to include space that will be between the quotation marks as an argument for the below example; this is a formula for three (3) names that will combine to be the full name=**CONCATENATE(A3," ", B3," "," ", C3).**

	A	B	C	D	E
1					
2	First Name	Last Name	Middle Name	Qualification	Full Name
3	Thompson	Wales	K	High School Diploma	Thompson Wales K
4	Burns	Carns	M	Associate Degree	Burns Carns M
5	Margi	Diego	T	First Professional Degree	Margi Diego T
6	Sileas	Vonny	D	Bachelor Degree	Sileas Vonny D

E3: =CONCATENATE(A3," ",B3," "," ",C3)

Using Average for Averaging Point Value

The **AVERAGE** function is used in determining the average point of a given data of a selected cell or a cell range. Let us take the below table as an instance by using the AVERAGE to estimate the average point score of the four students in three subjects. This is the structure of the AVERAGE function, =**AVERAGE(cell range).**

E4: =AVERAGE(B4:D4)

	A	B	C	D	E	F
2						
3		English	Maths	French	Average	
4	Alpha	80	50	60	63.33333	
5	Burney	70	50	40	53.33333	
6	Daves	40	80	90	70	
7	Hart	60	38	65	54.33333	

Excel exempts empty cells in the cell range during counting, but it regards zero (0) as part of the range and therefore computes for zero (0).

PMT For Estimating Periodic Payment of Loan

Have you borrowed a specific amount of money or you are about to take a loan but you are confused about the time it will take to repay the loan or how much can even borrow, no qualms, that is what PMT caters for, it describes the particular amount you can borrow at various interest rates and how much you will be paying on such loan yearly or monthly by dividing the yearly rate by 12 months to get the amount to be paid on monthly basis. To make use of the PMT function for calculating periodic payment, kindly observe this formula structure: =PMT(Interest rate, number of payment, amount of loan), let us check the structure worksheet for how PMT looks like:

	A	B	C	D	E
1					
2	Interest rate	No. of Payment	Amount of loan	Yearly Payment	Monthly payment
3	3.00%	120	$5,000	-$154.45	-$12.87
4	3.00%	120	$8,000	-$247.12	-$20.59
5	3.00%	120	$4,000	-$123.56	-$10.30
6	3.00%	120	$6,000	-$185.34	-$15.44

Formula in D4: =PMT(A4,B4,C4)

Explicit explanation:

a. **Interest rate**: do not put a percentage to the interest rate for it to be accepted as a number. After you are done typing the interest rate, move to the **Home** tab under number and go to percentage to format the column. That is, column (A).
b. **No of payment:** The no of time to redeem the loan is 10 years, long time loan payment ought to be paid every month, for the case of the loan in this illustration, it is 10 years, multiply it by 12 months in a calendar year, it equals 120 times in 10 years. That is column B.

c. **Amount of the loan:** insert the loan amount directly to column C, which is the amount you are calculating for what you want to borrow.
d. **Yearly payment of the loan:** this one will be having a formula in this structure: =PMT(A3, B3, C3), it is in column D.
e. **Monthly payment of the loan:** to get the amount to be paid every month, you have to divide the yearly payment with a 12-month calendar in formula (=D3/12) for cell E3.

Project Time Measuring with NETWORKDAY and TODAY

Networkday and Today measures the period of days to come, probably for a specific program, assignment, budget planning, etc. It is mainly concerned with workdays only and thus, excludes weekend (Saturday and Sunday), and therefore, the result of NETWORKDAY is for workdays alone. To make use of NETWORKDAY, structure its formula like this: =NETWORKDAY(Start date-End date).

	A	B	C	D	E	F
1	APRIL	JUNE				
2	01/04/2021	25/06/2021	64			
3	02/04/2021	26/06/2021				
4	03/04/2021	27/06/2021				
5	04/04/2021	28/06/2021				
6	05/04/2021	29/06/2021				

C2 fx =NETWORKDAYS(A2,B6,)

TODAY's function structure is like this: **=TODAY()** because it does not argue.

Note: to get the number of days between two dates, simply remove the latest date from the earlier date by using the minus sign. It will give you a total of the days between the selected dates without removing Saturday and Sunday, ="30/6/2021"-"1/4/2021". The enclosed quotation is for date identification to Excel.

LEN For Counting Text Character

LEN function in Excel is referred to as the length Excel function as long as it is used to ascertain the length or character of a given word, cell numbers, and many more. To get an in-depth understanding of this function, let us make use of it with the SUM function. =SUM(LEN(A2),LEN(B2)).

	A	B	C	D	E
1	First	Last	charater in total		
2	Catherine	ben	12		
3	Sabrina	Nick	12		
4	Sydney	Kyle	10		
5	Audrey	Vanessa	13		
6	Talor	Owen	9		
7	David	Henry	10		

C2: =SUM(LEN(A2),LEN(B2))

Note: LEN A2= 9 and B2= 3, the total is equal to 12, you will now use the auto-fill handle to copy the pattern of the formulas down.

Compares the Range of Values with LARGE And SMALL

LARGE and SMALL is used to compare which value is largest and which one is smallest within a given range, let us take for instance, the total number of the bag sold in the market.

- 100: maximum bag sold in one month in the market (**MAX**).
- 8: the least bag sold in one month in the market **(MIN)**.
- 93: the second maximum bag sold in one month in the market (**LARGE**).
- 10: the second least bag sold in one month in the market **(SMALL)**.

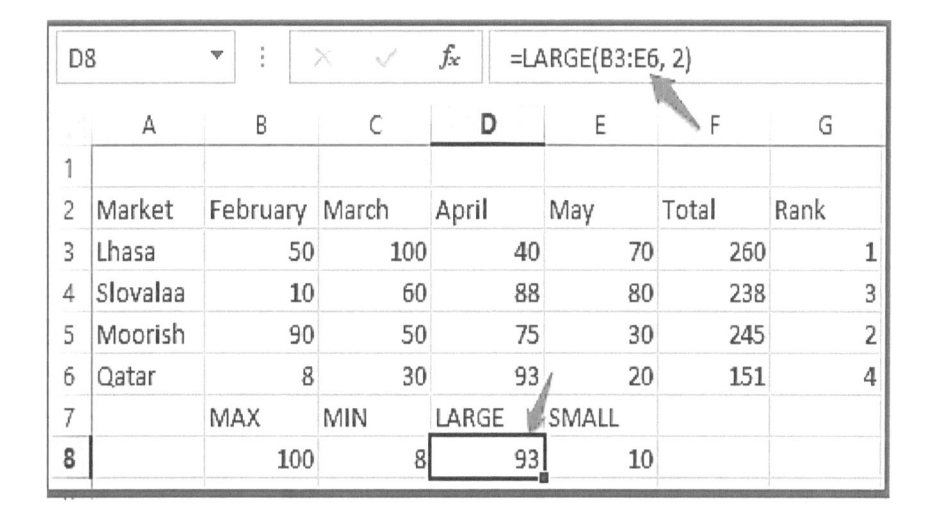

	A	B	C	D	E	F	G
1							
2	Market	February	March	April	May	Total	Rank
3	Lhasa	50	100	40	70	260	1
4	Slovalaa	10	60	88	80	238	3
5	Moorish	90	50	75	30	245	2
6	Qatar	8	30	93	20	151	4
7		MAX	MIN	LARGE	SMALL		
8		100	8	93	10		

D8: =LARGE(B3:E6, 2)

While you are having LARGE and SMALL, you may still at times have to use MAX and MIN. Let us check the use of the four functions in a jiffy with the above worksheet as an example:

1. **MIN:** it gives you the least number or value of the bags sold in the market throughout the whole four months with a given range of **=MIN(B3:E6).**

2. **MAX:** it gives the largest number or the values of the bags sold in the market throughout the four months with a given range of: **=MAX(B3:E6).**

3. **SMALL:** it gives you the nth position of the smallest value in the list. It will have two arguments, the first argument is the cell range and the second argument is the position of the nth lower value, which maybe 2nd or 3rd position, and the formula will be in a structure like this **=SMALL(B3:E6, 2) or =SMALL(B3:E6, 3)** depending on the nth position.

4. **LARGE:** it will give you the nth position of the largest value in the list. It will have two arguments as well, which are the cell range and nth position either 2nd or 3rd and the formula will be structured like this: **=LARGE(B3:E6, 2) or =LARGE(B3:E6, 3).**

5. **RANK:** it ranks the list of the data; the RANK function has three- arguments which are as follows:

	A	B	C	D	E	F	G
						=RANK(F5,F3:F6,0)	
1							
2	Market	February	March	April	May	Total	Rank
3	Lhasa	50	100	40	70	260	1
4	Slovalaa	10	60	88	80	238	3
5	Moorish	90	50	75	30	245	2
6	Qatar	8	30	93	20	151	4
7		MAX	MIN	LARGE	SMALL		
8		100	8	93	10		

Using cell G5, second-ranking

    a. The cell address with the value you are using for ranking. F5=245

    b. The cell range with which you will match the value in deciding the ranking, F3:F6

    c. The order of ranking, 0 for descending order, up to down, while 1 is for ascending order, down to up). 0

Text Capitalizing with PROPER Function

The **Proper** function is used to change editing text to upper, lower, or proper case. Excel does not have to confirm change case like MS word, though Excel's change case is not automatic like MS word but at the same time it is not difficult, it just requires some little processes. To change the case of the text you have used before, kindly:

    a. Create a momentary new column to the right of the column that has the text you want to change its case, which you will later delete when it completes its mission. To create the column:
        i. Select **the column** to the right where you want the new column to be situated.

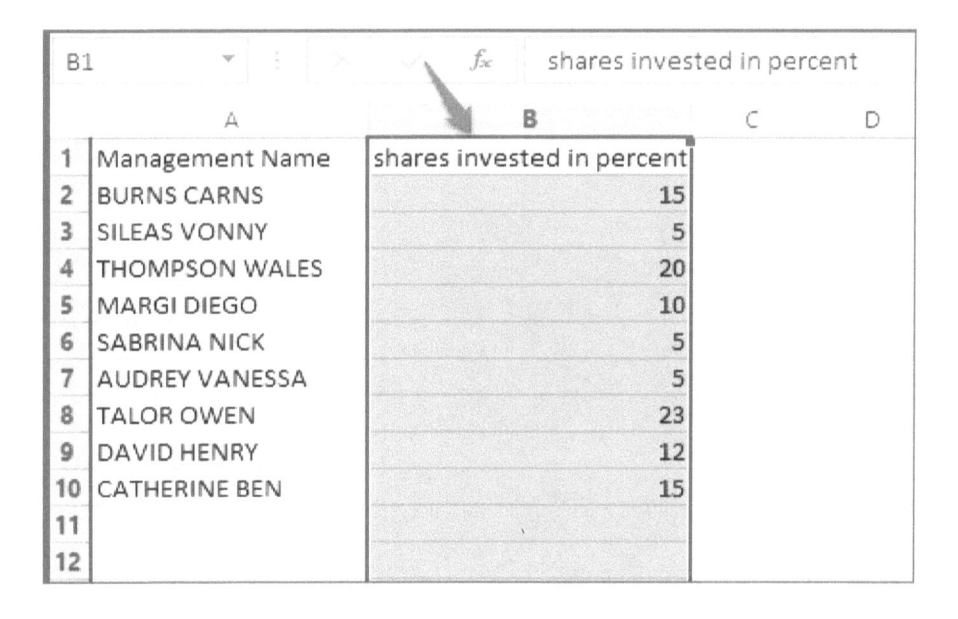

	A	B	C	D
		fx	shares invested in percent	
1	Management Name	shares invested in percent		
2	BURNS CARNS	15		
3	SILEAS VONNY	5		
4	THOMPSON WALES	20		
5	MARGI DIEGO	10		
6	SABRINA NICK	5		
7	AUDREY VANESSA	5		
8	TALOR OWEN	23		
9	DAVID HENRY	12		
10	CATHERINE BEN	15		
11				
12				

(B1 shown in name box)

ii. Right-click on the **selected column** and pick **Insert**.

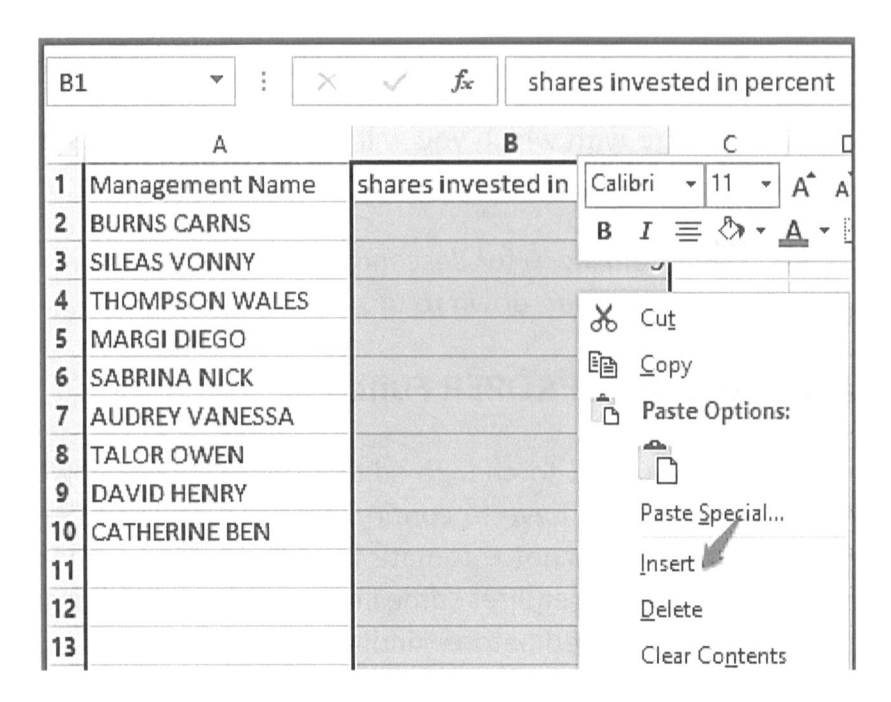

	A	B	C
1	Management Name	shares invested in	
2	BURNS CARNS		
3	SILEAS VONNY		
4	THOMPSON WALES		
5	MARGI DIEGO		
6	SABRINA NICK		
7	AUDREY VANESSA		
8	TALOR OWEN		
9	DAVID HENRY		
10	CATHERINE BEN		

(Context menu shown: Cut, Copy, Paste Options, Paste Special…, **Insert**, Delete, Clear Contents)

b. Immediately you are done with the insertion of the new column, tap on the **first column** on the column you have just created which is direct to the right side of the text you want to change its case.

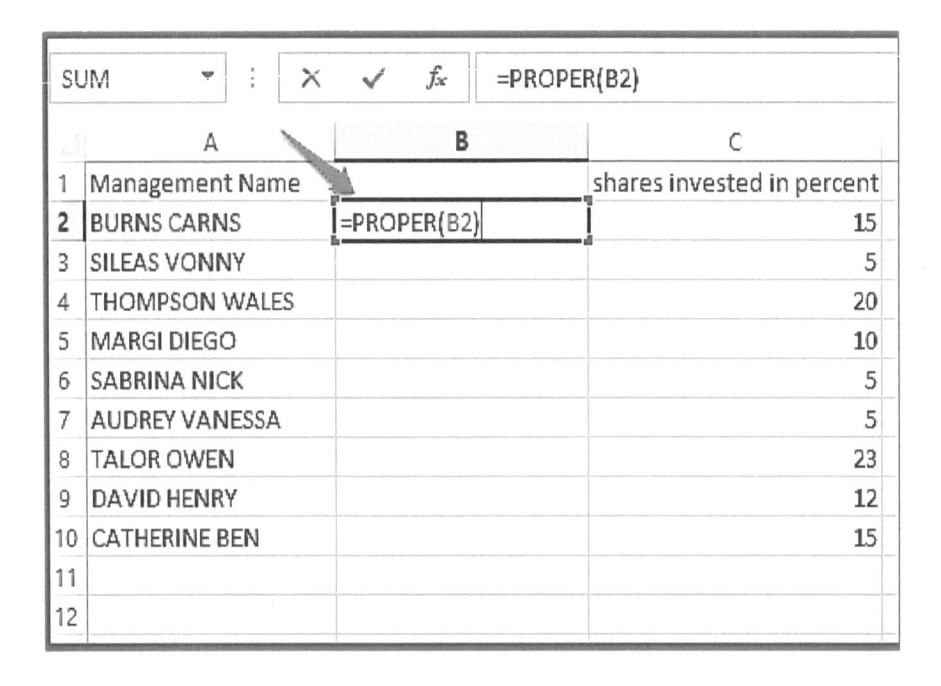

SUM fx =PROPER(B2)

	A	B	C
1	Management Name		shares invested in percent
2	BURNS CARNS	=PROPER(B2)	15
3	SILEAS VONNY		5
4	THOMPSON WALES		20
5	MARGI DIEGO		10
6	SABRINA NICK		5
7	AUDREY VANESSA		5
8	TALOR OWEN		23
9	DAVID HENRY		12
10	CATHERINE BEN		15

c. The column we want to change is in the upper case, but we want to change it to proper case. Now in the column, tap above in (b), insert a formula of this structure there: **=PROPER(B2)**. Perhaps we want to change it to a lower case, we would have replaced the **Proper** with **Lower** because we can only have upper, proper and lower. Immediately after the insertion of the formula, tap on the **Enter** key on the keyboard to initiate the process.

	A	B	C
1	Management Name		shares invested in percent
2	BURNS CARNS	Burns Carns	15
3	SILEAS VONNY		5
4	THOMPSON WALES		20
5	MARGI DIEGO		10
6	SABRINA NICK		5
7	AUDREY VANESSA		5
8	TALOR OWEN		23
9	DAVID HENRY		12
10	CATHERINE BEN		15
11			

B2 ▼ : ✗ ✓ ƒx =PROPER(A2)

d. If you observe, you will notice the text from the first cell A has been copied into the first cell of the new column (B) we created but in the proper case we desire.
e. Then use the auto-fill handle to copy down the process for the other names by dragging down the black arrow to the last name on the list.

	A	B	C
1	Management Name		shares invested in percent
2	BURNS CARNS	Burns Carns	15
3	SILEAS VONNY	Sileas Vonny	5
4	THOMPSON WALES	Thompson Wales	20
5	MARGI DIEGO	Margi Diego	10
6	SABRINA NICK	Sabrina Nick	5
7	AUDREY VANESSA	Audrey Vanessa	5
8	TALOR OWEN	Talor Owen	23
9	DAVID HENRY	David Henry	12
10	CATHERINE BEN	Catherine Ben	15

  f. At this moment, we have gotten the proper case in column B, all we have to do now is to copy the contents in the new column by selecting the names in the new column and press **Ctrl + C** to copy it.

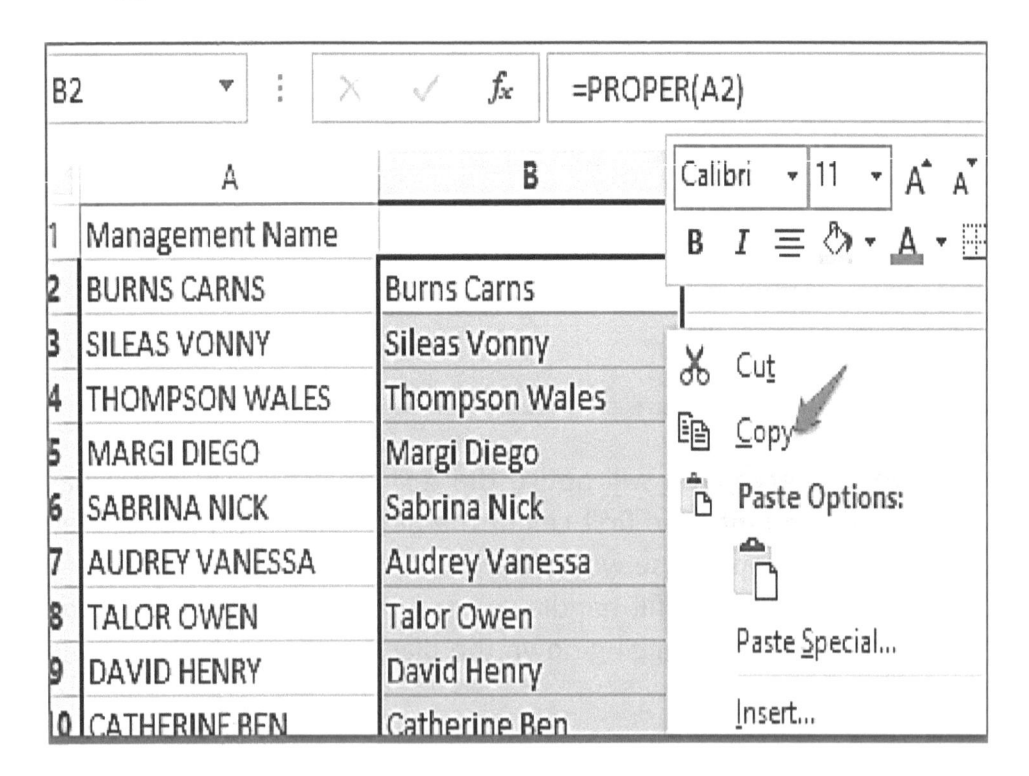

g. Then right-click **the beginning of the column** that you want to change, here, we have it as cell A2, tap on the **Paste** special menu for the values you copied.

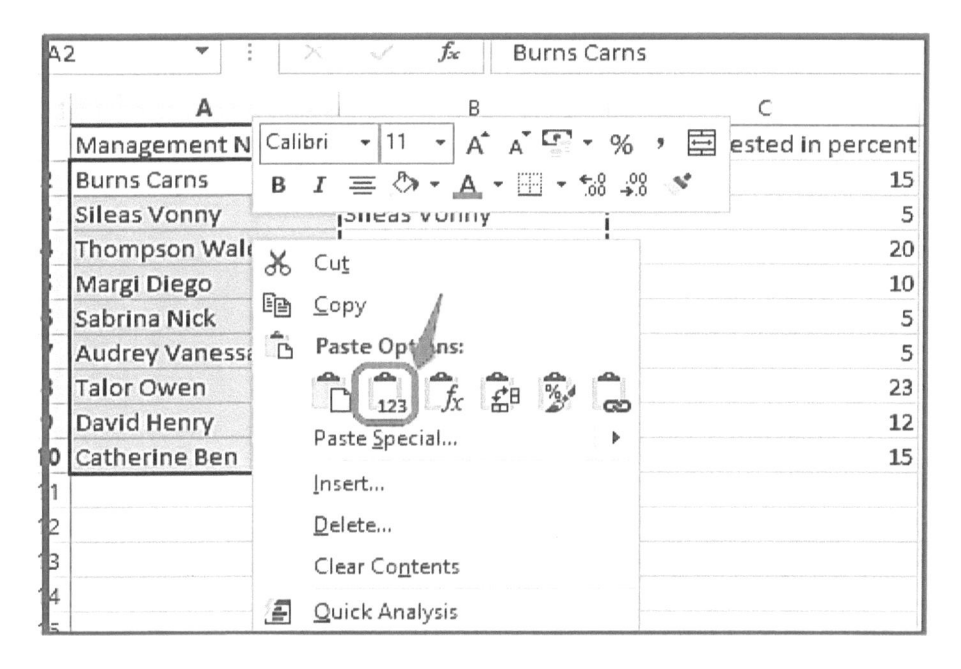

h. Now it is time to delete the momentary column that you used to format column A. this is done by selecting the column and right-click it, then pick the **Delete** option.

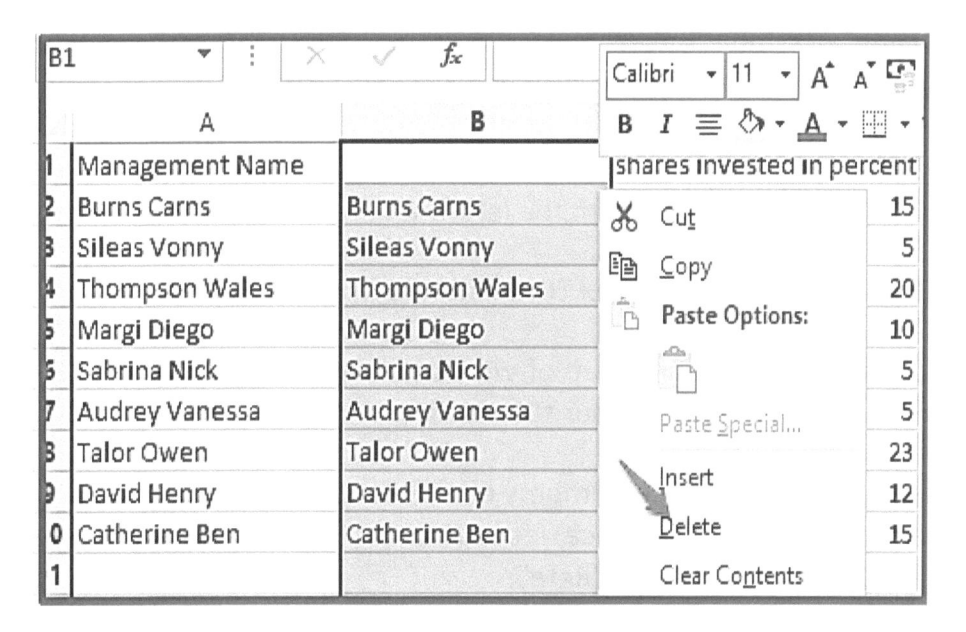

203

i. Column A is now having a set of **Proper cases** you want.

A	B
Management Name	shares invested in percent
Burns Carns	15
Sileas Vonny	5
Thompson Wales	20
Margi Diego	10
Sabrina Nick	5
Audrey Vanessa	5
Talor Owen	23
David Henry	12
Catherine Ben	15

LEFT, MID, AND RIGHT for Data Extraction

LEFT, MID, AND RIGHT are called text functions because they are made purposely to extract certain parts from a word or a group of words. As a means of explanation, you may need to extract the first two letters of a word, the last four letters, or the 6 letters from the middle of the sentence in LEFT, LAST, AND MID functions respectively.

- The **LEFT** function is used for middle extraction; let us put it to practice by starting with the left function.

=LEFT(text, num-chars) or =LEFT(cell address, num-chars)

Text: this is the word or group of words you type or the cell reference where you want to extract your sub word.

Num-chars: These are the numbers of characters you choose to extract from the left part. For instance, let us draw out 4 characters in the text "reference", the outcome is "Refe".

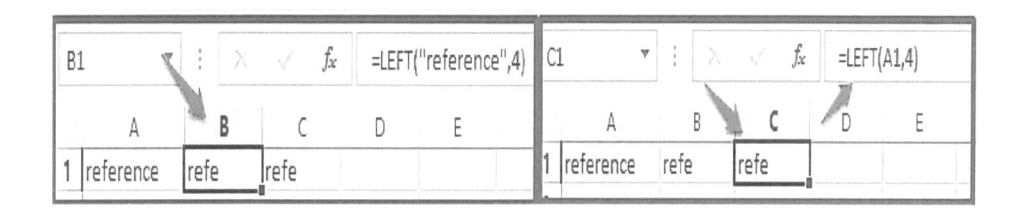

- Over to the **RIGHT** function, it is the exact opposite of the LEFT function, its structure is like this:

=RIGHT(text, num-chars) or =RIGHT(cell address, num-chars)

The explanation with the **LEFT** function is the same, except that you will extract from the right part. For instance, =**RIGHT("right choice", 3)**. This will give us the word "ice", which occurs to be the first three letter from the right.

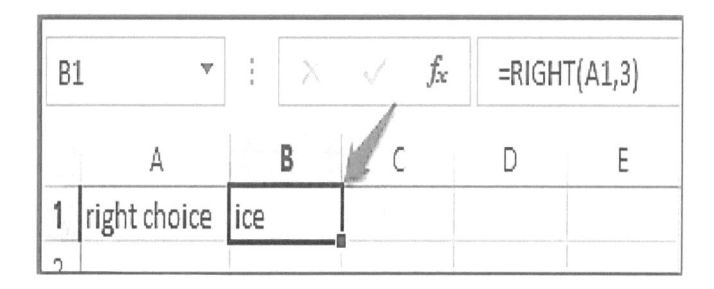

- The third function is the MID function and it is used in drawing out part of the middle letters from the text. It is will be in a structure like this:
  =MID(text, start-num, num chars) or =MID(cell address, start-num, num chars)
  Text: the text within where you wish to draw out words from.
  Start num: this is the number position where to start the extraction from.
  Num-chars: this is the number of characters it will be from the start-num.

Let us take for instance; we want to draw out the word **"key"** from the text **"the key of diligence"**. The formula will be structured like this = **MID("the key to diligence",5,3)**

	A	B	C	D
1	the key of diligence	key		

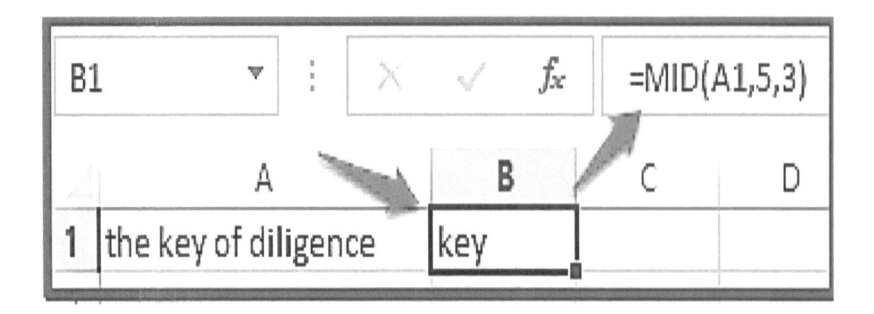

B1 =MID(A1,5,3)

a. **5: start-num** which happen to be the position of the starting point, we will count five (5) characters ("the" is 3 characters, space is recognized in MID function making it four-characters, from the beginning, in short, the 5th number start from K).
b. **3: num chars**, the total character to draw out from the text is 3 from the starting point which is K, and counting 3 characters from K will be the word "key".

IF For Analytical Identification

The IF function is the most recognized used function for analytical comparison between a particular value and your expectation. True return means your expectation is right and if it is otherwise, then your expectation is wrong.

For instance, =IF(D1=8, "True", "False"), It means IF D1=8, then it's True, but if otherwise, return False.

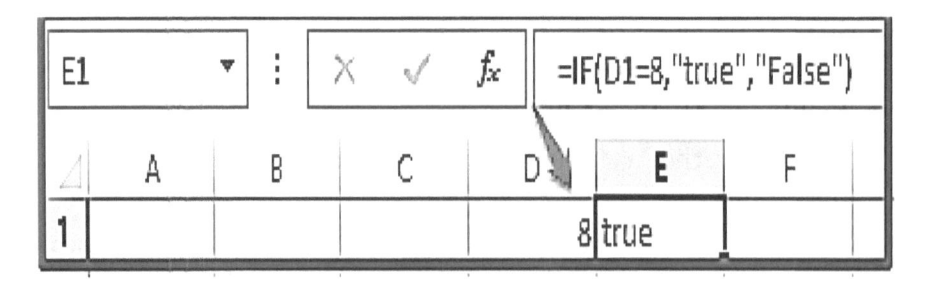

	A	B	C	D	E	F
1				8	true	

E1 =IF(D1=8,"true","False")

You can use the IF function to estimate text and values, it is called nest IFfunction, let us buttress more on the illustration below. IF(A4>B4," surplus" ", deficit").

	A	B	C	D	E	F
1	Income	Expenses	Difference	status		
2	400	300	100	Surplus		
3	600	800	-200	Deficit		
4	500	400	100	Surplus		
5	900	899	1	Surplus		

D4: =IF(A4>B4,"Surplus","Deficit")

The above illustration is saying IF(A4>B4, then return surplus, IF otherwise return deficit).

CHAPTER FIVE
CONSTRUCT WORKSHEET FOR EASY COMPREHENSION

Spreading Out Worksheet in An Orderly Manner

As you lay your bed, you shall lie on it, so they say. The same principle applies to the worksheet, if you learn how to manage the worksheet effectively, you will enjoy the result, even before and after you print it out, it will be wonderful and more comprehensive.

Managing a worksheet has a lot to do with how you arrange your worksheet and its contents, such as number formatting probably with percentage or dollars will make the reader understand the actual value of what you put inside the worksheet. Other worksheet management are change character, decorating with color and others that we will be discussing in length in this chapter.

Numbers and Text Alignment in Rows and Columns

The default alignment of the text in the worksheet is to the left, while that of the number is to the right; both default alignments can be adjusted if the need arises. The data inside the cell can be adjusted to the left, right, or middle or from bottom to center, top, and vice versa. You may as well justify cell data. At the time you have to change the alignment of the subject heading so that its look within the cell will be outstanding and that of the worksheet at large.

To change the alignment of the text and number, kindly do the following:

   A. **For horizontal alignment** (left to right or side to side alignment.).
      a. Select **the cells** that need alignment.
      b. Move to the **Home tab** and click on **the respective button** (left align, center align and middle align button).

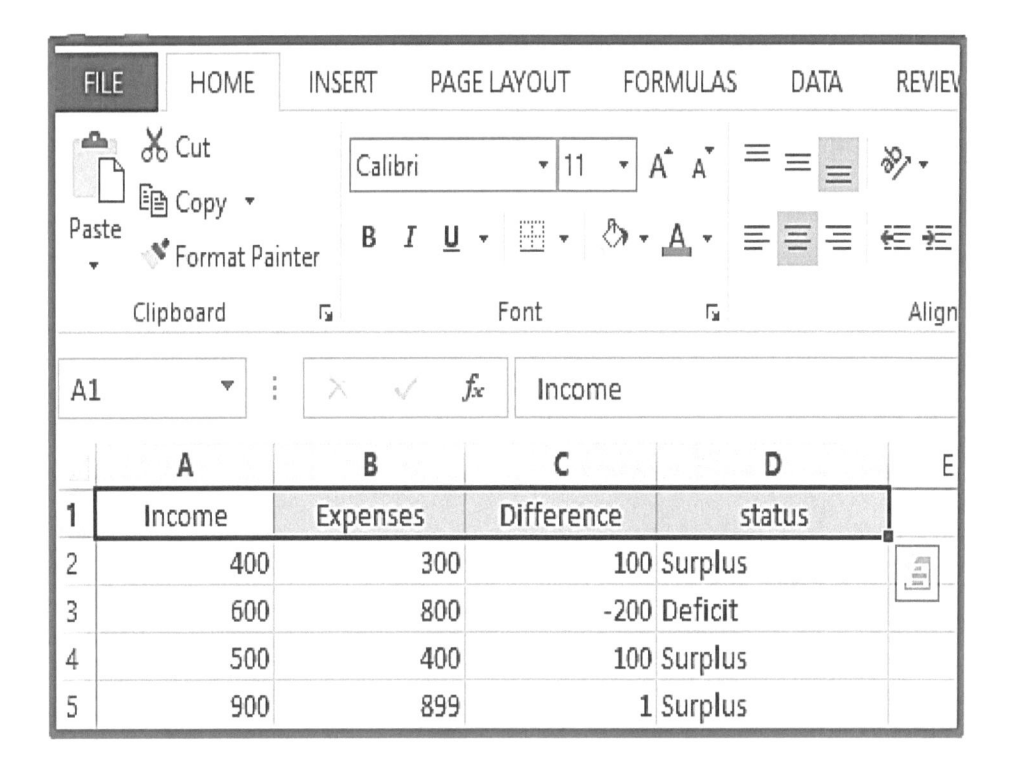

ALTERNATIVELY,

a. Tap on the **Alignment** group button and pick the **Format Cell Alignment** option from the drop-down list.

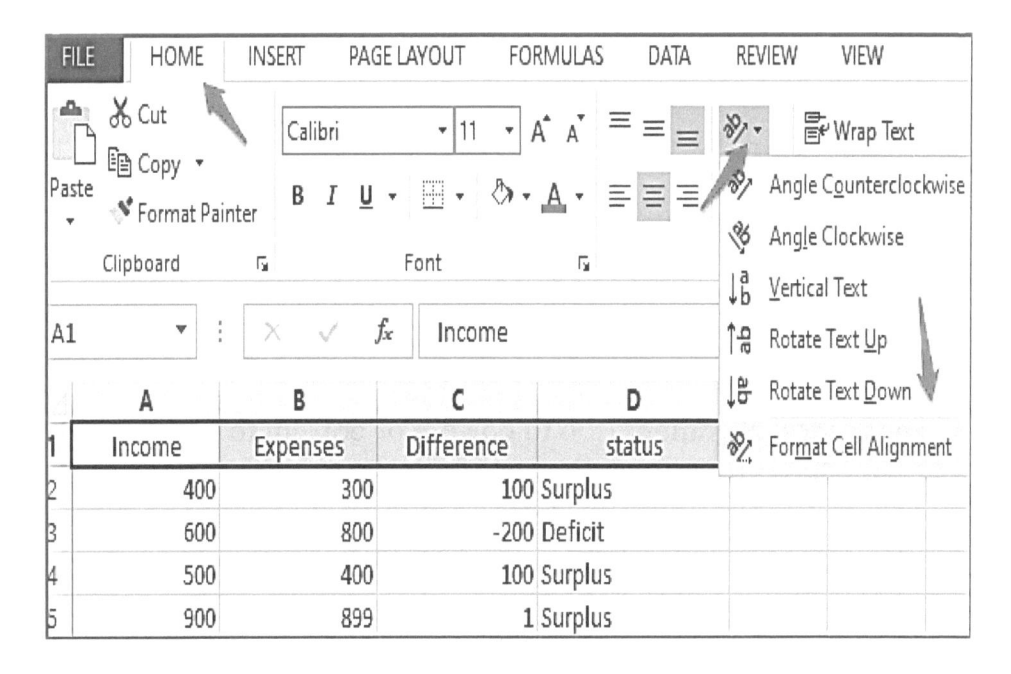

209

b. Tap on the **Alignment** tab inside the format cell dialog box.
c. Click on the **Horizontal section** and pick your desired alignment including justify that will fit your letter to the cell.

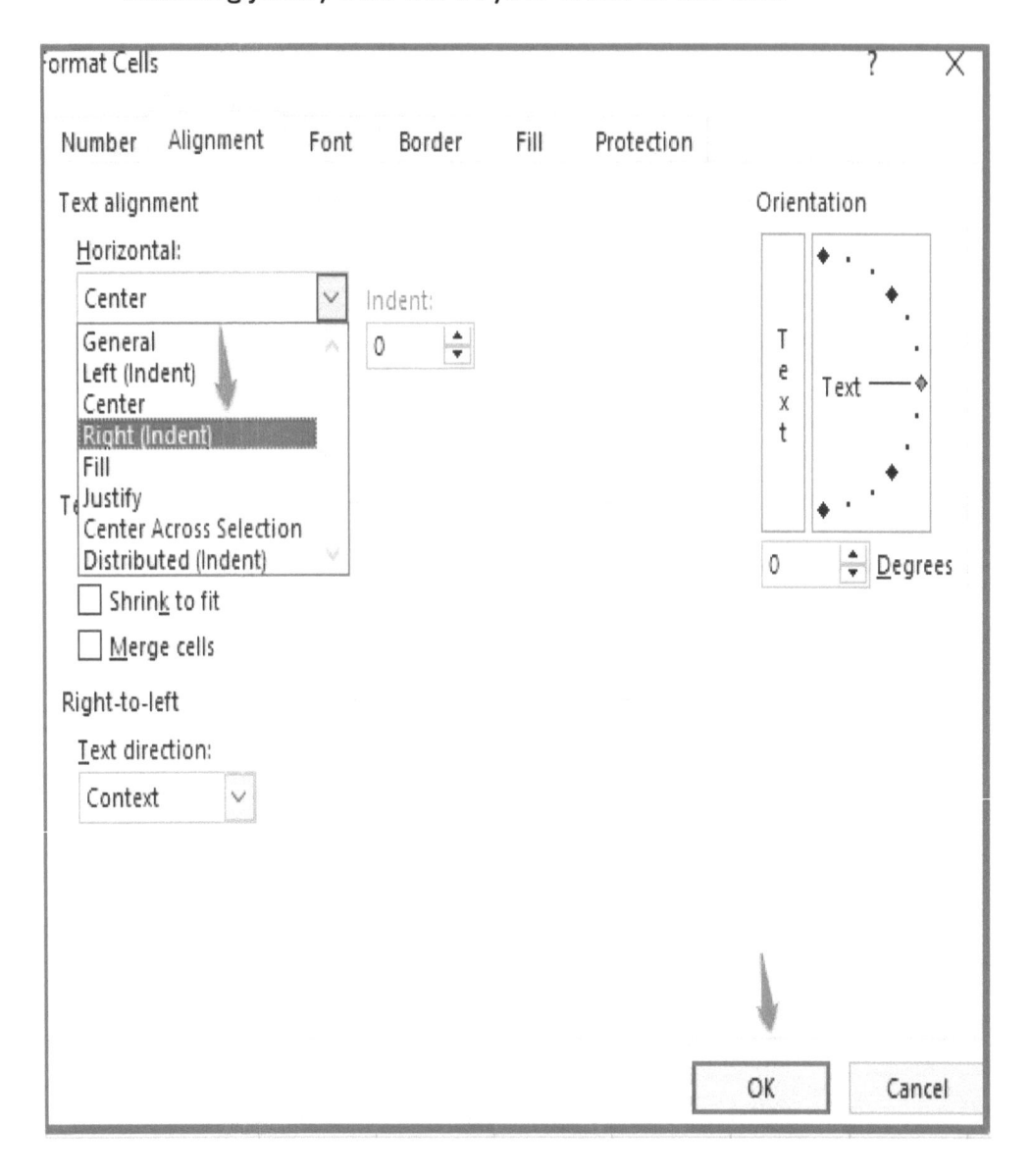

B. **For vertical alignment** (top to bottom or bottom to top):
   a. Select the **cells** that need alignment.
   b. Move to the **Home tab** and click on **respective alignment** (top align, middle align, and bottom align).

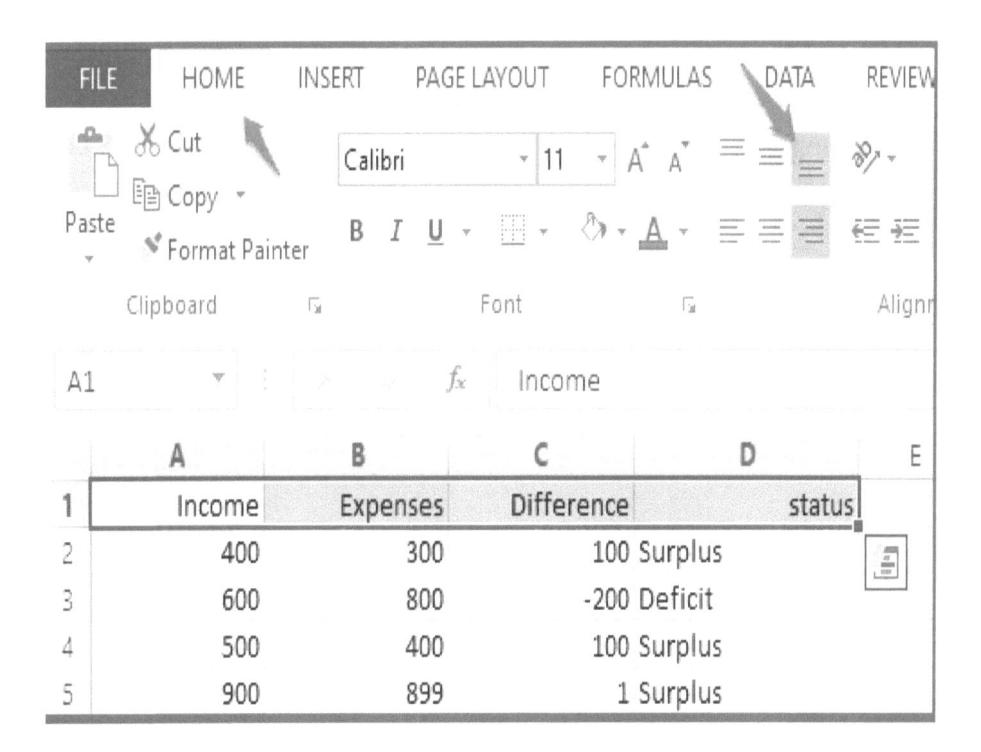

ALTERNATIVELY,

a. Tap on the **alignment group button** and pick the **format cell** button from the drop-down list.

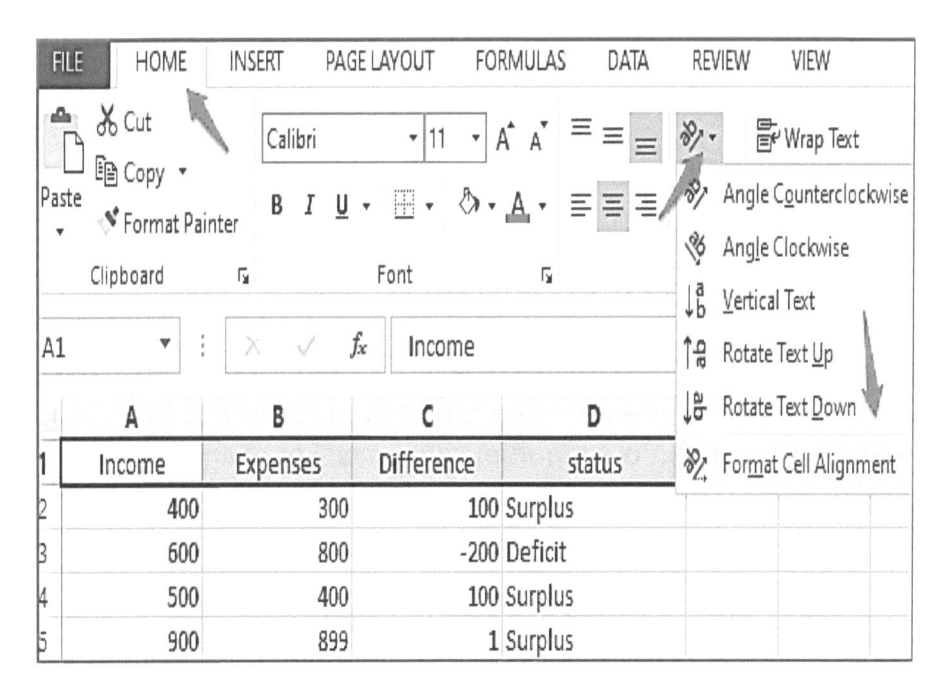

b. Tap on the **Alignment** tab inside the format cell dialog box.
c. Click on the **vertical section** and pick your desired **alignment** including justify that will fit your letter to the cell.

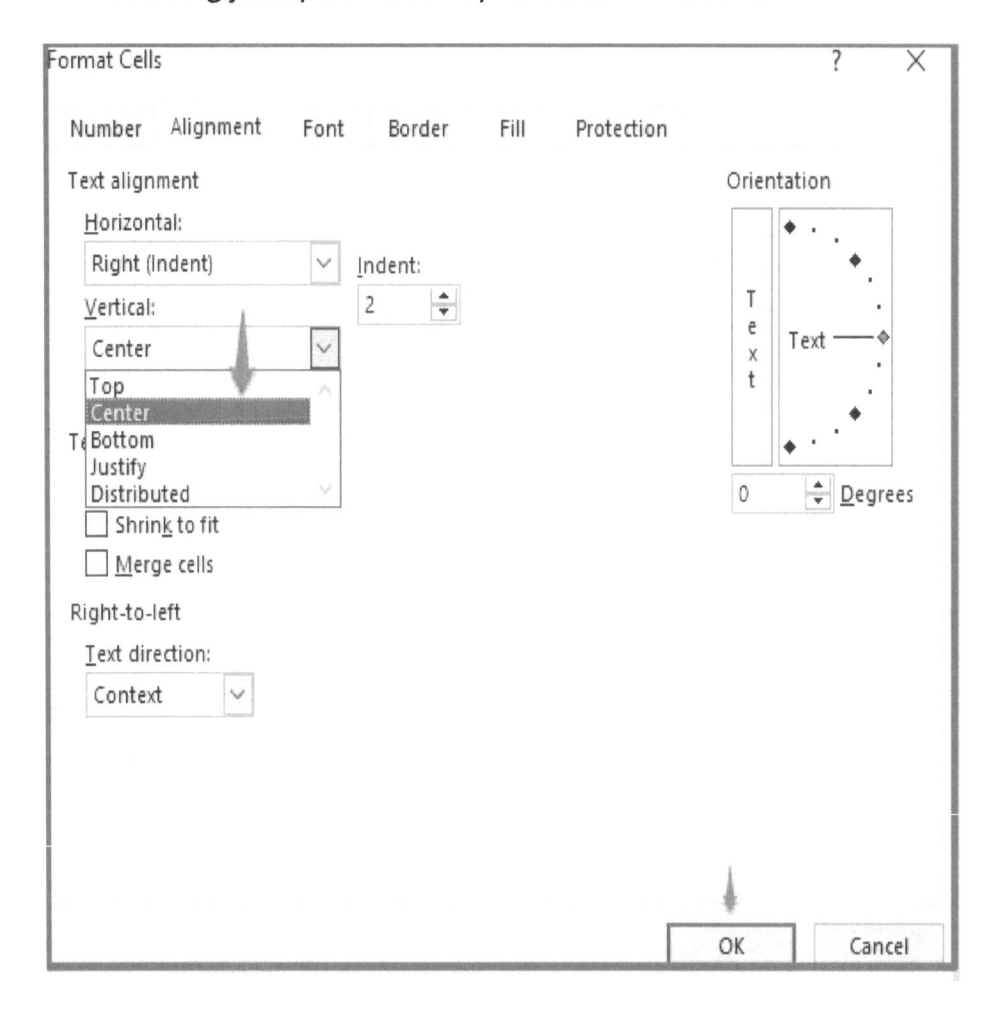

Text Merging and Centering Over Multiple Cells

Text is centered at times to show the information contained in the cell outstandingly or to create a sense of beautification. It helps you to present pieces of text over multiple columns. For example, the words "Local Government Chairman" is centered over five separate cells. To center and merge cells, do the following:

1. Drag your mouse over those cells to select them.

212

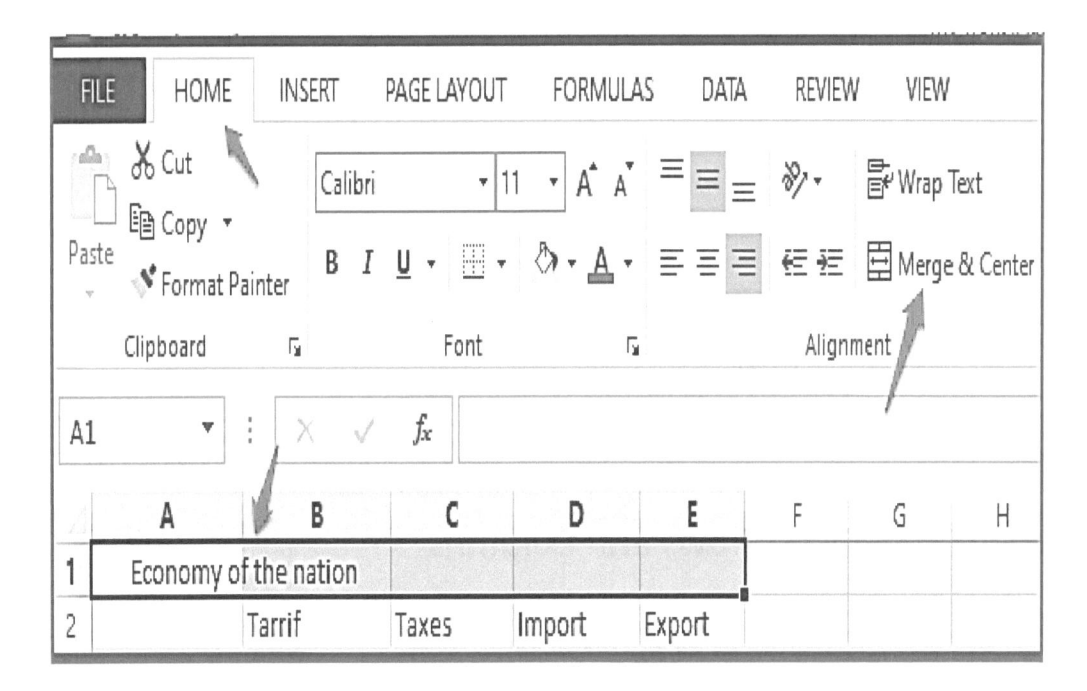

2. Maneuver to the **Home** tab, and then choose the **Merge and Center** button.

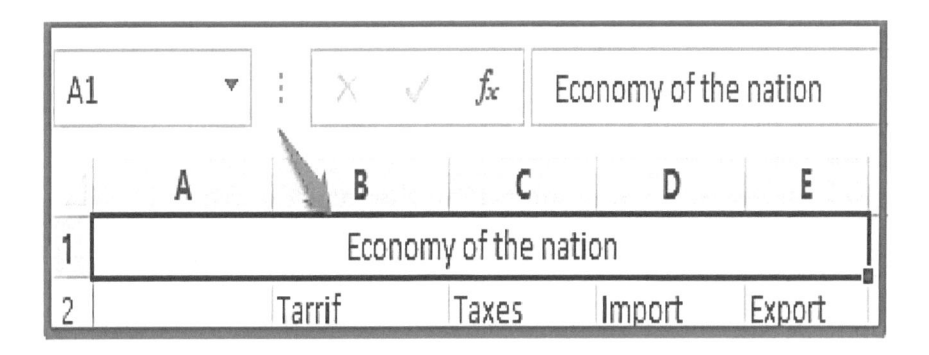

Note: when merging and centering, you will write the text to be merged in one cell, make sure the cell to its left and right side are empty; otherwise, it will be showing you that it's an error.

How do I "unmerge and uncenter" the cells that have been previously merged and centered? You can do that by following these simple steps:

 a. Click on the "**Merge & Center**" option from the **Home tab**.
 b. Pick **unmerge cells** from the "Merge & Center" drop-down list.

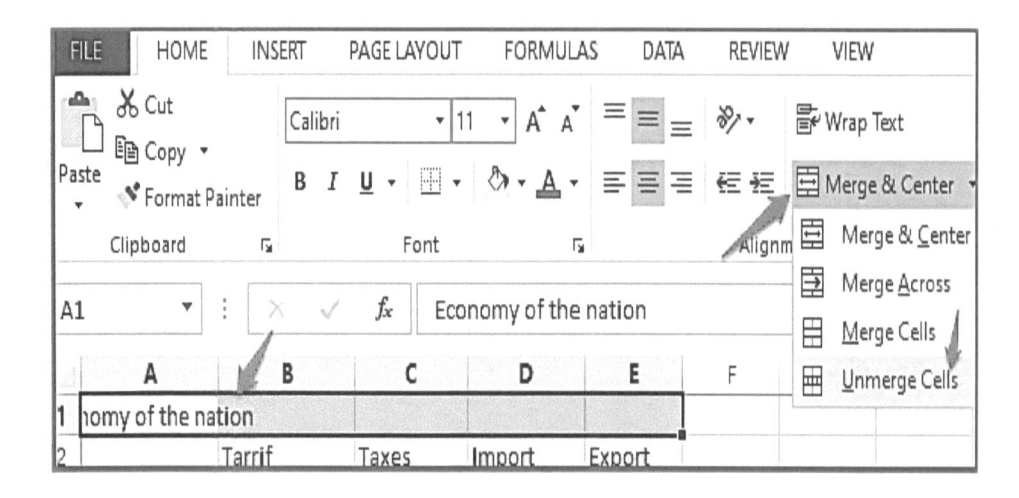

Delete and Insert Rows and Columns

There is always a motive behind deleting or inserting rows or columns, you have to insert a new row or column when you have skipped a particular heading or subject. Rows and columns are mainly deleted when they are not needed anymore.

To insert a new row, kindly do these:

a. Select **the row** that will be below the new row you are about to create.
b. Click on the **Home tab** and tap on the **Insert** button.

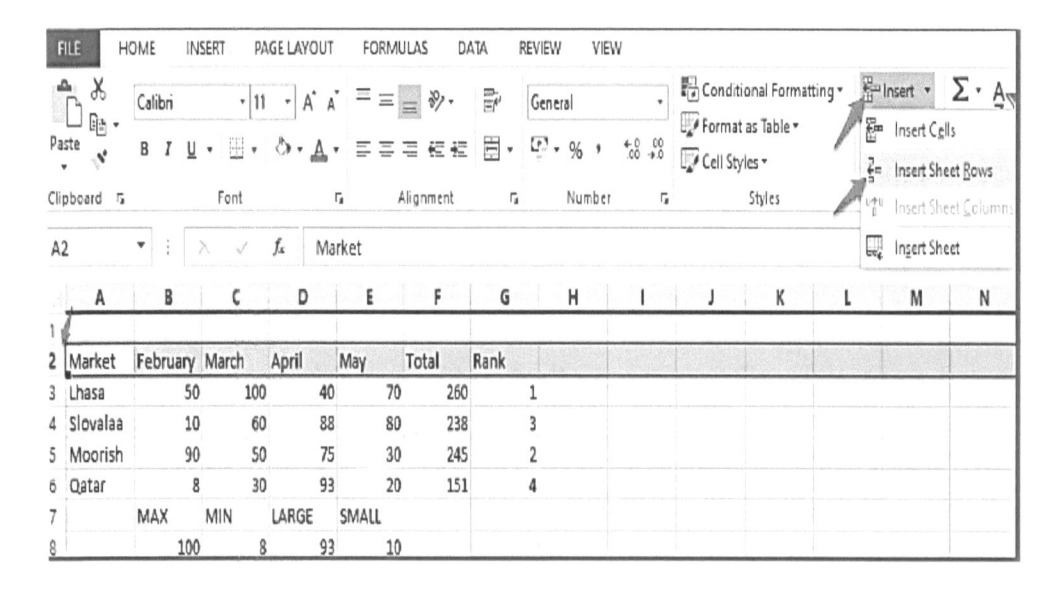

214

c. Then pick the **Insert Sheet Rows** option from the insert button drop-down menu as seen above.

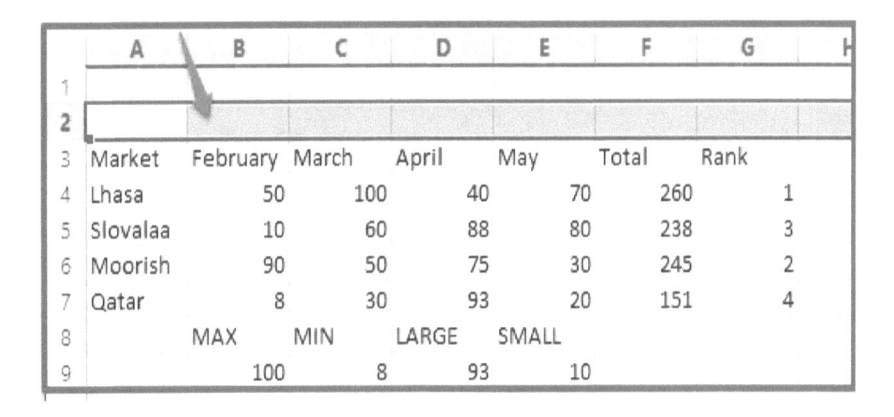

	A	B	C	D	E	F	G
1							
2							
3	Market	February	March	April	May	Total	Rank
4	Lhasa	50	100	40	70	260	1
5	Slovalaa	10	60	88	80	238	3
6	Moorish	90	50	75	30	245	2
7	Qatar	8	30	93	20	151	4
8		MAX	MIN	LARGE	SMALL		
9		100	8	93	10		

ALTERNATIVELY,

a. Right-click on **the row** which will be below the new row you want to create.
b. Pick **Insert** from the drop-down menu.

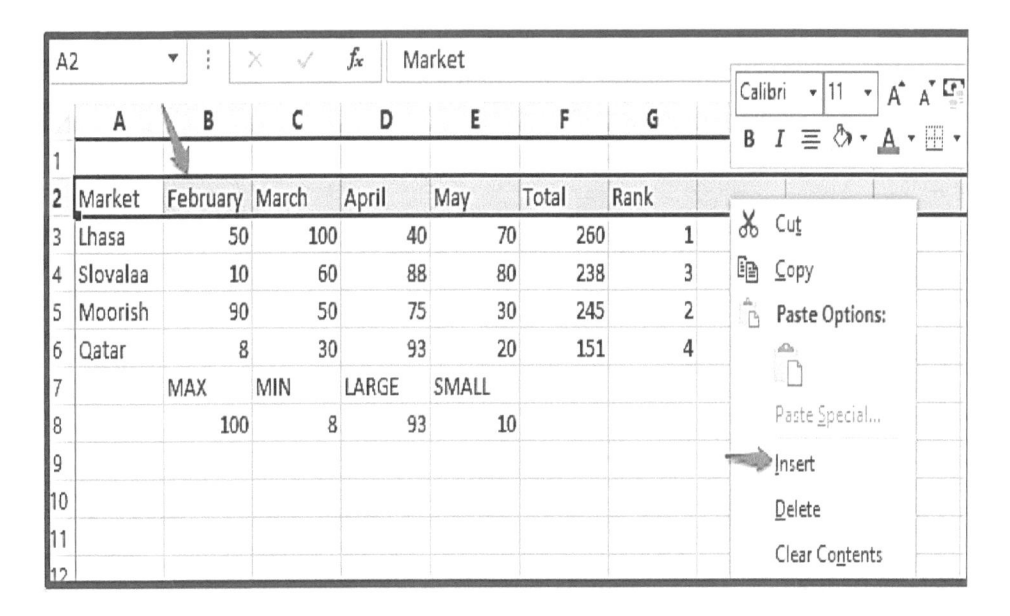

	A	B	C	D	E	F	G
1							
2	Market	February	March	April	May	Total	Rank
3	Lhasa	50	100	40	70	260	1
4	Slovalaa	10	60	88	80	238	3
5	Moorish	90	50	75	30	245	2
6	Qatar	8	30	93	20	151	4
7		MAX	MIN	LARGE	SMALL		
8		100	8	93	10		

Right-click menu options: Cut, Copy, Paste Options, Paste Special..., Insert, Delete, Clear Contents

How do you insert a column? By simply:

a. Selecting **the column** that will be to the right of the new column you want to create.

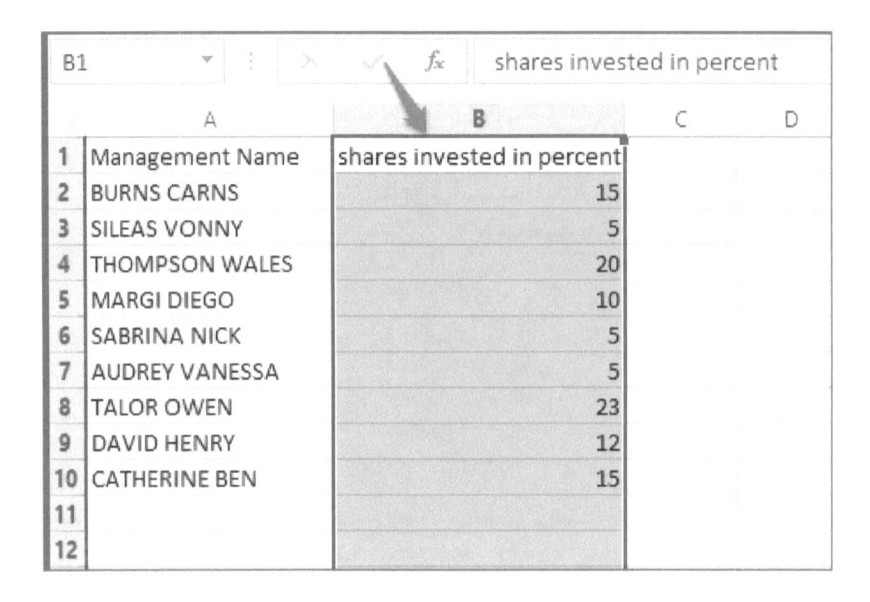

b. Click on the **Home** tab and tap on the **Insert** button.
c. Then pick the **Insert Sheet Column** option from the insert button drop-down menu.

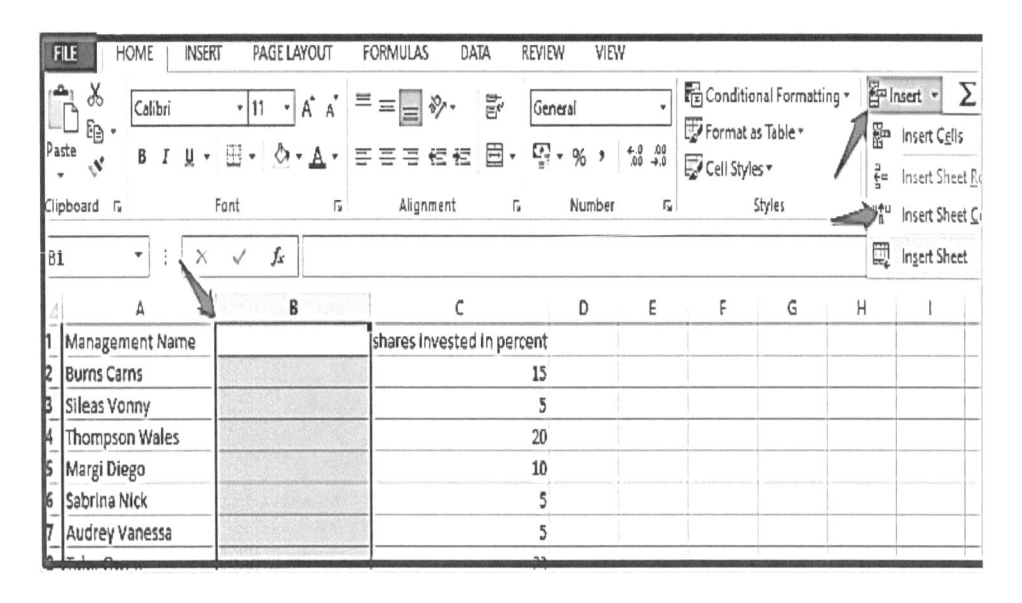

ALTERNATIVELY,

a. Right-click on **the column** which will be to the right of the new column you want to create.
b. Click on I**nsert** from the drop-down menu.

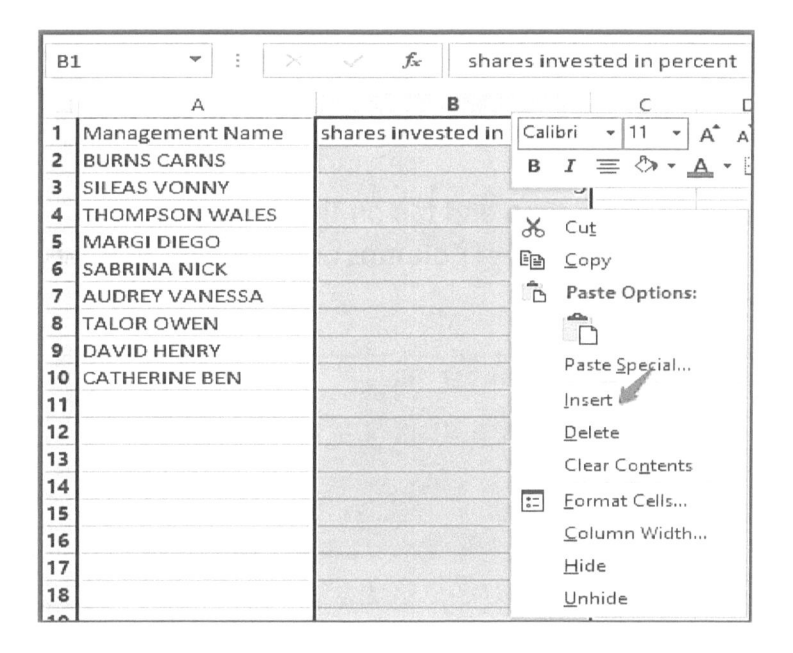

Deleting rows or columns

To delete rows or columns, you have to:

> a. Select the **row** or **column** you want to delete or you can drag over the rows and columns and then right-click over them.
> b. Pick **delete** from the drop-down list.

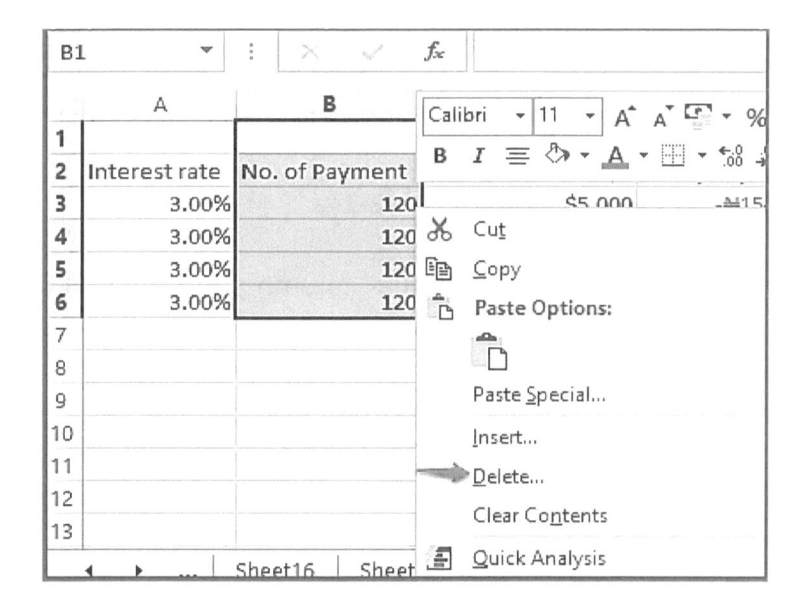

ALTERNATIVELY,

After the selection of the rows or columns to be deleted:

a. Move to the **Home** tab and tap on the **Delete** button.
b. Click on the **Delete Sheet Columns** or **Delete Sheet Rows** from the drop-down list.

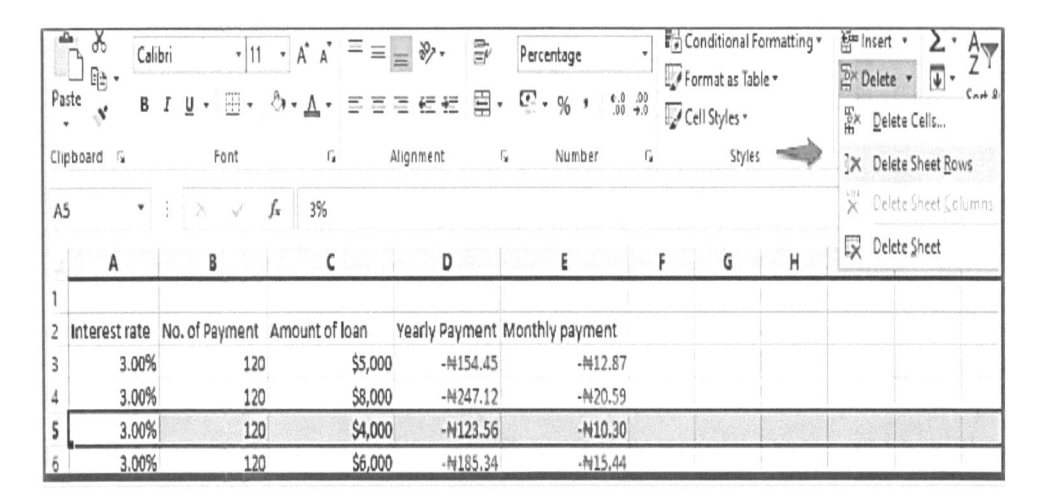

Note: you will see the Insert row and column options when are done inserting rows and columns, tap on it and pick the same format or different ones to the new columns and rows you have created from the pop-up menu.

Be careful not to delete a row that you will still later need because Immediately You Delete It, It Is Gone Forever.

Adjusting Rows and Columns Size

Excel programs the cell box (rectangular column and row box) to be 8.4 characters wide and 15 points high to column and row respectively. But at some point, Excel programming may not work when it comes to entering certain data which are wider than 8.4 in character and higher than 15points in height, as a result, Excel has made diverse preparations as a way of adjusting the sizes of columns and rows depending on what each user has to insert in the cell.

Adjusting the Height of The Rows

The following are the things to note in adjusting the height of the rows:

1. **Adjusting a single row**
    a. Click over the **row** number to select the row that needs adjustment.
    b. Place the mouse pointer into the boundary between two rows number with which the selected cell should share a boundary with.
    c. Shift the pointer a little to change the pointer to a black plus (+) sign, then double-click and drag the boundary between the rows up and down to the measurement you are looking for.

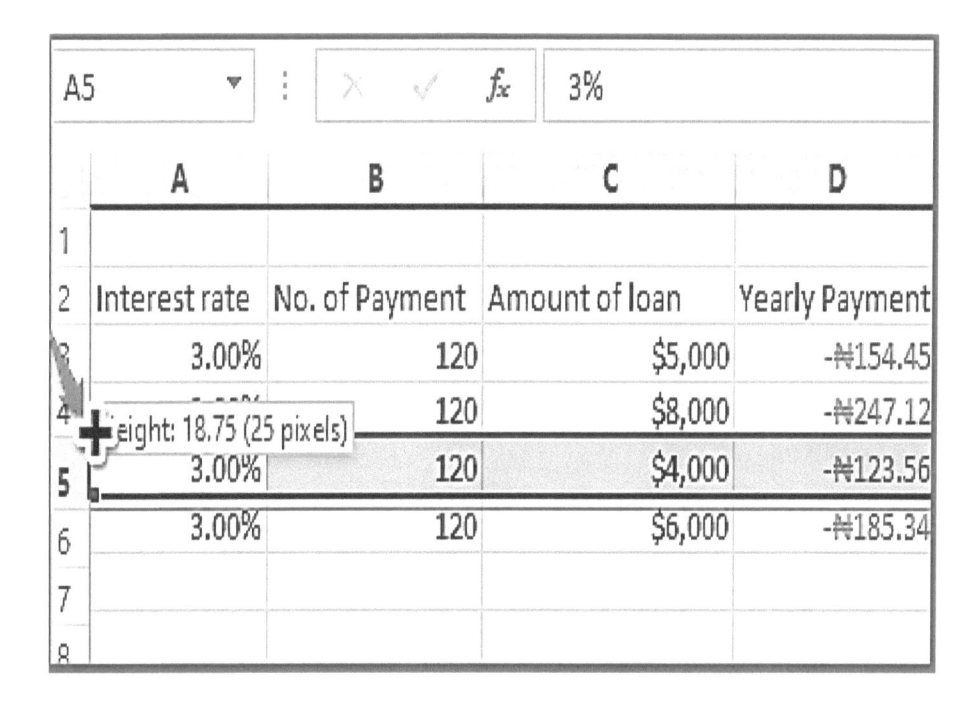

	A	B	C	D
1				
2	Interest rate	No. of Payment	Amount of loan	Yearly Payment
3	3.00%	120	$5,000	-₦154.45
4		120	$8,000	-₦247.12
5	3.00%	120	$4,000	-₦123.56
6	3.00%	120	$6,000	-₦185.34
7				

Height: 18.75 (25 pixels)

    d. As you are shifting the boundary, there will be a prompt pop-up note giving you a hint about the row height measurement you have just reached and to guide you to the measurement you are aiming to reach.

A5				fx	3%	
	A	B		C		D
1						
2	Interest rate	No. of Payment		Amount of loan		Yearly Payment
3	3.00%	120		$5,000		-₦154.45
4	Height: 18.75 (25 pixels)	120		$8,000		-₦247.12
5	3.00%	120		$4,000		-₦123.56
6	3.00%	120		$6,000		-₦185.34
7						
8						

e. Then release the mouse button after you double-click to complete the process.

2. **Adjusting Multiple rows height at once:**
   a. Click on the **multiple rows** you want to adjust or drag over them for selection.

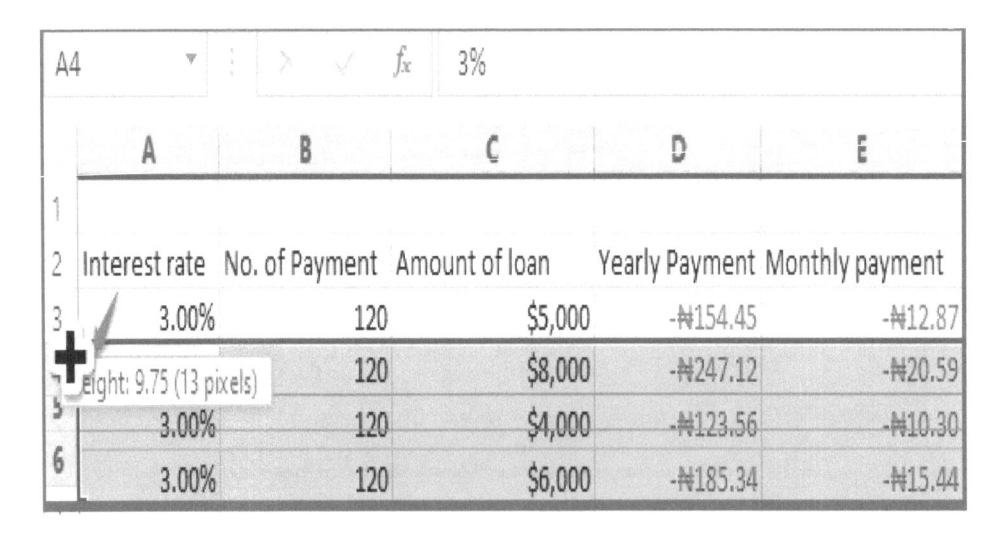

A4				fx	3%		
	A	B		C		D	E
1							
2	Interest rate	No. of Payment		Amount of loan		Yearly Payment	Monthly payment
3	3.00%	120		$5,000		-₦154.45	-₦12.87
4	Height: 9.75 (13 pixels)	120		$8,000		-₦247.12	-₦20.59
5	3.00%	120		$4,000		-₦123.56	-₦10.30
6	3.00%	120		$6,000		-₦185.34	-₦15.44

b. Then double-click and drag the boundary between one of the selected cells and all the other rows selected with it will be adjusted to the new measurement. Immediately, release the mouse after the double-clicking.

ALTERNATIVELY,

    a. Maneuver to the **Home** tab and tap on the **Format** button.

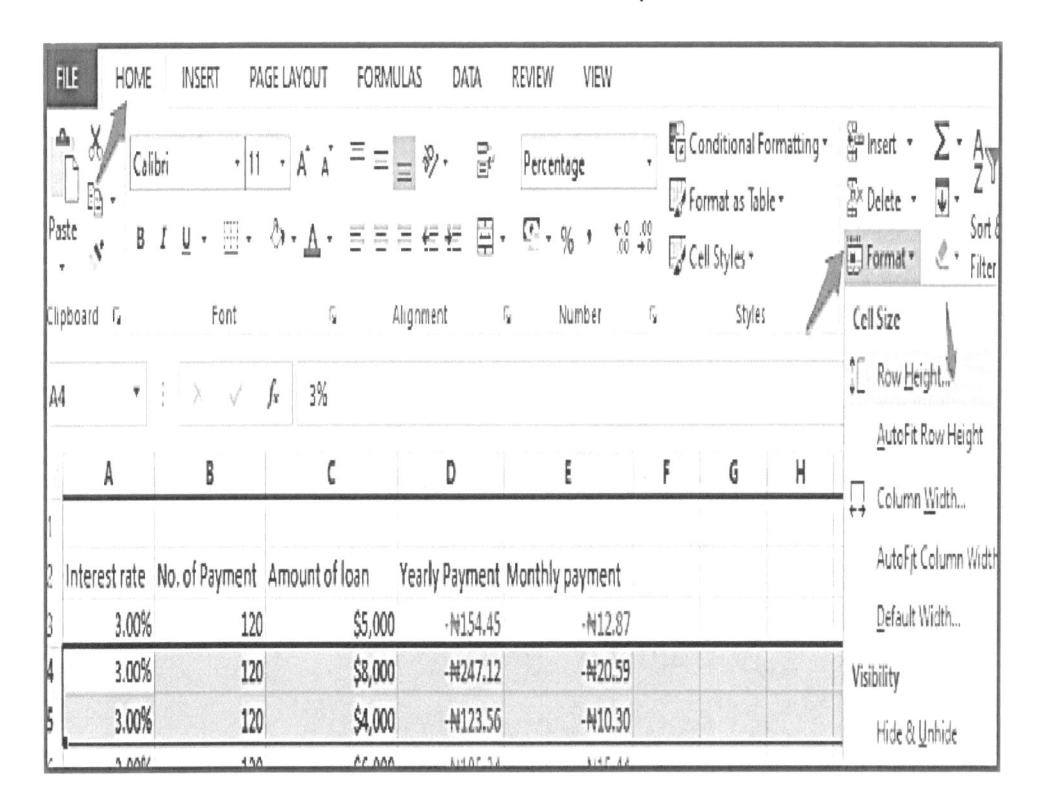

    b. Select the **Row Height** option, and then insert the **row height** you prefer in the Row Height dialog box.

3. **Adjusting cell entry to Autofit the row height:**
   You can adjust your row height automatically to make the data entry fit inside the cell accurately and so that row size will contain the data entry appropriately. Adjust your row height to fit in your data entry by:

   a. Moving to the **Home** tab and tap on the **Format** button.

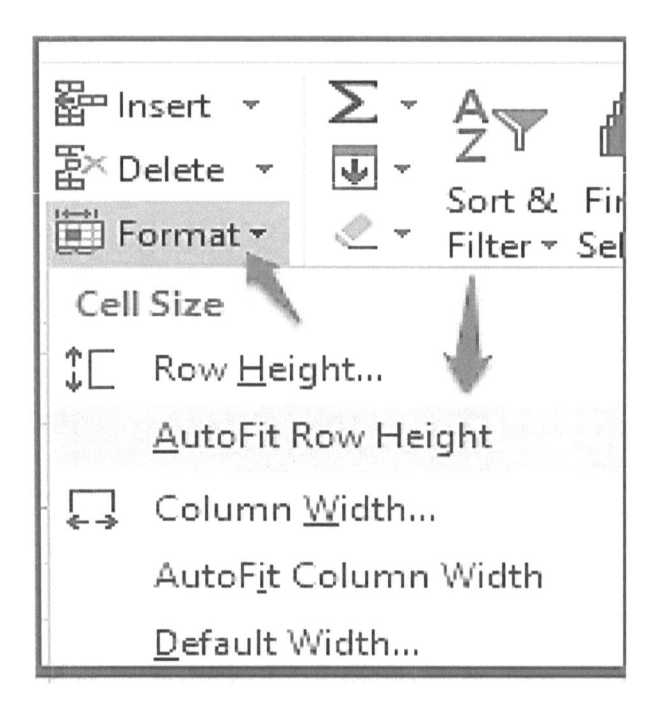

   b. Then choose **AutoFit Row Height.**

Adjusting the Column Width

To adjust the column width, below are the steps.

1. **Adjusting a single column:**
    a. Select **the column** to be adjusted.
    b. Place the mouse pointer into the boundary between two column letters with which the selected cell shares a boundary with.
    c. Shift the pointer a little to change the pointer to a black plus (+) sign, then double-click and drag the boundary between the columns up and down to the measurement you are looking for.

	A	B	C	D
1				
2	Interest rate	No. of Payment	Amount of loan	Yearly Payment
3	3.00%	120	$5,000	-₦154.45
4	3.00%	120	$8,000	-₦247.12
5	3.00%	120	$4,000	-₦123.56
6	3.00%	120	$6,000	-₦185.34
7				

Width: 17.86 (130 pixels)

   d. As you are shifting the boundary, there will be a prompt pop-up note giving you a hint about the column width measurement you have just reached and to guide you to the measurement you are aiming to reach.
   e. Then release the mouse after double-clicking to complete the process.
2. **Adjusting multiple columns:**
    a. Click on the **multiple columns** you want to adjust or drag over them for selection.

b. Then double-click and drag the boundary between one of the selected cells and all other columns selected with it will be adjusted to the new measurement immediately you release the mouse after double-clicking it also.

	A	B	C	D	E
1					
2	Interest rate	No. of Payment	Amount of loan	Yearly Payment	Monthly payment
3	3.00%	120	$5,000	-₦154.45	-₦12.87
4	3.00%	120	$8,000	-₦247.12	-₦20.59
5	3.00%	120	$4,000	-₦123.56	-₦10.30
6	3.00%	120	$6,000	-₦185.34	-₦15.44
7					

ALTERNATIVELY,

a. Maneuver to the **Home** tab, and tap on the **Format** button.
b. Select the **Column Width** button, and then insert the column width you prefer in the Column dialog box.

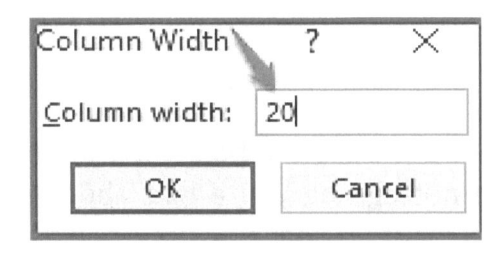

3. **Adjusting cell entry to Autofit the column width:**
You can adjust the width of your columns automatically to make the data entry fit inside the column accurately and so that the column size will contain data entries appropriately. Adjust your column width to make data entry fit into it, by:
- Moving to the **Home** tab and tap on the **Format** button.

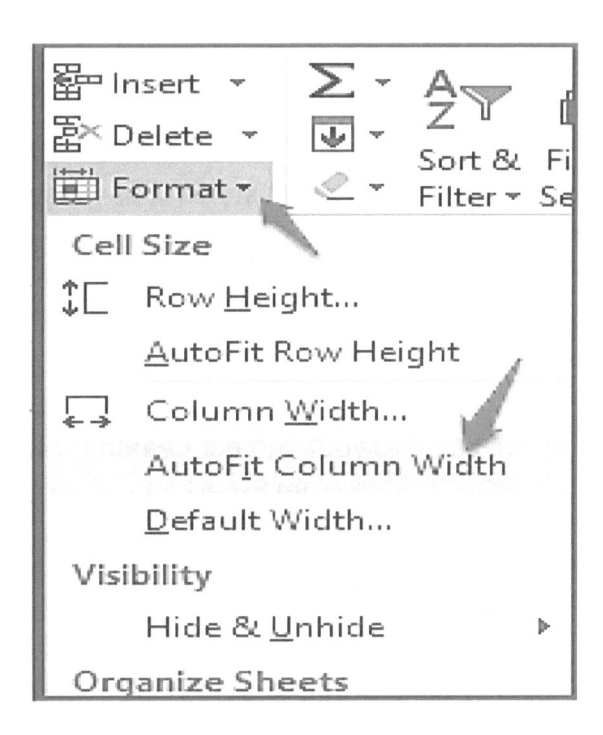

- Then choose the **AutoFit Column Width.**

Furnishing A Worksheet with Borders and Colors

Worksheet cell is arranged in a gridline format. The gridline is mainly for proper arrangement of your Excel work and thus, when you print Excel work, the grid background will not reflect. Nevertheless, if you prefer that your Excel work should look more presentable and meaningful, you must create something creative within the area of your Excel work, particularly an area that catches the reader's attention such as column heading, aggregate heading, and other essential parts. At the same time, it is of utmost importance to use color to decorate the background of your Excel work to add more life to your work.

Quick Way of Formatting Worksheet with Cell Style

Formatting simply means the appearance of things to make it better. For instance, formatting a worksheet is a way of changing its appearance for better improvement such as text, color, and drawing a table to surround your cells. The most pressing thing about formatting is that the look and appearances you desire can come out in a jiffy with a little process. It does not take much time, and indeed it is a quick way of formatting a worksheet. There are two ways to format the worksheet either by choosing from thousands of built-in cell styles that comes with Excel or by customizing your cell style to suit your taste.

Making Use of Excel Built-In Cell Style

With Excel built-in cell style, you have limitless access to the collection of cell styles which you can apply to your subject headings or title to capture the attention of the reader. To pick from Excel cell style collection, simply:

a. Choose the **cells** to be formatted.
b. Move to the **Home** tab and tap on the **Cell style** button, to make the cell style collection open.
c. Pick a preferred cell style from the available collection of cell styles to add value to your Excel work.

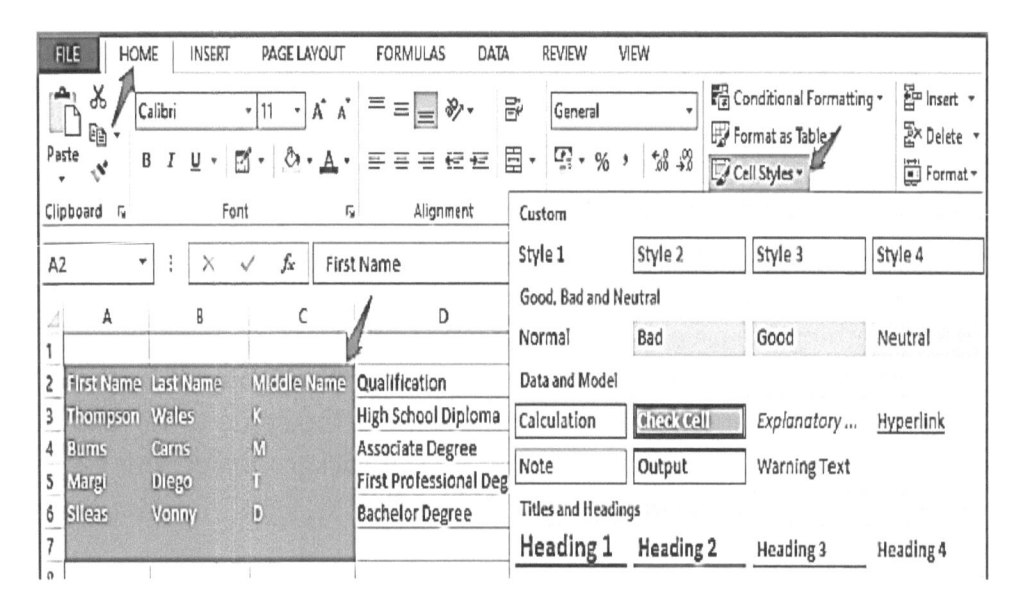

How can I remove cell style from the cell? By:

a. Selecting the cells with the formatting effect and move to the **Home** tab and tap on the **Cell style** button to make the cell style collection open.

226

b. Pick the **Normal** style from the available collection (the Normal style is under the group of good, bad, neutral, and normal).

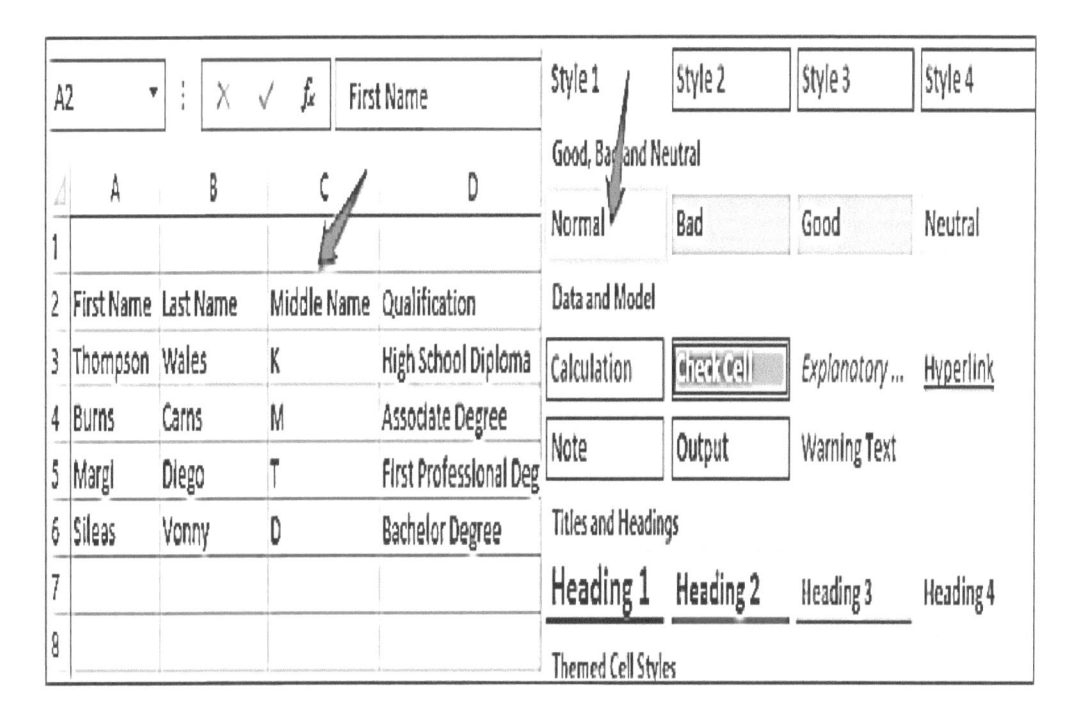

Customizing Your Cell Style

Excel allows for skill development and thus, it grants every user who is innovative an opportunity of building their cell style to suit their personalities. The cell style name you created will be on top of the cell collection under a customized heading for easy identification. To create your style, do the following:

a. Choose the formatting type you prefer for your style in a single cell, such as change case, change font, center alignment or middle alignment, and so on.
b. Move to the **Home** tab and click on the **Cell style** button, then choose the **New Cell Style** option as seen below from the drop-down of **Cell Styles** collection.

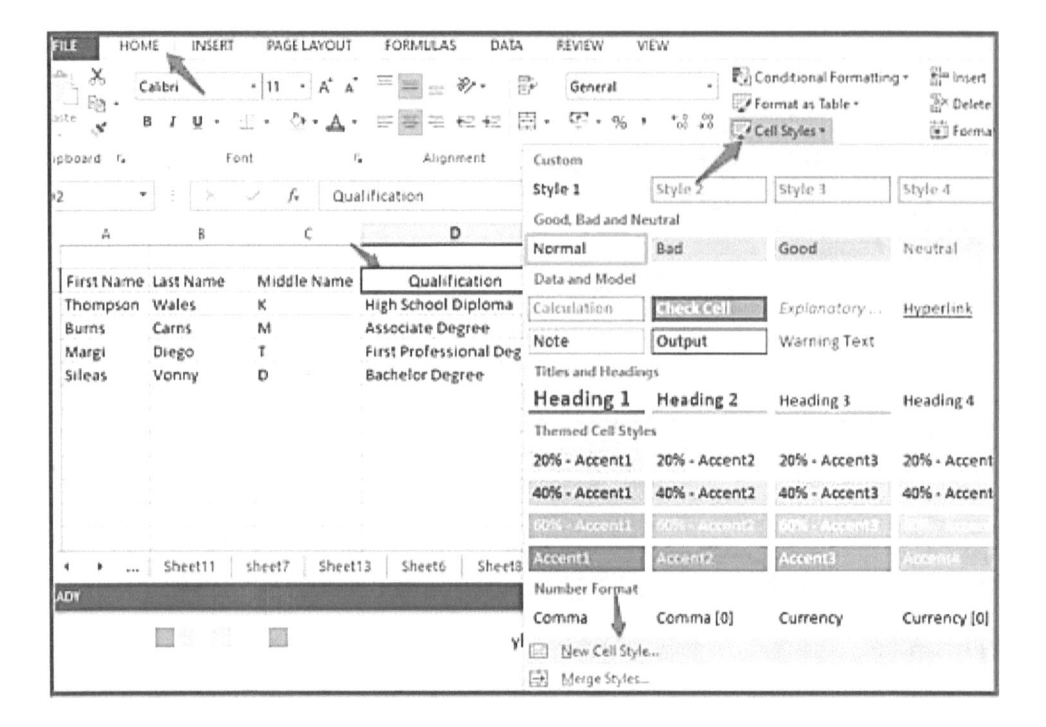

c. The Style dialog box will come forth with the style specification you entered at (a) above, if you wish to change that specification again, you can click on the **format** button to restructure the format at the upper right side of the dialog box.

d. Insert a brief and meaningful name to the style in the Name text box above for your style and tap **Ok**.

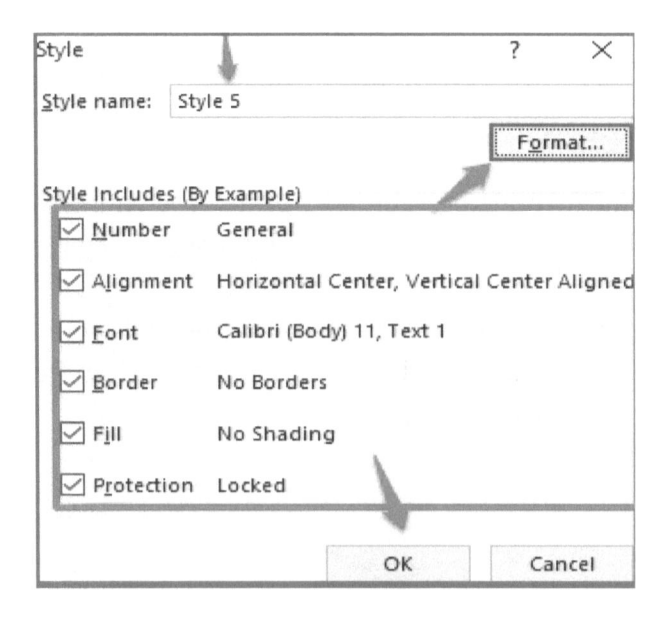

Note: you can remove the manual cell style you created by right-clicking on the name in the cell style collection box and choose the **Delete** option from the drop-down list.

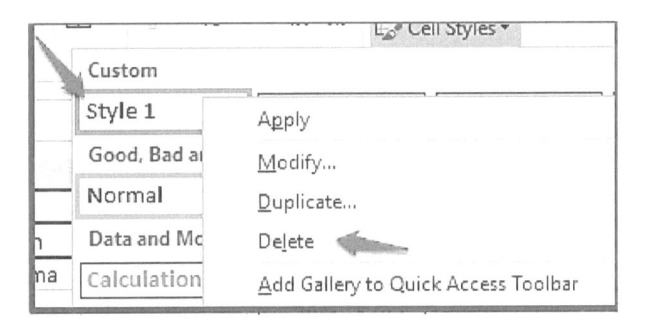

Using Table Style to Format A Cell

Table styles are used to add more decoration to the worksheet data; it gives more neatness and value to the contents inside the cells by creating a wall around them. Check the below steps to explore table style in Excels:

a. Choose the **cells** you want to add table style to.
b. Move to the **Home** tab and click on the **"Format as Table"** button.
c. Then navigate to pick a **table style** from the collection of table styles from the "Format as table" drop-down options.

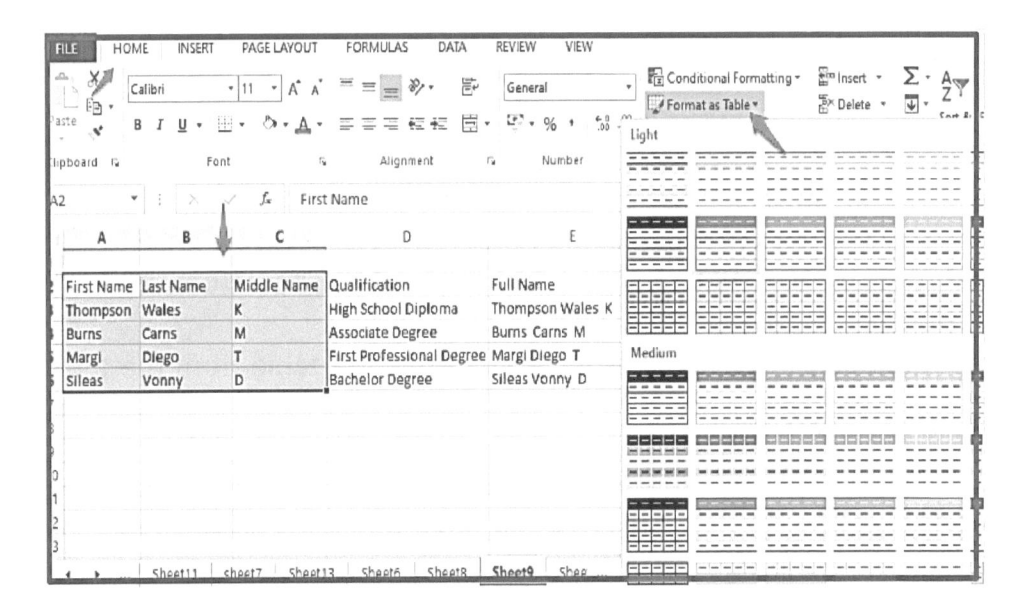

d. Immediately you pick one, you will see a small table style dialog box, tick **"My table headers"** if you have header, label, or title at the top of the column.

```
Format As Table                              ?    X
Where is the data for your table?
   =$A$2:$C$6
   ☑ My table has headers
              OK              Cancel
```

e. Tap **Ok** in the "Format as table" dialog box.

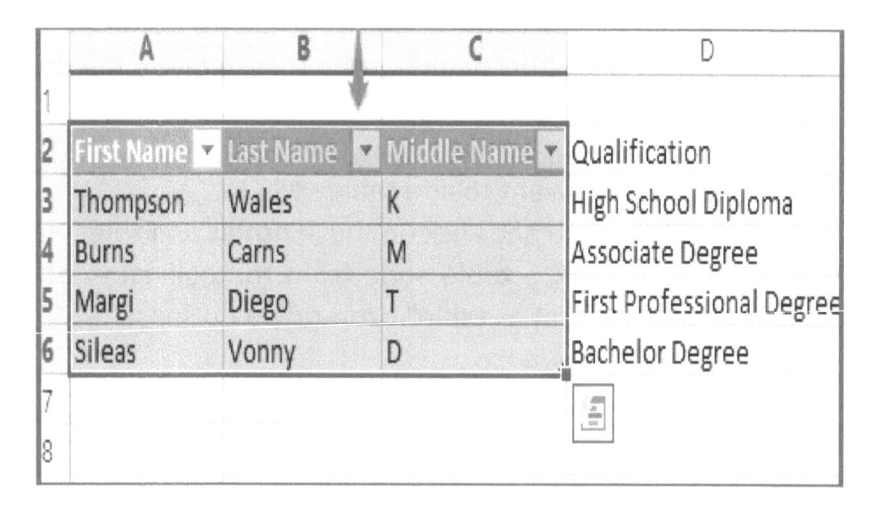

	A	B	C	D
1				
2	First Name	Last Name	Middle Name	Qualification
3	Thompson	Wales	K	High School Diploma
4	Burns	Carns	M	Associate Degree
5	Margi	Diego	T	First Professional Degree
6	Sileas	Vonny	D	Bachelor Degree
7				
8				

Note: you can improve the design of the table by:

a. Clicking on the **quick style** option or the **table tool** from the Table design.
b. Then select **"More Designs"** to improve the table from the table tool drop-down styles.

You can as well get the table removed from the quick style or table tool as well by moving to the bottom of the table tool and choose **"Clear"** in the table style collection.

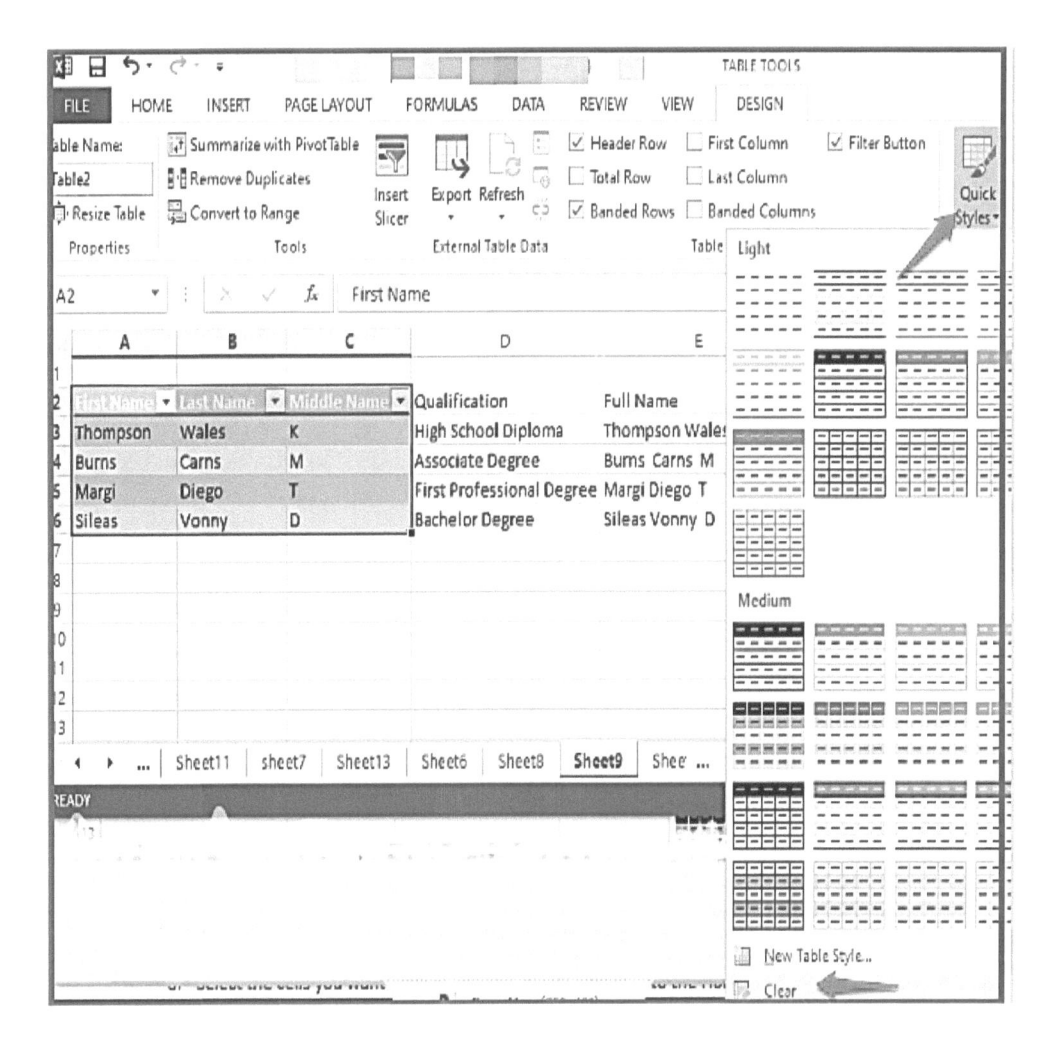

Creating Border on The Worksheet Cells

Borders are the lines that you can use to create a distinct zone between worksheet data and a specific area of worksheet that calls for special attention than the other data. Borders are used to give those items special attention, so that decision can be made with those values rather than glancing through the whole worksheet data. For instance, putting a borderline below the column data for totaling the data item gives the reader and user a hint of the peculiarities of that area because decision can be made quickly with those distinct zones. Are you confused on how to draw the border on your worksheet, okay, no problem; we have you covered with this one-on-one process:

Create the border using the Format cell dialog box:

a. Select the **cells** you want to draw a border around and move to the **Home** tab to select the **Format** button.
b. Then select the **Format Cells** options from the Format button drop-down list to open the Format cell dialog box.

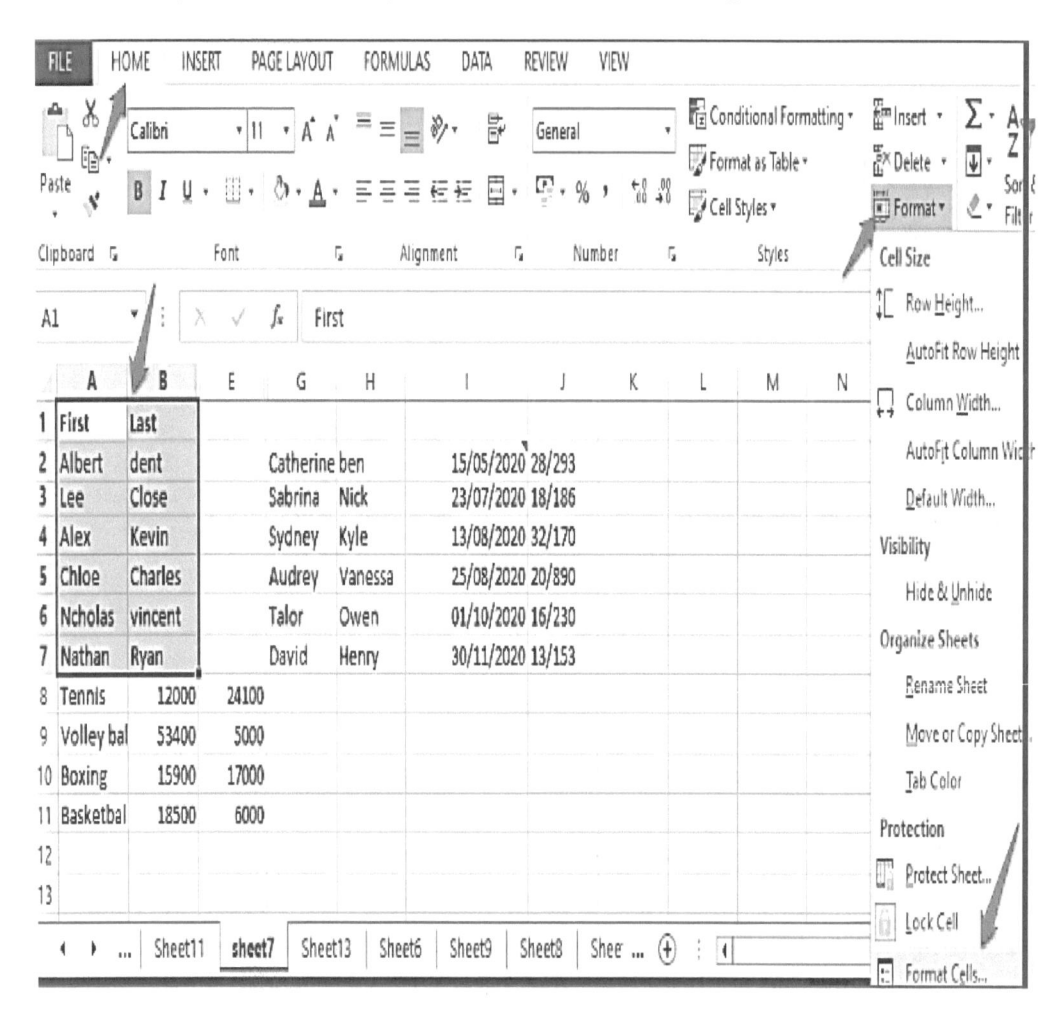

c. Tap on the **borders** tab inside the Format cell dialog box and select a border style for the cells you have selected in (a) above.
d. Click on the **"Preset"** button to show the preview of the border you chose and for the border to be reflected in the worksheet.

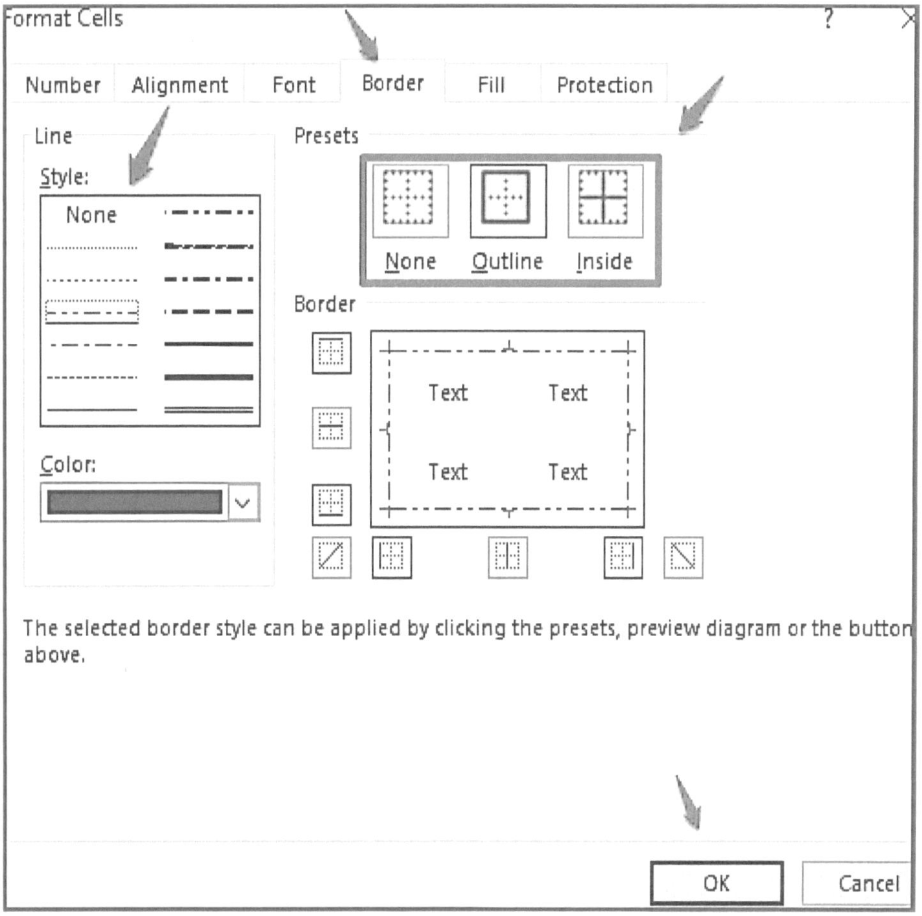
Format Cells
Number
Alignment
Font
Border
Fill
Protection
Line
Style:
None
Color:
Presets
None
Outline
Inside
Border
Text
Text
Text
Text
The selected border style can be applied by clicking the presets, preview diagram or the button above.
OK
Cancel

Note: border gives you the chance to use varieties of lines and colors for border, which makes it worthwhile.

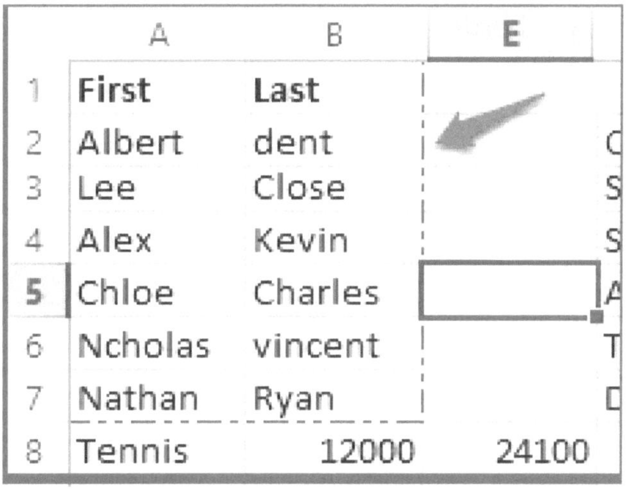
A
B
E
1 First Last
2 Albert dent
3 Lee Close
4 Alex Kevin
5 Chloe Charles
6 Ncholas vincent
7 Nathan Ryan
8 Tennis 12000 24100

Using drawing to add a border to the worksheet:

a. Moving to the **Home** tab and click on the **Border** button.
b. You can either choose **Border or Border Grid** from the border button drop-down list.

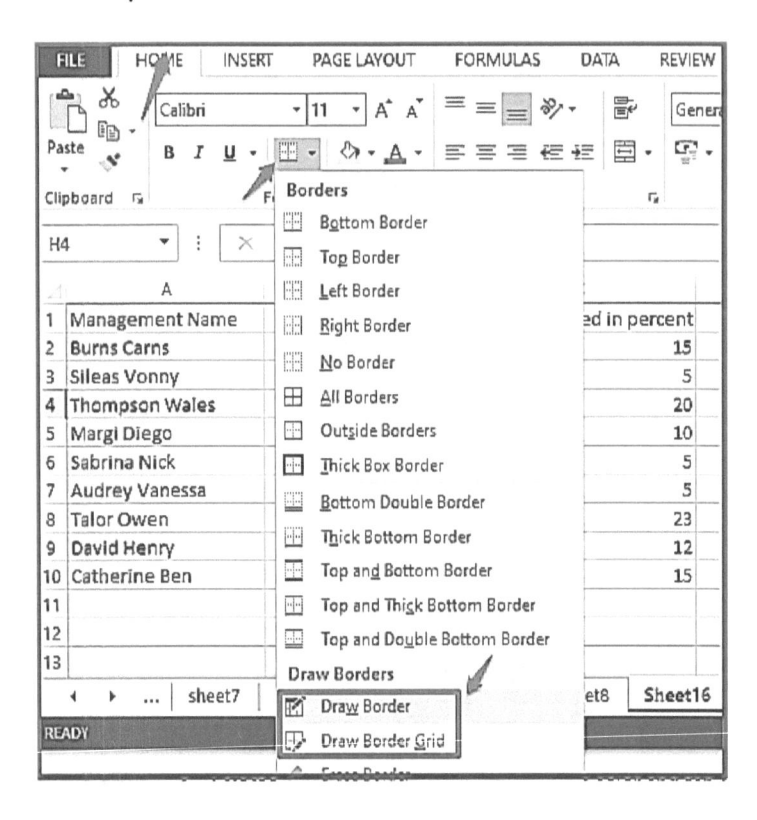

c. Before you draw the border, you can pick the **border style and color** from the border button drop-down list.

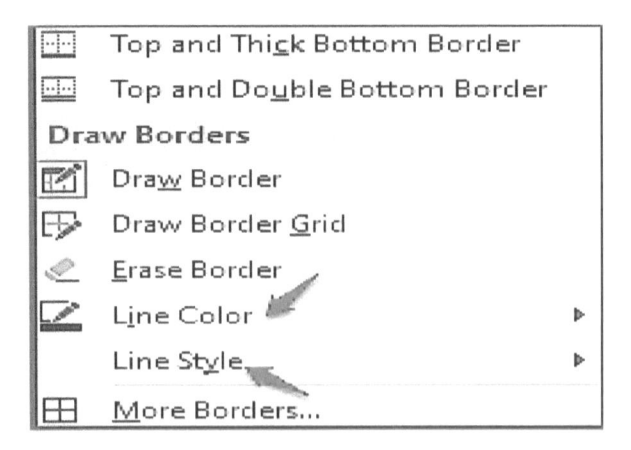

d. Then drag over to the position where you want to see your border. As soon as you are done with the border, tap on **Esc** to release the border pen.

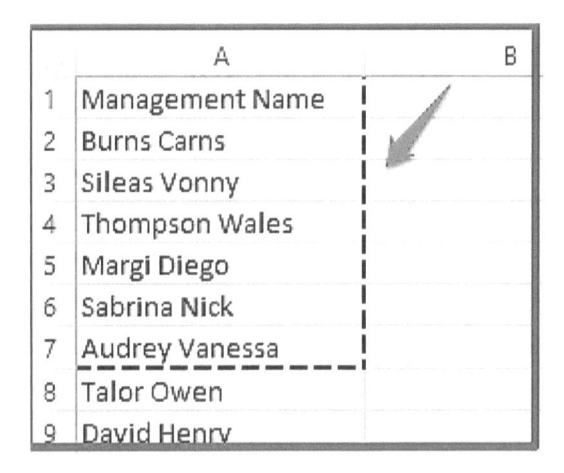

Note: You can remove the border from the cells. This can be done by:

a. Selecting the cells with border, from the **Home** tab, tap on **Border**
b. Then choose the **No Border** option from the border button drop-down list.

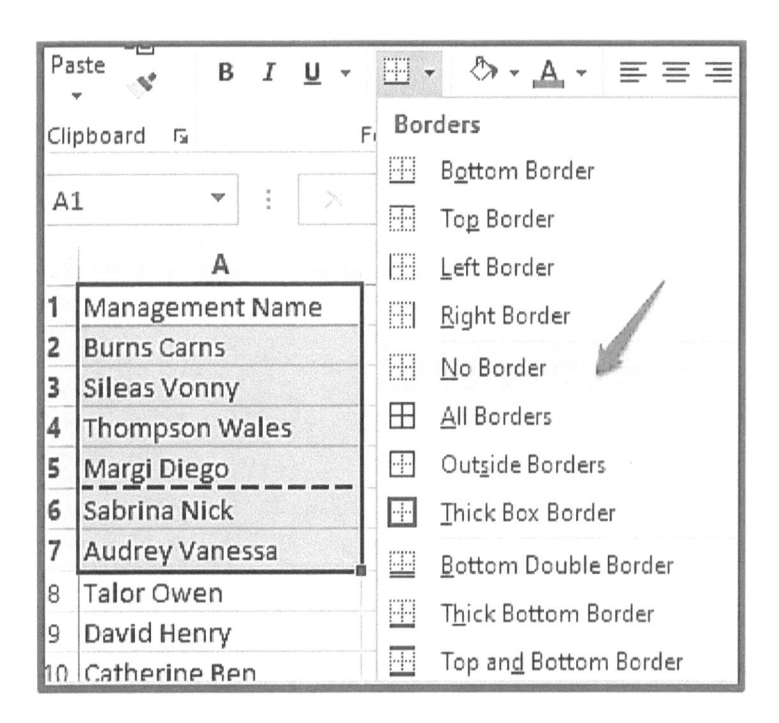

Colorize Your Worksheet

Colors add value and life to an object. Excel color is used to improve the Excel background to entice the interest of the reader to review it. When you are adding color to the worksheet, you have to pick a nice color, some colors are too harsh, do not pick such. To add color to Excel background, do the following:

a. Select **the cells** where you want to put the color and tap on the **Format** button.
b. Choose **Format cell** from the format button drop-down list and the format cell dialog box will come forth.

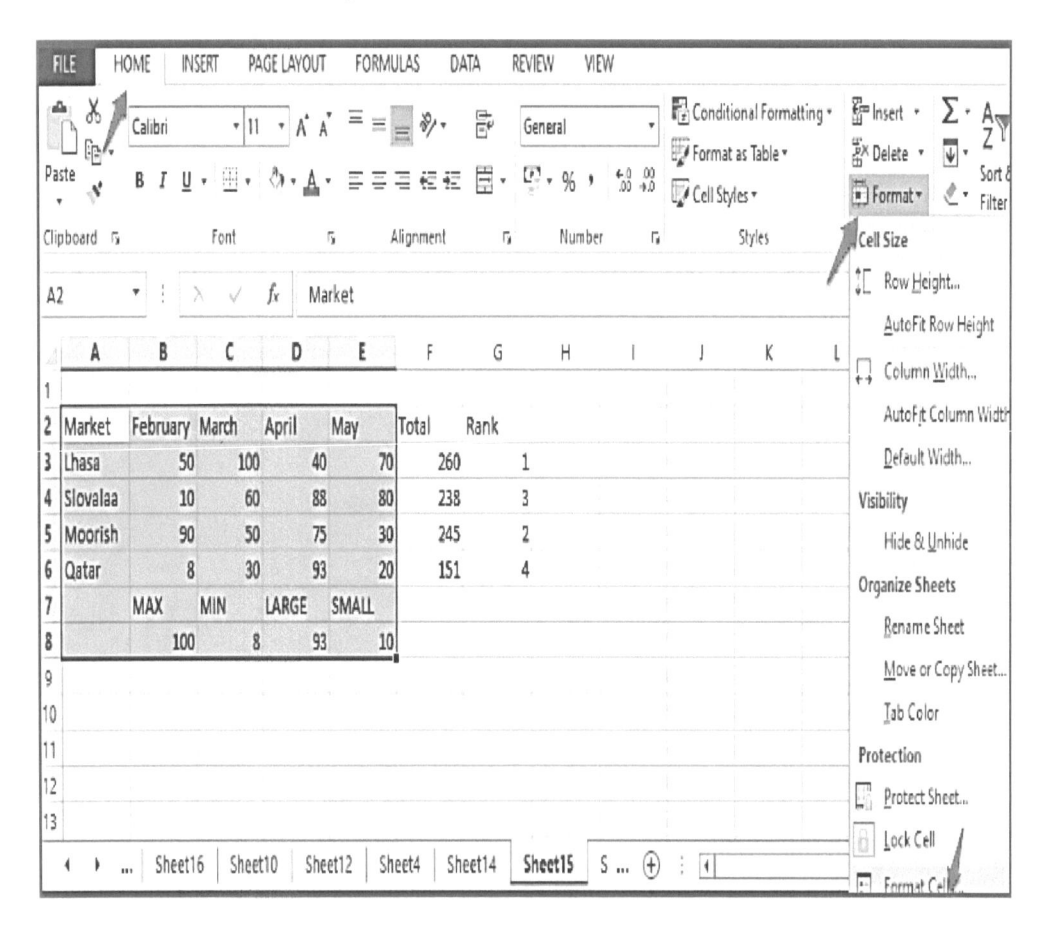

c. Select the **Fill** bar from the Format cell dialog box and choose an appropriate color from the collection, then click on **Ok**.

236

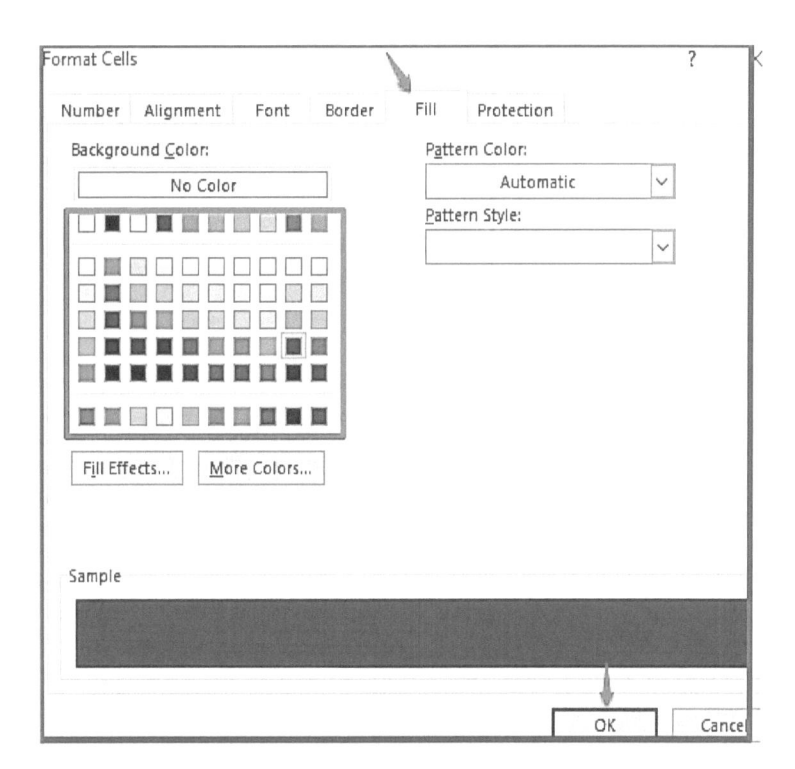

Be Prepared to Print A Worksheet

You have to prepare yourself ahead of printing a worksheet, don't just press Ctrl + P to print anyhow, there are certain steps to follow before you eventually print so that you will not end up printing what you do not want to print. The first process of printing is to check if the worksheet is rightly arranged on a single page so that you will not have a page break and end up printing a half page. To do that, you have to check these two sides of the worksheet (the bottom and right side of the worksheet) to confirm if the contents you are about to print is rightfully set very well.

Setting Up A Worksheet to Fit the Page

Setting up a worksheet to fit the page for printing is very expedient so that you will not end up printing what you do not expect. Excel starts its printing from the first column and first row (A1) to the last cell with data to the right side. To avoid page break of any kind and printing the actual document without wasting paper resources, you have to take worksheet page set-up with seriousness.

Note: before you click on print, check the **page layout** of your worksheet by clicking on the **View** button and tap on both **page layout** and **page break preview** to see the glance of what you are about to print.

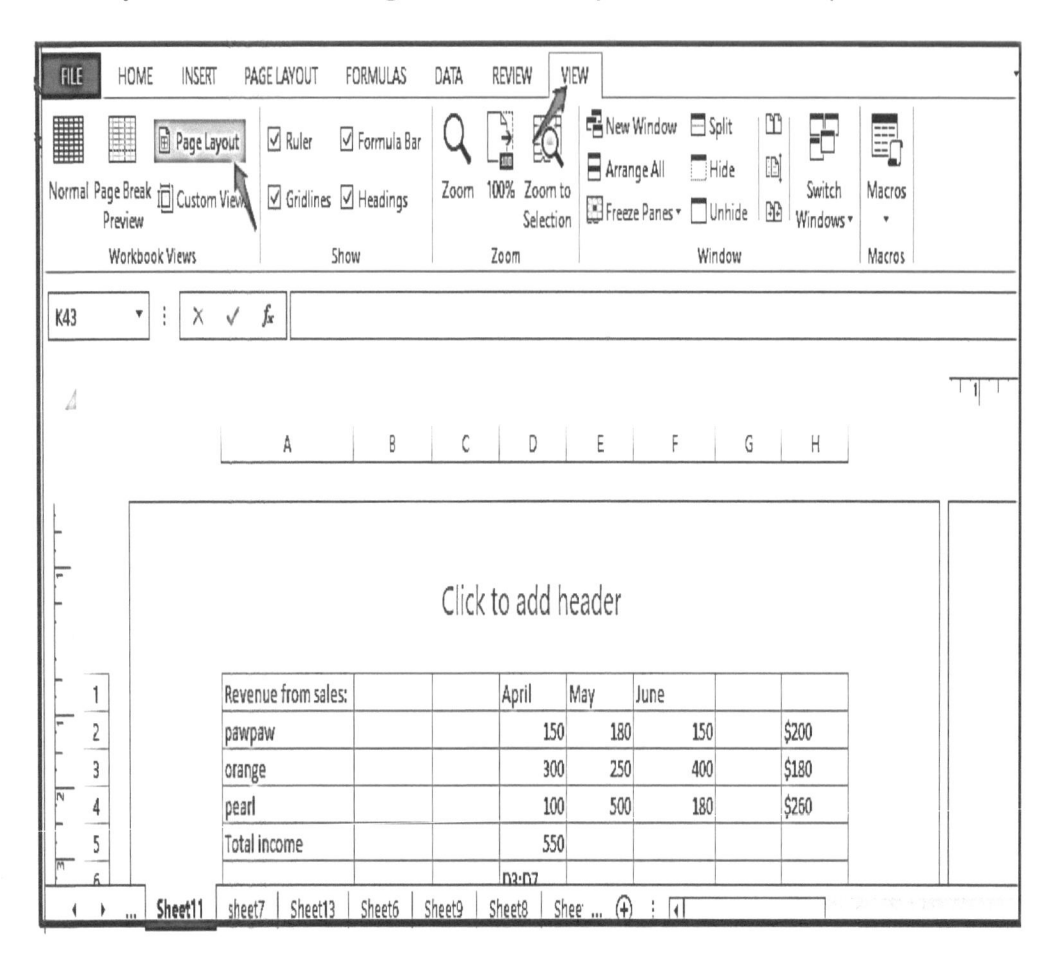

Printing section of the worksheet: you do not have to print the whole worksheet; you only have to print the useful part with contents that you need. To print a section of the worksheet, kindly:

a. Select **the cells** you want to print and move to the **Page Layout** tab.
b. Click on the **"Print Area"** button and select **"Set Print Area"** from the drop-down menu, and Excel will be authorized to print the only selected area.

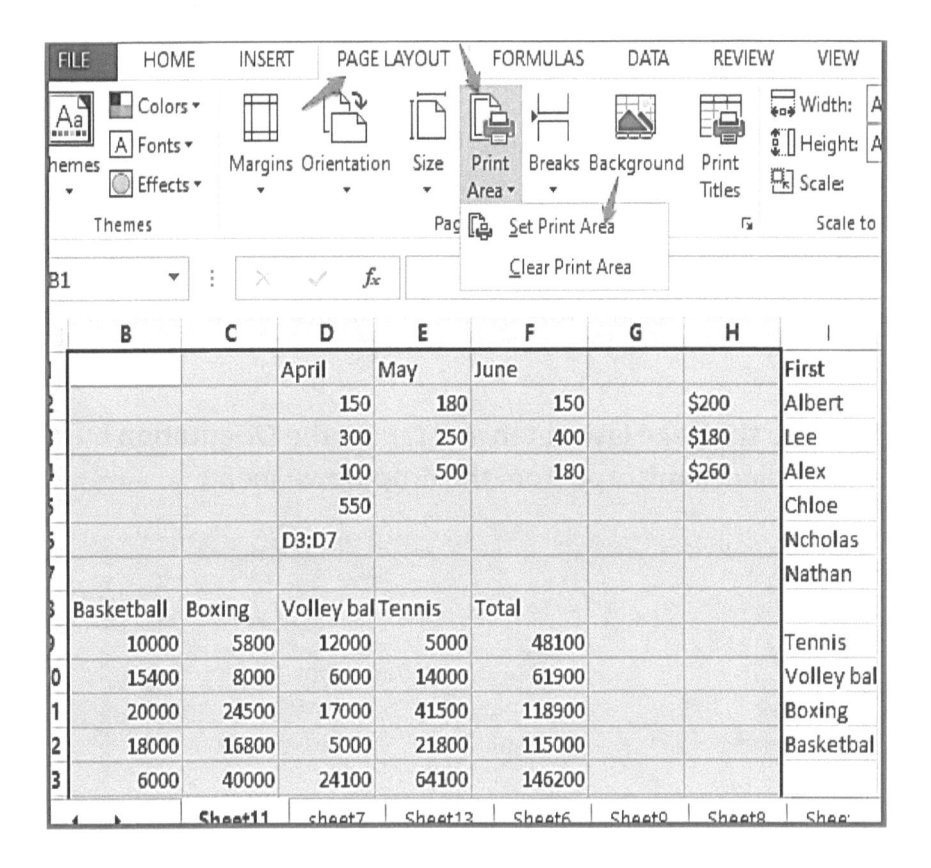

c. If you check your worksheet, you will notice an appearance of the box around the area you have selected for printing giving you an indication of the area you want to print.

Note: if you do not like to print the cells you have selected again, you can remove it by choosing "**Clear Print Area**" from the **"Print Area Button"** drop-down list.

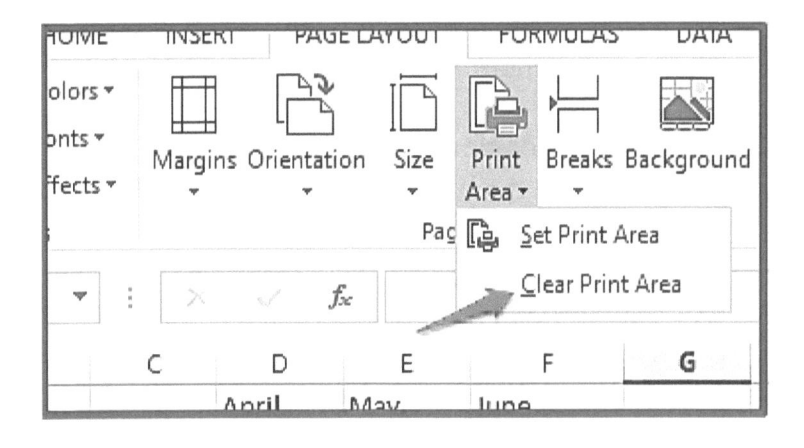

Printing a landscape worksheet:

The landscape is a horizontal printing, Excel users switch to landscape any time they perceive that the worksheet is too wide more than what portrait can accommodate. The beauty of landscape printing is that it permits Excel users to print a worksheet with a wider coverage which is not feasible with portrait printing. Print in a landscape format by simply doing these:

a. Move to the **page layout** tab and tap on the **Orientation button.**
b. Then, select **landscape** from the drop-down menu.

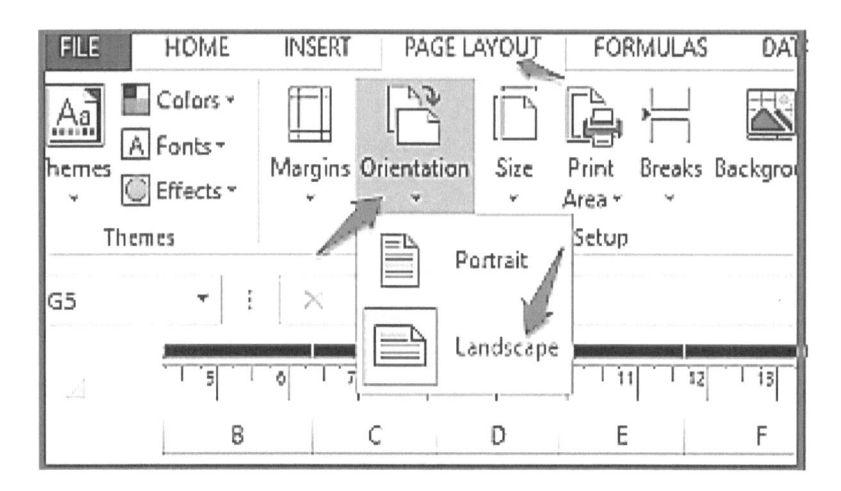

Dealing appropriately with the page break:

Page break is simply the same spot of the start point of one area and the endpoint of another area. There are ways to handle page breaks so that you will not want to have page breaks on page 10 and you will be having it on page 8. Let us quickly check how to manage page break:

1. **Viewing the actual position of the page break by:**
    a. Navigating to the **View** bar and tap on the **Page Break Preview** button.
    b. Inside the **Page Break Preview** view, under **"In this view"**, you will see all the worksheet page numbers and their respective dashed lines which signify the point where each page break will occur.

2. **Adjusting the position of the page break:**
   a. Inside the "page break preview view", double-click to drag the dashed line to adjust the page break position. Immediately you succeed in moving the page break, the previous dashed line will not be there anymore, but that point will be replaced with a solid line, and as a result, the page will not beak at that point anymore but on the new page break page position that you have just created. Be careful not to adjust the page break too much so that your contents worksheet will not be shortened.

3. **Inserting a page break:**
    a. Select the cell below the point where you want the horizontal break to take place and right to where you want the vertical break to set in.
    b. Move to the **Page Layout tab** and click the **Break** button.

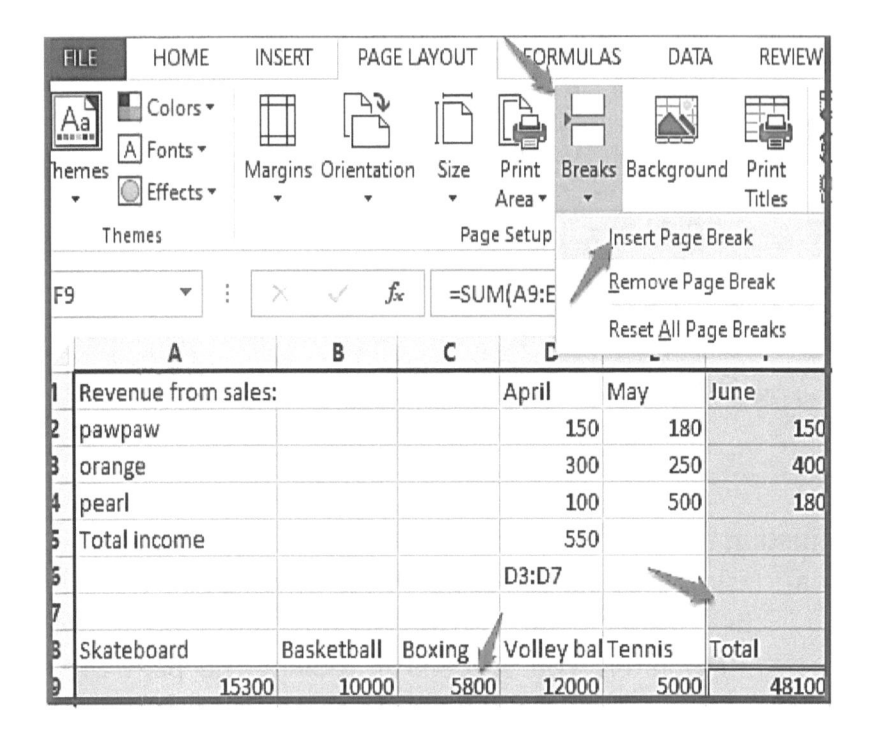

    c. Select the **Insert Page Break** from the break button drop-down list and then drag the page break to adjust its location.

4. **Removing a page break**:
    a. Select **the cell** below and to the right of the page break and navigate the **Page Layout** tab to click the break button.
    b. Choose **"Remove Page Break"** from the Break button drop-down menu.

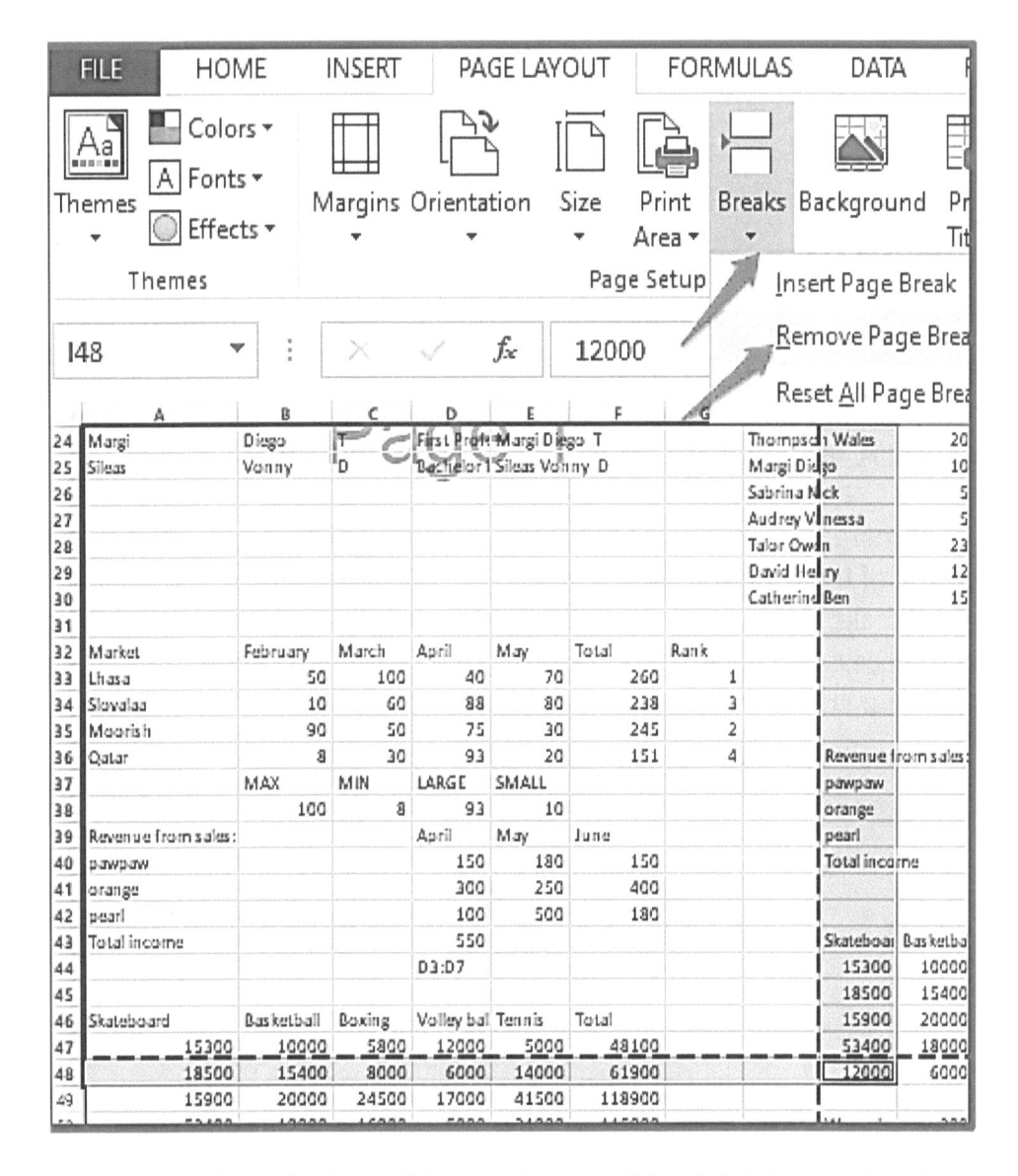

5. **Removing all the solid page breaks (the initial page break you shifted):** move to the **Page Layout Tab** and tap on the **Break** button, then choose "Reset all the page breaks".

243

Present A Worksheet in An Attractive Manner

Your ultimate objective is how the work you want to print will get the attention of those people who will read it. You can adjust your worksheet more to make it the best one out there by navigating to the page-set up box. To access the page-set up box, move to the **Page Layout Tab** in the Page set-up group and click on the drop-down arrow.

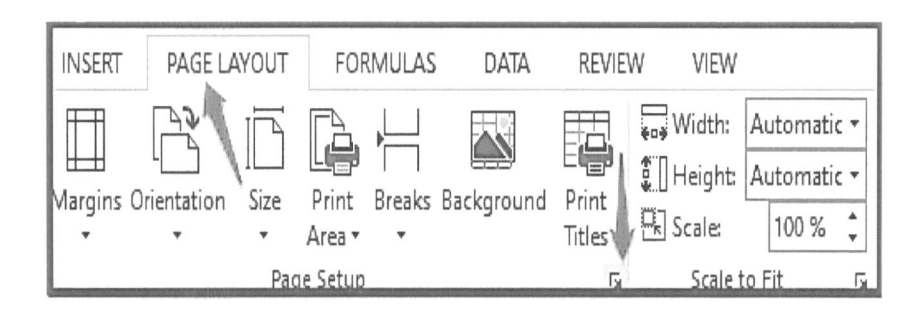

What can I do with the page set-up box? The following are certain things you can adjust inside the page set-up box:

a. **Numbering your worksheet page:** to number your page,
- Maneuver to the **Page** tab inside the page set-up box and insert **1** into the "First-page number text box".

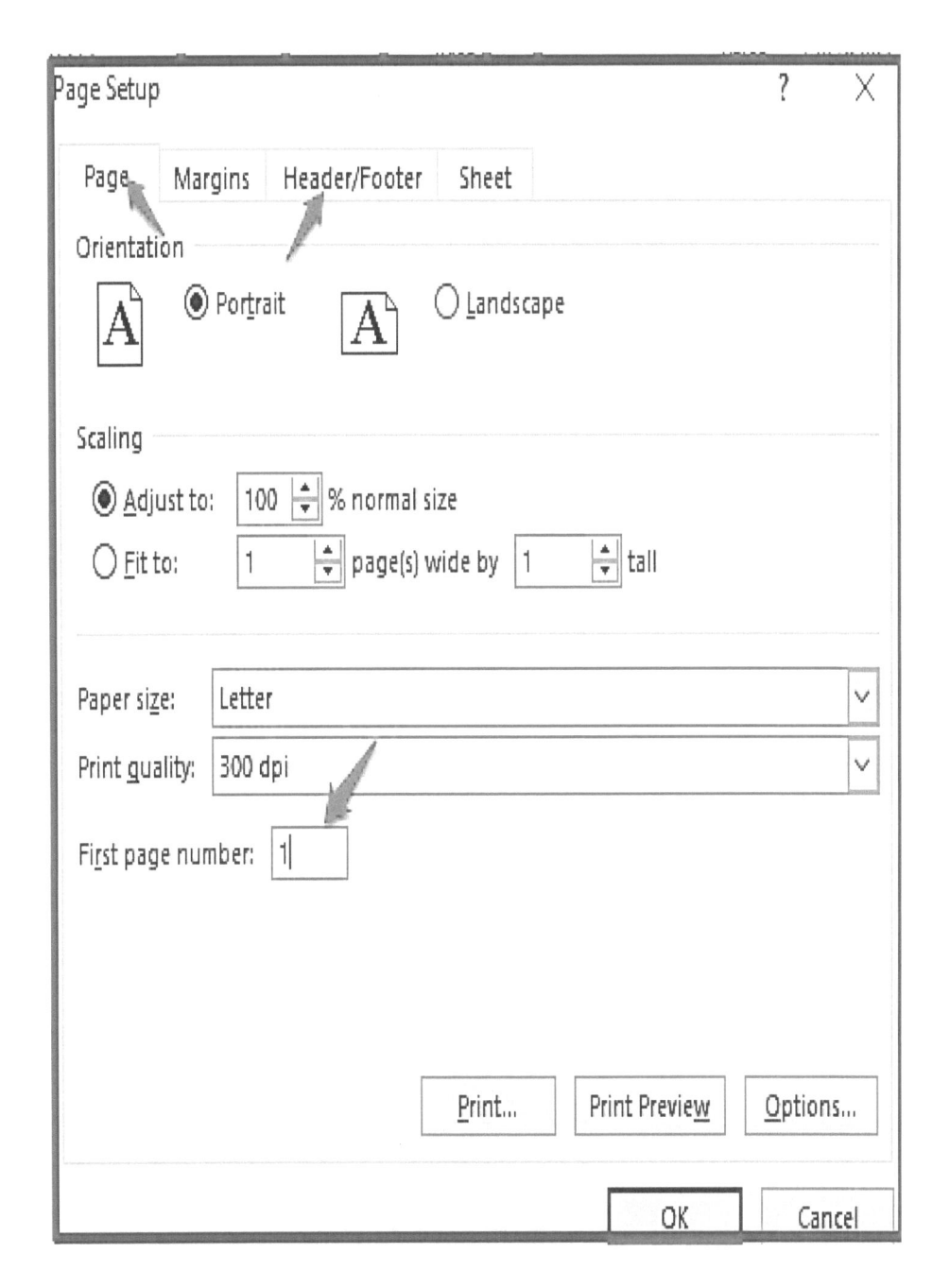

- then move to the header and footer tab and tap on either **footer or header** and pick **"page 1 of?"** from the drop-down list, that is page 1 of (?) the total worksheet pages. You will enter the number of the page number and the total number you are having in your worksheet to the header or footer.

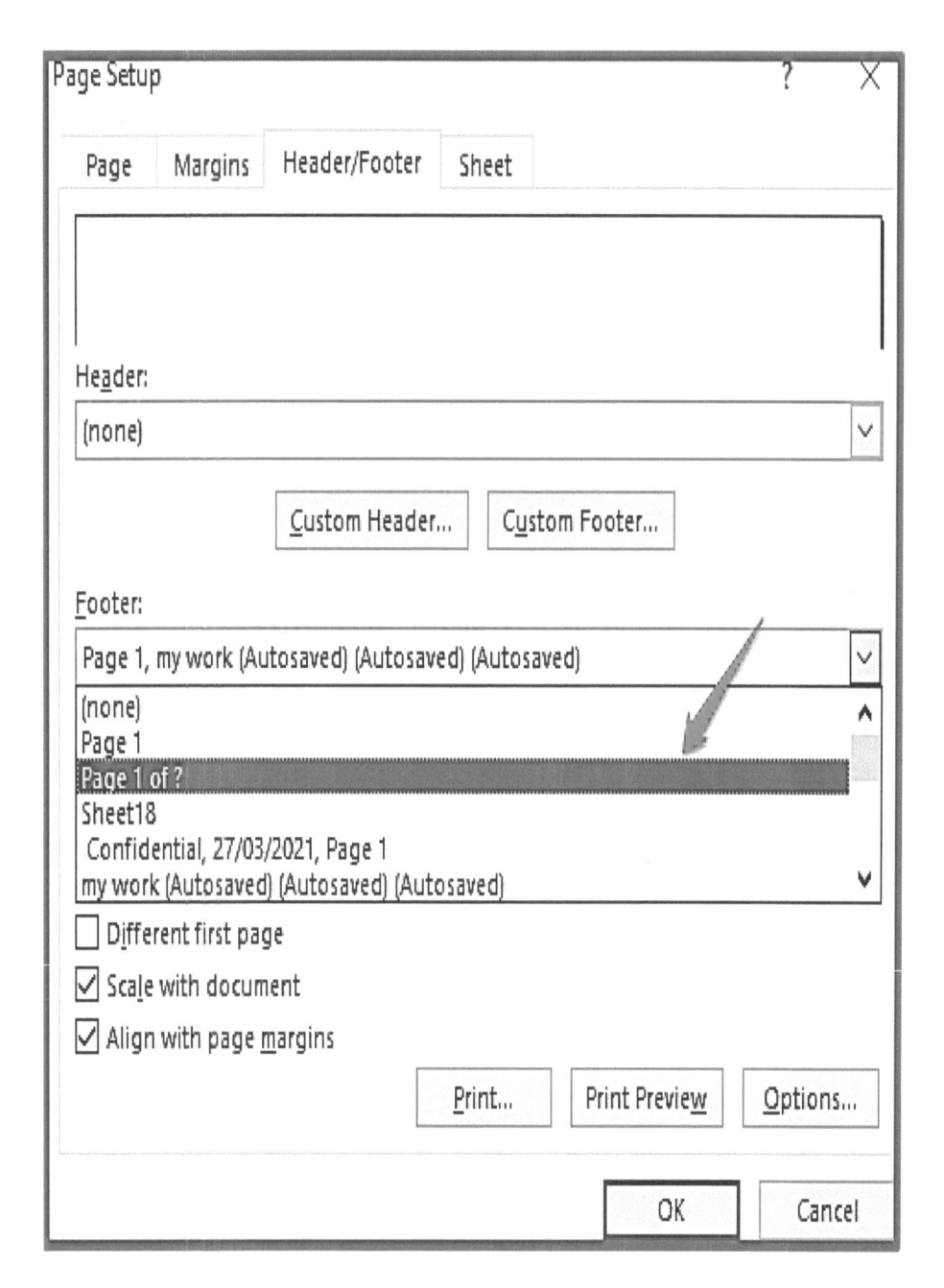

b. **Including headers and footers on page:** tap on the **header and footer** tab on the page set-up dialog box and then click on the "**Custom Header or Custom Footer**" option which will open you up to enter some actions such as, format text, sheet name, page numbers, file name, date, and your name.

247

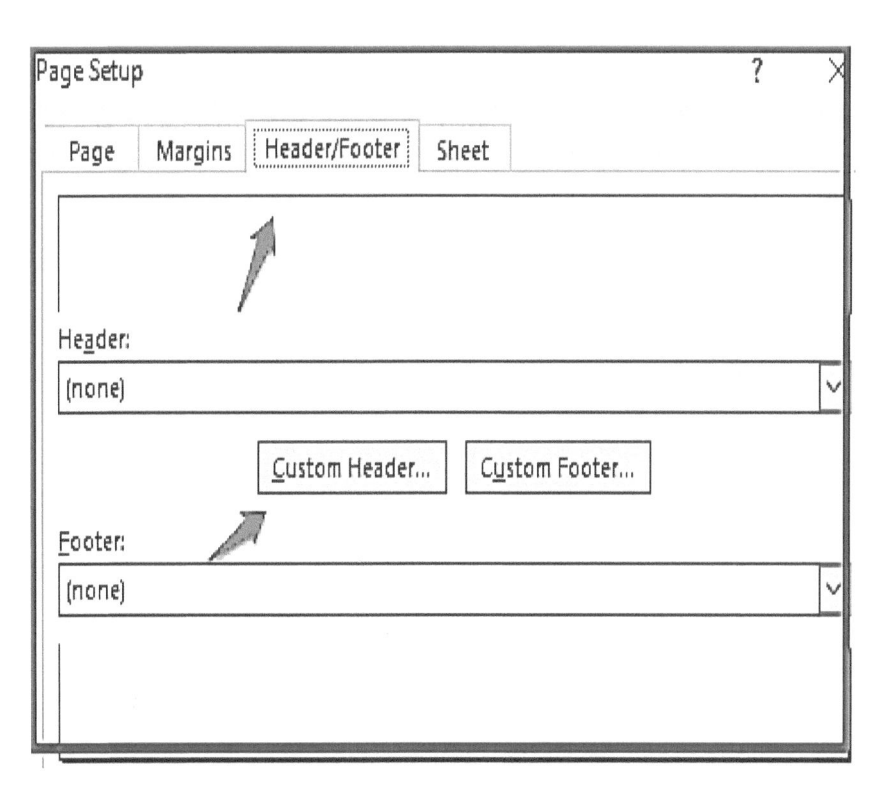

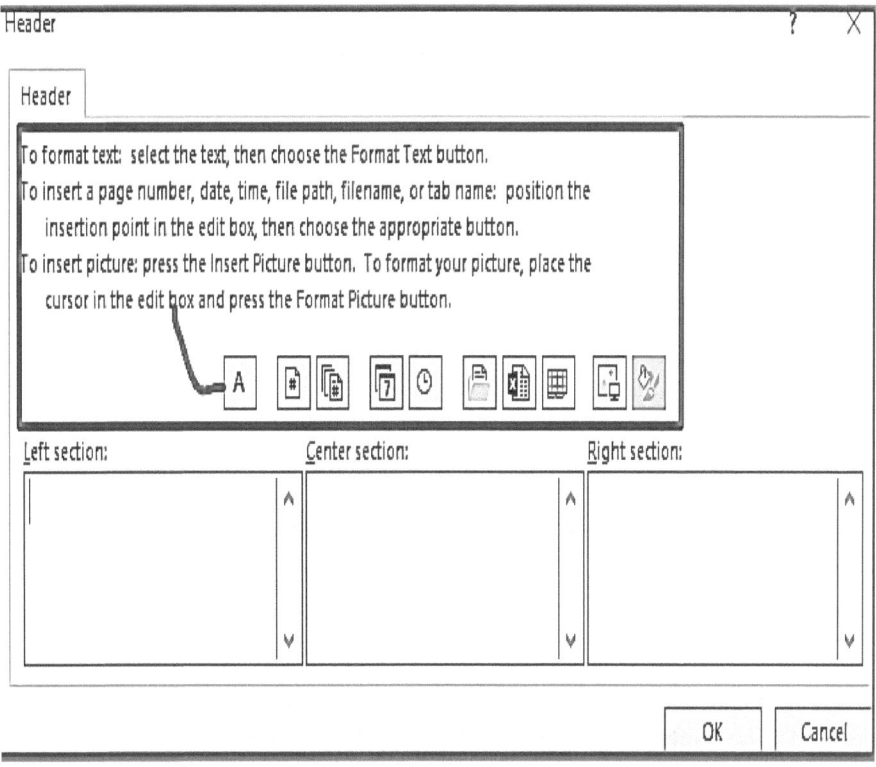

c. **Aligning worksheet page to the center:** click on the **Margin** tab inside the page set-up dialog, where you can either pick horizontal or vertical or both to center the page of the worksheet so as to center it accurately at the center of the sheet.

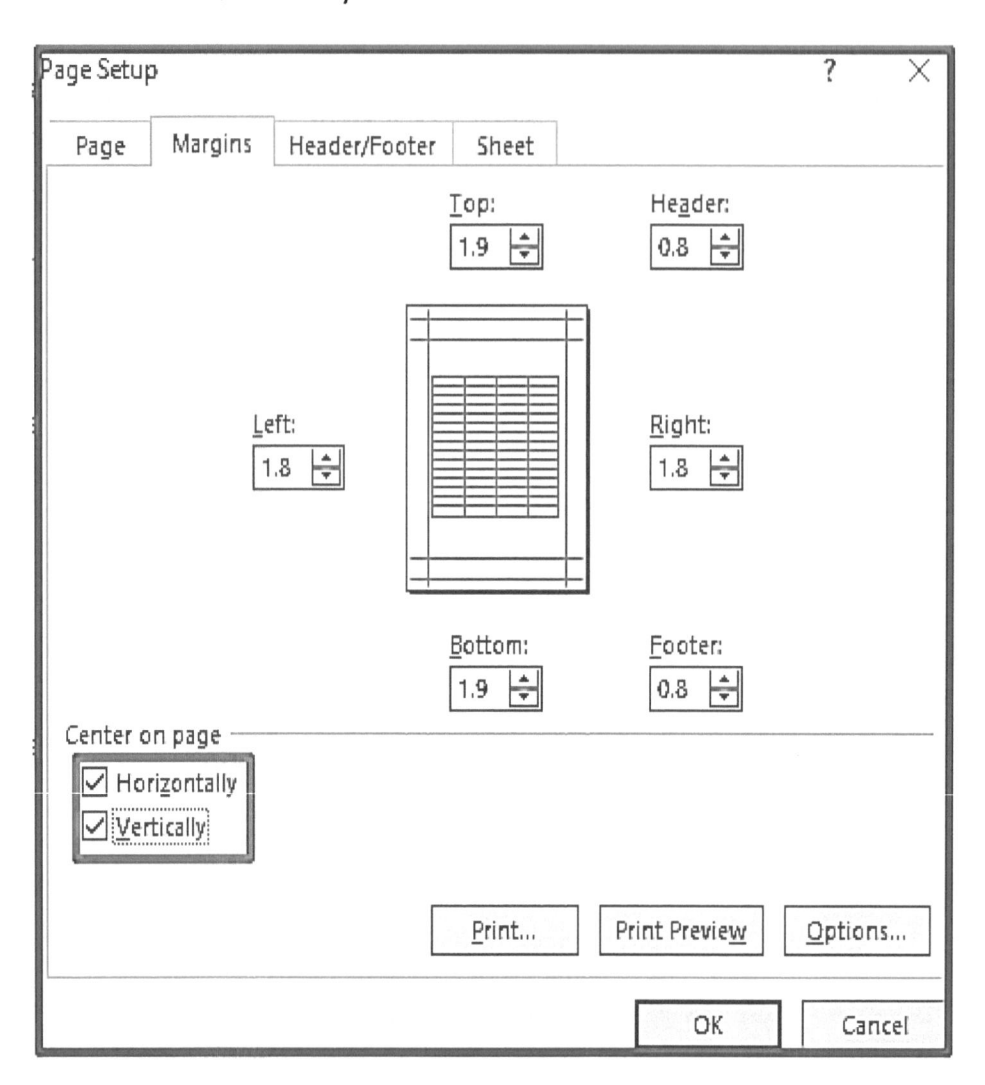

d. **Adjustment for cell gridline, column letters, and row numbers:** Excel neither print the gridline nor columns letters and row numbers by default, the features that give your worksheet an arrangement, but if you choose to print them, you can do that by clicking the **Sheet** tab inside the page set-up dialog box and select whatever feature you desire in the check box.

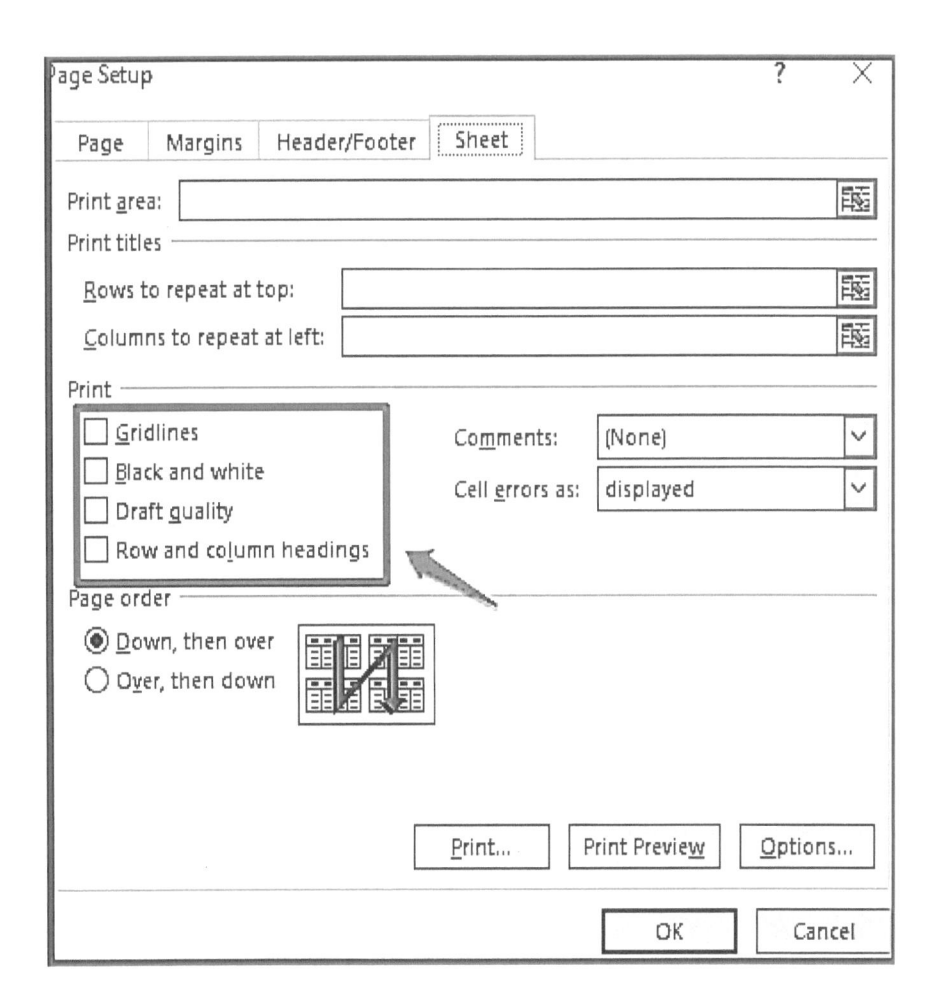

Repeat Rows and Columns Heading on Every Page

Perhaps your worksheet has multiple pages, and Excel does not print title page to every other page by default, and thus if you do not want your worksheet to look absurd because of missing heading on subsequent rows and columns because if the reader finds it difficult to see the title heading, they will as well find it difficult to get the main contents, then you are obliged to set the repeat row and column headings for document that has more than one page. To activate the repeated row and column headings on every page, you have to:

a. Move to the **Page Layout** tab and tap on the **Print Titles** icon, in a jiffy, you will see the page setup dialog box open.
b. Tap on the **Sheet** tab in the page setup dialog box.

c. Locate **row and column references** under the print title.
d. Click the reference selector button that relates to the type you set to be repeated. For example, "Row to repeat at the top" and for column "Column to repeat at the left" in the box provided for each heading.

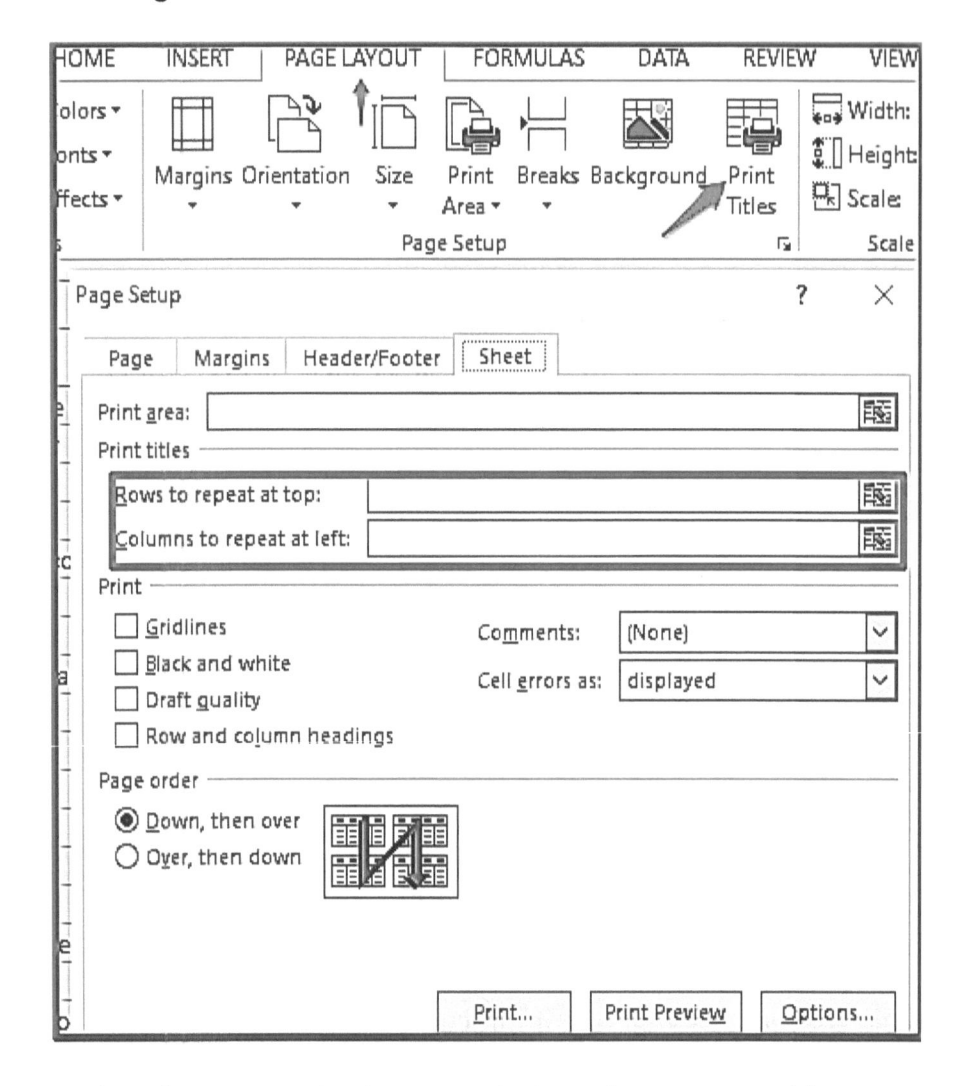

e. Select the rows and columns with the references or addresses you need either by typing their address or by dragging over them if they next are to each other.
f. By now, the respective headings you selected as the cell range must have been listed in the print title section under respective headings.

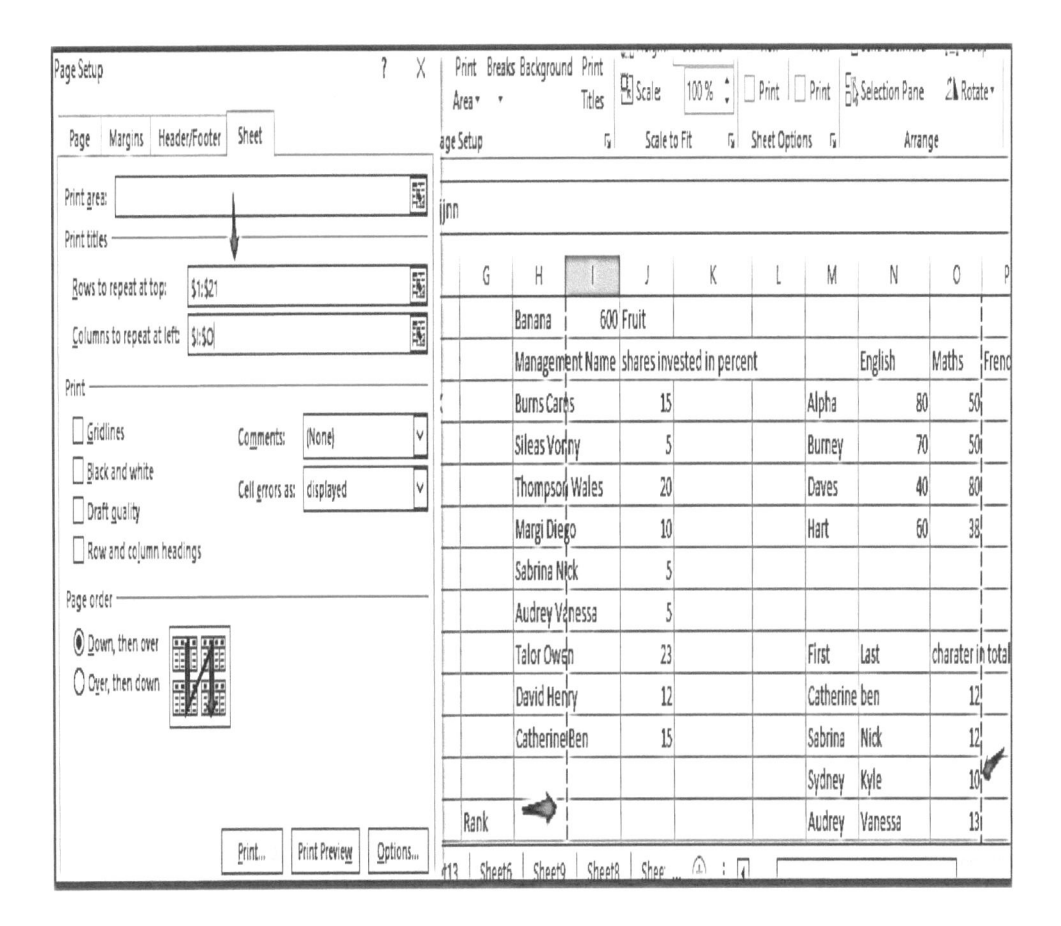

g. This is the pattern you will be repeating if you want to set up repeating row and column heading from step (d) – (f).
h. Tap **Ok** as soon as you are done with the page setup dialog box.

Tips: Before printing a document, check the print preview button in the page setup dialog box to confirm, if the row and column heading repeat themselves on the pages you selected.

Removing Row and Column Headings

To remove row and column headings, do well to:

a. Click on the **sheet** tab in the page setup dialog box.
b. Clear all the cell addresses in the rows to repeat at the top and column to repeat at the left in their respective box.

Page Setup

- Page
- Margins
- Header/Footer
- **Sheet**

Print area:

Print titles

Rows to repeat at top: $1:$21

Columns to repeat at left: $I:$O

Print

- ☐ Gridlines
- ☐ Black and white
- ☐ Draft quality
- ☐ Row and column headings

Comments: (None)

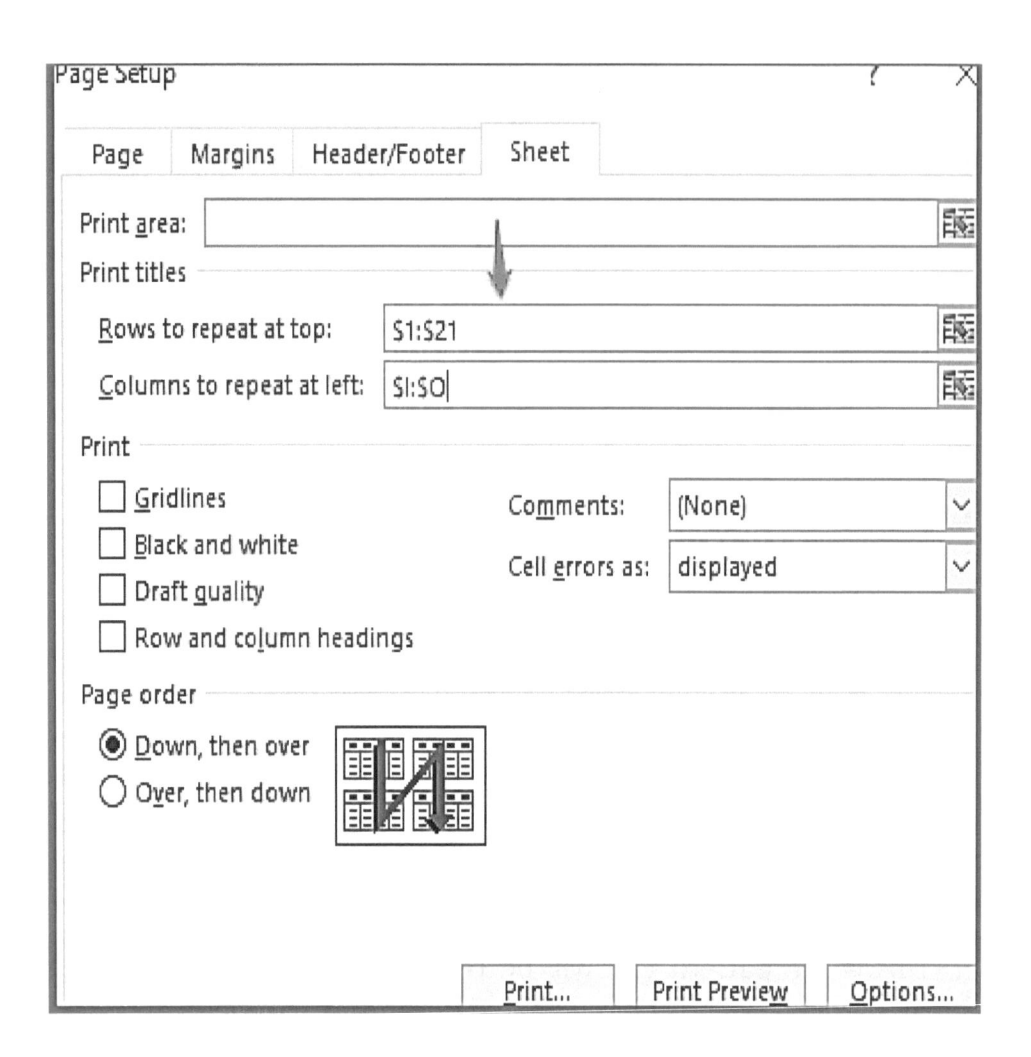

Cell errors as: displayed

Page order

- ◉ Down, then over
- ○ Over, then down

Print... | Print Preview | Options...

CHAPTER SIX

TOOLS AND TECHNIQUES FOR DATA ANALYSIS

What Are the Sparklines?

Sparklines are the tiny lines that live inside a cell; they show the variation in the dataset. Sparklines are of three types; line, column, and Win/Loss, compares to Excel graph. Sparklines are not graphs; they reside in the cell as a cell background. Let us quickly create one sparklines chart:

a. Select the **exact cell** where you want the chart to show up.
b. Click on the **Line, Column, or Win/loss icon** to open up "create sparklines" dialog box from the insert bar.

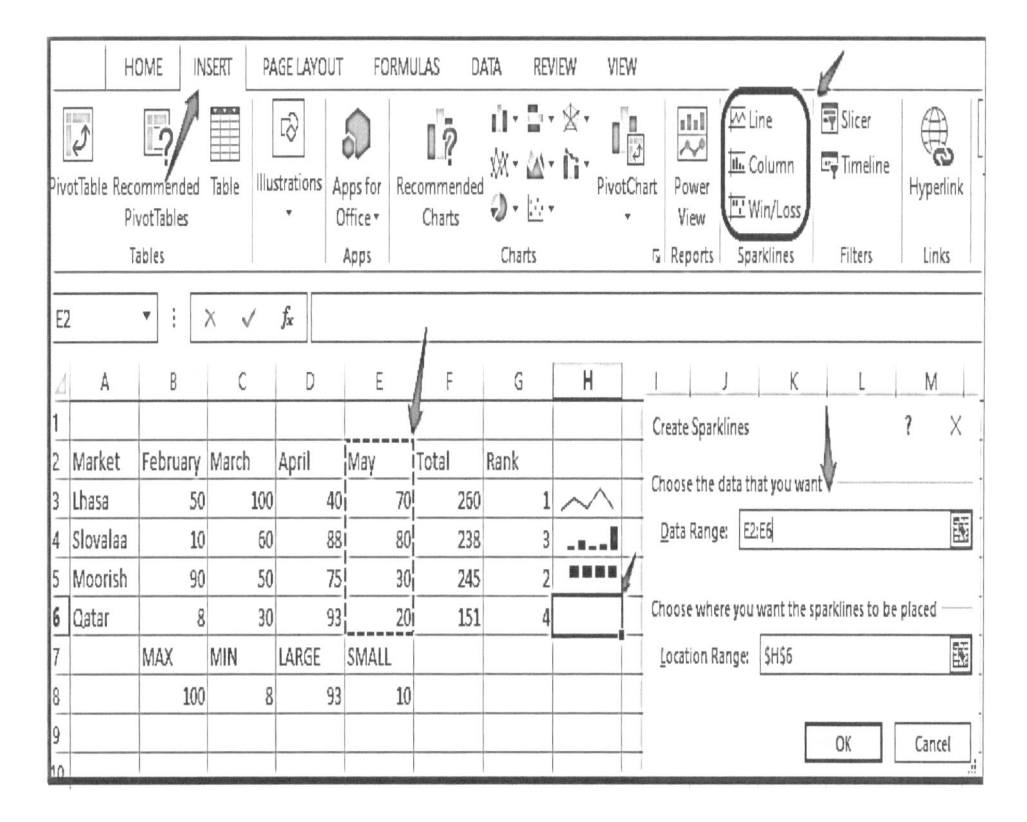

c. Input the range of cells name or drag over a row or column in your worksheet to select the cells from which the data is to be analyzed.

d. Tap on **Ok** to create the sparklines inside the Create Sparklines dialog box.

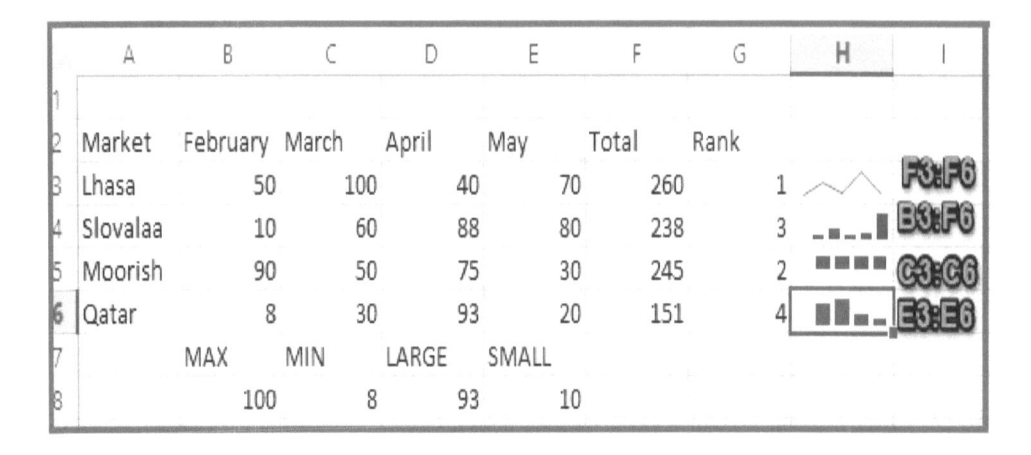

	A	B	C	D	E	F	G	H	I
1									
2	Market	February	March	April	May	Total	Rank		
3	Lhasa	50	100	40	70	260	1	∧∧	F3:F6
4	Slovalaa	10	60	88	80	238	3	_._.∎	B3:F6
5	Moorish	90	50	75	30	245	2	∎∎∎∎	C3:C6
6	Qatar	8	30	93	20	151	4	∎∎_ _	E3:E6
7		MAX	MIN	LARGE	SMALL				
8		100	8	93	10				

To remove the sparklines, click on the **Sparkline** and tap on the **Clear** button.

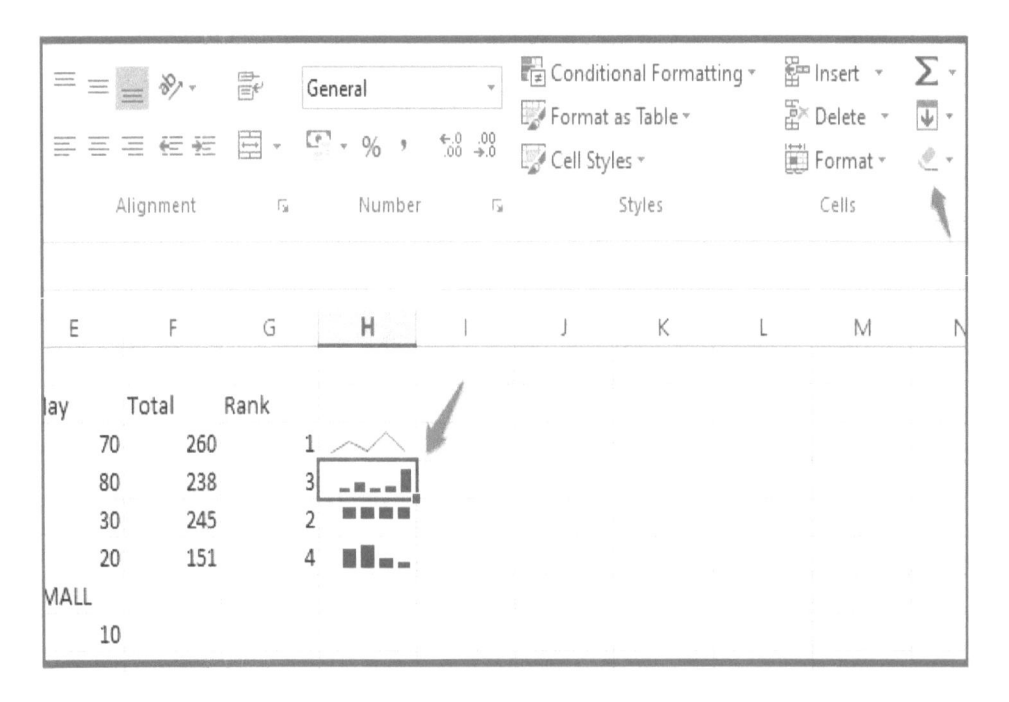

The sparklines' appearance can be improved by moving to the **Design tab** to locate the **sparklines tool** where you can pick some features to change the sparkline's appearance such as bar color, line color, and other various types of sparklines that you can pick as well.

254

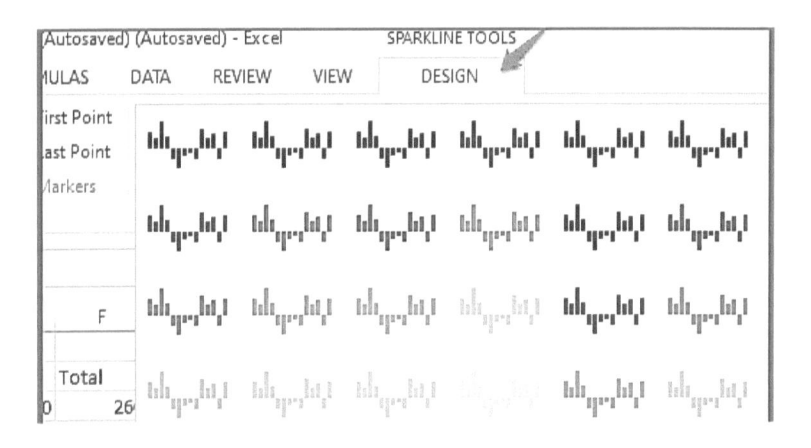

Conditional Format Application for Certain Data That Need Important Attention

The major aim of conditional formatting is to apply a conditional format to data and check if they will meet specific condition or criteria and call attention to it on meeting such condition setup, such as risk-tasks and budget item, it will then tell Excel to highlight those data. For instance, select blue for meeting positive criteria and red or black for meeting negative criteria. Conditional formats give you more understanding of the data. To understand the application of conditional formatting, follow this step-by-step guide listed below:

1. Select the **range values or cells** you want to apply conditional formatting to.
2. Move to the **Home** tab and click on the **"Conditional Formatting"** button.
3. Pick **Highlight cells rule or Top/bottom rules** from conditional formatting button drop-down list:
    a. **Picking highlight cells rules:** this is a rule that is demanding attention from a data that is lesser or greater than a certain value or that falls to a specific range of data or numbers. For example, you may decide to highlight a product that has less than 150 in any quantity.
    b. **Picking Top/bottom rules:** request for attention from any data that falls within a specific number or percentage within the range of the selected cells.

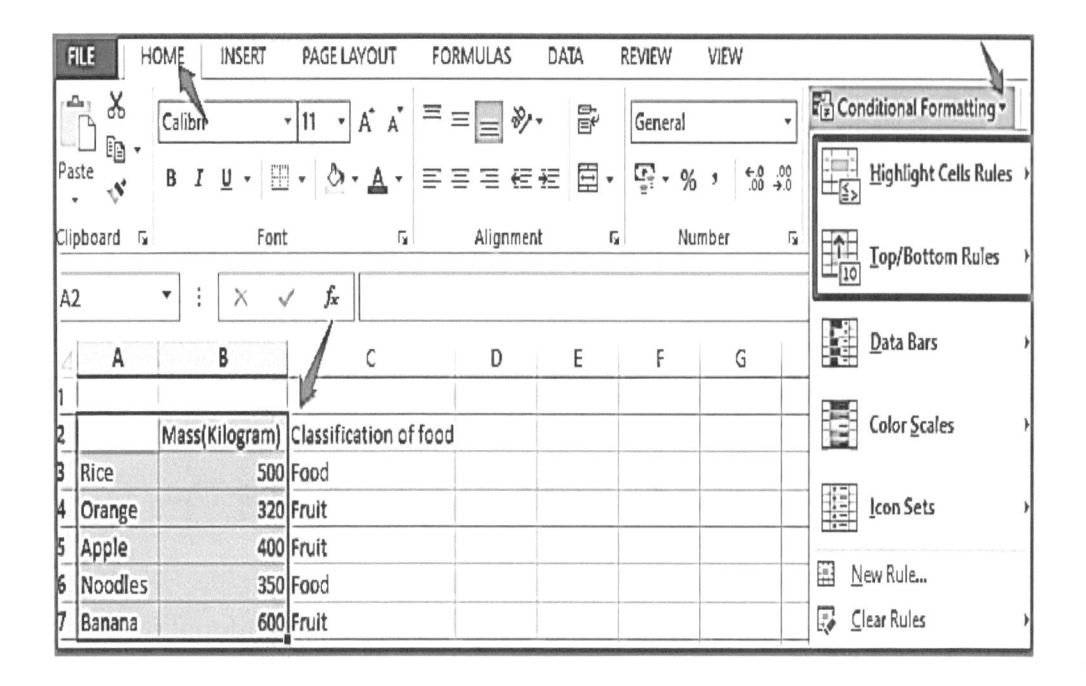

4. Pick an option for the headings you choose above in (3).

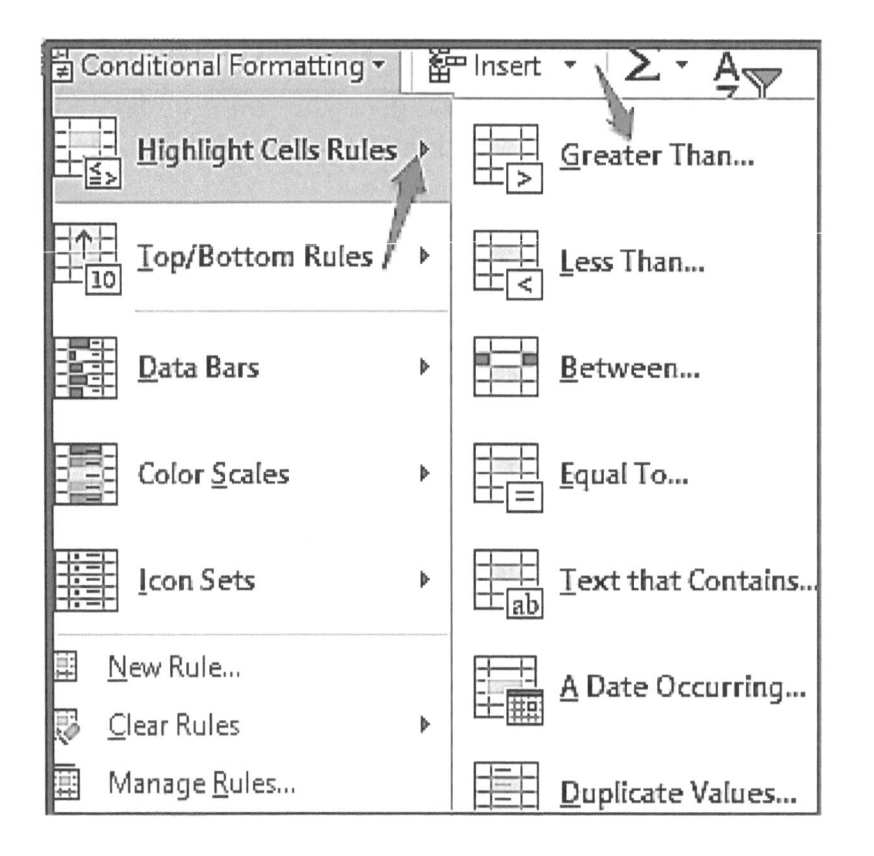

256

5. Set specific data rules for the cells you selected on the left side of the dialog box. For instance, greater than or less than, texts that contain a specific word or figure, and so on.
6. Select the specific attention you want each data that meet up with the condition to show. For instance, showing blue or red for meeting up with positive criteria or showing red or yellow, for meeting up negative criteria for easy identification, and you may as well refuse to use color at all.

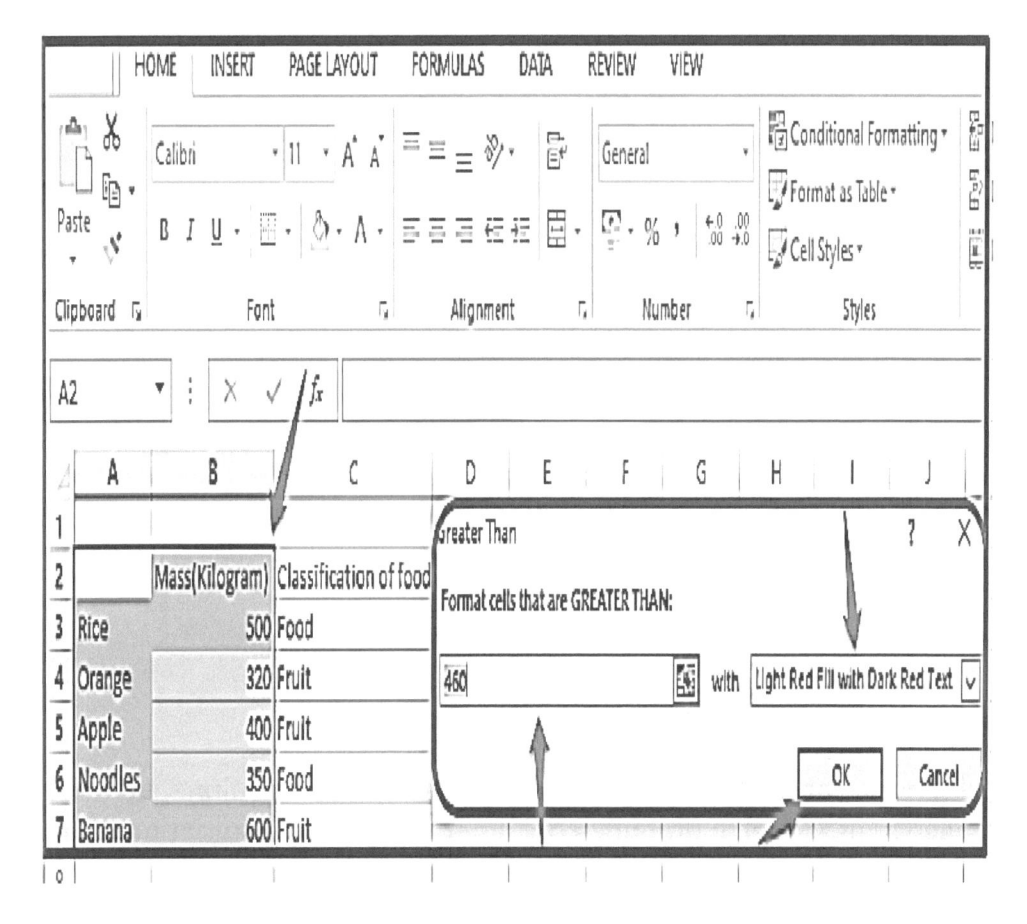

7. Tap on **Ok** to authenticate the process.

How do I remove conditional formats? It is not difficult, kindly:

a. Select **the cells** that have conditional format and move to the **Home** tab to click the **Conditional Formatting** button.

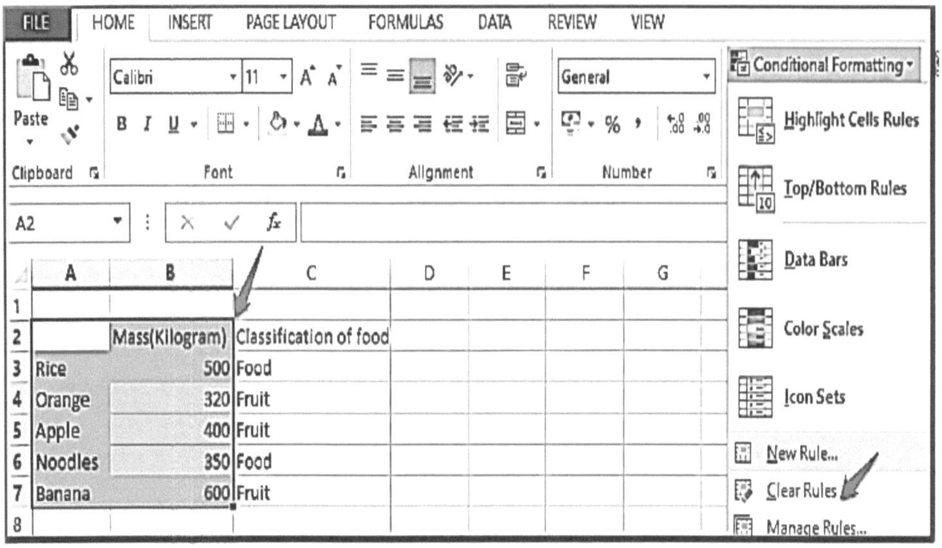
FILE
HOME
INSERT
PAGE LAYOUT
FORMULAS
DATA
REVIEW
VIEW
Paste
Calibri
11
General
Clipboard
Font
Alignment
Number
Conditional Formatting
Highlight Cells Rules
Top/Bottom Rules
Data Bars
Color Scales
Icon Sets
New Rule...
Clear Rules
Manage Rules...
A2
Mass(Kilogram)
Classification of food
Rice 500 Food
Orange 320 Fruit
Apple 400 Fruit
Noodles 350 Food
Banana 600 Fruit

b. Pick the **Clear rules** option, then select "**clear rule from selected cells"** from the clear rule drop-down list.

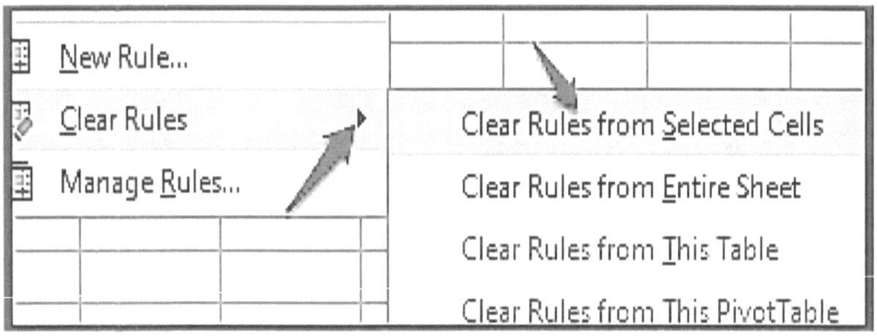
New Rule...
Clear Rules
Manage Rules...
Clear Rules from Selected Cells
Clear Rules from Entire Sheet
Clear Rules from This Table
Clear Rules from This PivotTable

Taking Care of The Information List

Excel is not all about preparing a document for office use alone, at times you have to use Excel to prepare a document for your consumption, even if it is for office use, such document may be prepared on occasion for a later use and such has to be arranged very well so that it will not be confusing next time you are to check it and thus, sorting has to come up for arranging document such as customer information and sort them maybe in numerical or alphabetical order. Filtering is also used to separate essential documents to the safer side, that is, selecting the necessary information by hiding other data and keeping the information required available.

Sorting List of a Data

Sorting data means to organize a full detailed worksheet row based on the data in the column, take for instance, you may logically organize a list by the first name. Data may be sorted numerically, alphabetically and in various other means to meet your need. When sorting, you can choose to sort a column or multiple columns.

To sort a column: if you want to sort a single column, kindly ensure you attach a header to each column for perfect identification and an effective function of Sorting;

- Select **any cell** which will represent other cells in that same column for sorting. Select the cell that has the data type you want to sort, and Excel will update it with other cells in the column.
- Move to the **Data** tab and tap on **Sort & Filter** group, then pick the **Sort type**, probably A-Z(ascending to descending) or Z-A(descending to ascending).

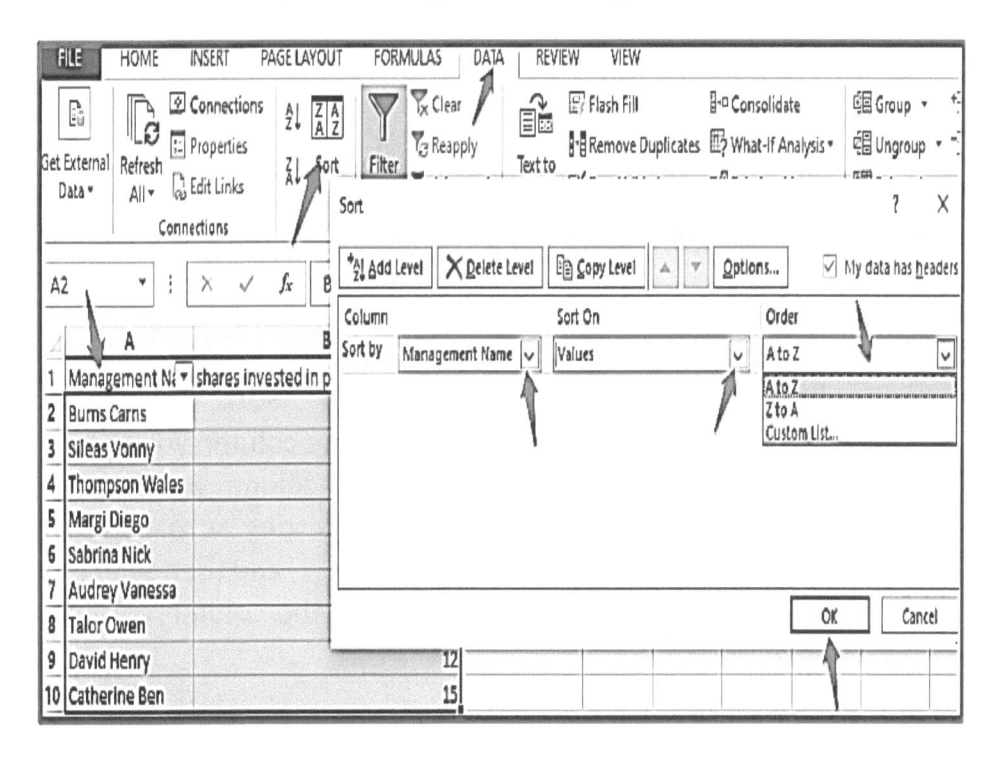

- Tap on a **column heading** and pick "**sort by**" perhaps by the headings and the order you prefer, from top to bottom or bottom to top.

	A	B
1	Management Na	Management Name
2	Audrey Vanessa	5
3	Burns Carns	15
4	Catherine Ben	15
5	David Henry	12
6	Margi Diego	10
7	Sabrina Nick	5
8	Sileas Vonny	5
9	Talor Owen	23
10	Thompson Wales	20
11		

To sort multiple columns: if you want to sort more than one column, kindly:

a. Select the **first cell** in the first column
b. Maneuver to the **Data** tab to open the "**Sort**" dialog box.
c. Inside the Sort dialog box, indicate the column you want to sort under the column for the first column and keep on tapping on **"Add level"** to keep on getting as many as the number of the column you want to sort, and then select the **Sorting order** you will prefer for all the column you have selected.

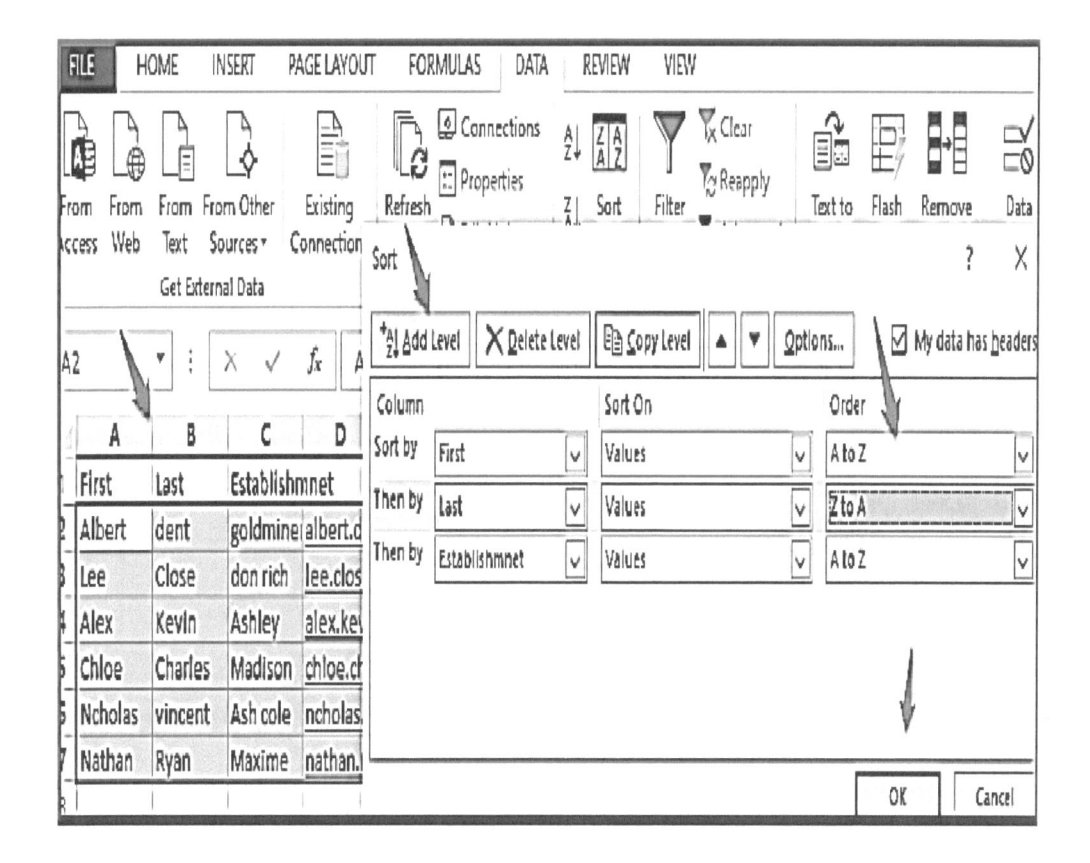

d. Tap **Ok** for authentication.

Filtering List of Data

Filtering list of data is used to analyze data and pick out only the rows that meet the filter condition and thus hide all the other data, provided the data that satisfy the criteria for the filter is established. Filtering will clean up the list of data except for the types of rows of data you demand and at the end of the filtering criteria, the list would have shortened down the worksheet data, so, you can view only the information you desire to see. To filter a list of data, endeavor to the following:

- Ensure you attach a header row for each column to make filtering work effectively.
- Select the data you want to filter, move to the **Data** tab, click on **Filter** under the Sort & Filter group.

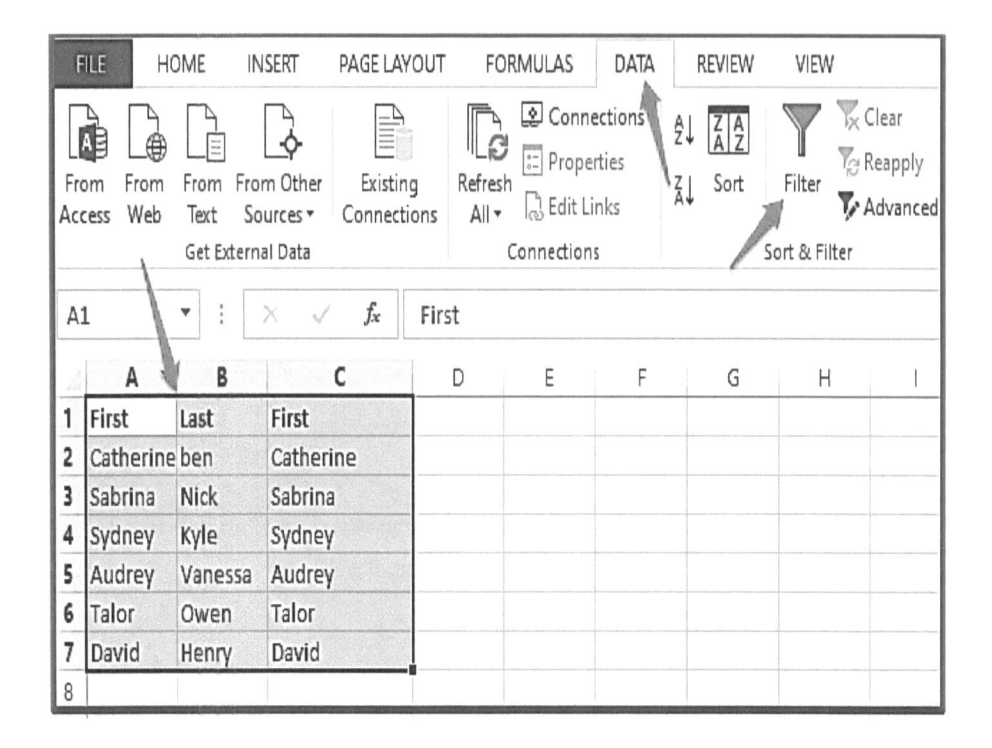

- Tap on each Filter arrow you want to filter and navigate to **Text Filters** to open the options that are available under filter.

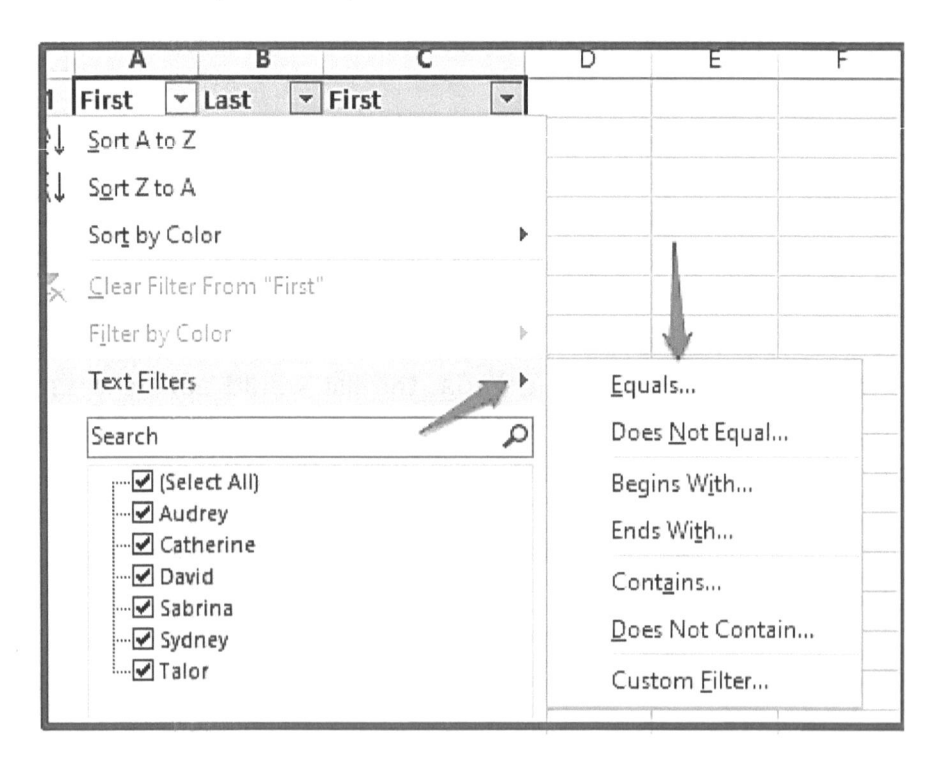

- Tap on the option you want and the Auto filter dialog box will open, supply the condition of the data you are looking for, and tap **Ok**.

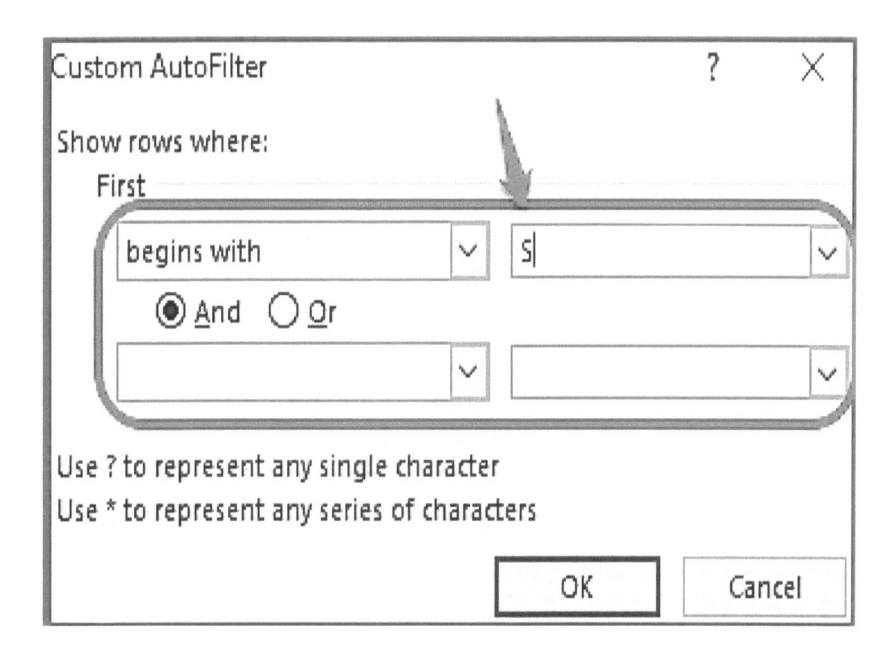

- As soon as you click **Ok**, the filtering will show only the row that meets the criteria with the cells that have that data.

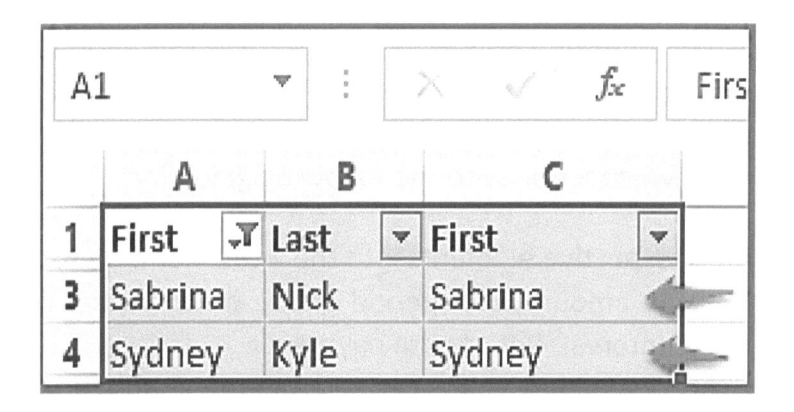

How can I clear all the filters from the worksheet, and get the total information back?

Move to the **Data** tab and click on the **Clear** button from Sort & Filter group.

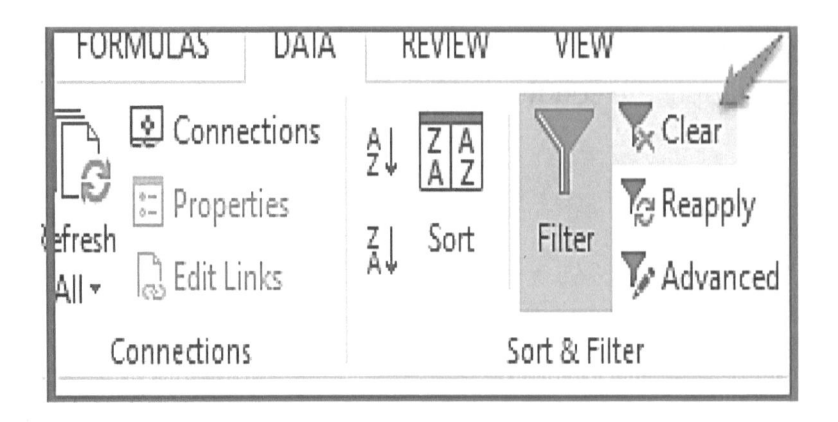

Exploiting Goal Seek Command

Goal seek command is simply a technique of data analysis that focuses more on the result by using the result to formulate an analysis that will help in getting the raw data which will give one the actual result one wants to achieve. Goal seek command is an order you give Excel to experiment result to get the raw data based on the result you desire to achieve coupled with necessary Excel argument.

Goal seek analysis input value in the place of raw data, for instance, you want to borrow money, you know how much to borrow and you have the ability to pay off the loan, and also know the period you will use to pay off the whole loan, but you do not know the exact rate of interest that you will pay in acquiring such loan, Goal seek command will help you in that area. Let us do the computation of interest rate to pay in acquiring a loan with the PMT function with the following guideline:

1. Enter the respective elements into the worksheet, for instance:
   - B1= Loan amount, B2= period of the payment monthly, B3= Rate of interest, B4= month payment.
2. Enter the **respective value** for each element above in (1), for instance,
   - Cell C1= $120000, that is the amount you prefer to borrow.
   - Cell C2= 180, the number of times to pay off the loan if paid monthly.
   - Cell C3= the interest rate we are about to calculate for the loan amount.

- Cell C4= the amount of payment every month, but you are not going to insert it here, it will be used in the Goal seek computation because it is the data result.

	A	B	C
1		Amount of loan	120000
2		Number of payment (Monthly)	180
3		Interest rate	
4		Payment	

3. Insert the formula into **Cell C4** by putting in **Cell 4=PMT(C3/12, C2, C1)**, this will give you the formula result for the monthly payment value. In this scenario, you wish to be paying $1200 each month, but you will not enter it, it will be using in Goal seek dialog box for interest rate computation. The formula breakdown:
   - **C1** is the loan amount
   - **C2** is the period it will take for paying off the loan.
   - **C3** is the Interest rate that "Goal seek" seeks to find, and the 12 is 12 months, PMT calculates on yearly basis, and thus you have to divide it by 12 to convert it to a monthly basis. But, because cell B3 does not have anything inside, Excel will assume it to be Zero (0).

C4 =PMT(C3/12,C2,C1)

	A	B	C
1		Amount of loan	120000
2		Number of payment (Monthly)	180
3		Interest rate	
4		Payment	-$667

4. Move to the **Data** tab and tap on **What-if Analysis** and then choose the "**Goal Seek**" button from the What-if Analysis drop-down list.

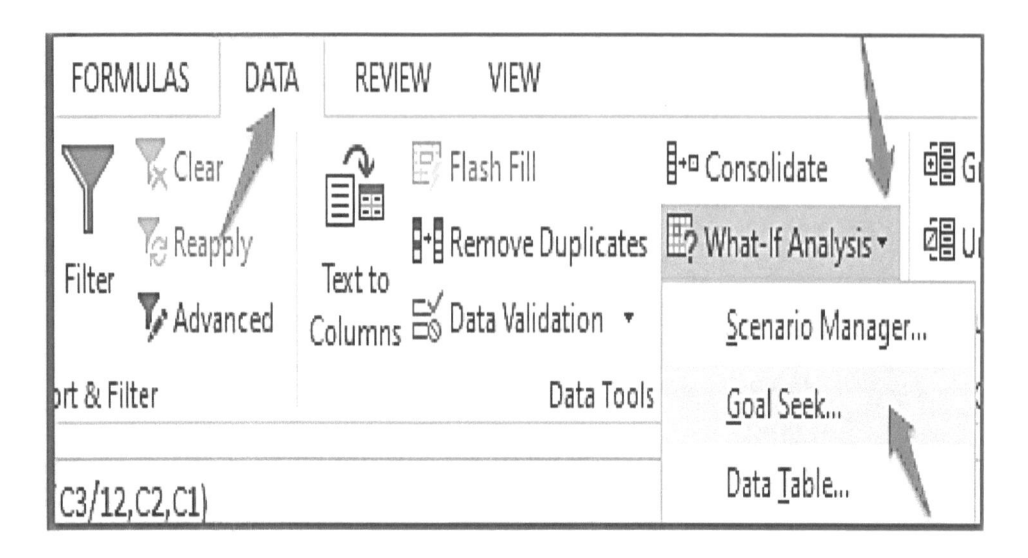

5. Once the "Goal Seeks" dialog box opens, insert the **cell reference** that comprises the formula you are looking at, in this case, it is C4.
6. Then type the formula result into the "**To Value box**", this is representing -1200 because it is the outflow.
7. Insert the **cell address** that comprises the value you want to change inside the **"Changing cell box"**; in this case, it is cell C3.

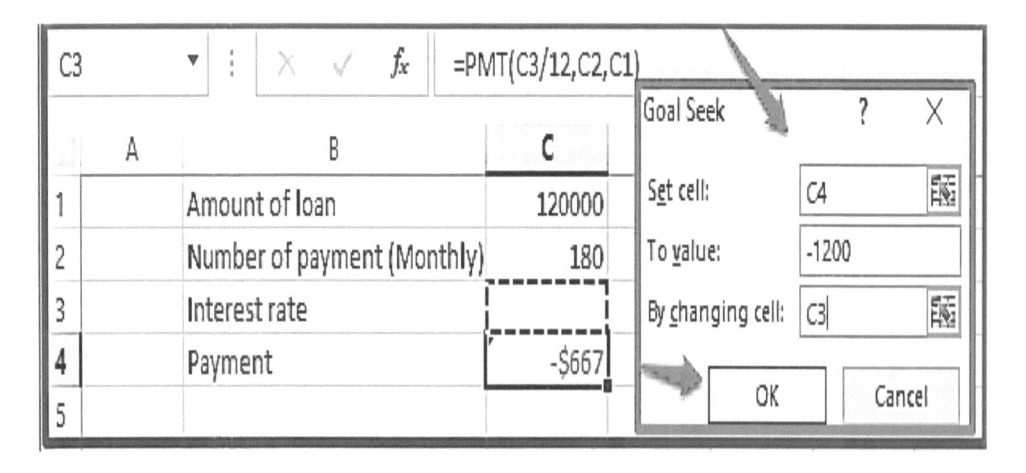

8. Tap **Ok** and Goal seek will run the check for you and provide you with the result.

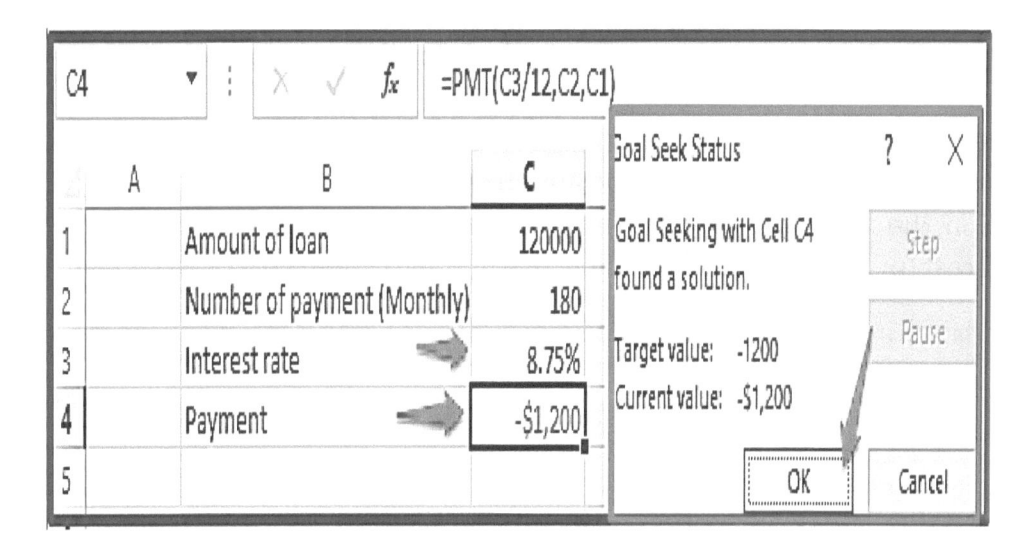

C4	▼ : × ✓ fx	=PMT(C3/12,C2,C1)		
	A	B	C	
1		Amount of loan	120000	
2		Number of payment (Monthly)	180	
3		Interest rate	8.75%	
4		Payment	-$1,200	
5				

Goal Seek Status
Goal Seeking with Cell C4 found a solution.
Target value: -1200
Current value: -$1,200

9. Then format the cells to display the actual face value by navigating to the **Home** tab, then, click on the **"Number"** group, then move to currency to format it.

	A	B	C
1		Amount of loan	$120,000
2		Number of payment (Monthly)	180
3		Interest rate	8.75%
4		Payment	-$1,200
5			

Analysing Data with Data Table and What If Analysis

Data tables with What-if analysis are combined to address a complex computation. This technique helps to alter the range of data on a single table and extract the cause of adjusting such on the formula results. Goal seeks and data table are almost the same thing except for multiple variables of data that data table uses in carrying out its process and experiment at once.

Using A One Input Data Table for Analysis

One input data table structures its experiment in a single table and provides the results of each formula to be per the change on the input cell in the formula. To get it right at this level, let us use the rate of interest for this scenario by making use of the following set of data below.

△	A	B	C
1		Amount of loan	$120,000
2		Number of payment (Monthly)	180
3		Interest rate	8.75%
4		Payment	-$1,200
5			

In the above information, we are having:

- The amount of the loan, interest rate on the loan, number of payments every month. The monthly payment value is calculated on the other three (3) elements (it is in red), because it is cash outflow or payment.
- The amount of the loan in cell C1 is $120000, the number of payments every month in cell C2 is 180 times, the rate of interest in cell C3 is 8.75%, and the payment value (monthly) in C4 is calculated based on the first three (3) elements; it has to be in red because it is the cash outflow or payment. It is calculated based on: =PMT(C3/12, C2, C1).

We will be using the above information and analysis to check the number of the monthly payment that will befit you. If your monthly payment capacity will not exceed $1000 compared to $1200 you have been paying before by making use of the data in the above table to formulate different number of payments per month and select the numbers of payment that will give us below $1000.

Let us forge ahead to check what we have to do to formulate different number of payment (monthly) and monthly payment, kindly:

1. Insert different number payment (monthly) to column E from above the 180 we are having above because you are paying lesser than $1200, enter the number to column E2 down to column E12.
2. Insert, = C4 in cell F1, because it is one row above the value to the column we want to test and thus, it gives reference to cell C4. In referencing, cell C4 you have to refer it, not by inserting the value so that the formula can work but kindly type "=" in F1 and click on C4 to refer it.

F1			fx	=C4		
	A	B		C	D	E	F
1		Amount of loan		$120,000			-$1,200
2		Number of payment (Monthly)		180		185	
3		Interest rate		8.75%		193	
4		Payment		-$1,200		207	
5						220	
6						250	
7						280	
8						300	
9						330	
10						350	
11						380	
12						400	

3. Now, select the cell in E1 to F12 and move to the **Data** tab, and tap on **What-if analysis**, then click on **Data table** from What-if analysis drop-down to open Data table dialog box.

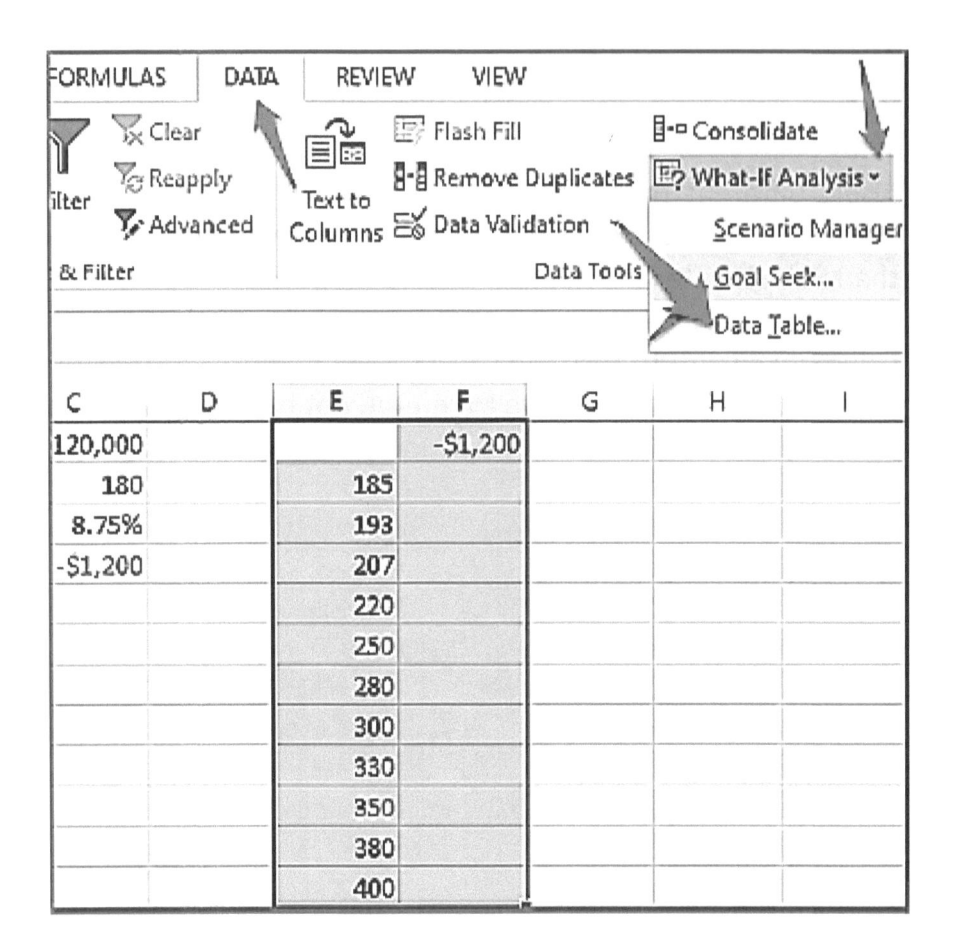

C	D	E	F	G	H	I
120,000			-$1,200			
180		185				
8.75%		193				
-$1,200		207				
		220				
		250				
		280				
		300				
		330				
		350				
		380				
		400				

4. Inside the **"Data Table"**, give reference to cell C2 in "Column input cell field"; we will be using the column cell field alone because we are calculating with one input data table.

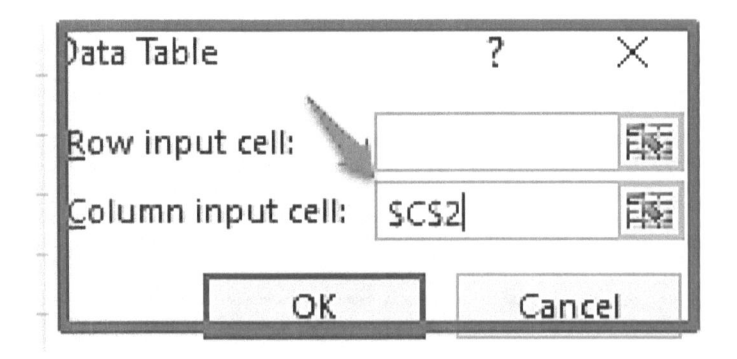

5. Tap **Ok**, and the Data table will process the result and insert the data process into their respective cells.

	A	B	C	D	E	F
1		Amount of loan	$120,000			-$1,200
2		Number of payment (Monthly)	180		185	-1184.01
3		Interest rate	8.75%		193	-1160.89
4		Payment	-$1,200		207	-1125.39
5					220	-1097.14
6					250	-1045.28
7					280	-1007
8					300	-986.937
9					330	-962.911
10					350	-950.068
11					380	-934.462
12					400	-926.016

Note: One Input Data table is done with the calculation, by following the calculation, you can pick E8 which gives you 300 of a monthly payment with monthly payment lesser than &1000 ($986).

Clear the Data table you created by:

- Selecting the whole **Data Table** and tap on the **Delete** button. Note that you cannot delete part of the table, that's why you have to select the whole Data Table.

Using A Two Input Data Table for Analysis

As the name indicates, two input data table permits you to test two input elements rather than one input table, taking for instance the above One input unit that we used in calculating the number of the monthly payment in the column, you can as well add another variable such as loan amount to the row so that the computation will cover both sides and be more detailed by combining loan amount and number of monthly payments to meet a specific need.

For instance, you may want to combine loan amount and the number of payments that will give you less than $700, it is that computation that will give you the actual loan amount with the period of time that will give you such. Without much ado, let us analyze the data with two input data table by observing this one-on-one process:

1. Let us get a diverse number of monthly payments to the column and different levels of the loan amount to the row located above the column one cell above to the right.

	A	B	C	D	E	F	G	H	I	J	K
1		Amount of loan	$120,000			$50,000	60000	70000	90000	105000	120000
2		Number of payment (Monthly)	180		185						
3		Interest rate	8.75%		193						
4		Payment	-$1,200		207						
5					220						
6					250						
7					300						
8					350						
9					400						
10					420						
11					500						
12					550						
13											

2. Insert: **= C4 in cell E1** as it represents row above the values in the column. Remember we are working with two input variables and thus, E1 is dependent on both variables (number of monthly payment and amount of the loan), you will not insert C4 directly, you have to reference it, so that the formula can work effectively. Reference it by typing "=" into cell E1 and then move to click on cell C4.
3. Then select **cell (E1:K12)**, and navigate to the **Data** tab to click on the **What-if analysis**, then tap on the **Data Table** from the What-if analysis drop-down, to open the Data table dialog box.

	A	B	C	D	E	F	G	H	I	J	K
1		Amount of loan	$120,000		-$1,200	$50,000	60000	70000	90000	105000	120000
2		Number of payment (Monthly)	180		185						
3		Interest rate	8.75%		193						
4		Payment	-$1,200		207						
5					220						
6					250						
7					300						
8					350						
9					400						
10					420						
11					500						
12					550						

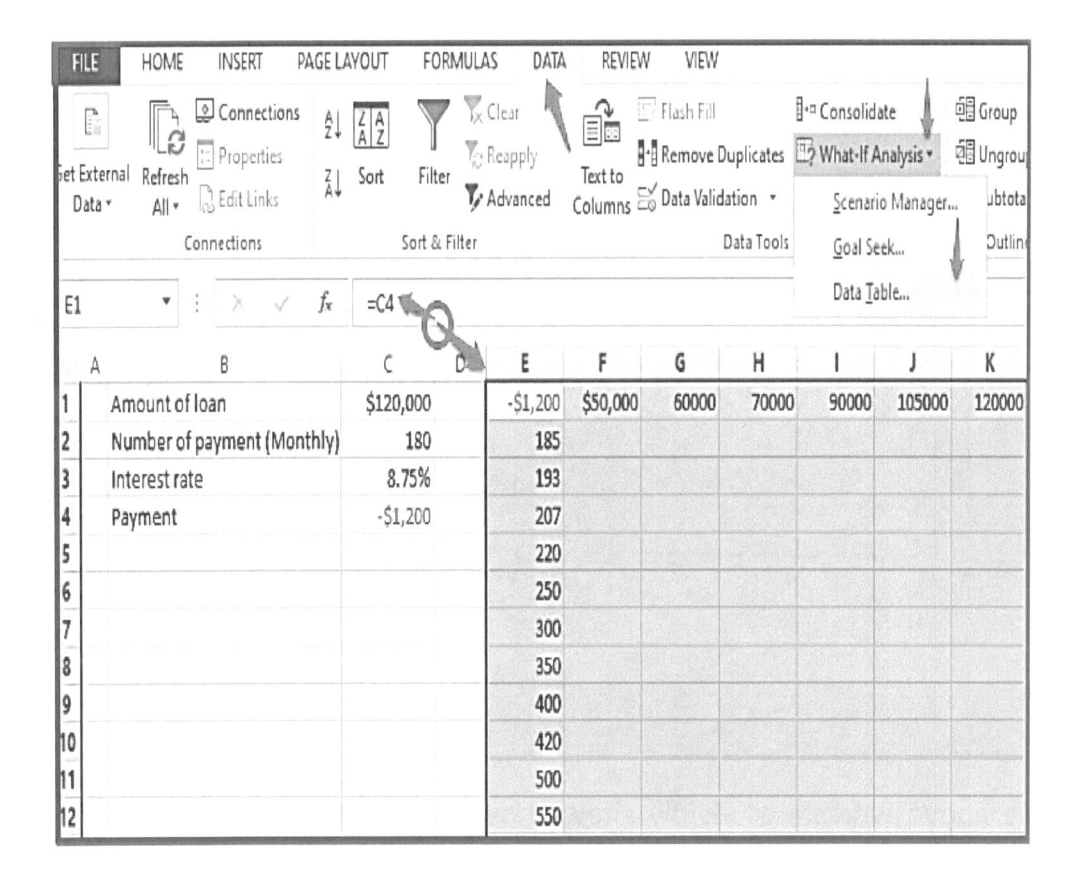

4. Right inside the Data table dialog box, insert into the:
    i. **Row input cell, $C$1**
    ii. **Column input cell, $C$2**

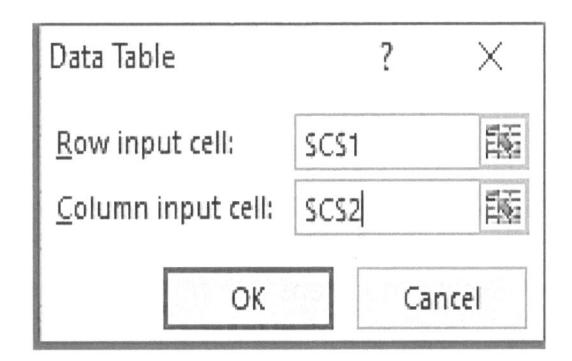

5. Tap **Ok** and Excel will quickly run the check and fill the selected range which you can check carefully to select the combination of the loan amount and number of the monthly payment that best suits you.

	A	B	C	D	E	F	G	H	I	J	K
1		Amount of loan	$120,000		-$1,200	$50,000	60000	70000	90000	105000	120000
2		Number of payment (Monthly)	180		185	-493.336	-592.003	-690.67	-888.004	-1036	-1184.01
3		Interest rate	8.75%		193	-483.704	-580.445	-677.186	-870.668	-1015.78	-1160.89
4		Payment	-$1,200		207	-468.911	-562.693	-656.475	-844.04	-984.713	-1125.39
5					220	-457.143	-548.571	-640	-822.857	-960	-1097.14
6					250	-435.533	-522.64	-609.746	-783.96	-914.62	-1045.28
7					300	-411.224	-493.469	-575.713	-740.203	-863.57	-986.937
8					350	-395.862	-475.034	-554.206	-712.551	-831.309	-950.068
9					400	-385.84	-463.008	-540.176	-694.512	-810.264	-926.016
10					420	-382.848	-459.417	-535.987	-689.126	-803.98	-918.834
11					500	-374.66	-449.592	-524.524	-674.388	-786.786	-899.184
12					550	-371.59	-445.908	-520.226	-668.862	-780.339	-891.816

The above worksheet vividly shows how much you can borrow with respective numbers of payment from which you can extract monthly payment that is below $600.

Clear the Data table created by:

- Selecting the whole **Data Table** and tap on the **Delete** button. You cannot delete part of the table and that is why you need to select the whole table.

Using Pivot Table for Data Analysis

Pivot table is one of Excel's indispensable features that grants you the privilege of arranging a large set of data in a worksheet and rationally analyze them. The pivot table works soundly by changing the column to row and also changing the row to column.

Note: Pivot table works perfectly with a set of data that has a column heading label which Excel will use to identify each column.

Using Recommended Pivot Table

Excel provides a means of generating automatic pivot table; there are many recommended pivot table options that are available for Excel users.

To explore and make use of a readymade pivot table, observe the followings steps:

1. Select **any cell** that contains data inside it in the worksheet.
2. Move to the **Insert** tab and tap on the **Recommended Pivot Table** option

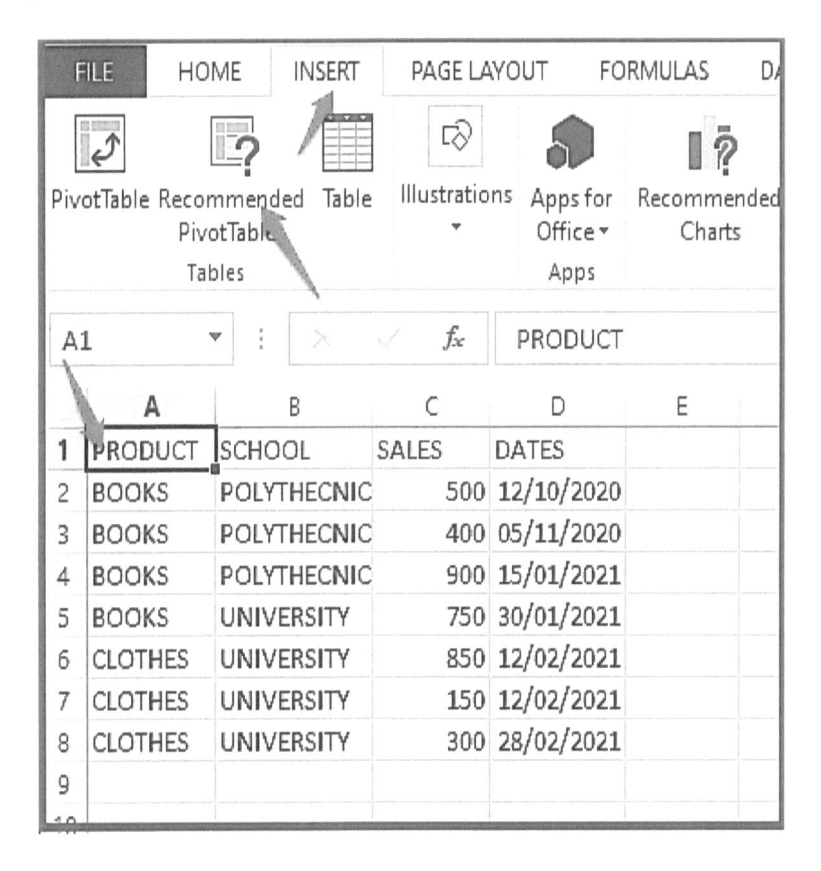

	A	B	C	D	E
1	PRODUCT	SCHOOL	SALES	DATES	
2	BOOKS	POLYTHECNIC	500	12/10/2020	
3	BOOKS	POLYTHECNIC	400	05/11/2020	
4	BOOKS	POLYTHECNIC	900	15/01/2021	
5	BOOKS	UNIVERSITY	750	30/01/2021	
6	CLOTHES	UNIVERSITY	850	12/02/2021	
7	CLOTHES	UNIVERSITY	150	12/02/2021	
8	CLOTHES	UNIVERSITY	300	28/02/2021	
9					

3. And you will be provided with a recommended table dialog box for your worksheet data. Pick any format of the recommended pivot table that suits your needs. For this illustration, we will be choosing the **"Sum of SALES by PRODUCTS and SCHOOL.**

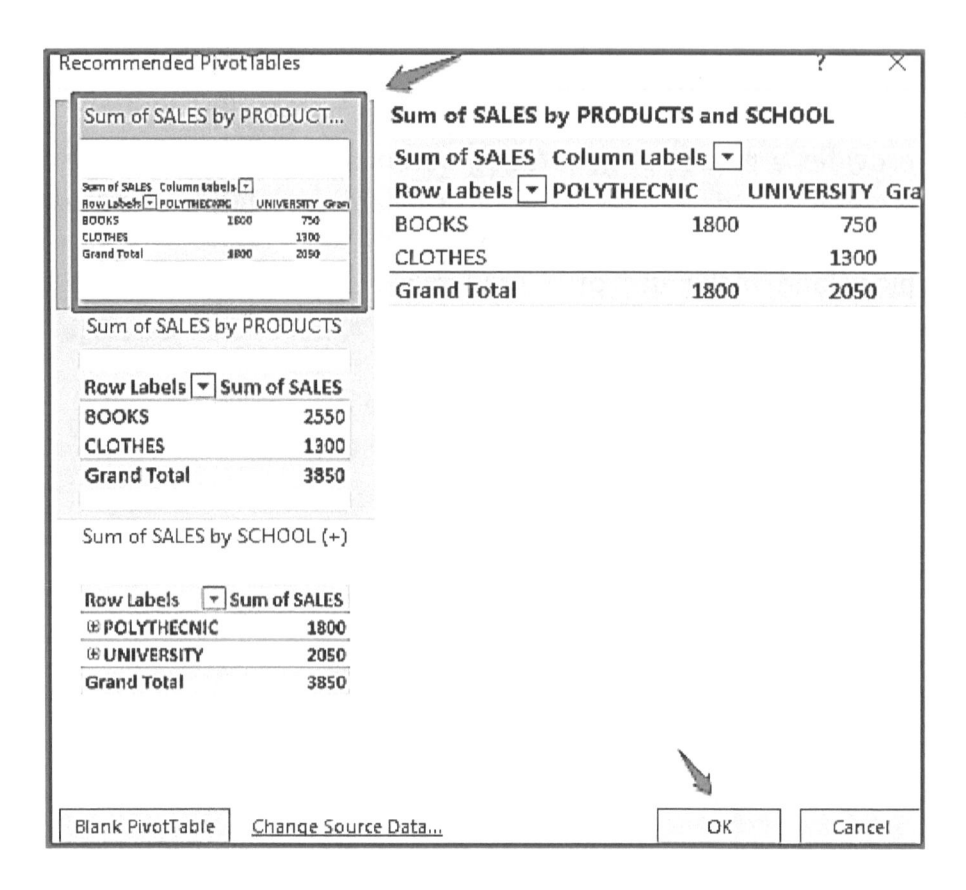

4. Then tap **Ok** and you will see the generated Pivot table.

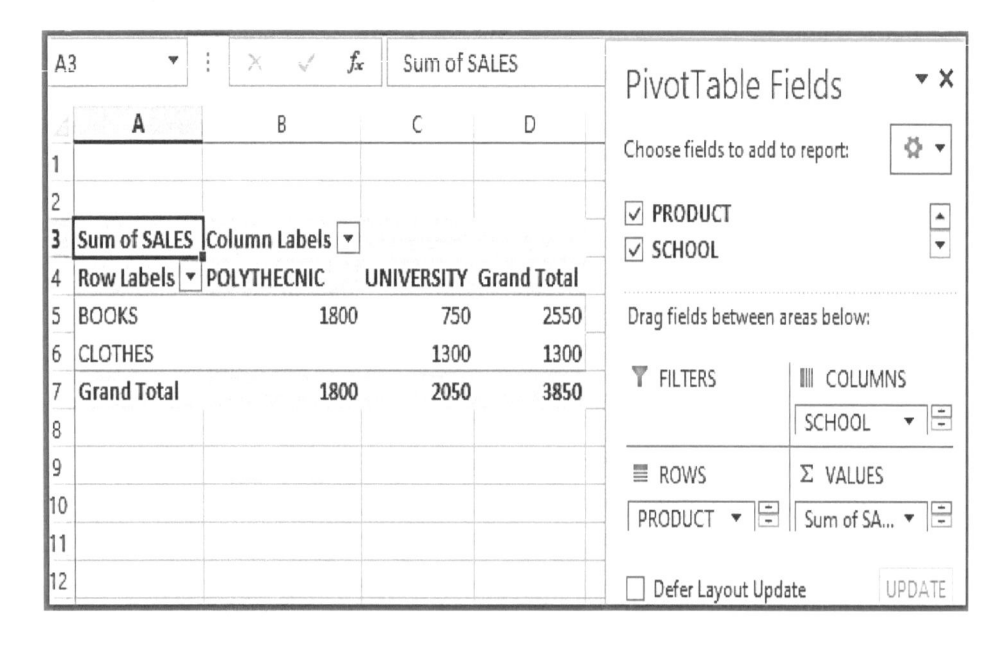

Creating A New Pivot Table

You can create your Pivot table. If the structure of the recommended Pivot table does not correlate with your information, creating a pivot table by yourself will help you to organize list around any of the command label, such as ordering by date to indicate the highest and lowest date order, arrange the price of the product to check the best and least sales and many more. Check the below guide to create a new Pivot table of your choice:

1. Select **a cell** that contains data anywhere in the list.
2. Go to the **Insert** tab and click on the **Pivot Table** button; Excel will select the entire list in your worksheet and use it to open a Created Pivot Table Dialog box.

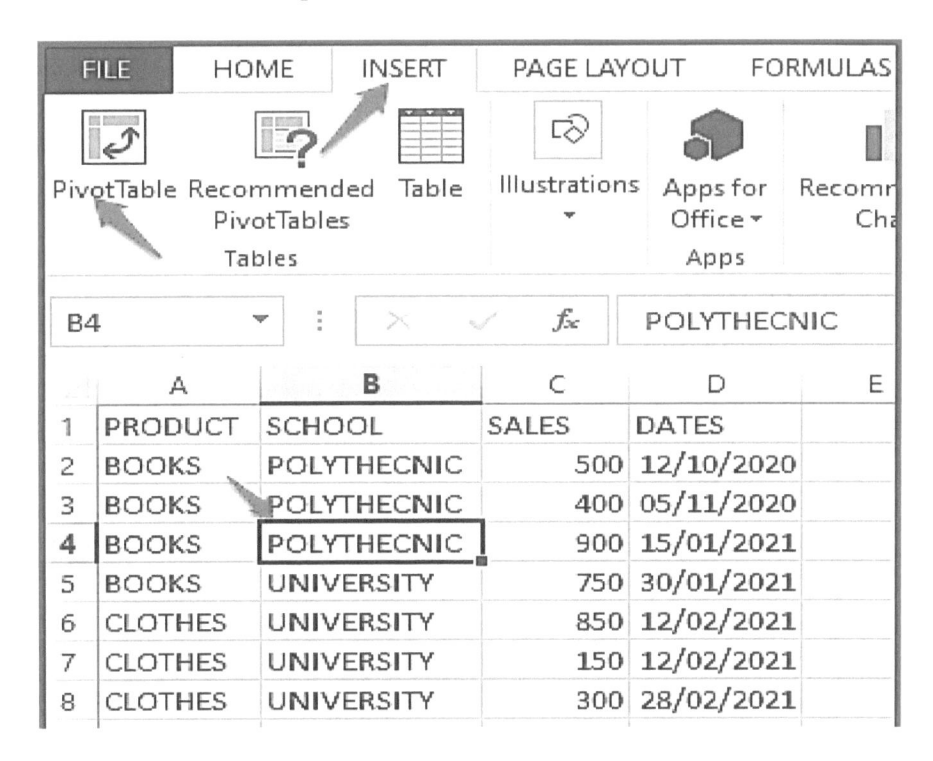

3. Pick **"select a table or range"** button, while the new worksheet will be there on default mode which is the best option. You will edit in the new worksheet and later transfer it to the existing worksheet.

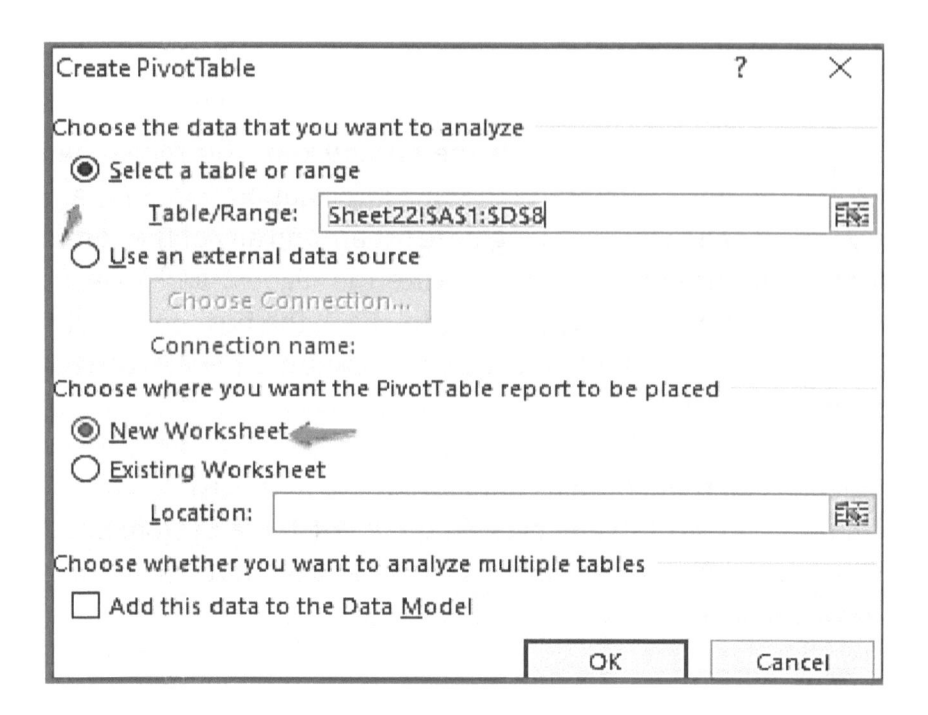

4. Tap on **Ok** and you will be provided with a PivotTable field, select each field you want and drag them to any of the four areas of the Pivot table which are: Rows, Columns, Filters, and Values.

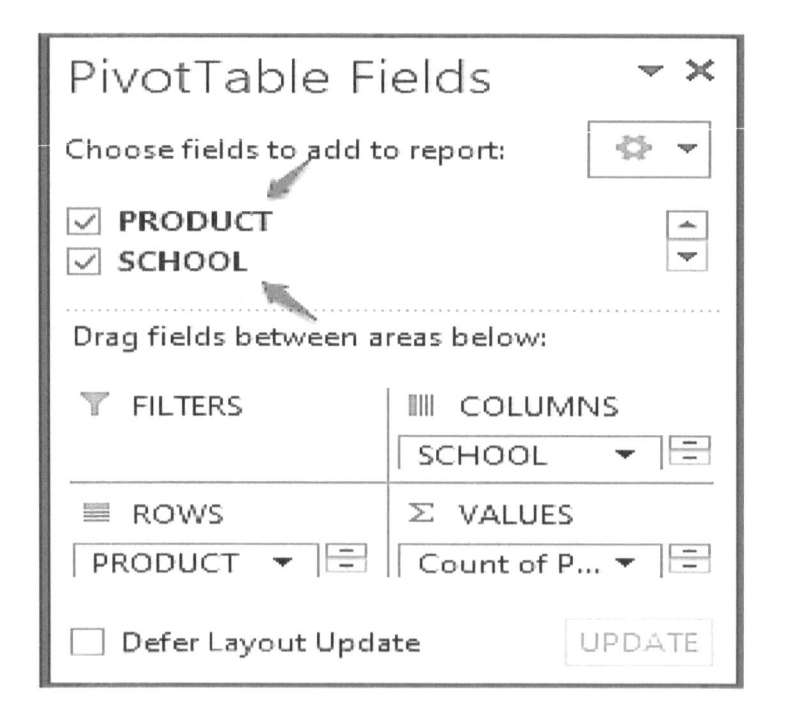

5. In this case, **PRODUCT is added to Value while SCHOOL is added to Column.**

	A	B	C	D	E
4	Row Labels	POLYTHECNIC	UNIVERSITY	Grand Total	
5	BOOKS	3	1	4	
6	CLOTHES		3	3	
7	Grand Total	3	4	7	
8					

(A3 — Count of PRODUCT)

Note: you can choose the field with the mouse by placing your mouse on the field, then click and drag it to any of the four areas as you desire, immediately, the Pivot table will compute the selected field and the summation of the amount of products sold in each field.

You may as well sort and filter the Pivot table with the "Sort & Filter" button situated at the upper right side of the **Home** tab.

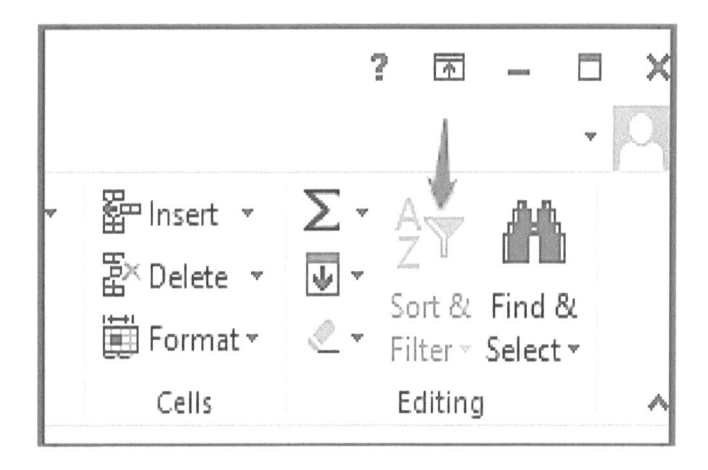

ADDING FINAL TOUCHES TO THE PIVOT TABLE

You are permitted to touch or restructure the default pattern of your Pivot table with Grand total, Report layout, and pivot table styles. Let us check this one by one.

1. **Grand total:** Grand total is the addition of total value. Excel estimates the total value of the column and row by default, but if you are not pleased with it, navigate to the **Pivot Table** design and click on **Grand Total**, and then you can choose **"Remove either column or row or both"**.

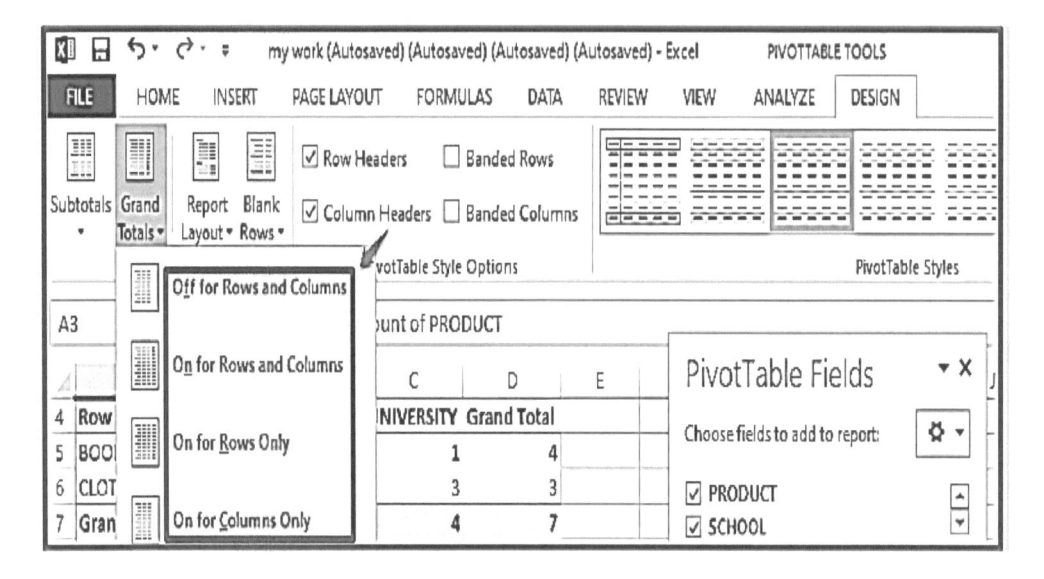

2. **Report layout:** Layout shows how your Pivot table is presented. From the **Pivot table design**, click on **Report layout** to choose diverse layout from various alternatives.

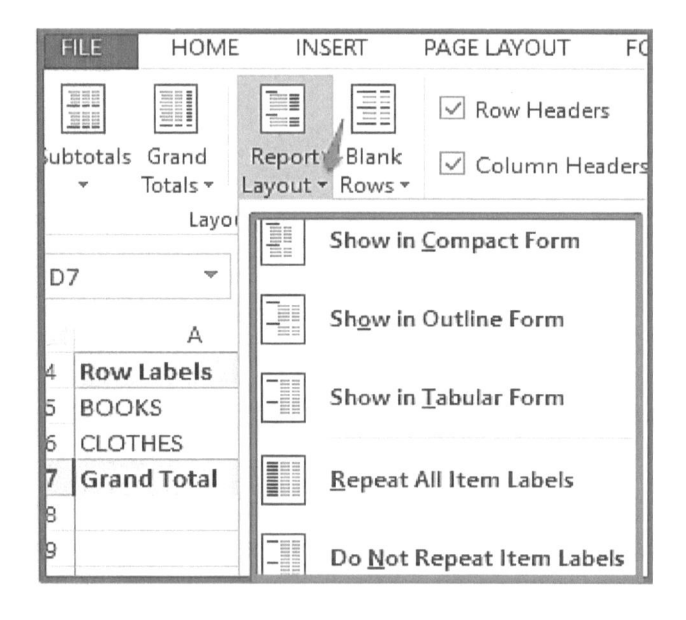

280

3. **Pivot table style:** Pivot table style breathes some color and design to your pivot table. Once you draw a pivot table, the pivot table style will be there by default, to change it, simply click on the drop-down arrow to see all the pivot table styles; the table style is there by default.

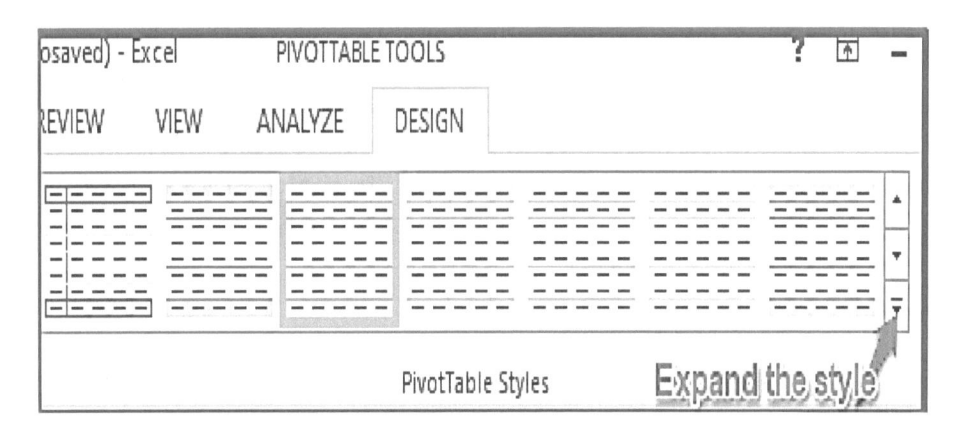

CHAPTER SEVEN
EXCEL 365 SHORTCUTS, TIPS AND TRICKS

Useful Shortcuts

When you find yourself making an exploit through keyboard shortcuts, that is the time you can gain speed in whatever you are doing in Excel. The following shortcuts are amazing shortcuts that you will find useful and necessary as you begin to use the Excel program:

Formula Shortcuts

SHORTCUTS CODE	USES
= Equal to	Start a formula.
Ctrl + '	Switch between formula and cell value.
Shift + F3	Enter a function.
Alt-=	Entering an AutoSum function.
Ctrl + `	From the cell above into the current one.
Ctrl + Shift + U	Expand or collapse the formula bar.
Alt + F8	Create, run and edit a macro.
Ctrl + shift + End	Select all texts from the cursor to the end in the formula bar
Ctrl + End	Inside the formula bar, move the cursor to the end of the text formula.

General Excel Shortcuts

SHORTCUTS CODE	USES
Ctrl + N	Open new workbook
Ctrl + O	Open exiting workbook
Ctrl + W	Close a workbook
Ctrl + F	Open the Find and Replace dialog box
Ctrl + 9	Hide the selected rows
Ctrl + O	Hide the selected columns
Ctrl + shift+ (	Unhide hidden row in a selection
Ctrl + shift +)	Unhide hidden column in a selection
Ctrl + '	Switch between displaying formula and cell value
Ctrl + shift + U	Expand or collapse the formula bar.
Ctrl + shift + %	Percentage formatting without decimal
Ctrl + shift + #	Date formatting with date, month, and year pattern.
Ctrl + shift + @	Time formatting with 12 hours pattern.
Ctrl + Q	Open the Quick analysis tools for selected cells with data.
Ctrl + 1	Open the Format cell dialog box.

Alt + `	Open the style dialog box.
Ctrl + shift + &	Apply a border-box.
Ctrl + shift + _	Remove a border from a cell or selection.
Ctrl + C	Copy cell's item into the clipboard.
Ctrl + X	Cut cell's item into the clipboard.
Ctrl + V	Paste from the clipboard into a cell.
Ctrl + Alt + V	Open paste special dialog box.
Enter	Moving to the next cell down
Shift + Enter	Moving to the next cell up
(Ctrl + A or Ctrl) + (shift + space bar)	Select the whole worksheet
Ctrl + Home	Navigating the selection to the beginning of the selected rows
Ctrl + Shift + Home	Navigating the selection to the beginning of the selected worksheet
Ctrl + space bar	Selecting a column.

Shift + spacebar	Selecting a column.
F5	Open "Go To" dialog box
Ctrl + left arrow	Move to the left end while you are still in a cell
Ctrl + right arrow	Move to the right while you are still in a cell
Esc	Erase your cell entry
Ctrl + ;	Enter the current date.
Ctrl + Shift + ;	Enter the current time.
Ctrl + T	Open the create table dialog box.
Tab	Move to the next cell to the right.
Up / down arrow key	Move the cell one up / down.
Home	Move to the beginning of a row.
Ctrl + Home	Move to the beginning of a worksheet.
Shift + tab	Move to the next cell to the left.
Ctrl + End	Move to the last cell that has contents inside.

Indispensable Tips And Trick For Quick Command

The following tricks and tips will not just help you to analyze or simplify an issue, but also save your time by simplifying things and aid you to crunch long data item. With these simple tools, do not worry, because you will move at a faster pace with Excel.

Absolute and Relative Reference

Excel references cells using an absolute or relative reference, or both. For instance,

a. **= C4*D1**, is referred to a relative referencing because it refers to a certain location by one cell to the left or three cells up the row.

	A	B	C	D	E	F
1			Rate	5%		
2						
3		Detail	Price	Rate	Total	
4		chair	300	15		
5		desk	230			
6		book	400			
7		pen	150			
8		bag	1000			

D4 — =C4*D1

b. And thus, if you decide to copy down the formula using Autofill, you will be getting an error notice, because each cell you copy will still be referring to one cell to the left and three cells up the row. In this case, it is either it will give you the wrong answer or give you an error because that D1 should apply to all formulas in that column. For instance, three cells above the row; in this case, it's a text (Rate), in the case of cell D6 =C6*D3, D3 is a text and it is because the formula is relative referencing.

D6				f_x	=C6*D3
	A	B	C	D	E
1			Rate	5%	
2					
3		Detail	Price	Rate	Total
4		chair	300	15	
5		desk	230	0	
6		book	00	#VALUE!	
7		pen	150	2250	
8		bag	1000	0	

c. In such a scenario like this, we will make use of absolute referencing by making D1 fixed to this location for all the rows, do this simply by highlighting it and press **F4** to switch between relative and absolute cell referencing.

SUM				f_x	=C4*D1
	A	B	C	D	E
1			Rate	5%	
2					
3		Detail	Price	Rate	Total
4		chair	300	=C4*D1	
5		desk	230	0	
6		book	400	#VALUE!	
7		pen	150	2250	
8		bag	1000	0	

	A	B	C	D	E	F
1			Rate	5%		
2						
3		Detail	Price	Rate	Total	
4		chair	300	=C4*$D$1		
5		desk	230	0		
6		book	400	#VALUE!		
7		pen	150	2250		
8		bag	1000	0		

d. Then, you can lock the column, row, and both; but in this scenario, we will keep cell D1 locked, then, if you copy it down now, it will copy the right formulas for each cell.

	A	B	C	D	E	F
1			Rate	5%		
2						
3		Detail	Price	Rate	Total	
4		chair	300	15		
5		desk	230	11.5		
6		book	400	20		
7		pen	150	7.5		
8		bag	1000	50		

Note: Anytime you copy a formula, make sure you set the relative or absolute referencing appropriately in respect of how the formula will be applied to the data.

Quick Analysis Tool

Quick analysis is used to perform numerous quick actions on the list of data in the worksheet, check this case:

   a. When you highlight the list of data and click on the "Quick Analysis" tool icon, it will show up a group of information.

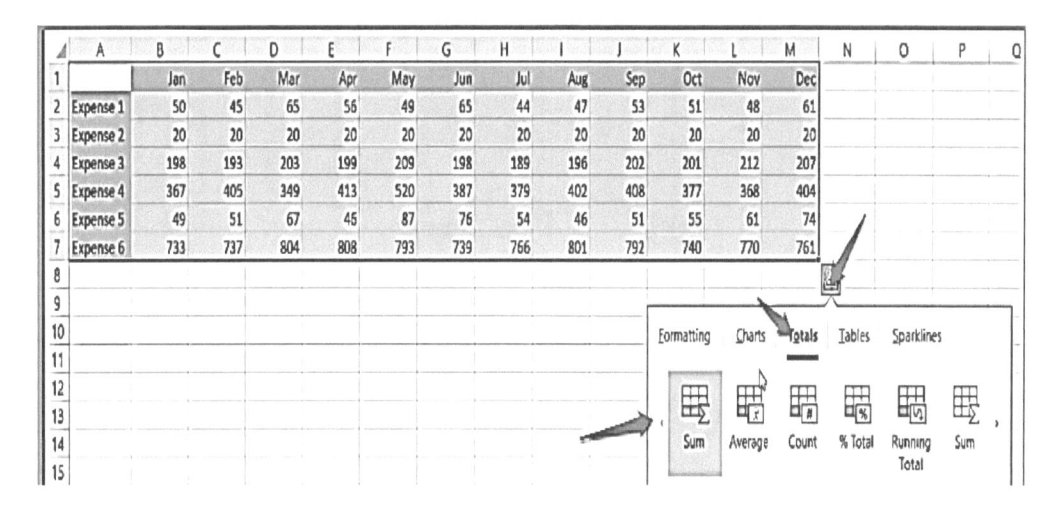

   b. Click on the **Total** tab where you will be able to select **SUM, AVERAGE,** and others. When you pick from SUM, there is also row sum, column sum, or Running total or percentage.

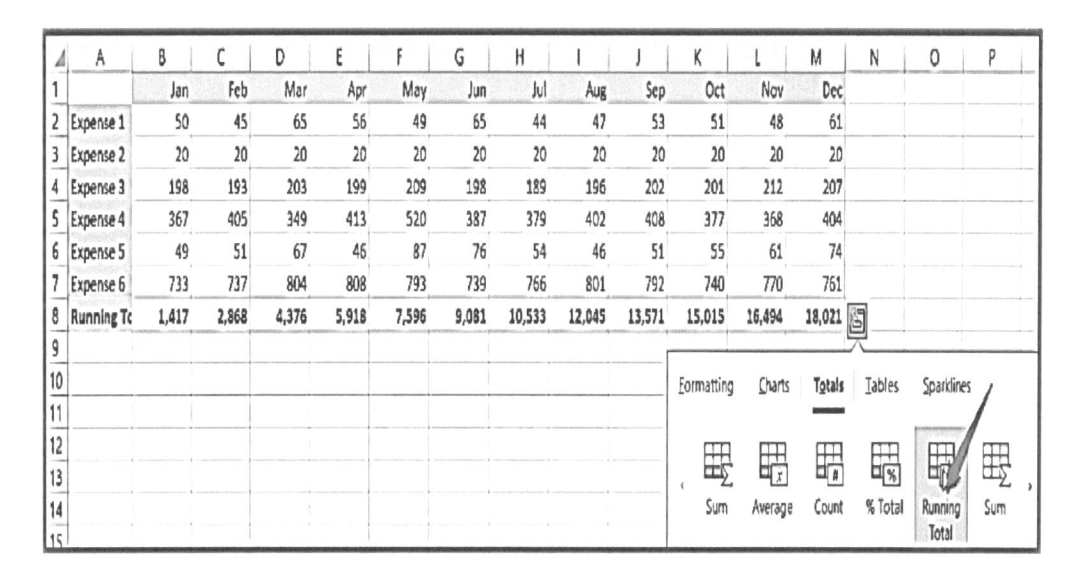

c. Click on the **Chart** option, and you will be given a line, clustered area, and so on.

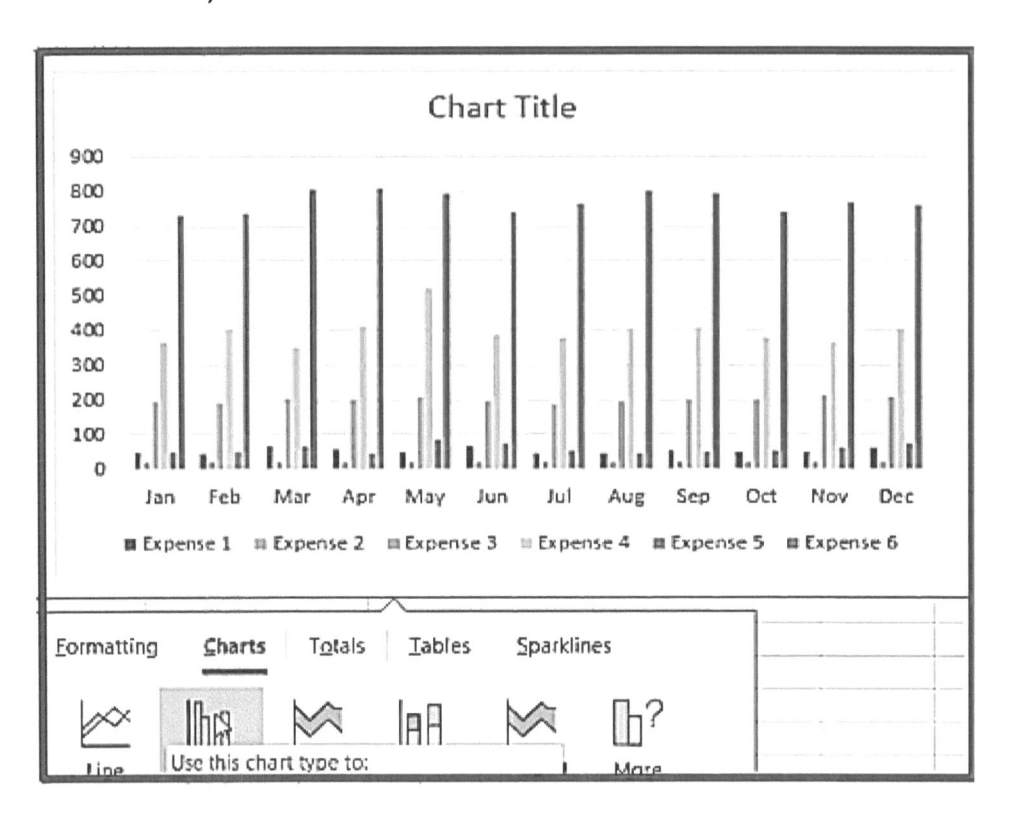

d. Click on **formatting** and you will be given Data bar, color scale, icon set, mark 10%, and others. With the Data tab, all your cells will be represented with a graph in respect of the value they have inside.

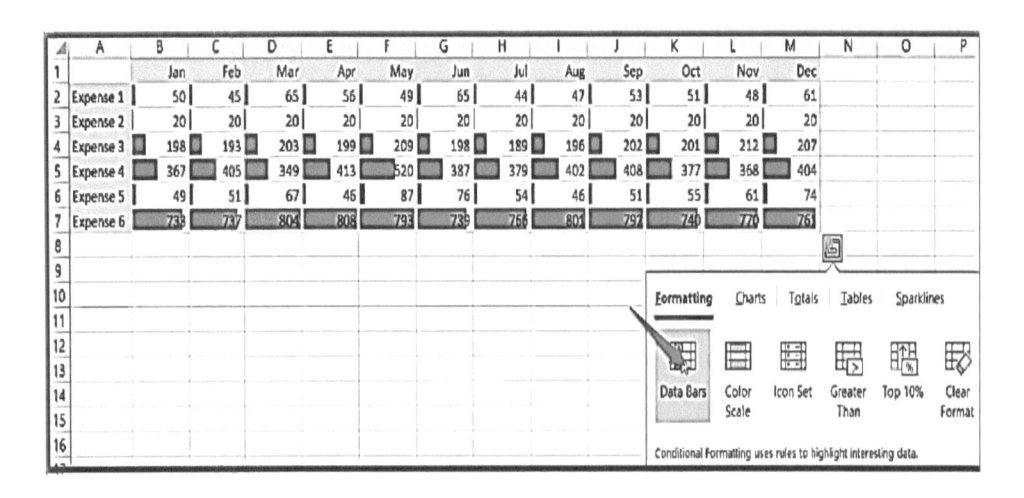

The color scale helps you to adjust the color.

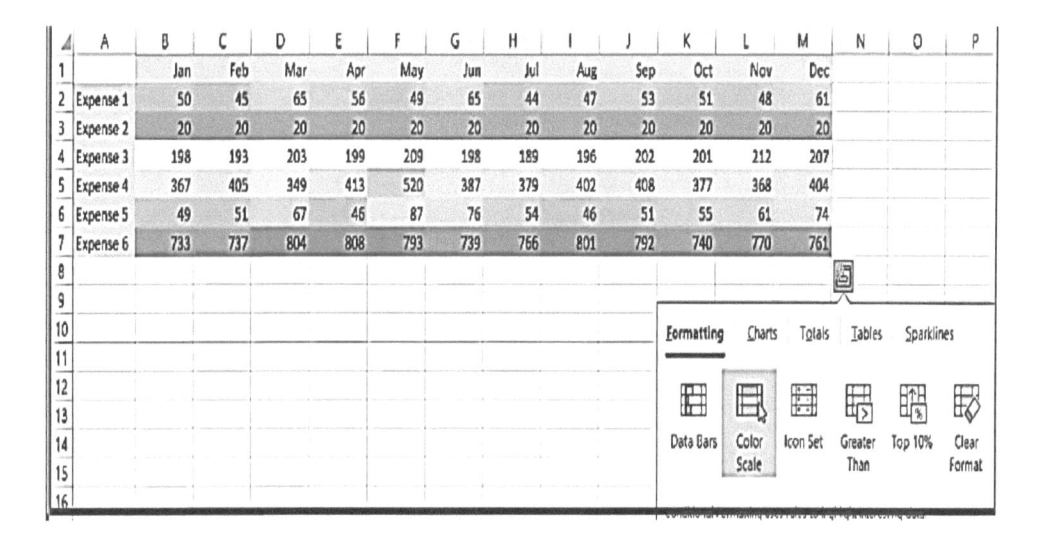

While icon set gives you a pictorial illustration of each data in the list and mark the top, 10% will mark top ten in the list. When you click on the Sparklines, it shows you the small chart of your data.

Autofit Column Width

The Autofit command is the quickest way of adjusting column, to use it;

    a. Move to a **boundary between any columns** until you see the cursor change to a black-headed arrow.

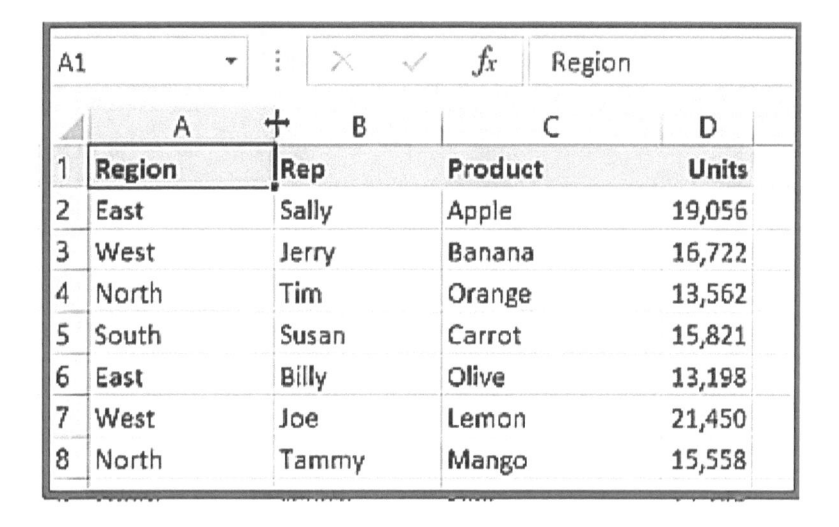

b. Then double-click it, immediately it will readjust the size of the column width to fit the data inside the cell in the column selected perfectly.

	A	B	C	D
1	Region	Rep	Product	Units
2	East	Sally	Apple	19,056
3	West	Jerry	Banana	16,722
4	North	Tim	Orange	13,562
5	South	Susan	Carrot	15,821
6	East	Billy	Olive	13,198
7	West	Joe	Lemon	21,450
8	North	Tammy	Mango	15,558
9	South	Nancy	Kiwi	17,146

c. You can as well highlight **multiple columns** and double-click any of them and all the column width in the column will be adjusted.

	A	B	C	D
1	Region	Rep	Product	Units
2	East	Sally	Apple	19,056
3	West	Jerry	Banana	16,722
4	North	Tim	Orange	13,562
5	South	Susan	Carrot	15,821
6	East	Billy	Olive	13,198
7	West	Joe	Lemon	21,450

| A1 | | ▼ | × | ✓ | *fx* | Region |

	A	B	C	D	E
1	Region	Rep	Product	Units	
2	East	Sally	Apple	19,056	
3	West	Jerry	Banana	16,722	
4	North	Tim	Orange	13,562	
5	South	Susan	Carrot	15,821	
6	East	Billy	Olive	13,198	
7	West	Joe	Lemon	21,450	
8	North	Tammy	Mango	15,558	
9	South	Nancy	Kiwi	17,146	

XLOOKUP Function

XLOOKUP is a powerful new function design to replace HLOOKUP and VLOOKUP. Take for instance:

a. We want to look up the name of John in this table and return a value from the February column.
b. You can quickly use **XLOOKUP** and the first element in this LOOKUP value is **John,** the array through which we are going to look up John's name in this area is the John row and we want to return the value from the February column.

	A	B	C	D	E	F	G
1	Name	Month	Amount				
2	John	Feb	=XLOOKUP(A2,A5:A12,E5:E12				
3			XLOOKUP(lookup_value, lookup_array, return_array, [if_not_found], [match_mo				
4	Name	Region	Discount	Jan	Feb	Mar	Apr
5	Jim	Region 1	55%	34,533	36,998	31,097	33,439
6	Karen	Region 2	60%	16,588	17,834	19,832	17,309
7	Sally	Region 3	45%	22,793	28,391	22,454	26,749
8	John	Region 4	65%	17,498	17,232	18,767	19,200
9	Jim	Region 5	45%	22,007	21,233	23,984	24,943
10	Sally	Region 6	40%	36,558	35,890	34,210	36,722
11	Karen	Region 7	55%	29,823	29,432	29,656	28,997

c. You will see the result it returns is **17232**, which is the meeting point of **John and February.**

	A	B	C	D	E	F	G	H	I
1	Name	Month	Amount						
2	John	Feb	17,232						
3									
4	Name	Region	Discount	Jan	Feb	Mar	Apr	May	Jun
5	Jim	Region 1	55%	34,533	36,998	31,097	33,439	37,876	29,57
6	Karen	Region 2	60%	16,588	17,834	19,832	17,309	18,085	19,13
7	Sally	Region 3	45%	22,793	28,391	22,454	26,749	28,845	26,99
8	John	Region 4	65%	17,498	17,232	18,767	19,200	20,921	19,63
9	Jim	Region 5	45%	22,007	21,233	23,984	24,943	23,278	22,79
10	Sally	Region 6	40%	36,558	35,890	34,210	36,722	37,646	35,21
11	Karen	Region 7	55%	29,823	29,432	29,656	28,997	29,041	28,87
12	Jim	Region 8	50%	30,678	30,943	31,298	31,884	32,190	32,39

Note: XLOOKUP has one merit and that merit is that it can perform horizontal XLOOKUP as well, let's say we want to lookup February in this list, we are going to return the value from John and it will be the same number **17232**, in the February column next to John.

	A	B	C	D	E	F	G	H	I
1	Name	Month	Amount						
2	John	Feb	=XLOOKUP(B2,D4:I4,D8:I8)						
3			XLOOKUP(lookup_value, lookup_array, **return_array**, [if_not_found], [match_mode], [search_mode])						
4	Name	Region	Discount	Jan	Feb	Mar	Apr	May	Jun
5	Jim	Region 1	55%	34,533	36,998	31,097	33,439	37,876	29,578
6	Karen	Region 2	60%	16,588	17,834	19,832	17,309	18,085	19,138
7	Sally	Region 3	45%	22,793	28,391	22,454	26,749	28,845	26,992
8	John	Region 4	65%	17,498	17,232	18,767	19,200	20,921	19,630
9	Jim	Region 5	45%	22,007	21,233	23,984	24,943	23,278	22,790
10	Sally	Region 6	40%	36,558	35,890	34,210	36,722	37,646	35,212
11	Karen	Region 7	55%	29,823	29,432	29,656	28,997	29,041	28,871
12	Jim	Region 8	50%	30,678	30,943	31,208	31,004	32,100	32,304

Remove BLANK

You may have multiple blank cells in a list of a given data; it will not be wise to remove them one by one. To remove multiple blank cells, kindly:

a. Highlight the **total list** of the data.
b. Navigate to the **Home** tab and select the **Find & Select** option from the home tab, then select "**Go to special**" from the drop-down list to open the "Go to special" dialog box.

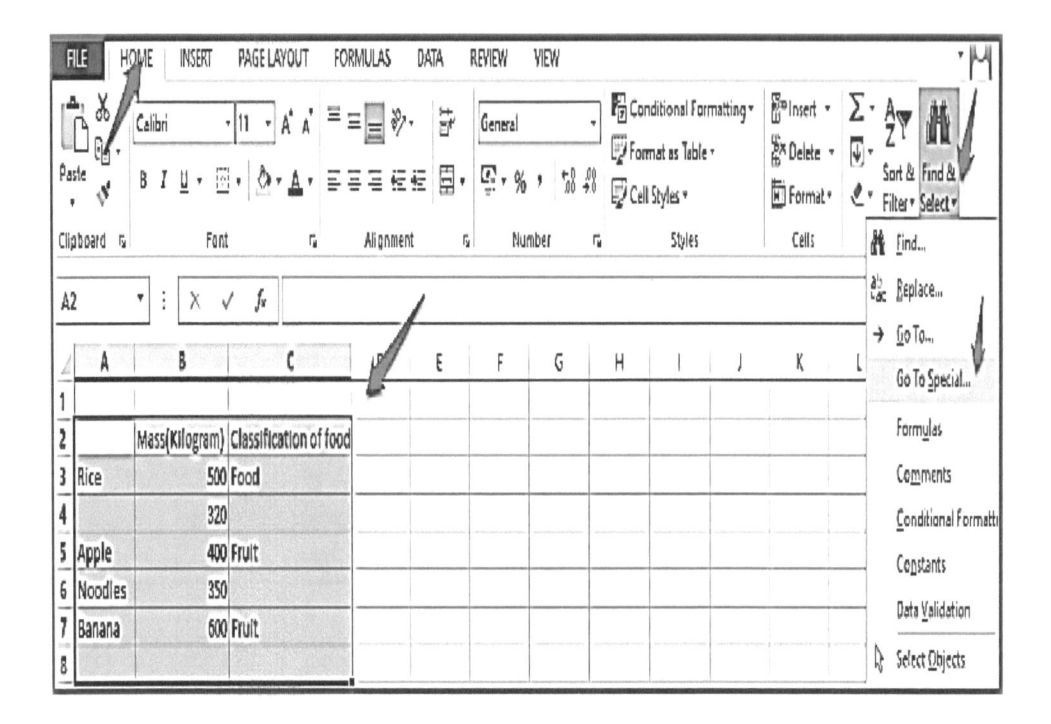

c. Pick **Blank** from the box and tap **ok,** immediately, Excel will highlight all the blank cells in the list.

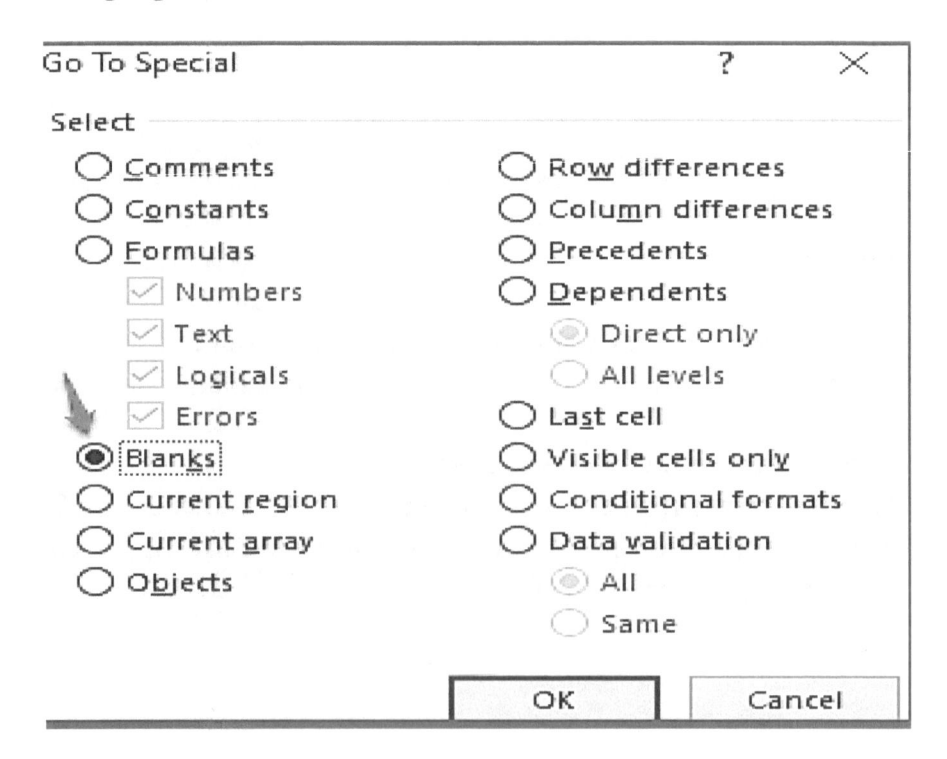

	A	B	C
1			
2		Mass(Kilogram)	Classification of food
3	Rice	500	Food
4		320	
5	Apple	400	Fruit
6	Noodles	350	
7	Banana	600	Fruit
8			

d. Simply right-click on any of the blank cells highlighted, then select **delete** from the drop-down list.

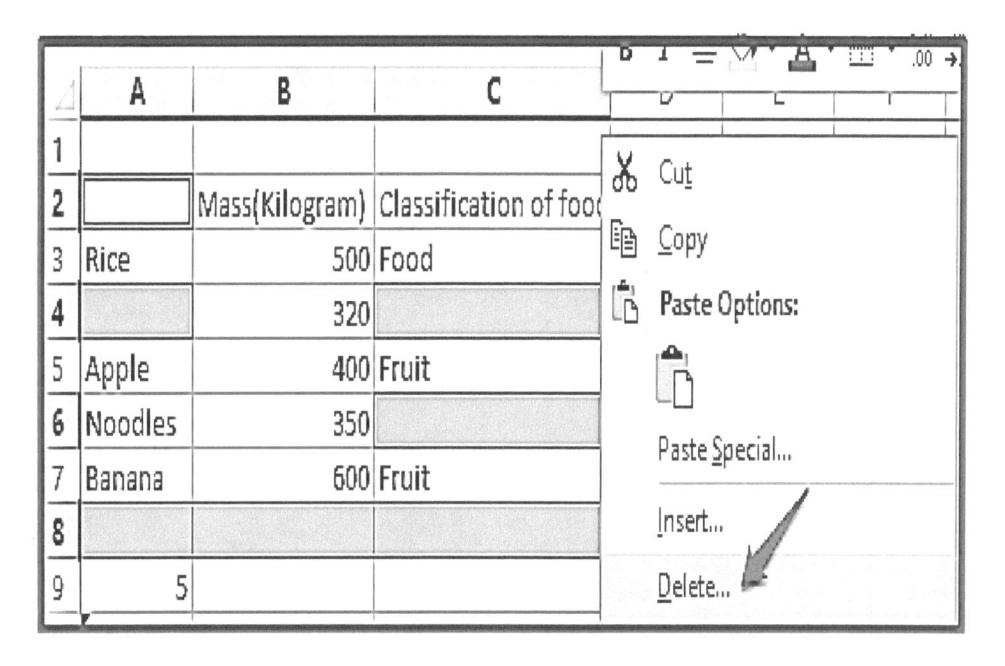

	A	B	C
1			
2		Mass(Kilogram)	Classification of food
3	Rice	500	Food
4		320	
5	Apple	400	Fruit
6	Noodles	350	
7	Banana	600	Fruit
8			
9	5		

- Cut
- Copy
- Paste Options:
- Paste Special...
- Insert...
- Delete...

e. You can now pick the "**Shift cells left**" option from the dialog box and tap **Ok**, instantly, all the blank cells will be cleaned up.

Delete   ?   ×

Delete

- ● Shift cells left
- ○ Shift cells up
- ○ Entire row
- ○ Entire column

OK   Cancel

Mass(Kilo	Classification of food	
Rice	500	Food
320	6090	price
Apple	400	Fruit
Noodles	350	
Banana	600	Fruit

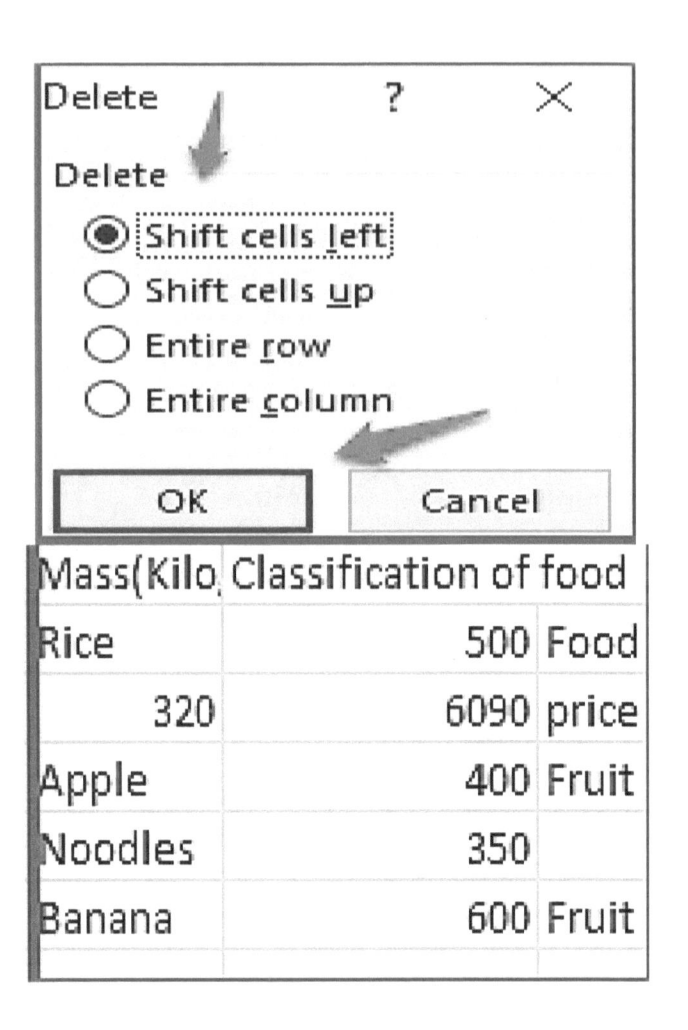

CONCLUSION

Excel 365 has been the talk of the whole world, not because Excel is just a spreadsheet program employed in recording and analyzing various data, but it has also been tested to be beneficial with its new features and updates for everyday business activities.

The idea of Excel 365 is to make Excel an essential part of business enterprises, and as a result of its best techniques used in analyzing various business issues, Excel has been the most used program in every office.

At this point, you will agree with me, that the method and technique analyses used inside this user guide as Excel 365 is capable of managing and analyzing every data and brings it under control, even if it is so large.

I so much believe you must have familiarized yourself with the formulation of formulas and functions that are necessary for executing data, including the techniques for coordinating and regulating data. I hope those techniques will give you a better chance of managing your lists of data and even extract the basic and most important information from the list of data within a given shortest period.

I must confess to you, that the major aim of the user guide is to give you an overview of Excel tools and functions which as improved over time in running our day-to-day Excel operation.

I hereby, wish you the very best of luck as you journey through the era of Excel 365, an online-based version.

INDEX

A

ABOUT FORMULAS, 76
Access, vi, 1, 2, 3, 4, 5, 6, 7, 10, 11, 12, 14, 17, 20, 28, 29, 30, 32, 35, 37, 38, 39, 40, 41, 47, 51, 52, 53, 55, 60, 72, 73, 74
address, 5, 8, 40, 73
Allowing whole numbers and decimal only, 34
analyze, vi
Append Only, 41
applications, vi, 1, 2, 3, 74
APPLYING FORMATTING TO NUMBERS, DATES, MONEY, AND TIMES VALUES, 30
Arithmetic Operators, 79
Arithmetic type, 79
array, 3
Arrow key, 41
audio, 8
Auto Fill, 25, 28
AutoFill handle, 30

B

BASIC KNOWLEDGE OF ENTERING DATA, 16
Binary, 8
business, 1, 74
bytes, 8

C

calculate, 6
caption, 39
Caption, 39
category, 14, 15, 20, 21, 23

Cell, 11, 13
Cell range, 13
CHANGING EXCEL ORDER WITH PARENTHESIS, 82
COLLABORATION, 5
columns, 4, 5, 26, 46, 61, 66
Columns, 11
Combining data with the Flash Fill, 25
commands, 3, 6, 53, 73
COMMENTS FOR DOCUMENTING YOUR WORKSHEET, 55
Comparison type, 81
components, 4, 6
computer, vi, 6, 74
COMPUTING DATA WITH FUNCTION AND FORMULAS, 76
Concatenation Operator, 80
COPYING DATA, 63
create, 1, 2, 3, 4, 5, 6, 9, 10, 11, 12, 14, 20, 26, 27, 29, 30, 31, 35, 36, 40, 42
CREATING AND OPENING A NEW EXCEL WORKBOOK, 8
CREATING CELL RANGE NAME FOR FORMULAS USES, 93
Currency, 8, 39
customizing, 2, 5

D

data, vi, 1, 2, 4, 5, 6, 7, 8, 9, 11, 27, 28, 29, 33, 35, 36, 37, 38, 39, 40, 41, 45, 47, 48, 51, 52, 66, 67, 74
Data, 15

database, vi, 1, 2, 3, 4, 5, 6, 7, 10, 11, 12, 13, 15, 17, 18, 20, 26, 27, 28, 29, 31, 32, 33, 35, 37, 38, 40, 41, 44, 47, 51, 52, 54, 55
Data-Entry List, 41
Datasheet, 33, 34, 35, 36, 52, 53, 59, 60, 61, 69, 71
Datatypes, 7
Date and Time, 39
decimal places, 8, 39
Default Value, 39
deleting, 7, 18, 20, 48, 50
Deleting all comments, 58
DELETING DATA, 63
description, 13, 35
Design View, 31, 33, 34, 35, 36, 37, 42, 44, 48, 49, 50, 52, 62, 64
DIFFERENCES BETWEEN EXCEL 365 AND TRADITIONAL EXCEL, 2
DISCOVER MORE ABOUT THE ERROR AND ADJUSTING IT, 102
DISCOVERING AND ADJUSTING FORMULAS ERROR, 101
document, vi, 54
DOCUMENT SAVING TYPES, 4
duplicate, 27, 28, 37, 48

E

Edit mode, 11
Editing a comment, 57
EDITING YOUR WORKSHEET DATA, 41
email addresses, 30
Enter mode, 11
entering, 5, 6, 28, 33, 41, 51
ENTERING DATA IN THE WORKSHEET CELL, 15
environments, 2

ESSENTIAL GUIDE TO DATA VALIDATION, 34
Excel document, 11
EXCEL INTERFACE, 10
Excel ribbon, 11
Excel Workbook, 14
Excel worksheets, 14
Extracting data with Flash Fill, 27

F

filter, 13
Finding comment, 57
Flash Fill, 25
FOREKNOWLEDGE OF ENTERING A FORMULA, 83
forms, 2, 4, 5, 6, 12, 13, 27, 30, 41, 59, 62
Freezing, 44
FREEZING AND SPLITTING COLUMNS AND ROWS, 44
Frequent message error for entering wrong formulas, 102
functionality, 3

G

GETTING FAMILIAR WITH EXCEL INTERFACE, 10
GIVING YOUR WORKSHEET A NEW APPEARANCE, 43
group, 14, 15, 16, 18, 23, 24, 25, 32, 56

H

Handling cell range name, 96
hardware, 3
Hide, 14, 18

HIDE AND UNHIDE THE COLUMNS AND ROWS, 47
HIDING YOUR WORKSHEET, 71
How do I enter Edit mode, 41
How do I enter Edit mode?, 41
How do I freeze or split rows or column on the screen, 44
How to add a new worksheet, 69
How to colorize your worksheet, 69
How to copy a worksheet, 69
How to delete a worksheet, 70
How to move a worksheet inside a workbook, 66
How to rearrange worksheet, 66
How to rename a worksheet, 68
How to select all cells, 63
How to select an individual cell, 60
How to select multiple individual cells, 61
How to select range of cells, 61
How to select worksheet(s), 67
hyperlink, 8, 72, 73

I

IMPORTANCE OF EXCEL 365, 7
IMPROVING YOUR WORKSHEET, 41
information, vi, 1, 2, 4, 5, 6, 26, 27, 28, 47, 52
INSERTING A CELL RANGE, 92
Inserting a comment, 56
Integer, 39
integrate, 2
internet, vi, 74
INTRODUCTION, 78
invalid data, 41
inventory, vi

K

keywords, 33

L

languages, 2
live, 6
Lookup, 41, 42, 44, 45, 58, 71

M

macros, 2, 4, 6, 7, 12, 13, 59, 62
maintenance, 2
management, vi, 1, 2
MANAGING THE WORKSHEETS IN A WORKBOOK, 66
manipulate, 2, 35, 51
Mask, 39
mathematical, 8
maximum, 8, 39
MEANING OF EXCEL, 1
Memo, 39
Microsoft, vi, 1, 2, 3, 6, 7, 10, 11, 74
Microsoft 365, vi, 1
module, 7, 59, 63
modules, 4, 7
MOVING DATA, 63

N

Name and formula bar, 11
NAVIGATING AROUND THE WORKSHEET, 42
navigation panel, 14
null, 37, 39
numbers, 8, 27, 30, 39
numerical, 8

O

objects, 4, 5, 7, 8, 13, 14, 15, 16, 17, 19, 20, 31, 33, 34
OPERATORS AND PRECEDENCE OF EXCEL FORMULAS, 79
Optimal Data Types, 51
Oracle, 2, 3
orders, 4, 26
organization, vi, 4, 26, 27, 74
ORIGIN OF EXCEL, 1
OVERVIEW OF MICROSOFT EXCEL, 1

P

Percentage, 39
permanently, 22
phone, 30, 39
Plus icon, 11
POINTING TO CELLS IN A WORKSHEET FOR FORMULAR PURPOSE IN A DIFFERENT WORKSHEET, 98
PREFACE, 76
PRICING METHODS, 2
primary, 5, 28, 37, 47, 48, 51
Professional, vi
proficient, vi, 74
programmer, 6
programming, 1, 3, 6
PROTECTING YOUR WORKSHEET, 73
purchase, 26

Q

queries, 2, 4, 5, 6, 12, 13, 30, 47, 59, 62
query, 5, 6, 28, 41, 47, 59, 60, 67

Quick Start, 30

R

Ready mode, 11
records, 5, 7, 28, 32, 51, 68
REFERENCE CELLS IN THE WORKSHEET BY CLICKING ON THE CELLS, 92
Reference Operator, 80
Reference type, 80
REFERENCING FORMULA RESULTS IN SUBSEQUENT EXCEL FORMULAS, 78
REFERENCING THE CELLS VIA FORMULAS, 76
RELEVANCE OF EXCEL, 1
renaming, 20
Replication, 8, 39
report, 2, 6, 7, 39, 59, 60, 62, 63, 68
reporting, 1, 2
reports, 2, 3, 4, 6, 12, 13, 30, 41, 62
RESTRICTING OTHERS FROM MEDDLING WITH YOUR WORKSHEETS, 71
Rows, 11

S

Scroll bar, 12
search, 5, 12, 13, 17, 28, 47, 53
SELECTING CELLS (S) IN A WORKSHEET, 60
server, 2, 3
Setting rules for text character length, 37
Shutter Bar, 13
SIMILARITIES BETWEEN EXCEL 365 AND TRADITIONAL EXCEL, 6

skills, 3
Smart Tags, 41
software, vi, 3, 74
SOL, 2
solution, 3
Splitting, 44
standalone object, 7
START YOUR EXPLOIT WITH EXCEL, 8
Status bar, 11
store, vi, 1, 4, 7, 8, 11, 28, 51
storing contact, 30
SUB RIBBON MENU, 6
suite, vi, 1, 2, 74

T

tables, 2, 4, 5, 6, 12, 13, 26, 27, 28, 29, 30, 31, 33, 35, 51, 52, 60, 62, 66, 71
tabular form, 36
TAKING ADVANTAGES OF FLASH FILL AND AUTO FILL COMMANDS, 25
teams, 3
template, vi, 10, 12, 13, 29, 30, 31
Text concatenation type, 80
Text Format, 41
texts, 8, 41
THE FAST-TRACK METHOD TO OBSERVE IN ENTERING A FORMULA, 85
Tracing dependents, 104
Tracing Precedent, 103
TRACING THE CELL REFERENCES, 103
TRADITIONAL EXCEL, 3
TYPING DATES AND TIME VALUES, 22
TYPING NUMERIC VALUE, 21

U

UNDERSTANDING ROWS, COLUMNS, AND CELL ADDRESSES, 12
unhide, 14, 18, 19
Unicode Expression, 40
UPDATED VERSIONS AND FEATURES, 3
users, 1, 2, 3, 4, 6, 7

V

Validating dates and times, 38
Validation Rule, 40
Validation Text, 40
VBA, 1, 3, 7
vendors, vi
version, vi, 41
video, 8
viewing, 2, 5, 18, 33, 50
Viewing a comment, 57

W

WAYS OF COPYING FORMULAS FROM ONE CELL TO OTHER CELL, 100
WHAT IS EXCEL 365?, 2
WORKBOOKS, 14
working with the database, 26
Worksheet, 11
WORKSHEET, 14
Worksheet navigation key, 11

Z

Zoom Slider, 12

Was this book helpful to you?
Are you pleased with the contents of this book?

We would love to hear from you, please kindly leave a review after buying/reading this book. Thanks

Made in United States
Troutdale, OR
02/05/2025